DEVIANCE AND IDENTITY

3⁰⁰

SE10

Soc/ sale shelf

DEVIANCE AND IDENTITY

by

JOHN LOFLAND

with the assistance of

LYN H. LOFLAND

PRENTICE-HALL, INC.

Englewood Cliffs, New Jersey

PRENTICE-HALL SOCIOLOGY SERIES

Neil J. Smelser, *Editor*

Current Printing (Last Digit):
10   9   8   7   6   5   4   3   2   1

13-208413-9

Library of Congress Catalog Card Number: 77-75630

Printed in the United States of America

PRENTICE-HALL INTERNATIONAL, INC., *London*
PRENTICE-HALL OF AUSTRALIA, PTY. LTD., *Sydney*
PRENTICE-HALL OF CANADA, LTD., *Toronto*
PRENTICE-HALL OF INDIA PRIVATE LTD., *New Delhi*
PRENTICE-HALL OF JAPAN, INC., *Tokyo*

Grateful acknowledgment is made to the following for permission to quote from copyrighted material. Material from:

The book, *My Shadow Ran Fast*, by Bill Sands is quoted by permission. © 1964 by Prentice-Hall, Inc. Published by Prentice-Hall, Inc., Englewood Cliffs, New Jersey.

Edwin M. Lemert, *Human Deviance, Social Problems and Social Control* (1967), is quoted by permission of the author and Prentice-Hall, Inc.

William J. Chambliss, "Two Gangs: A Study of Societal Responses to Deviance and Deviant Careers" (1967a), is quoted by permission of the author.

Edwin M. Lemert, *Social Pathology* (1951), is quoted by permission of the McGraw-Hill Book Company and the author.

Edwin M. Lemert, "An Isolation and Closure Theory of Naive Check Forgery," is quoted by permission of the author and is reprinted with special permission from the *Journal of Criminal Law, Criminology and Police Science*, Copyright © 1953 by the Northwestern University School of Law, Vol. 44, No. 3.

Sethard Fisher, "The Rehabilitative Effectiveness of a Community Correctional Residence for Narcotic Users," is reprinted with special permission from the *Journal of Criminal Law, Criminology and Police Science*, Copyright © 1965 by the Northwestern University School of Law, Vol. 56, No. 2.

Rita Volkman and Donald R. Cressey, "Differential Association and The Rehabilitation of Drug Addicts" (1963), is quoted by permission of the authors and reprinted from the *American Journal of Sociology* by permission of The University of Chicago Press. © Copyright 1963 by The University of Chicago Press.

Edwin M. Lemert, "Paranoia and the Dynamics of Exclusion" (1962), is quoted by permission of the author and the American Sociological Association.

"Richard Speck's Twisted Path," *Detroit Free Press*, July 24, 1966, is quoted by permission of the *Detroit Free Press*.

"Hoffa To Be Kingpin to Cons," *Detroit Free Press*, March 8, 1967, is quoted by permission of the *Detroit Free Press*.

Erving Goffman, *Asylums* (1961a), is quoted by permission of the author.

William Jewell, "A Case of a 'Psychotic' Navaho Indian Male" (1960), is quoted by permission of The Society for Applied Anthropology.

Frank Tannenbaum, *Crime and the Community* (1938), is quoted by permission of Columbia University Press.

The Death and Life of Great American Cities, by Jane Jacobs, © Copyright 1961 by Jane Jacobs is reprinted by permission of Random House, Inc.

Lou Harris, "Conformity: The New American Way" (1965), is quoted by permission of Louis Harris & Assoc., Inc.

Eric Hoffer, *The Passionate State of Mind* (1954), is quoted by permission of Harper & Row, Publishers.

Gordon Allport, "An Autobiography," in *The Person in Psychology: Selected Essays* (1968), is quoted by permission of Appleton-Century-Crofts.

Evelyn Hooker, "The Homosexual Community" (1961), is quoted by permission of the author.

As social beings we live with our eyes upon our reflection, but have no assurance of the tranquility of the waters in which we see it. In the days of witchcraft it used to be believed that if one person secretly made a waxen image of another and stuck pins into the image, its counterpart would suffer tortures, and that if the image was melted the person would die. This superstition is almost realized in the relation between the private self and its social reflection. They seem separate but are darkly united, and what is done to the one is done to the other.

CHARLES HORTON COOLEY

[An] . . . older sociology . . . tended to rest heavily on the idea that deviance leads to social control. I have come to believe that the reverse idea, i.e., social control leads to deviance, is equally tenable and the potentially richer premise for studying deviance in modern society.

EDWIN M. LEMERT

Charles Horton Cooley, *Human Nature and the Social Order*, p. 247.
Edwin M. Lemert, *Human Deviance, Social Problems and Social Control*, p. v.

PREFACE

The two terms "deviance" and "identity" that comprise the title of this work reflect the duality of its commitment. The prime substantive topic is behavior called deviant, but such behavior is approached from within a more general theoretical orientation. That orientation is captured in part by the concept of identity and is known to sociologists as the "symbolic interactionist" or, simply, "interactionist" perspective. Although I have here attempted to codify and extend an interactionist approach to deviance, I have also tried, more generally, to extend and articulate this general approach to sociological social psychology. I hope this work may be useful in understanding deviance and/or identity, each separately or in combination.

As the author of a piece of writing which, in order to effect some larger and more abstract order, is intentionally constructed from other writing, my debts are many and various. First, there are debts of a personal and diffuse sort.

The most personal of these are the multidimensional debts owed my spouse, Lyn H. Lofland. She assisted with every phase of the book, from initial conceptualization through struggles over composition to construction of the index. Her name on the title page indicates her scholarly contributions, but beyond these contributions, I want also to say that she is the *compleat* colleague, friend and intimate. There is a private and significant sense in which she made this work possible.

My interest in sociological social psychology was first aroused by Herbert Blumer, a man to whom I have a profound and abiding debt. My interest in deviance as combined with more general issues stems from contact with Erving Goffman. The influence of his specific ideas, as well as his more general stance, can be seen throughout. Although of a different theoretical tradition, I have been much impressed by the logic of the analyses carried on by Neil Smelser. Somewhat adapted, the kind of logic he has sponsored is applied here. The almost incredible imagination and insight of Gerald Suttles have strongly influenced my approach to deviance and social life. I am particularly indebted to his highlighting of relations between distrust, fear and social organization. My understanding of, and faith in, the possibility of a truly sociological social psychology have been extended through contact with the social organizational perspectives of Max Heirich, Leon H. Mayhew, Albert J. Reiss and Guy E. Swanson.

The researches and writings of a number of other scholars, whom I have not known personally, have been particularly important to me in thinking about deviance and identity. Concerning identity, the writings of Ernest Becker and Peter Berger have been extremely enlightening. The views they have so vigorously advanced have helped to place the minutiae of social science in a proper human perspective. Concerning deviance, the kinds of analyses carried on by Donald R. Cressey and Edwin M. Lemert have been continuing points of reference. The lines of analysis developed by Professor Lemert are indeed central to the present effort. And, I should like to comment more generally that Professor Lemert's persistence and independence during the fifties, when sociological fashion was directed elsewhere, allow all our thinking about deviance today to be considerably more rich and acute. I am happy to see that he is finally receiving from the discipline the recognition and honor long ago his due.

I also have a debt to the author of every other work cited. A task of the present sort is possible only on the basis of the materials they have created. Among these authors, David Matza, Thomas J. Scheff and Howard S. Becker are due a special word of thanks. And, I offer my apologies to authors of equally or more relevant works which happen not to be drawn upon. Many crucial omissions are doubtless due to my own oversight, but others were made necessary by a lack of space in which to utilize or cite every relevant work on every topic discussed.

Given the fact that there is here an attempt to bring together the separate but interrelated efforts of many scholars, I have been somewhat embarrassed by reactions of some readers to earlier drafts. Some have seen the present work as, in one or another sense, discontinuous with, or a departure from, the lines of thought expressed by, among other scholars, the people named above. I have concluded that this perception arises from the logic and vocabulary used, which are in some ways not standard. I want here to emphasize that no discontinuity or departure is intended or exists. There is, rather, an attempt to articulate, extend, integrate and generalize existing conceptualizations. In order effectively to do this, a slight change of packaging has seemed necessary. The product itself is intact, hopefully with some improvements in design. A judgment concerning the merits of this packaging must, of course, rest with the reader.

A number of people have given generously of their time and of their constructively critical capacities in eliminating errors, improving clarity of exposition, modulating overly emotional statements, extending the range of illustrations, pointing out necessary qualifications and the like. Many of their suggestions are incorporated without specific mention. I extend my sincere and heartfelt thanks to: Donald Black, Donald Dickson, Kenneth Feldman, Max Heirich, Martin Kane, Edwin Lemert, Peter K. Manning, Marvin B. Scott, Neil Smelser and Gerald Suttles. Thomas Moore, John Slosar and Don Spencer ably assisted me at various points. The students of my course on deviant behavior have been a continuous source of stimulating commentary.

Cordelia Thomas managed the book's production with skill, tact and perseverance. My thanks to her for making the process a pleasant experience.

Miss Sharon McEndarfer, Miss Judith McEndarfer and Mrs. Aled Wold expertly typed an early draft of sequential blurbs and created continuous text. Their aid and other assistance provided through the Center for Research on Social Organization, The University of Michigan, are gratefully acknowledged. Mrs. LaRae Newby transformed a later version from a scissored and stapled mass to duplicatable elegance.

Although I have been the beneficiary of the works, ideas and specific advice of the people mentioned, they, of course, have had no control over my final decisions. Indeed, some of these decisions are contrary to either their published and public advisements or their personal and private recommendations. It follows that responsibility for what is misguided and erroneous rests entirely upon myself.

JOHN LOFLAND

Ann Arbor, Michigan, and
San Francisco, California,
Summer and Fall, 1968

CONTENTS

DEVIANCE AND IDENTITY

This is a book about some of the stronger and more dramatic ways in which people can feel about and act toward one another. It is a book about behavior and about persons toward whom there is experienced fear, hate, threat and defensiveness and, on occasion, compassion, concern and hope of redemption. It is a book about what sociologists call deviant behavior—behavior which is said to violate important social rules and which is therefore strongly disapproved of. Homicide, suicide, alcoholism, mental illness, prostitution and homosexuality are among the forms of behavior typically called deviant, and they are among the kinds of behavior that will be analyzed.

CHAPTER 1
INTRODUCTION: IDEOLOGICAL MATTERS

Each of these types of behavior and many others that might be called deviant have, of course, been addressed in print on numerous occasions. Each has associated with it a very large body of specialized literature; moreover, each has associated with it a body of persons who are publicly considered experts on "their" category of problematic activities or problematic persons. This high degree of specialization, with its associated outpouring of specialized literature, has reached the point where it is difficult for an individual to keep up even with his own specialty, much less attempt to follow and comprehend the total corpus of materials on everything that might be called deviant. In the face of, and in spite of, this fact, the attitude of some sociologists can only be seen as presumptuous; they persist in their belief in the reasonableness of attempting to comprehend deviance as a general category of human activity and of attempting to make statements that apply to many if not all of its forms. They have sought to surmount the strong tendency to specialization among investigators and practitioners. They have mounted theoretical constructs that encompass and unite, at some level, what threaten to become isolated and parochial camps. The present work is an expression of that presumptuousness and of that synthesizing line of endeavor.

This work seeks to codify and to extend recent developments in the sociology of deviance. It will delineate an analytic category of what is deviant and will attempt to specify problem areas that cross-cut common-sense, technical and popularly identified concrete designations. Three such analytic problem areas will be proposed. On the basis of what amounts to three questions that require answers, three sets of generalized explanatory constructs applicable to the three generic dependent variables will be developed.

However, before engaging in this exercise in technical sociology, it is necessary to place it in context. Works of all kinds, written and otherwise, are typically undertaken in response to, in reaction against and/or in furtherance of, what already exists. The present work is likewise conceived in social cor-

1

ruption. The context is primarily that of the history, traditions and disputes of the field of sociology and of the specialty called deviance. To understand better what sociologists have of late called deviance and, therefore, the relation of the present work to it, it is reasonable to review some aspects of the historical background and contemporary backdrop that constitute the stage upon which one more act is to be played out.

Given the peculiarly moral character of sociology and given the existence of various substantive critiques of the history which is to be reviewed here, it seems additionally proper to emphasize selectively the ideological and value-laden aspects of the far past, recent past and present.[1]

CHANGING PERSPECTIVES AND THE TOPICS OF DEVIANCE

The term deviance is a mere infant compared to such major and long-standing terms as stratification, community, institution and society. Deviance is, in fact, less than twenty years of age, having "made the scene," as it were, after World War II and primarily after 1950. It and its variants, deviant, deviation and deviancy, entered the field very quickly, without eliciting much debate and almost without eliciting any reflection upon or conscious regard for what was happening. One of the lonely commentaries on this occurrence was felt by its author to merit but a footnote.

> It is remarkable that those who live around the social sciences have so quickly become comfortable with the term "deviant." . . . Just as there are iatrogenic disorders caused by the work that physicians do (which gives them more work to do), so there are categories of persons who are created by students of society, then studied by them. (Goffman, 1963a: 140.)

The unheralded advent and sweeping acceptance of deviance as a name for a subset of sociological topics pose an important question in the sociology of sociology. This question is relevant to understanding the more ideological texture and context of recent studies of a very old and standard set of topics. The coming of deviance as a sociological rubric poses, simply, the question of the conditions under which this occurred.

---

[1] For histories emphasizing the substantive dimensions of the ideological shifts, see the references in notes 8 and 12 of this chapter and note 8 of Chap. 2. General readers who are unacquainted and unconcerned with "inside" sociology should be warned that this chapter will be parochial in the sense that it deals with topics over which sociologists fight among themselves. Readers who simply want to know what a sociologist says about "problem" behavior and "problem" people may wish to begin with Chap. 2.

SOCIOLOGY AND THE TOPICS OF DEVIANCE PRIOR TO WORLD WAR II

If we are adequately to understand the advent of the concept of deviance, it is necessary also to understand something of the concepts which deviance replaced. For, although the name of the sociological subfield has changed, the concrete topics of study have remained much the same. Furthermore, to understand these replaced concepts, we must also understand *who* practiced sociology in what kind of *social context*.

From the discipline's beginning in the United States at the turn of the 20th century, and for some forty years thereafter, sociologists often had a conventionally reformist-social problem-social work orientation. Many early sociologists were the products of training grounds in ideal morality, either as the result of exposure to Protestant ministerial fathers or as the result of their own earlier careers as clergymen. Others came to sociology from backgrounds in what was then called "social reform" (but has since been tamed to "social work").[2] These pioneers on the frontiers of sociology were unabashedly moral men. Their overt aim was to understand society so as to solve its problems. Although they considered themselves men of science, theirs was a science in the service of ethical ideals. Unencumbered by the doctrines of value neutrality that would make moral eunuchs of a later generation, their writing could be charmingly explicit on moral matters, as in the following passages from a popular text of the period.

Sin, vice, crime, corruption, all consciously directed antisocial forces, offer a primrose path of pleasurable activity, albeit they eventually lead to destruction. Beguiled by clever leaders and the desires of the moment, man is continually selling his soul for a mess of pottage.

※　　　　※　　　　※

Those unhappy creatures who offer themselves for sex hire represent the most demoralized of all sex offenders.

※　　　　※　　　　※

Women are seldom "sold" or "forced" into lives of shame or compelled to remain in houses of prostitution any longer than they desire. It is a sad but valid fact that there are thousands of women in large cities who are

[2] See Mills, 1942, to whom I am indebted for rendition of the relevant parts of pre-World War II sociology. See also Strauss, 1961 and 1968.

willing to become prostitutes voluntarily. (Elliott and Merrill, 1934:44, 182, 188.)

Only in a world of moral certitude can "clever leaders" "beguile" the souls of "unhappy creatures" in the light of "sad but valid facts."

The more explicitly conceptual side of their work was hardly less moralistic. In place of the deviance framework of today stood such concepts as social disorganization, social pathology, and social maladjustment. All these concepts assume the existence and knowledge of standards against which polities and persons can be judged to be organized or disorganized, normal or pathological, adjusted or maladjusted. These "social pathologists"—as C. W. Mills called them—were not, however, very explicit as to the exact nature of the standards by which their judgments were made. Nonetheless, investigation into the moral backgrounds and outlooks of these men and knowledge of those objects which they conceived as disorganized, pathological or maladjusted allow one to infer their underlying standards or assumptions with some certainty.

Like millions of Americans prior to World War II, many early sociologists were of Anglo-American descent, were reared in rural Protestant areas and were migrants to the burgeoning cities. Interestingly enough, the disorganization, pathology and maladjustment they discerned were peculiarly confined to urban areas. In the early part of this century there were indeed many acute urban "problems," problems that were possibly much more acute than those now plaguing contemporary America. Successive waves of immigrants were undergoing the painful process of accommodating themselves to a new land, a land that was itself undergoing profound and rapid change. From a rural society of independent landholders, America was being transformed into the most urbanized and industrialized country in the history of the world. If the social change witnessed by the social pathologists in the cities of the time was upsetting to them, it was understandably so. For the change they witnessed was, in an important sense, something new. They were parties to the birth of a new kind of social order—a social order based on elaborate mechanization, technological innovation and occupational differentiation, a social order whose new bases were overlaying and tending to supplant the more traditional bonds of kinship, territorial anchorings and historic cultural tradition.

Because these social scientists were essentially rural persons who were also new to the big cities, they tended to view the urban complex from the perspective of their early learned conceptions or assumptions about what constituted a normal society. They had an image of a normal society as one which was small in population, compact in territory and homogeneous in cultural tradition —an image which fit the classic American small towns. Cities were exactly the opposite: large in population, sprawling in territory and heterogeneous in cultural tradition. If small towns were normal, then other places must be abnormal, pathological or disorganized. In addition, they tended to assume that a normal society was one in which people agreed about most things and did not (at least, not openly) dispute one another. The good life (i.e., the mythical utopia of small-town America) was one in which harmony characterized public and private relations. Cities, however, were arenas of conflicting groups, battling for what were thought to be scarce resources. A multitude of groups in conflict and therefore out of harmony indicated a condition of social disorganization. Furthermore, the "normal" or "adjusted" person was, in the natural order of things, a bourgeois, Sunday-go-to-meeting, stable booster of Small Town's Main Street. He was Protestant, temperate, married only once, a parent and the like. For the social pathologists,

> the ideally adjusted man is "socialized." This term seems to operate ethically as the opposite of "selfish"; it implies that the adjusted man conforms to middle-class morality and motives and "participates" in the gradual progress of respectable institutions. If he is not a "joiner," he certainly gets around and into many community organizations. If he is socialized, the individual thinks of others and is kindly toward them. He does not brood or mope about but is somewhat extravert, eagerly participating in his community's institutions. His mother and father were not divorced, nor was his home ever broken. He is "successful"—at least in a modest way—since he is ambitious, but he does not speculate about matters too far above his means, lest he become "a fantasy thinker," and the little men don't scramble after the big money. The less abstract the traits and fulfilled "needs" of the "adjusted man" are, the more they gravitate toward the norms of independent middle-class persons verbally living out Protestant ideals in the small towns of America. (Mills, 1942:180.)

Woefully, cities were glutted with foreigners, workmen, Catholics, nonchurchgoers and a variety of even less savory types, such as prostitutes and hoboes, whose behavior flew in the face of the middle-class small-town ethic. Hence masses of people in the city were maladjusted or abnormal.

SOCIOLOGY AND THE
TOPICS OF DEVIANCE
IN THE FIFTIES

It was partly with reference to and against this ideological scenery (as well as some Marxist tendencies of the thirties) that sociologists after World War II began to seek some more modern and scientific posture. This posture emerged as the doctrine of value-free sociology, the position that the work of sociologists must be purged of moral taint. Sociologists should work with ethically neutral concepts and hold themselves aloof from moral musings. The prestigious Max Weber's lecture entitled "Science as a Vocation" was the primary ideological document of this movement.[3]

---

[3] Weber, 1946:129–56 (originally published in 1922). A more detailed analysis of the fifties, upon which I have drawn, is presented in Gouldner, 1962.

The doctrine of value-free sociology is potentially revolutionary in its implication (e.g., if one is truly value-free, he avoids loyalty to the state; therefore he
is disloyal), but as a matter of operating application and consequence it was
conveniently congruent with and supportive of the political climate and technological developments of postwar America. The crystallization of the East-
West blocs and the coming of the not-so-cold war generated considerable
domestic concern over the nature and meaning of loyalty. In the period surrounding the McCarthy era, value-free sociology seemed mostly to mean politically conventional, neutral or harmless sociology. It thus helped to remove
sociologists and other social scientists from too close and too continuous scrutiny or harassment by the polity. Along with this, the increasing technological
complexity of the military and the economy promoted government concern
over, and support of, research and development. In addition to the vast sums
made available for the development of more conventional types of hardware,
funds were allocated for research into the solving of "human problems," such as
group morale and efficiency, mental illness and juvenile delinquency. The
value-free ideology contributed to the training of moral conventionalists and
amoral technicians and thus helped to ensure that social scientists would abun-
dantly benefit from this largesse.[4]

Thus, with the coming of a belief in value-free sociology in the fifties, concepts such as social disorganization and social pathology, with their associated
moral ideology, came to be thought of as inconsistent with a strictly scientific
perspective. These and kindred concepts became disreputable, at least in the
leading universities. Their fall from grace created a conceptual vacuum. Desirous of retaining the traditional and juicy topics studied under these rubrics,
sociologists needed some new concept or concepts under which the appropriate
materials could continue to huddle. Enter, unheralded, the rubrics "deviance"
and "deviant." Emanating primarily from Harvard and Columbia,[5] the leading
centers of sociology in the fifties, the deviance framework moved quickly and
quietly into a position of supremacy.

For some people a new name may offer a new lease on life. But for the
topics which it was intended to designate, the new concept, deviance, seemed
less helpful. Beyond some concern with anomie, the presumed discovery that
people have to have opportunities to act in certain ways, and two statements on
adolescent males labeled delinquent,[6] the field lay in relative quiescence. Traditional types of research studies on the topics of deviance continued, of course,
at a high rate, but few of them appear to have accomplished more than a repli-

[4] Although written in writhing anger, screeching voice and nasty tone, Mills' *The Sociological Imagination* (1959) is a valuable commentary on and document of sociology in the
fifties. As in other matters, one must be careful not to throw the baby out with the bath.
   [5] From Harvard: Parsons, 1951:Chap. 7; and Cohen, 1955 and 1959; from Columbia:
Merton, 1938, 1949 and 1957:Chaps. 4 and 5. These strangely brief treatments of the field
were ubiquitously recounted, cited as major statements and read seriously by active sociologists of the time.
   [6] Cohen, 1955; and Cloward and Ohlin, 1960.

cation of prewar findings (now cast in deviance terminology) or a reiteration of
the still active social pathological perspective.[7]

DISSENT IN THE SIXTIES

By the beginning of the sixties an increasing number of restive musings became noticeable. In sociology generally and in deviance in particular, scholars
announced doubts about sociological studies being in fact value-free.[8] Among
deviance scholars, Howard S. Becker's pungent distinction between conventional and unconventional sentimentality was an important expression of these
doubts. Defining sentimentality as "a disposition on the part of the researcher
to leave certain variables in a problem unexamined,"[9] he pointed out the conventionally sentimental tendency of deviance scholars to accept lay assumptions
about the acts and qualities of "normals" and "deviants." Given their conventional sentimentality, they tended to design their studies in ways that revealed
only the morally crediting aspects of normals and the morally discrediting aspects of deviants. As a consequence, much deviance research served mainly
to reinforce the layman's conception of the world as divided into thoroughly
"good people" and thoroughly "evil people," with perhaps a few in between.
Thus studies focusing strictly on the backgrounds and psychological characteristics of people classified as criminals, for example, conveniently ignored their
normal conduct, the conventional social processes in which they participated
and the conventional acts and qualities of their interaction partners. Put another way, the conventionally sentimental tended to conceive their research
problems in ways that overlooked the aspects of normals that were morally
blemished and the aspects of deviants that were morally crediting. Expanding
on Becker, we should observe that the conventional sentimentality of the fifties

[7] As T. Kuhn (1962) has noted, conceptual frameworks in science are not replaced by
scientists' abandoning their former views and taking up the new. Scientists, like religionists,
tend to espouse a single perspective over their entire careers. New perspectives spread,
rather, through their adoption by young and relatively unknowledgeable newcomers to the
field, either while in graduate training or early in their professional careers. Unencumbered
by prior commitments and not understanding the orthodox very well in any case, novices
more readily comprehend the new, or, if one prefers, more easily fall prey to folly.
[8] E.g., Dahrendorf, 1958; and Gouldner, 1962. Interestingly enough, pre-World War II
expressions of the same theme seem to have gone into eclipse during this period, even when
propounded by otherwise widely read men such as Lynd, 1939; and Myrdal, 1944:Appendix
2. Moving deep into the psychedelic sixties and into increasing involvement with questions
of public policy, matters of moral stance became a prime object of dispute during which one
work even put "sociology on trial" and another declared a "new sociology." The interested
reader will find this diatribe conveniently chronicled in the pages of The American Sociologist, a magazine instituted in 1965. See also Horowitz, 1967; H. S. Becker, 1967; Tumin,
1968; and Manis, 1968. On the substantive and ideological texture of sociology more generally, see Horowitz, 1965; Lipset and Smelser, 1961; Gouldner, 1968; and Horton, 1966;
the works collected in Demerath and Peterson, eds., 1967; and the historical interpretation
advanced by E. Becker, 1968:especially Chap. 4.
[9] H. S. Becker, ed., 1964:4.

was more invidious than that of earlier social pathologists, because it was less naïve and less obvious, wearing as it did the facade of value-free sociology. Beneath this facade, however, lay an essentially normative—even conservative— status quo orientation.

In the same way that all perspectives tend to generate counterperspectives, a different (if not new) genre of deviance researchers arose with some force in the early sixties. Acting as both spokesman for the motif and as skeptical on-looker, Becker characterized the equally noticeable bias of this new perspective as "unconventional sentimentality," a disposition to assume that normals are less moral than typically portrayed and a disposition to assume that deviants are considerably more moral than is commonly thought. The unconventional sentimentalist "assumes . . . that the underdog is always right and those in authority always wrong."[10] As editor (1962–64) of a scholarly journal with the ironic title *Social Problems*, Becker was particularly disposed to articles of an unconventionally sentimental cast,[11] a policy that was continued by his succes-sors. The error of the unconventionally sentimental was justified, according to Becker, because "if one outrages certain conventional assumptions by being unconventionally sentimental, a large body of opinion will be sure to tell [schol-ars] about it. But conventional sentimentality is less often attacked and spe-cious premises stand unchallenged" (H. S. Becker, 1964:5–6).[12]

It needs hastily to be added that none of this controversy over value-bias is an attack on science per se. Science is only a set of procedures which disci-plines the collection and analysis of data. The scientific outlook concerns itself with matters of appropriate sampling, measurement, adequate controls and comparisons, demonstrations of hypothetical associations and legitimate inter-pretation of data. Science cannot tell researchers what questions to ask, what problems to pose, what aspects of reality to single out for study, what concepts to employ in analyzing some situation or what assumptions to make about the nature of some problematic phenomenon. The present questions of value neu-trality or tacit commitment have to do with these latter concerns. They are not issues of appropriate scientific procedure. Scholars of any value orientation can be equally scientific and yet still be at odds because they do not agree on what questions to ask or how to ask them, or, if they agree at this level, because they differ in their assessment of the fundamental characteristics of the same object. These are matters of perspective.

---

[10] *Ibid.*, p. 5.

[11] Becker later collected many of these articles in a book he entitled *The Other Side* (H. S. Becker, ed., 1964), an overt expression of unconventional sentimentality.

[12] There has, of course, been a concomitant, substantive shift from a focus on deviant acts and persons to a focus on "normals" and their various relations to deviance, particularly cen-tering on the concept of labeling. The latter questions will occupy us below, especially in Part II. For histories emphasizing the substantive character of the dissent or shift, see Gibbs, 1966; Reiss, 1966; Bordua, 1967; and Douglas, 1969. See also the substantively critical statements cited in footnote 8 of Chap. 2.

SOME MORAL RESERVATIONS
OF THE PRESENT WORK

Despite the extensive dissent of the unconventionally sentimental sociologists —a dissent that has provided much of the recent excitement in sociology—they did not, in one important respect, go far enough. As intellectual heirs of the deviance framework, they retained the concepts of deviance and deviant. Howard S. Becker's influential book *Outsiders* (1963), for example, bears the unapologetic subtitle "Studies in the Sociology of Deviance."

It can be suggested that the dissent from conventional sentimentality should have included a certain skepticism about the term used in the fifties to name the field. The concepts of deviance and deviant carry a value-bias and represent moral judgments not dissimilar to those implied in the concepts of the social pathologists. Regardless of the intent of the scholars who utilize them, the terms deviance and deviant carry a conservative moral loading. Both terms are quite similar to the popular concept deviate, which, in turn, conjures up the modifier sexual, producing that darling of the mass press, "sexual deviate." From there it is but a short step to pervert, especially sexual pervert.

As a term in everyday language, deviant seems to evoke a range of fairly standardized images of miserable creatures. When college students are asked, for example, to list those things or types of persons whom they regard as deviant, they produce in large percentages such categories as homosexuals, drug addicts, alcoholics, prostitutes, murderers and criminals, among others (Simmons, 1965:223–25). Although people may not agree on exactly what is deviant, it is important to note that, when presented with the word, they have no difficulty producing a list of types.

If the term deviant evokes such categories, then what characteristics do these categories themselves evoke? When sociologist J. L. Simmons asked college students to write sketches of selected deviant types, the majority were found to present rather negative portraits. Marijuana smokers, beatniks, adulterers, homosexuals and political radicals—the types presented—emerged with a majority stereotype as a "dark, haunted creature beyond the pale of ordinary life" (Simmons, 1965:226). Thus one person characterized the marijuana smoker as

> . . . a greasy Puerto Rican boy or the shaky little Skid Row bum . . . . As for the life led, it is shiftless, unhappy, dog-eat-dog for survival. I guess marijuana is used as a means of avoiding reality. The pleasure that comes from the drug outweighs the pleasure of life as it really is. (Simmons, 1965:226.)

Simmons additionally found that, when college students were presented with a check list of 70 "character traits" that might apply to the five types, they most frequently indicated negative attributes for each type. Neutral or positive traits that were also on the list were generally not attributed.

> The marijuana-smoker stereotype emerges as an insecure escapist, lacking self-control and looking for kicks; the beatnik is sloppy, immature non-conformist; the adulterer is immoral, promiscuous and insecure; the homosexual is perverted and mentally ill; the political radical is ambitious, aggressive, stubborn and dangerous. The only characteristic imputed frequently to all five types was irresponsibility—lacking self-control. All but the radicals were described as lonely and frustrated. Immaturity was encircled by at least some fraction of respondents for each of the types. (Simmons, 1965:228.)

The negative imputations made by these college students are probably not much different than those which might be elicited from the total population. It even seems likely that many social scientists themselves hold much the same imagery. It strikes me as peculiar, then, that scholars should take as their central concepts words which have such enormous moral meaning and which therefore dispose them, however unintentional the disposition, to set about their work in a rather conventionally sentimental way. By using the terms deviant and deviance, they participate, knowingly or not, intentionally or not, in the reinforcement of popular ideology. (This is the case despite the fact that, within some limited sociological circles, to call someone a deviant is to compliment him.) It is perhaps of little wonder that social scientific theories of these matters tend to reproduce, in more abstruse language and in a more complicated manner, the folk theories of mass culture.[13]

It is usual at this point to make a resounding call for the development of value-free concepts. I will not do this, because I am not at all certain that morally neutral languages are possible in the social sciences. Insofar as social scientists draw upon "natural language," the language of everyday or more esoteric discourse, they fish in a pool of already moralized possibilities. All categories of reality are moral categories, if only in the assertion that *this*—whatever the this—should be designated. The sociological quest for abstruse, coined and neologistic words is, at least in part, an attempt to escape the moral meanings inherent in natural language. Once adopted, however, even these words acquire moral valence or are constantly translated into their everyday synonyms, which themselves have moral valence. Entire sociologistic-scientific languages presented as candidates for the sociological lexicon, once accepted, would seem eventually doomed to the same fate.

But even if morally neutral languages were possible, as a person and a citi-

---

[13] I am indebted to Gerald Suttles for instructive conversations on this parallelism. Also instructive have been the writings of students in courses on juvenile delinquency who, upon being asked on the first day of the course to write what they believed to be the causes of delinquency, could handily produce reasonably accurate versions of Cohen, 1955; Cloward and Ohlin, 1960; and various psychologistic perspectives.

zen I am not certain that they are desirable. Morally neutral languages tend to be sponsored by persons who put the building of knowledge above all other human values. Such an operating orientation rather easily falls prey to, and is rather easily exploited by, groups who would use the science for their own ends. Amoral language and science seems to mean politically exploitable language and science. Perhaps moderately moralized language and science are somewhat more resistant. This is not to advocate a thoroughly politicized scientific enterprise, but merely to recommend a continuing consciousness among social scientists of the moral meaning, relevance and consequence of their work. Social science is a social force in a technological society. As such, it can serve, dominate or make treaties with other political interests. Whatever may eventually crystallize as the political role of social science, a consciousness of the moral meaning and "loading" of social science work may at least ensure that the alignment will not be forged by default and external manipulation.

More specifically, concepts tend to reflect and, by their choice and phrasing, to serve the social interests of the social category which sponsors them. As an illustration of this point, one need only recall the links between the social location of the sociologists who earlier used the concept social disorganization and the connotations of that term and between the social location of later sociologists and their term, deviance. All sociology—nay, all human communication—is communication from a point of view—from the point of view of one or another social category and that category's objective interests. We, the reader and writer alike, are doomed to be involved as partisans if we are to live at all (cf., Seeley, 1963; Halmos, 1966:106–123). But because, as human beings, it is possible for us to recognize, to be aware of, the constrictions and limitations of social location, it is also possible for us to make explicit the social location and resultant point of view from which we speak. I personally feel that it is the moral obligation, especially of professional promoters of some point of view, to make as clear as they can the connection between their views and that which serves their social interests. I owe to the reader, in the present case, some sense of the social location out of which the present work and sociological efforts of a similar nature grow.

Occupational differentiation in American civilization has made it possible for some persons to make a rather decent living while at the same time having available large blocks of free time during which they may observe and contemplate, either as outsiders or as marginally involved insiders, the events that transpire in various institutional realms. Located in colleges and universities, these persons occupy the role normally labeled "professor," a role which has come to be reasonably secure against short-term attack upon its occupants. By means of such arrangements as three-year contracts and tenure, the role occupants are relatively immune from sanction by their opponents, at least for a time and at least in what are, by definition, the better colleges and universities. Although possibly representing only a relative minority of all professors, there are recruited to the role persons who are not strong partisans or defenders of established institutions or of reigning conceptions of the good, the true and the beautiful. Within the academic setting such persons are relatively free (in terms of time and social pressure) to pursue their interests.

Professors who turn their attention to institutions external to the university and who are not already partisans of such external institutions are located, then, as relatively protected and affluent outsiders, free from any constraint to adopt the point of view of those whom they observe. Such is my location, or, at least, my conception of it, which is in some sense all that matters. What follows, then, need not be, and is not, an apology for any set of government officials, of so-called therapeutic professionals or of criminals, prostitutes or other categories involved in the deviance game. If anything, this work is the kind of apology that is best written and perhaps only written by the professional and secure outsider to a social institution: it is an apology for the broadest of all social categories conceived by human beings, the category of humanity.[14] Despite the fact that such observers may render a short-term disservice to the objective interests of some social categories, it is to be hoped that they render an important long-term service to all social categories.

Let me say, nonetheless, that I continue to share somewhat in the unconventionally sentimental bias. What has been done in the past and is done today to those humans classified as deviant (and even to those classified as normal) is in many respects a crime against humanity. Indeed, if throughout what follows, I appear somewhat less friendly toward normals than toward some sorts of deviants, it is because I am.

All this brings us back to the question of the moral loading inherent in the term deviance. Although I am highly dissatisfied with the term, I am also at a loss to find an alternative that will perform the same work and be equally succinct. As a creature of tradition and training, I will continue to use the term, but on the understanding that it carries only that meaning to be spelled out in Chap. 2.

[14] See further on the character and implications of such a posture and perspective: Berger, 1961; Mills, 1959; Gouldner, 1968:116; and Etzioni, 1968a. See, in particular, Etzioni's view of elements necessary to what he terms an active society; Etzioni, 1968a:Chaps. 8, 12 and 18, especially pp. 181–88 and pp. 537–41.

Hopefully having provided some sense of the larger context in which study of the present topics is set, we may turn now to more formal matters. These include questions of what might be denoted by the concept deviance, how one might set about more specifically to delineate items requiring explanation and how explanatory accounts of them might be organized.

CHAPTER 2

INTRODUCTION: LOGICAL MATTERS

DEVIANCE AS A TYPE OF SOCIAL CONFLICT

As used by sociologists, the concept of deviance and its variants are merely somewhat more abstract versions of common-sense, everyday designations. Such popular designations include "crime," "criminal," "deviate," "pervert," "nut," "kook," "lunatic," "oddball," "wierdo," and the like. The deviance vocabulary represents sociologists' attempt to encompass these more colorful words of the layman. Sociologists and laymen alike bracket together certain acts and categories of persons as deserving a kind of attention that is different from that accorded all other acts and categories of persons. One way, then, to approach a definition of deviance is in terms of the basis upon which sociologists and laymen accomplish this broad bracketing.

Parties in Conflict

The basis of this bracketing can best be pursued, not through a search for distinctive features of deviance per se, but rather in terms of general and generic dimensions of social organization and social response. Within such dimensions, the defining of persons and acts as deviant can be seen as a particular instance of generalized ways in which social organization and social definition can differ. At the level of a single and *total society*, such a basis is found in the dynamics of what proportion of a society, how well organized and how powerful, are *fearful* of, and feel *threatened* by, some other portion of the society. Organized social life can be viewed as a game in which actors and collectivities defend themselves against distrusted and suspected others. Suspicion, distrust, fear and threat are central themes in all large-scale and differentiated societies. A political constitution like that of the United States even builds in a division of powers to take account of such feelings and to institutionalize their expression.

The parties playing the game around these basic themes can, of course, differ considerably along a variety of dimensions. Taking first *who is feared* or felt to be threatening, some basic distinctions reside in the *population size* of the feared party, the degree of its *organization* and the amount of its *power* relative to the size, organization and power of those who fear it. Taking only size and degree of organization together, some typically identified feared parties are: (1) individuals or small groups who have a limited degree of organization; (2) relatively small but thoroughly organized groups with leaders; and (3) large, well-organized groups within a total society.

On the other side, that of *who is fearful* or is perceiving a threat, parties may vary along the dimensions of: (1) the proportion of the society which feels threatened (e.g., a small minority, a sizable minority or a majority); (2) how strongly the party feels threatened (ranging from mere amusement to a "basic threat to our way of life"); (3) the extent to which the party is organized; and (4) how much power, relative to the feared party, is possessed by those threatened. The amount of power of who is threatened refers in particular to their ability to bring the resources of the state to bear upon the party felt to be threatening. Those fearful parties who can voice their fears at the public level, who receive at least some public legitimation, and who have the legal structure act in compliance with their wishes (namely, to incarcerate or banish the feared party) are parties with the greatest amount of power.

These variations in size, organization, degree of fear and amount of power among factions of a society provide a basis upon which we can roughly define deviance and see its relation to some other kinds of power games. What is called deviance is but one of a series of generically related situations, some of the more popular forms of which are identified in Chart 2.1.[1] Deviance is the name of the conflict game in which individuals or loosely organized small groups with little power are strongly feared by a well-organized, sizable minority or majority who have a large amount of power.

Under different levels of fear, size, organization and power between parties in conflict, there are corresponding changes in public definitions of the situation. Persons and acts in a small, powerless minority that are at one time regarded as merely deviant may, at another time, be felt to constitute a civil uprising, social movement or civil war. Theft, arson, assault, torture and murder perpetrated by individuals is simply deviance; when perpetrated by a loosely organized minority acting in concert such acts might be imputed to have a political meaning, and, when performed in the context of a civil or revolutionary war—that is, by a well-organized minority—they are acts of war or of liberation or legitimate defense. (When undertaken in conflicts between nations, such acts can be among the highest forms of patriotic display. When Audie Murphy killed German soldiers, he was a hero. When Charles Whitman shot Texas civilians, he was a mad killer.)

------

[1] It is testimony to the rich diversity of human life that Chart 2.1 represents only a few of several hundred possible conflict situations. For example, if one combines the three dimensions of party feared (size, organization and power) and the four dimensions of party fearing (size, organization, power and degree of fear), and if each dimension is merely dichotomized (a massive oversimplification), the result is 128 different conflict situations.

The imputation of even greatly feared acts and persons as deviant seems to depend less upon particular behavior per se than upon the respective size, degree of power and degree of organization of parties to an issue.

Beyond the excluded conflict situations indicated in Chart 2.1, there are two other items which some investigators have defined as deviant or as a basis for defining deviance. First, acts that are only *mildly* feared, even if so feared by a large and powerful majority in relation to single powerless individuals or small groups, seem more cogently considered simply as *inappropriate* behavior. Social life is replete with occurrences of tardiness, rudeness, impoliteness, overfamiliarity, embarrassments, *faux pas*, etc.[2] These continuing but mild vexations are better analyzed as features of the sociology of everyday life.[3] Second, strong fears of some act or class of actors that emanate from a relatively small

CHART 2.1. *CONFLICT SITUATIONS*

Dimensions of the Character and Relations of
Parties in Conflict

Resulting Popular Definition of the Conflict Situation	Size and Organization of Party Feared	Economic and Political Power of Party Feared Relative to Party Fearing	Degree to Which the Well-organized Opposing Large Minority or Majority Feels Fearful or Threatened
Deviance ("Crime," etc.)	*Individual or small, loosely organized groups*	*Almost none*	*Very high*
Civil Uprising or Disorder	*Small loosely organized minority*	*Relatively low*	*Very high*
Social Movement	*Sizable organized minority*	*Relatively low*	*Mild*
Civil War	*Large, well-organized minority*	*Relatively high or almost equal*	*Very high*
Mainstream Party Politics in the United States	*Large, organized minority*	*About equal*	*Mild*

[2] Definitions of the field like "behavior which violates institutionalized expectations" (Cohen, 1959:462) thus seem much too broad and group together items of too many varieties.

[3] Within perspectives such as presented by Goffman, 1959, 1961b and 1967.

and not very powerful minority involves *special pleading* and, at the level of the total society, the objects of these fears are not rendered deviant.   The Prohibition Party's fear of alcoholic consumption and the people who consume it defines a class of deviance for the Prohibitionists, but they are largely bereft of following and social power.   Militants of the left and right of both races, who see wisdom in stockpiling firearms to defend against oppressors, apparently have very strong fears of "leftists," "whites," "blacks," or those felt to be ubiquitous Communists in disguise.   As long as such groups remain small minorities and lack much power, the objects they define as fearful are merely matters of some slight controversy.   Any such group can, of course, come into a position of some power, perhaps to the extent of forcing the game of civil war, or, with sufficient power, of creating a new game of who is defined as deviant about what.   Consider, for example, what former Alabama Governor George Wallace and his followers define as deviant:

> Bearded professors on some of our college campuses . . . are sympathizing with the enemy, they are encouraging youths to burn draft cards, and some are saying openly, the Viet Cong should win and furnishin' food, blood and clothes to the enemy.
>
> If I were President I would hale 'em before a grand jury and prosecute 'em for treason for that is what it is and traitors is what they are . . . never mind the thin line that we haven't declared war.   (Vestal, 1967.)

Given the wide range of groups and perspectives in American civilization, it is probably the case that almost any act or person is strongly feared by *some* social category or organized group.   If it is to be possible to isolate a category of deviance rather than simply a multitude of conflicts, it is essential that there be involved at least a powerful minority—even if not a majority—who feel a strong sense of threat and fear.   And, as is already evident from the foregoing, the system focus for defining and analyzing deviance is the total society, most typically the nation-state.   Items that might be called deviant but that have only a local interest—that can only be of concern within less inclusive or "lower-level" systems such as formal organizations and face-to-face groups—seem best left as topics of analysis within their respective formal areas.[4]

FURTHER SPECIFICATION

The foregoing is a very general guide to types of conflict situations and is lacking in specificity.   How, more concretely, may an investigator determine that he is witnessing the deviance game rather than some other kind of con-

---

[4] Cf., Goffman, 1963a:140–47, on "in-group deviants."   A different conception is presented by Cohen, 1966.

flict? How can one know when he is viewing a constellation of a large and powerful well-organized minority or majority that is highly fearful of lone individuals or small, loosely organized groups with little power? Issues of specificity center, in particular, on the concepts or variables of fear and power. What does it mean to say that a party is highly fearful or feels highly threatened or has a great deal of power?

Leaving aside fear and threat arising from relations to extrahuman objects (e.g., other kinds of animals, the supernatural, floods, explosions), the perception that another human is a fearful object centers significantly on the belief that the human impedes or inhibits the pursuit of one's objectives. The threatening party is seen as actually or potentially disrupting or placing in jeopardy one's activities. Disruption and jeopardy are most commonly conceived in terms of possible or actual physical harm or loss of material resources, but I should here like to take a broader view of the matter. The possibility of physical harm or loss of material resources are not the only ways in which the accomplishment of planned activities can be made problematic. The possibilities of being murdered or robbed are not the only ways in which there can exist serious ambiguity or unpredictability and consequent anxiety about reasonably getting through a day and negotiating a life course generally. Since human plans, under the best of circumstances, are only ambiguously accomplishable, it is reasonable for humans to seek to reduce extraneous sources of ambiguity and unpredictability.

While the more spectacular possible acts, like murder or robbery, are clear-cut sources or forms of ambiguity, it is also true that serious ambiguity is an essential feature of other items defined as deviant. Persons defined as mentally ill are precisely so defined because of the havoc of ambiguity they inflict upon the interactional order of the everyday lives of those around them. More than simply violating understandings of face-to-face interaction, they are also unpredictable as to when and in what manner they will commit these violations, and this creates what can be thought of by persons who must associate with them as unreasonable contingencies. In the larger perspective of institutional orders, categories of persons who defy existing conceptions of possible and proper being serve to create ambiguity about that order. Homosexuals of both sexes serve to make ambiguous the institutionalized division between the sexes. Prostitutes make ambiguous the sexual benefits of the familial order.[5]

When the actual or potential disruptive ambiguity is believed to affect the

---

[5] When considered in the light of threat, fear, jeopardy and ambiguity, it is not unreasonable to contemplate the possibility that the blind, the physically handicapped and the retarded are deviant. In much the same way that the thief creates extraneous anxiety and ambiguity by his acts, these categories create what can be felt to be extraneous anxiety and ambiguity by their being. Their disabilities block the normal and smooth flow of everyday interaction and special account must be taken of them. Note that the kind of account taken of them is much the same kind as that taken of other rather powerless and unorganized categories; namely, incarceration and other exclusion from civil society. Despite this, in the analysis which follows, they will not be so defined.

activities most fundamental or central to the pursuit of the initial party's objectives, there is likely to arise a range of demands and practices which are intended to prevent and inhibit such disruption. The demands and practices that ensue will be a function of the size, degree of organization and, especially, power of the involved parties. Within nation-states, powerful, large and well-organized parties, whose activities are actually or potentially disrupted by small, powerless and unorganized parties, are in a position to demand and perhaps to effect various kinds of exclusions relative to the offensive party. The exclusion may be in the form of banishment or exile (one of the more popular practices, historically), or it may be in the form of ritualized, state-conducted annihilation. In more recent times exclusion by incarceration has become popular, as seen by the growth of such exile institutions as prisons and mental hospitals (as well as homes for the elderly, schools for the blind, sheltered workshops, training schools, etc.).

In modern civil states, one obtains something like a formal measure of power by noting the differential capacity of interest groups to have enacted by the state exclusionary rules and practices which are protective of their activities. The advocates of banishing or annihilating all Blacks or Jews differ from the advocates of incarcerating embezzlers or committing the mentally ill primarily in the degree to which they are able to mobilize the state to enact such rulings. Indeed, in at least one modern state, a group could come to have the power to banish and finally to annihilate Jews, a policy still advocated by some citizens of the United States.

The ideology of democratic societies which asserts that state rulings must have popular support should not obscure the more fundamental fact that large portions of the populous of any society are typically indifferent to and ignorant of any given possible ruling and that any proposed ruling is likely to have one or more groups that vigorously oppose it. Although there is likely to be some degree of support for a given ruling in democratic societies, it should not be assumed that such support is strong or necessarily arises from a majority sense of strong fear. The advent of an exclusionary ruling might only mean that some highly fearful, well-organized and powerful interest group has been able to muster relatively large minority support, perhaps in the midst of widespread apathy or ignorance, and therefore has been successful in having its interests sponsored and protected by the state. The important point is that such a course of events is possible only in relation to people of little power who are not very well organized. If this were not the case, overt political struggles, perhaps even civil war, would ensue. (See, e.g., H. S. Becker, 1963:135–46; Dickson, 1968.)

A primary indicator of "this is the type of conflict called deviance," in a total society is, then, the existence of state rulings and corresponding enforcement mechanisms that provide for the possibility of forceably removing actors from civil society, either by banishment, annihilation or incarceration. Again, it is precisely those actors who have little power and who are not organized toward whom such actions can most successfully be undertaken.

Readers who are familiar with sociological definitions of deviance will note that this approach departs somewhat from the more typical emphasis upon deviance as rule breaking or norm violation. It is certainly true that deviance involves the breaking of somebody's rules; but it is also true that the breaking of somebody's rules is not peculiar or unique to the type of conflict called deviance. The types of conflict labeled civil disorder, rebellion, revolutionary and social movements, civil war and even staid American politics also involve one party's feeling that another party is abridging or will abridge proper rules of conduct. "People are in fact always *forcing* their rules on others," as Howard S. Becker has put it (1963:17). The issue, then, is not rule violation per se; rather, it is rule violation *in the context of* relative power, size, degree of organization and sense of fear among parties in conflict. Deviance is rule violation only in the limited sense that it involves violating the rules of relatively large minorities or majorities who are powerful, well organized and highly fearful of individuals or loosely organized or small groups who lack power.

It is in the situation of a very powerful party opposing a very weak one that the powerful party sponsors the *idea* that the weak party is breaking the rules of society. The very concepts of "society" and its "rules" are appropriated by powerful parties and made synonymous with their interests (and, of course, believed in by the naïve, e.g., the undergraduate penchant for the phrases "society says . . . ," "society expects . . . ," "society does . . ."). It is not so easy to sponsor such notions of a solid society in conflicts with organized opponents who possess some power. Hence conflicts with such opponents are conceived in different terms and given different names, as in Chart 2.1 (cf., the discussion in Chap. 6).

This point brings us to a further, more general observation. To the degree that sociologists emphasize, *about modern nation-states,* the idea of there being abstract social rules of society, they tend ideologically to align themselves with powerful groups. They sponsor a conception that is congruent with the interests of such groups. The notions of the social rules of the society may have some relevance for smaller, more homogeneous tribal societies and other relatively face-to-face collectivities. But such concepts seem to mislead more than lead in addressing the sprawling, highly diverse, mediated, amorphous and conflictual object that is the technological nation-state (see, further, Douglas, 1969).

CONFLICT OVER THE NAME OF THE CONFLICT

The degree to which rulings are expressions of strong, reasonably widespread beliefs in the threatening character of an act or type of actor is likely to vary quite widely. Almost 100 per cent of a society might feel that premeditated homicide not involving self-defense is highly threatening and that child molesting or the rape of a female by multiple males unknown to her is equally so. But beyond such instances, consensus on strong fear appears to diminish, especially in the area of what are called "crimes without victims," for example, abortion, homosexuality between consenting adults and the use of such drugs as marijuana (Schur, 1965). Indeed, even for items often presumed to be rather strongly disapproved or feared, there seem to be significant portions of the population who do not care much at all about them. A public-opinion poll conducted by the Harris organization asked this question:

> America has many different types of people in it. But we would like to know whether you think each of these different types of people is more helpful or more harmful to American life, or don't they help or harm things much one way or the other? (L. Harris, 1965.)

Often-mentioned deviant categories on the list elicited the following distributions:

	MORE HARMFUL	MORE HELPFUL OR DOESN'T MATTER
American Communist Party *members*	89%	11%
Homosexuals	70%	30%
Prostitutes	70%	30%

Other categories that some people regard as deviant can be seen (at least in the poll year of 1965) to be not all that widely feared.

	MORE HARMFUL	MORE HELPFUL OR DOESN'T MATTER
Anti-Vietnam War picketers	68%	32%
Civil rights demonstrators	68%	32%
Student demonstrators at *colleges*	65%	35%
Young men with beards and *long hair*	52%	48%
Beatniks	52%	48%
Members of the John Birch *Society*	48%	52%

Indeed, at least as measured by the Harris poll, some categories not usually mentioned as deviant turn up, in the popular view, to be almost as widely feared or disapproved as more usual kinds of deviance.

	MORE HARMFUL	MORE HELPFUL OR DOESN'T MATTER
People who don't believe *in God*	72%	28%
Women who gossip all the *time*	65%	35%

Note that on this measure, atheists, agnostics and gossips draw a response distribution rather similar to that drawn by homosexuals and prostitutes. The two sets of categories are perhaps most distinguished by the degree to which powerful organized interests are fearful enough to mobilize themselves for the purpose of making rulings. One set winds up as deviant and the other merely as objects of popular suspicion.

The Harris poll also supplies some material on the point that at least some segment of the population is likely to be fearful of almost anything that can be named. Witness these objects:

	MORE HARMFUL	MORE HELPFUL OR DOESN'T MATTER
High school students more interested in athletics than studies	45%	55%
College professors active in unpopular causes	58%	42%
Working career women with young children	50%	50%
Women who wear bikini bathing suits	36%	65%
Lawyers who defend notorious criminals	34%	66%
Young people who like rock and roll	10%	90%
Young people who read books most of the time	10%	90%

An act or type of actor over which there is attenuated consensus can come to have a relatively organized set of defenders, despite the fact that some others continue strongly to fear the object and despite the fact that the legal ruling remains in existence and is enforced. This was once the case for workers attempting to organize unions and is the case today relative to the use of marijuana, the obtaining of abortions and engagement in homosexuality. Like workers at the turn of the 20th century, advocates of the use of marijuana and LSD and of homosexuality have organized to promote their interests (H. S. Becker, 1965).

The process of beginning not "to take it" from the political order, the development of organized efforts at change and the creation of a sympathetic segment among the public at large are early steps in the removal of an item from the purview of the deviance game. The revolutionary sect that draws support begins to play at the politics of insurrection and revolutionary upheaval. The advocates of easy abortion who draw support begin to play at the social movement or conventional politics game. Those who refuse to fight in a war and who draw large minority support engage in the vicissitudes of political strife. While that which is deviant accumulates power, those who still fear it and who continue to have the rules and state apparatus in their favor tend to persist in defining the growing opposition as deviant. The question is then posed: At what point is something no longer deviant? It seems most reasonable to confront this question on the same grounds that initially make it problematic for the sociologist. Those grounds are that the participants can themselves be divided and that whether something is deviant or not can be at issue in public discourse. To be true to the character of his materials, the sociologist must reflect ambiguity as well as more or less consensual public definitions. The point here is that there are likely, at any time, to be acts and persons about which it is difficult to make a decision as to their deviance. This ambiguity and conflict over the name of the conflict is an important feature of that act or type of person. By being attentive to such conflict and ambiguity, it becomes possible to follow the dynamics of how items can come to be defined in terms of kinds of conflict other than deviance, or can reach consensual normality (as well as how they can come to be defined as deviant).

In the American sixties, civil disorder among Blacks in urban ghettos has been an outstanding instance of such conflict and ambiguity over the name of the conflict. The pronouncements of some political authorities that rioting and civil disorder "have nothing to do with civil rights" but are simply *crimes* is an attempt to define the conflict as a deviance game. That position is opposed by those who argue that rioting and civil disorders represent at least protopolitical movements which must be defined and dealt with in a political manner. Reviewing the history of articulate protest in the form of riots in England, Allen Silver observes the following:

> Lacking a strong tradition of urban violence in the form of articulate protest [in America], it is all the easier to define ["violence, criminality and riot"] as merely criminal. Such definitions work not only on the respectable but also on the riotous poor. Like American society as a whole, the American poor lack a traditional past: on neither side of the boundaries of class and race do the conditions for "articulate riot" exist in generous measure. "Criminal" acts like looting and violent assault are likely to dominate riotous protest, rather than explicitly political gestures. Similarly, the propertied and respectable are ill-prepared to react in terms other than a confrontation with uncontained and shapeless criminality. Articulate riot, however, requires that both rioters and their target or audience jointly define the meaning of riotous acts. The frequency with which recent riots by Negroes in American cities are interpreted officially as "meaningless" . . . contrasts with the ability of the English elite [in the 19th century] . . . to interpret the meaning of riotous behavior.
>
> Current concern over violence and riot, then, involves a problem of the political language in which these events are described and interpreted. (Silver, 1967:22–23.)

From the point of view of sociological analysis, whether Black rioting in particular is deviant or not must rest upon an assessment of how powerful interests

choose to define it.[6]   In the late sixties it is perhaps best said that the matter is
still at issue, and that feature is itself a prime topic of sociological interest.

CAUGHT AND UNCAUGHT

It is perhaps obvious but should nonetheless be said that deviance is here
defined with reference to public definitions embodied in civil rulings and detection and apprehension procedures—not with reference to any human bodies
that actually get detected and apprehended. Definition hinges upon the *possibility* of detection and apprehension, not upon *actual* detection and apprehension. The domain of deviance is all that behavior that *could* become an object
of defensible apprehension, processing and punishment were the activity
known to civil authorities and should they choose to act. Indeed, the fact that
much behavior that could be defined as deviant is unknown to civil authorities
and that these authorities choose not to take action toward much that is known
sets up a central dynamic in the study of deviant behavior.

ABSOLUTE AND RELATIVE
DEFINITIONS OF DEVIANCE

The foregoing statement is but one variant of a broader approach to de-
lineating behavior called deviant. Prime reference to social organization and
social definition as a way in which to delineate analytic categories is a variety
of relativistic definition. What is deviant or not is entirely a matter of what
participants in a social category judge to be deviant. (In this case the categorical referent is the nation-state.) Although this is a relatively common perspective in sociology, it should be said that not all investigators, sociological or
otherwise, accept it.

There are those who prefer, rather, an absolutist definition of deviance. The
absolutist asserts that, regardless of time and social context, certain culture-free
standards, such as how fully persons develop their innate potential or how
closely they approach the fulfillment of the highest human values, enable one
to detect deviance. Thus suicide or alcoholism destroys or inhibits the possibility of the actor's developing his full human potential and is therefore always
deviant. The perception of objects obviously not present (hallucinations) is a
failure to confront reality fully, thus inhibiting the actor's optimal adaptation to
that reality. Hallucinations, too, are always deviant. The absolutist believes
that he knows what reality *is*, what people *should be* and what constitutes full

---

[6] A somewhat similar view is taken by Horowitz and Liebowitz, 1968, although they appear to believe that some items of deviance are really instances of political conflict, that is,
to believe that sociologists can decide what is "really political" as opposed to "really deviant." See also Vold, 1958:Chap. 11; and Gusfield, 1967.

and appropriate development. In the case of suicide, for example, he believes that life is obviously and almost always better than death. He feels that he can properly judge what *other people* should do with their lives and that he is very often a better judge than other people about how they should be acting and feeling. The relativist, on the other hand, takes a somewhat more existential stance. Confronting a world of conflicting standards and a universe without obvious moral meaning, he is less certain of his ability to judge for others. If another wishes to take his own life, the relativist questions *his* right to interfere. He may well hold strong beliefs and standards by which he judges himself, but he is hesitant to impose these beliefs and standards upon others who view the world quite differently. He looks upon the absolutist as a special pleader for the adoption of his own quite arbitrary conceptions of what people are and should be. The relativist suspects, in contrast, that each man is his own best judge.

It can be suggested that the most pertinent comment to be made about *both* the relativist and absolutist positions is that they proceed from primitive *value premises* regarding the nature and meaning of human life and the relations that should obtain between people. Each is its own respective *article of faith,* and, like all articles of faith, each lies quite beyond matters of science. In the same way that the parade of arguments over the existence of God does little more than reinforce prior beliefs on either side, arguments between relativists and absolutists over their extraempirical premises or axioms about life can serve little purpose. Let us not, nonetheless, decry such differences in the moral predicates of science. Moral premises are inescapable. They are the evaluative stances upon which science is predicated. They may lead in different directions, not because one is right and the other is wrong, but because they emphasize or highlight aspects disattended by their alternatives.

TENTATIVENESS

The analytic category of materials constituted on the above bases leaves intact and, in effect, further sponsors the notion that there is a meaningful batch of items that can reasonably be called deviance. This assumption must in itself be regarded as highly tentative and subject to reassessment. We must remain open to the possibility that the materials so grouped do not have enough in common to make meaningful their conjoint analysis.

Analytic theory in sociology is not well enough developed at this time to make an informed judgment on the theoretical cogency of the category of deviance. It may well turn out that deviance is not of itself a reasonable element of sociological theory. In the future it may seem more reasonable to parcel out materials that huddle beneath it into such candidate elements of theory as socialization, person perception, stigma, social roles, formal organiza-

tion or the general theory of conflict.[7] Because a priori judgment is not possible, the best way eventually to make such decisions is through actually performing analysis in each candidate manner and assessing its resultant fruitful-
ness. It is in a spirit of tentativeness, then, that I have accepted the notion
that a work on deviance is at all reasonable. As will subsequently become
clear, I am not at all convinced that the category is much more than one type
of vehicle upon which to address analytic questions that are far more general
than deviance itself.

SPECIFICATION OF
DEPENDENT VARIABLES

Although it marks off a range of relevant materials, the concept of deviance
remains highly general and highly abstract. It seems likely that statements
about, and explanations of, deviance at the level of any and all deviance are
bound to be equally abstract, possibly to the point of being vacuous. There
must be an attempt, then, to break down this general category into more
amenable patches of concern.

CONCRETE AND ANALYTIC
CATEGORIES

As mentioned at the outset, the traditional means of doing this is simply to
adopt the phenomenologically concrete and common-sense groupings appearing in folk culture or invented by scientific folk culture and later accepted by
the host population. Such designations often form the titles of books or the
chapter headings of omnibus textbooks, e.g., suicide, homicide, alcoholism,
prostitution, crime, mental illness. Each one of such categories becomes the
dependent variable in terms of which causes and cures, as independent variables, are explored. The employment of these major subdivisions of deviance is
not predicated on any conceptual or theoretical grounds; the subdivisions are
simply assumed to be meaningful and relevant because folk culture has defined
them as such. (However, for some purposes, such categories may be highly
relevant. See Chap. 6.)

A commitment to the theoretical grounding of deviance, in contrast, requires
that one seek to surmount such common-sense categories; to focus upon features and processes that occur across many such categories and to develop
generalizations applicable to analytically defined kinds of deviance. Phenomena associated with a variety of common-sense categories of deviance

---

[7] Further reflections on this question are presented in Goffman, 1963a:Chap. 5; and
Glaser and Strauss, 1967:Chap. 5.

become instances of more general social processes. (Cf. Blumer, 1956:684 on "generic variables.")

Despite attempts, such a goal remains a vision rather than an accomplishment. Various suggestions in this direction have received notice but have not been widely adopted. Among the most noticed has been Robert Merton's typology of deviant types. Five patterns are generated by conceiving all deviance in terms of acceptance or rejection of social ends (values) or means (norms): the conformer (accepts ends and means and is not deviant); the ritualist (rejects ends, accepts means); the innovator (accepts ends, rejects means); the retreatist (rejects ends and means); and the rebel (rejects established ends and means and adopts a different set of them). The beauty in a classification such as this lies in the way in which it directs one's attention *across* particular concrete forms of deviance and into a search for commonality and variation along these more abstract lines of conceptualization (in this case, orientation to social ends and means). It becomes possible for the investigator to classify items together that do not conventionally go together and to conceive them as essentially similar instances of the same thing. The hope is, of course, that they are essentially similar in enough respects to make such a reconceptualization fruitful. Thus, in Merton's scheme, "psychotics . . . vagrants . . . tramps . . . drunkards and drug addicts" (Merton, 1957:153) become concrete forms of "retreatism," promoting, therefore, a search for their *other* common features and their differences. Despite the apparent fact that the Mertonian scheme has not been fruitful,[8] one can still admire the elegance of its logical form and commend Merton's pioneering of this type of endeavor.[9]

INVOLVEMENT IN DEVIANCE

Aside from Merton and the tradition he represents, sporadic and unprosecuted attempts at analytic categories of deviance have centered upon ways in which and degrees to which persons are implicated in deviant activities. Possibly inspired in part by the concept of career borrowed from sociological studies of occupations, there has been raised the question of the degree to which a given deviant activity can possibly provide a career and the degree to which persons become oriented to deviance as a major basis of personal identity and long-term involvement.[10] Such a concern will be our point of departure here.

Surveying forms of deviance, one finds considerable variation in (1) the fre-

[8] See, e.g., the critiques in Clinard, ed., 1964; and by Short and Strodbeck, 1965; Douglas, 1969.

[9] Other efforts of an analytic kind include: Parsons, 1951:Chap. 7; H. S. Becker, 1963: 19–22; Gibbons, 1965 and 1968; Friedson, 1966; Clinard and Quinney, 1967:Chap. 1. On the character of some such schemes, see Chap. 6 of this book.

[10] Cf., Lemert, 1951; H. S. Becker, 1963; and references in note 9.

quency of a given actor's performance or display of deviance, ranging from performing the deviance but once in his life to regularized, even daily performance or display; (2) the degree to which the actor organizes his everyday life in terms of, or for purposes of, a deviant activity, ranging from almost no organization specifically oriented to deviance to total life organization around a deviant activity; (3) the degree to which the actor conceives of himself as the kind of deviant person who would engage in the given deviance, ranging from viewing himself as a perfectly normal sort of person to viewing himself centrally as a deviant person; and (4) the degree to which others in the actor's world define him as a deviant kind of person, ranging from viewing him as an unremarkable normal to viewing him as a thoroughly deviant human.

Even if these dimensions of variation are crudely dichotomized, there are sixteen degrees to which or ways in which persons can be implicated in deviance, as indicated in Chart 2.2. Among the possibilities, the *lowest* degree of involvement and the *highest* degree of involvement suggest themselves as strategic foci. The former case brings into focus the situation in which a deviant act is performed by an actor who minimally organizes his life for deviance, does not see himself as deviant and is not so viewed by others (upper-left-hand cell, Chart 2.2). It is the situation of deviance among normals, or what might be referred to as the isolated or episodic deviant act. Such acts are not untypically a *first* performance of a given concrete kind of deviant act. The latter case brings into focus the maximally contrastive situation—that of an actor who continually engages in deviance, who totally organizes his activity in terms of this fact and who views himself as a deviant sort of person in the midst of others who likewise so view him. This is the situation of the fully public and committed or social deviant.[11]

Between the two extremes exist various degrees of marginal and/or secret involvement in deviance. Intriguing as such in-between patterns may be, *we shall here focus only upon what might be considered the beginning and end points of implication in activity or states defined as deviant.* It is assumed that, if we can first come to understand initiations and terminations, we might later arrive at a clearer conception of what lies between the two.

Relative to the empirical frequency of the occurrence of instances of the patterns delineated in Chart 2.2, it seems likely that the number of persons involved in any pattern declines as degree of involvement increases. Studies in which presumed normals are asked anonymously to report deviant indiscretions tend to show that a very high proportion of the population (perhaps in excess of 80 per cent) have engaged in at least one deviant act of some publically defined seriousness.[12] And a significant proportion of presumed normals claim

---

[11] These two extreme cases are essentially the same as Lemert's distinction between primary and secondary deviance. See Lemert, 1951:Chap. 4; 1967a:Chap. 3.

[12] See Leighton *et al.*, 1963; Srole *et al.*, 1962; Wheeler, 1960; Short and Nye, 1958; Kinsey, Pomeroy and Martin, 1953; Porterfield, 1949; Wallerstein and Wyle, 1947; Murphy, Shirley and Witmer, 1946; Cohen, 1966:25–29.

CHART 2.2.   *DEGREES OF INVOLVEMENT IN DEVIANCE*

		Low Frequency of Deviance		High Frequency of Deviance	
		Low Organization for Deviance	High Organization for Deviance	Low Organization for Deviance	High Organization for Deviance
Actor Does Not View Himself as Deviant	Others Do Not View Actor as Deviant	*Isolated or episodic deviant acts*			
	Others View Actor as Deviant				
Actor Views Himself as Deviant	Others Do Not View Actor as Deviant				
	Others View Actor as Deviant				*Social or pivotal deviants*

to have engaged in several or even a large number of deviant acts. Moving from a degree of involvement in deviance, where the empirical frequency is almost the same as the size of the population itself, frequencies decline rapidly, down to the perhaps one or possibly few per cent who are full social deviants. These would include a proportion of those humans who are at any time confined to mental hospitals, prisons, juvenile reformatories and the like and those actors who carry on deviant life styles in civil society, such as the professional hustler, homosexual, prostitute or thief. In deviance, as in other pursuits, it would seem that many are called but few are chosen.

The categories of the deviant act and the social deviant serve to cross-cut phenomenologically concrete and common-sense designations and make central not the common-sense name of the act but the *context* (of the four dimensions of involvement) in which it is performed. The fact that the behavior labeled homicide, drug use, juvenile delinquency, homosexuality or prostitution, for example, can occur in either context (or others shown in Chart 2.2) leads to a central consideration of the context rather than the label. It may be the case, indeed, that the prevalent tendency to focus on labels in the search for causes of the designated behavior has been an important analytic roadblock.

If it is provisionally reasonable to delineate a category of the deviant act and a category of the social deviant, what about them should be made problematic?

What questions can then be posed? The study of deviance traditionally centers on questions of conditions or causes of occurrence. This work is traditional. We will inquire in Part I into the generalized circumstances under which an isolated or episodic deviant act can or will occur. Part II addresses the question of the conditions surrounding the assumption of social deviance. In Part III the most traditional of all concerns will be yet again addressed: once social deviance has been assumed, under what sort of circumstances can there be a return to identity as a normal? In the course of subsequent discussion a variety of other foci will also be utilized in terms of their relevance to the present questions.

It should be clear that, although questions of occurrence and of change have consumed investigators of deviance since the inception of such studies, they are not the only sorts of questions that can be asked. Although it will not concern us here, it would be equally legitimate and useful to focus, for example, on how social deviants manage their roles—how, in a positive sense, they manage to keep together and coherent and meaningful their world—much in the same way that we might analyze life styles of other kinds.[13] Changing the analytic level altogether, there can also be questions of the conditions under which deviant organizations or "subcultures" themselves emerge and are maintained.[14]

ORGANIZATION OF INDEPENDENT VARIABLES

If we want to explain deviant acts and the coming and going from social deviance, it becomes necessary to consider the logical or formal character of how explanatory units can be brought to bear on that which is to be explained. We must thus concern ourselves with the following kinds of issues: the conceptualization of what is to be brought to bear, the logical form in which to arrange whatever it is that is to be adduced, and the causal logic of how elements operate.

THREE LEVELS OF VARIABLES

Since we are focusing on actors and their acts, it is not unreasonable to take actor as a central vantage point from which to think about explanations of his enmeshments. He may be taken as a vantage point in terms of an initial concern with his subjective or phenomenological assessment of what he is doing, what is happening around him and what is happening to him. And he may be

[13] See, for example, Goffman, 1963a; F. Davis, 1961; Anderson, 1923; J. Lofland, 1966; Simmons, 1964; Simon and Gagnon, 1967.
[14] See the materials reprinted in Rubington and Weinberg, eds. 1968:Part III, "The Rise of Subcultures." Unfortunately, much material (including the aforementioned) said to deal with "subculture" and the like confuses or equates the simple situation of the deviant act with social worlds and the organized social life of deviants.

taken as a vantage point in terms of the character of his immediate circumstances, apart from his subjective assessment of them. Such subjective and objective immediate circumstances form an on-line explanation of action, be it performing a deviant act or becoming a social deviant or normal. These may be isolated as a *first level* of independent variables. When analyzing the deviant *act*, first-level independent variables will include the degree to which the actor is threatened, the degree to which he might be said to be encapsulated and the determinants of a process to be called closure. First-level independent variables in connection with entering and leaving *social deviance* will be the degree of social identification and the variability of a process of escalation.

The objective and subjective structure of the actor's most immediate circumstances is not capricious, but it is itself a function of still rather immediate but one step removed *second-level* independent variables. Upon what, in a reasonably proximate sense, do the features of first-level processes depend? Viewed in abstract terms, features of immediate circumstances may be a function of four classes of variables of a sort so obvious that many investigators have not taken them seriously, although I will here argue for the cruciality of their *conjoint* operation. First, immediately around actor there are likely to be other human beings, or what might be called, generically, a complement of *others*. The developing character of immediate circumstances will be a function of others being present or not, the ways in which they can be arranged about actor, the view they have of actor, the ways in which they act toward him and the skills they possess. Second, an immediate circumstance must everywhere and always be geographically and socially located in what are typically called *places*. There may or may not be access to a sort of place conducive to a given kind of immediate circumstance. The ways in which accessible social places vary will affect what can likely develop in them. Third, immediate subjective and actual circumstances are structured by variations in the presence and availability of relatively movable physical objects that might be termed, generically, *hardware*. Fourth, the development of an immediate circumstance is a function of what *actor* brings to it in terms of his capacities, his technical skills, his self-esteem, his conception of himself and the ways in which he defines events.

These categories of second-level independent variables are intended to constrain at least an initial focus on matters that are temporally and spatially proximate. To make the presence and character of hardware and places problematic, in particular, is to ask about variations that, for actor, involve perhaps only minutes or hours and feet or miles as determinants of outcomes. Variations of this relatively immediate kind as determinants make more possible an appreciation of the possibility that whether deviance as an act or role occurs or not can have to do with variations that are, from actor's perspective, quite random and fortuitous, even if discernably patterned within a broader frame of reference.

Such a broader frame of reference involves a *third level* of independent variables. Bracketing together others, places, hardware and actor as elements of a proximate system, there can be raised the question: Upon what does a given variation in each of them depend? Taking the humans involved, others and actor, their second-level relevant features will be a function of a course of biographical experience, which is itself largely a function of enmeshment in given types of social organization. Pushing one step further, there is the question of the determinants of the type of social organization in which persons could experience given kinds of biographies. We thus reach the level of the comparative study of societies themselves, the ways in which they are similar and different and the lines along which they develop, thereby structuring personal biography. Variations in the presence and character of hardware and places may likewise be scrutinized for the social organizational sources of the development of given types of them, the ways in which they vary and their distribution within a population.

Inquiry into the determinants of the presence and features of others, places, hardware and actor, then, is intimately involved with the nature and operation of the standard elements of societies themselves; their cultural patterns and their institutions. *However, in what follows, greatest attention is given to the level of immediate circumstances and second-level determinants of these circumstances.* It has seemed proper to do this because there has been a lack of effort at these levels. For whatever reason, investigators have been more enamored with remote matters of biography and larger units such as communities, institutions and societies than with the "nitty-gritty" matters of the ways in which there will or will not be concrete conjunctions of others, places, hardware, and actors that are productive of deviance. However, at some points in the text, I have taken excursions into the third level of independent variables, the better to provide a sense of how some seemingly private and microscopic matters have very public connections; how they are, in the final analysis, not at all private, but inextricably implicated in the macroscopic.

It should be clear that the foregoing distinctions among three levels of proximity to a dependent variable, and the distinctions made within these levels, only make up what is sometimes called an organizing scheme, that is, classes of items to take into account. It is not in any sense a theory, because theoretical concepts have yet to be added and propositions propounded. It is merely a vehicle by means of which such work can be performed. The main body of this work is directed to the task of this theoretical explication and specification.

AN IMAGERY OF CONSTRUCTION AND FACILITATION

There are at least two kinds of linguistic devices and perhaps broader causal imageries within which empirical materials on the causes of phenomena can be cast. On the one hand there is the language of cause itself, employing the phraseology of "what are the causes of X?" Thus posed, investigators seem easily led into a scattered quest for any variable or item that might be found associated with the differential outcomes, and this quest can culminate in a simple list of causes, the relations among which are moot. Such language also incorporates a "push" imagery of how some item X varies, promoting a search for anything that might push X into existence and "make it" assume various strengths.

On the other hand, there is an imagery which likewise pursues causes but which is phrased in terms of how X can be built up, constructed or produced or its occurrence facilitated. Such language leads to a somewhat different kind of thinking about how X varies. It becomes more possible to consider the role that a variety of items may play in making possible, facilitating, or constructing, let us say, an act of homicide or the assumption of the role of prostitute. Thinking is organized in the same way that it might be if one were to consider ways to facilitate the existence of a car or of a Broadway play. It seems significant that people who manufacture cars, radios, Broadway plays and the like could as well conceive their efforts in the language of cause, asking, for example, "What are the causes of cars?" They apparently do not do so because it would not be a very clear or pertinent manner in which to organize the business of accomplishing practical activities.[15] The language of cause employed in social science may likewise serve to spawn more confusion than clarity in doing the work of detailing the means by which one or another outcome can be facilitated, fabricated or constructed.

Attention to models of practical activity may help to broaden social scientific conceptions of causality. Social scientists could be more attentive, in particular, to the following. First, perpetrators of practicality who aim at the construction of some outcome are attuned to ways in which necessary elements must often be *phased* in order to constitute a facilitative contribution to a product. If an item is present too soon or too late, it may either be irrelevant or it may actively inhibit a sequence of production. Second, it is often the case that a necessary element may be derived from more than one source. A variety of tertiary suppliers of materials for a sequence of activity can suffice to meet current requirements; that is, a relatively determinate requirement can derive from alternatively sufficient but diverse sources. Third, although one sort of material may be preferred as maximally facilitating a process, it is sometimes possible to make do with less auspicious and amenable materials upon which hurried and jerry-built adaptations to the moment are performed. Fourth, there are likely to be plateau periods during which elements are present but not combined, such that there is any perceptible change in the state of the practical activity. The addition of a single additional element or operation upon existing elements can serve to crystallize what is already present into a new configuration. The slow building up of elements can at some point pre-

[15] See, e.g., Amber and Amber, 1962.

cipitate a "critical mass," such that the arrangement of things is now believed to have reached a "new stage" (Boulding, 1953:333–35). Fifth, the attainment of critical mass may be possible on the basis of a variety of different combinations of strengths of a single relevant set of elements. In the simplest case of only two elements, X at a high level and Y at a low level may be equivalent in the attainment of critical mass to the existence of X at a low level and Y at a high level. Neither alone may be necessary, but either alone may be sufficient.

Perpetrators of practical activities thus recognize, to use the vernacular, that there is more than one way to skin a cat. They make discriminations between more effective and less effective ways in which outcomes can be attained or can occur. They evaluate alternatively sufficient sequences in terms of certainty of outcome attainment and amount of effort that must be expended. I will here make the assumption that human action generally displays the features of such practical activities. It should therefore be the case that those who undertake to explain human action must take account of these features and attempt to incorporate them, however vaguely, into their accounts.

Having assumed that there is more than one way to skin a cat—to phase facilitants, to combine elements, etc.—there is then the question of how many ways one will choose to trace. *I have chosen throughout to present what appear to be the most maximally effective combinations and strengths of elements in producing one of the three outcomes that will occupy us.* These will be contrasted with situations of the same elements in weaker form, the weakness of which does not make an outcome impossible but only less likely if other elements are not sufficiently operative. *Emphasis is also placed upon the variety of ways in which various conceptual components within the categories of others, places, hardware and actor can be alternatively sufficient in facilitating an act or the assumption of a role.* Within such a logic it is hopefully possible to move beyond debate over whether something is a cause or not, or an important cause in spite of its empirical association, and into a consideration of the question of under what combinations and strengths of elements will this—whatever the empirically associated this—operate to facilitate or be irrelevant to an outcome.

EMPIRICAL MATERIALS

Two notes of caution are in order regarding the character of the empirical materials to be employed.

First, the concrete materials to be introduced should be taken as illustrations rather than demonstrations of particular points or of total arguments. This is the case because the complex and full range of materials required for demonstration seem not to exist. This is also the case because the materials used vary enormously in terms of the faith one might wish to place in them. They are drawn from sources as varied as the popular press and research journals. They were originally assembled by persons as varied as free-lance writers and highly competent researchers. Some of the materials are of questionable reliability, some are extremely reliable and most probably fall somewhere in between. (I excuse the more popular, and possibly less reliable, references partly on the ground of their being the best available and partly on the ground of their being the most forceful means for conveying abstract, and sometimes abstruse, notions.)

Second, it must be noted that I make more frequent reference to a few concrete forms of deviance than I do to the wide variety of other forms that could conceivably be described and analyzed. I have attempted to make reference to as wide a range of concrete forms of deviance as possible. But the sad fact is that those aspects of deviance which I consider crucial for analysis have not, except for a few forms of deviance, been intensively investigated. Although I have reasonable confidence in the applicability of the general conceptions to those concrete forms that are mentioned, I cannot project such applicability to those forms that are not.

The perspective here employed requires for its application rather detailed, close observation. It requires, particularly, information about face-to-face interactional dynamics and immediate human phenomenology. Such an emphasis is apparently being carried out at present by only a limited number of investigators. Thus in Part I, "The Deviant Act," I draw rather heavily on certain studies of homicide, embezzlement, "naïve" check forgery, suicide and a few other acts. These studies happen to have "brought back" relevant materials. For good interactional materials on suicide, it has even been necessary to draw on a study where the action takes place in the confounding setting of a mental hospital. Although unfortunate from the point of view of sorting out deviant acts from deviant identities, such a setting is one of the few places where detailed interactional chronicles and phenomenologies are assembled *prior* to the act of suicide. The standard hospital practice of maintaining daily ward notes, to which a variety of staff members contribute, created a unique source of information. From it the authors of the study (Kobler and Stotland, 1964) could construct an interactional view of that act. Likewise, in discussing the assumption of deviant identity (Part II) and the assumption of normal identity (Part III), there is heavy reference to certain studies of paranoia, "mental illness" more generally, and Alcoholics Anonymous and Synanon. Again, the use of these and other references is a function of both the available interactional material and the selective focus of the present framework.

It may be, and indeed is likely, that existing relevant data not known to me or data yet to be collected will limit the generality of what follows.

DRAMATIS PERSONAE

In the course of these preliminaries, the main characters of the drama have made an unannounced and perhaps bashful appearance. Let me now formally, if belatedly, introduce them. There are only four, and each is derived from two sets of dichotomous distinctions. The first distinction is between the object of analytic focus around which all else is arranged, here called *Actor*, and everyone else who may be involved with this focus, here called *Others*. The second distinction is between the character of the public identity imputed to either of these parties, which may be either *normal* or *deviant*. Humans involved in deviance may be either a normal Actor or a deviant Actor or a deviant Other or a normal Other. The important point about these characters is that the labels normal and deviant are not to be taken as my judgments of their "personalities" or personality dynamics. In using these labels, I am saying nothing about what the involved humans might "really" be. The labels are to be construed, rather, as attempts to *report* what participants believe to be true about one another (and perhaps themselves) and to relate the character of the treatment they accord one another on the basis of having classified an Actor or Other as normal or deviant.

Sociologically speaking, the question of who or what is "really" normal or deviant is an irrelevant question. What is important for the social analyst is not what people are by his lights or by his standards, but what it is that people construe one another and themselves to be for what reasons and with what consequences. The labels of normal and deviant should be taken, then, as highly abstract or encompassing characterizations of distinctions made in social life.

In these two introductory chapters I have attempted to sketch out a perspective within which deviance can be approached, to define the character of the area, to specify what is to be made problematic and to provide an overview of how these problematic phenomena will be analyzed. We turn now to the first of the substantive topics: the deviant act.

PART I

THE DEVIANT ACT

Action is built up in coping with the world instead of merely being released from a pre-existing psychological structure by factors playing upon that structure. By making indications to himself and by interpreting what he indicates, the human being has to forge or piece together a line of action.

HERBERT BLUMER

Herbert Blumer, "Sociological Implications of the Thought of George Herbert Mead," p. 536.

The analytic category of the deviant act here denotes that class of strongly feared human actions undertaken by persons who neither define themselves as deviant nor are defined as such by Others, at least not at the time the act occurs. We want to deal, in other words, with deviance among normals—normals in the sense that the persons involved have not been publicly defined as deviant kinds of persons either by themselves or by Others. The category is further intended to denote those acts that are either a *first* occasion or a relatively unpracticed and isolated or episodic occurrence. In contrast, repeated deviant acts of a given kind that have, for Actor, become prac-

ticed, routine and unremarkable are more auspiciously viewed in terms of role behavior, for such acts are implicated in matters of personal and social identity. Deviant acts of this sort represent compliance to a role and are problematic only to the degree that all role behavior is problematic. The different character thus assumed requires a correspondingly appropriate explanatory construct concerning the taking up of roles. This question will occupy us in Part II, "The Assumption of Deviant Identity."

The question of the conditions or causes of deviant acts may be approached by asking what arrangement of elements most strongly facilitates the occurrence of such acts. If, as engineers of some sort, we wanted to produce a deviant act, what conditions and relations among conditions would be well advised to construct? For the manufacture of social action, as for other items of human concern, there likely exists a plurality of construction methods and sequences which will eventually attain the same end but which differ in their efficiency, effectiveness and certainty of producing a desired outcome.

DEFENSIVE AND ADVENTUROUS DEVIANT ACTS

It is not my purpose to explore all the possible sequences that will produce an instance of the deviant act. I want, rather, to explore what appear to be the most facilitative sequences. I want to do so relative to two classes of deviant acts. Primary emphasis will be on the most facilitative sequence leading to what is here called the *defensive* deviant act. This is to be distinguished from another class of deviant acts that social scientists have explored considerably less extensively, here labeled the *adventurous* deviant act. The difference between the two resides primarily in the character of the perception and arousal elicited from the organism in response to immediately occurring events. In the defensive act a sense of *threat* is felt and becomes a key experience around which Actor organizes his action. In the adventurous deviant act the key subjective experience is a sense of *positive excitement* and the perception of enchanting possibilities.

The adventurous deviant act will be discussed separately in Chap. 5. However, it is with some ambivalence that I postpone its consideration until after a discussion of the three phases of the defensive deviant act. On the one hand, the distinction between threat and adventure is a pure-type division. It is an overly strong distinction in dealing with empirical cases where the two states of arousal sometimes seem to be compounded. Although there are deviant acts based upon a pure state of threat and deviant acts based upon a pure experience of adventure, there are also many acts where these experiences are mixed in various proportions. For that reason, conjoint treatment seems most reasonable.

On the other hand, there is considerably less empirical material on adventurous deviant acts than on defensive ones. I am therefore uncertain whether they are sufficiently similar to justify my creating the impression that all the processes involved are essentially the same. I question, for example, whether the operation of the three phases of the defensive deviant act—threat, encapsulation and closure—is the same for the adventurous deviant act. It would be easy enough to engage in speculation about a similar set of phases in the adventurous act, in the absence of even minimally adequate reports, but it seems pointless to do so.

This separation of defensive and adventurous deviant acts is performed, then, for reasons of insufficient data and for reasons of conceptual clarity. It is *not* performed because I want to maintain that deviant acts in general are simply, only, mostly, or merely a matter of people being threatened. Part I should *not* leave the reader with the impression that deviant acts *only* involve "those poor threatened people who act out of desperation." Although such a statement is true, it is only part of the story. If in what follows, it appears to be the greater part of the story, the reader should keep in mind that this is merely a reflection of past social science emphasis. Since social scientists have said more about defensive actions, more can be said here. However, we shall see in Chap. 5 that deviant acts can, in contrast and as well, involve the more ornery dispositions of human beings. Indeed, illustrations used in explicating the defensive deviant act will sometimes suggest a coexisting element of adventure along with the manifest element of threat.

An additional important, if obvious, point must be made. A deviant act cannot be classified as defensive or as adventurous only on the basis of common sense and popular beliefs about it. The defensive or adventurous character of a deviant act is determined by the Actor's *experience* of it as one, the other, or some combination of the two. Thus the act of raping a female may be adventurous for one adult male but defensive for another, as in a case where the male is fending off a female's aspersions on his manhood. Although some deviant acts may more frequently have associated with them a defensive or adventurous orientation, this still does not allow one unequivocally to classify it as one or the other. From available empirical studies it appears that most homicides and embezzlements are of a phenomenologically defensive sort (see pp. 42–48), but at least a small minority of such acts may be performed from within an adventurous orientation. And despite the psychoanalytically inclined studies which assert their "underlying" defensive nature, some drug use, deviant sexual activity and youthful vandalism seem very often to have a phenomenologically adventurous character. And, of course, for any given Actor and act there can also be a compounding of these orientations.

PHASES OF THE DEFENSIVE DEVIANT ACT

The task of creating conditions most strongly facilitative of the occurrence of a defensive deviant act may be conceived, at the most general level, in terms of three sequential and cumulating phases of Actor's subjective experience. First, it is strongly facilitative for there to occur an event or events which, for whatever reason, Actor defines as a *threat* to him in some manner. Second, within the occurrence of events defined as a threat, the perpetration of a defensive deviant act is facilitated if there additionally occurs the phenomenon of psychosocial *encapsulation,* a foreshortening of the temporal and social span to which action is referred in order to judge its appropriateness. Third, the occurrence of a defensive deviant act is facilitated if, within existing threat and encapsulation, Others, places, hardware and certain definitions by Actor combine to make the deviant act (among the range of all feasible acts) the most objectively and subjectively available action. The phase of selecting an act from the class of all more or less proximate and available acts may be referred to as the process of *closure* upon an act.[1]

These three phases are relatively independent of one another in the sense that threat does not in and of itself lead to encapsulation, and encapsulation does not in and of itself lead to closure on a *deviant* act. Indeed, in what follows, what is of central concern is the question of what factors lead from mere threat to encapsulation and, in turn, from encapsulation to closure on a deviant act. Or, in the vocabulary preferred here, what arrangements of elements most strongly facilitate the occurrence of threat, the occurrence of encapsulation after threat and the occurrence of closure on a deviant act after encapsulation? Threat, encapsulation and closure are related to one another in terms of the closing off of alternative possible actions at each phase. Threat is the most general facilitant, meaning that it can easily lead (and typically does lead) to

---

[1] The concept of closure is borrowed (and expanded) from Lemert's usage, 1953:304–7.

states other than encapsulation and to acts other than deviant ones. If, however, encapsulation follows threat, a deviant act becomes more likely; that is, the total range of possible acts is reduced, and, for reasons to be specified, acts having a deviant character become more likely. The theoretical imagery involved is that of a funnel with numerous holes at the top and fewer holes toward the bottom. As fluid moves through the funnel, there is an enormous initial slippage or loss (alternatives) but rapidly decreasing loss (a decrease of alternatives) as the fluid moves downward.[2] The aim here is to specify, at least in a provisional way, elements and states and combinations of elements that facilitate movement through the entire funnel or set of phases, eventuating in a deviant act.

THREAT

THE CHARACTER OF THREAT

A first step in facilitating the occurrence of a deviant act is the production of an event that Actor will construe as a clear and present threat to him. The construal of threat may be connected to (1) his possible *physical* destruction or (2) his possible social destruction as the kind of object he believes himself to be and has been believed to be by others who are significant to him.

1. A fair number of acts later coded by the social-control establishment as criminal homicide appear to involve a basic defense of the physical body. In a study of what he calls "victim-precipitated" criminal homicide, Wolfgang relates a series of altercations involving such primitive reactivity.

> A husband accused his wife of giving money to another man, and, while she was making breakfast, he attacked her with a milk bottle, then a brick and finally a piece of concrete block. Having a butcher knife in hand, she stabbed him during the fight.
> A husband had beaten his wife on several occasions. In the present instance, she insisted that he take her to the hospital. He refused, and a violent quarrel followed, during which he slapped her several times, and she concluded by stabbing him.

❁   ❁   ❁

> During a lovers' quarrel, the male (victim) hit his mistress and threw a can of kerosene at her. She retaliated by throwing the liquid on him and then tossed a lighted match in his direction. He died from the burns.

❁   ❁   ❁

> A victim became incensed when his eventual slayer asked for money which the victim owed him. The victim grabbed a hatchet and started

---

[2] For a fuller discussion and application of this logic, see Smelser, 1963:especially 12–21; Turner, 1953; H. S. Becker, 1963:22–25; Lindesmith, 1968:17–22.

in the direction of his creditor, who pulled out a knife and stabbed him.

A victim attempted to commit sodomy with his girl friend, who refused his overtures. He struck her several times on the side of her head with his fists before she grabbed a butcher knife and cut him fatally.

✻   ✻   ✻

During an argument in which a male called a female many vile names, she tried to telephone the police. But he grabbed the phone from her hands, knocked her down, kicked her, and hit her with a tire gauge. She ran to the kitchen, grabbed a butcher knife, and stabbed him in the stomach. (Wolfgang, 1957:3. See also Wolfgang, 1958:Chap. 10.)

The literally self-defensive features of these situations may have made such homicides more or less understandable to outsiders, but they did not gainsay either the later definition of these homicides as criminal or the criminal trials which resulted from this definition. Despite the courts, the theme of the primitive rightness of self-defense is celebrated in folkways and enshrined in popular writings. In John Steinbeck's *Grapes of Wrath*, for example, Tom Jod, telling us of the homicide he perpetrated, proclaims, "I'd do what I done—again."

In advanced technological societies, where a large part of the population has been brought under the control of civil authorities and a kind of civil order prevails, threats are more likely to arise from the clear and present possibility of social defacement or disgrace than from the clear and present possibility of physical destruction or annihilation. Yet, even in the most "advanced" societies, man remains an animal, and one should not underestimate his concern with physical survival or his capacity to take action to preserve his physical being. At least among the vertebrates, within which man is possibly distinctive merely in his capacity for symbolization, there is a rather well-developed reactive capacity for defensive aggression against objects defined as threatening to bodily survival. Man shares with snakes and tigers and rats the presocial reactive capacity to resist and attack when threatened. Indeed, there is some evidence to suggest that man may be even more volatile and even stronger in his capacity for defensive reactivity than are animals with less complex cortical structures. D. O. Hebb has concluded that there is a strong positive relation between position on the phylogenetic scale and capacity for rage, volatile reactivity and behavior disorganization and that this relation is a function of the complexity of the central nervous system. That is, the most complex neural systems seem to be those that are most capable of strong and possibly disorganized responses. As the creature with the most complex neural system yet to evolve, man may also be the most threatenable (Hebb and Thompson, 1968).

Because such reactivity in man involves a certain unpredictability and disorder, within societies an effort is often made to subdue it in the name of civil order and safety. To ensure the safety of social participants, many defensive actions are defined as constituting deviance and are punished. In fact, one way in which to view a social order is to conceive of it as an arrangement wherein the legitimacy of presocial reactive defense against threat is taken from the actors involved and lodged in a noninvolved third party, acting in the name of broader social interests, the society at large or the state.

2. The development of such a third-party arrangement and the declaration that there is a society are made possible by man's capacity to symbolize. The symbolic capacity and practice involve the invention of an arbitrary set of labels which carve out of the flux of raw reality those objects to which one can attend. Symbolization makes possible, in turn, the practice of attending and respond-ing to symbols themselves, rather than merely to the objects in raw reality that they were intended to set apart. Furthermore, the symbolic capacity makes possible the invention of symbols that have no empirical referents, in the sense of being depictions of objects in any known or claimed-to-be-knowable external stimulus situation. Symbols may be said to provide meaning if, by the term "meaning" we intend the designation of possibilities for action (E. Becker, 1962). A symbolically designated object is meaningful if it evokes in its user some possibilities for acting toward it. Among humans, within the limits set by communication boundaries (such as features of terrain, etc.), invented sym-bols diffuse and tend to be shared in the form of language or, more broadly, culture. The bearers of such a shared set of symbols or meanings tend to go to great lengths to ensure that new human creatures in their midst (mainly what are called children) become apprised of and believe in common symbols. The inculcation of existing and common symbols tends to ensure a certain predictability and regularity of behavior by restrictively designating what ob-jects exist out there, their meaning and the appropriate manner in which to act toward each of them.

Being a mobile, flesh-bound creature, it becomes possible for instances of the species Homo sapiens not only to designate other objects but to have a sense of themselves as separate objects in the world. However, humans tend not to see themselves, first and most importantly, as unique objects, but rather, in the manner of other objects, as *instances* of one or more classes or categories of human objects. Thus they view themselves (and others) as instances of some sex, age, kin relation, territorial position, race or ethnicity, occupation and the like. They may also view themselves as instances of some emotional state, mood or, in some societies, personality type. So, although there is an object that *is* Actor, this "is" is constructed from the categories available to him in terms of which he can construe himself to be an example. Humans are thought to be properly socialized when they view themselves not merely as instances of presumably shared categories, but as *being* really, after all and indeed, these categories, whatever the "these." A human who says, "But, after all, I *really am* female," or "I *really am* 21 years old," or "I *really am* white," or "I *really am* an American" or "I *really am* an extrovert," has been successfully socialized.

Such a human has been conned in the oldest of all con games. That this identity con game is necessary for there to be human society and social life does not gainsay its essential feature as a symbolic fiction.

In human societies, categories of sex, age, territory, race, occupation and the like are employed as the basis upon which human beings organize their action toward one another. Each category has a meaning in the sense that there is associated with it a repertoire of possible, proper or appropriate ways to treat the human body imputed to be an instance of it. Equally as important, because human beings can believe themselves really to be instances of given categories, they organize action *toward themselves as objects* on the basis of the action possibilities associated with their kind of person. So it is that humans can say of themselves such things as, "A nice girl doesn't do that sort of thing."

Categorical designations, however, are merely overlays on a defensively volatile, highly reactive and anxiety-prone creature. Behind his categories of social identity, there lurks an enormously threatenable being. As a number of theorists have noted, a basic corollary of the meanings associated with all human categories of identity is the highly protective and gingerly fashion in which humans treat one another. Aggressive interaction is controlled. Failure is communicated in an oblique and often awkward fashion. Games of self and other face-saving are played. It would appear that humans are able to play the game of social life mainly because they are constantly being fed symbolic supports to their sense of social worth. They are able to bear up under the possibility of threat posed by being in the presence of other human beings mainly because sufficient self-esteem is generated out of their own faith, and that of others, in the categories they believe themselves to be.

Because of symbolization and because of identification of self in terms of being a certain kind of person, threat among social humans takes on a special character. In civil society there is little likelihood of immediate threat to physical survival, but the reactive (and highly adaptive) capacity for threat persists. As noted, all categories of identity specify standards of what is appropriate treatment toward, and action on the part of, the category; these form the meaning of the category. If and when treatment and action are made problematic, fear, defensiveness and the capacity for reactive correction are aroused. Because of variations in social categories and associated definitions of proper treatment, human beings, as a function of their categorical occupancies, are highly variable with regard to the kinds of social treatment or situations, short of sheer physical assault, which will arouse in them a sense of threat and a felt need for defensive action. Threat can thus become attached to occurrences which forebode loss of prestigious and proper occupancy of one's categories. For example, persons in the position of having other people's money entrusted to them can sometimes become involved in situations which they can define as threatening to a good public reputation. Cressey relates the following:

During 1944 and 1945 real estate men, building contractors, automobile dealers and others sometimes considered as nonsharable the fact that the financial structure of the business had become precarious because of the shortage of building materials and cars. Many of those who subsequently violated positions of trust complained that *in order to maintain their business or social position* they "had to keep up a good front," or "had to take risks" (including conversion of entrusted funds) which they otherwise would not have taken. (Cressey, 1953:49–50, italics added.)

That is, a conception of self invested in a category such as "being a good real estate man" defines a range of events and occurrences that are destructive of that self-conception. Thus a French chef who loses his restaurant's listing in the *Guide Michelin* can be so defaced as to kill himself (*Newsweek*, Oct. 24, 1966). The self-conception is itself, of course, rooted in an audience before whom Actor can be defined as *not* maintaining a business or social position. The demography of suicide is also in part explicable in such terms.

The rate of suicide among males (who lose jobs) goes up more in depression periods than does the suicide rate for females; persons living in higher rental areas (who may have to leave them) show more increase in suicide rate during depressions than those in lower rental areas (who cannot leave their area); white persons (who have more stable social roles in normal times) increase their rate of suicide during depressions more than Negroes.

           ✻   ✻   ✻

Persons who have recently fallen into poverty have a high rate . . . as do the newly unemployed. (Kobler and Stotland, 1964:13.)

Clear and present dangers arising from imminent threats to Actor's esteem among the public to which he plays are hardly confined to the more advantaged categories of a society. More disadvantaged categories have exactly the same potential for threat. Perhaps the current combination of disadvantaged categories *par excellance* is the young male Harlemite, one of whom relates:

Horse [heroin] was a new thing, not only in our neighborhood but in Brooklyn, the Bronx, and everyplace. I went uptown and downtown. It was like horse had just taken over. Everybody was talking about it. All the hip people were using it and snorting it and getting this new high. To know what was going on and to be in on things, you had to do that. And the only way I felt I could come out of Wiltwyck [reformatory] and be up to date, the only way to take up where I left off and be the same hip guy I was before I went to Wiltwyck was to get in on the hippest thing, and the hippest thing was horse. (C. Brown, 1965:99.)

           ✻   ✻   ✻

It would be a drag for someone to come up to you and say, "Man, you ever snort any horse?" and you would have to say, "No." Hell, I wanted to be able to say, "Yeah, man."[3]

Along somewhat the same lines, observations made of low-income male street-corner youth groups suggest that intergang violence is highly associated with threats to territorial integrity or to the stability of the rather amorphous leader-ship structure. Threats to territorial integrity and to the sense of self and safety that attach to territory are especially likely in low-income settings where the territories in question are likely to be public thoroughfares and thus highly subject to unwitting or willful violation (Suttles, 1968). Likewise, in groups without formalized structure, where leadership is a *de facto* matter, power and control are relatively precarious, making threats to them quite likely and more drastic responses to the threats quite possible. So it is that leaders with the most precarious positions in their gangs are likely to foster aggression against outside groups, i.e., to foster the commission of deviant acts (Short and Strodt-beck: 1963, 1965:Chaps. 8 and 9).

Beyond sheer physical assault, what can be a threat, then, is very much a matter of what the Actor believes will put him in social jeopardy or possible disgrace before some category or categories of human Others in whose terms he constructs his action and for whose favor he plays out some sort of self. Middle-class, sedate males may be unmoved and bemused over having the epitaph "motherfucker" hurled at them by one of their own kind; but the same word among low-income male youth represents the ultimate insult and may be a ground for a very strong, decisive, defensive attack.[4] Through learning a self —the social categories that compose it—humans learn in what situations they must display shame or pride, grace or disgrace, self-esteem or defacement.

---

[3] C. Brown, 1965:101. Although Brown's reputation was threatened by not using heroin, his further remarks suggest an additional admixture of adventurous arousal, suggesting the way in which there can be a compound arousal of defensive and adventurous orientation.

> Those guys seemed to feel like they were flying, like they were way up in the air; they felt a way they'd never felt before. And to see so many people going around on those streets feeling so good—I just knew I was missing out on some-thing really big. (C. Brown, 1965:101.)

Throughout, we must, of course, be wary of "account biases." That is, Actor may skew the relative emphasis of his account of his immediate subjective experience in order to fit his conception of what his audience will honor as a reasonable or understandable account (see Scott and Lyman, 1968). This seems, however, a minor pitfall compared to the havoc ren-dered upon theories which are relatively uninformed by *any* accounts. On the character of the skewed theoretical emphasis that can thus result, see Bordua's insightful explication (1961) of shifting sociological conceptions of the delinquent act (and over-conceptualization as "the juvenile delinquent").

[4] On the variety of substantive forms or "meanings" that the threat, associated even with a single type of product act, can assume, see Douglas' explication of four "common patterns of meanings" in suicide. (Douglas, 1967:Chap. 17.) On the structured vulnerabilities of young males in particular to various sorts of socially defined threats, see, further, Wolfgang, 1967:149–50; Short and Strodtbeck, 1965:Chap. 10; Suttles, 1968; and Matza, 1964:53–59, 156–58 on membership and masculinity anxiety.

The definition of *social* threat (as distinguished from mere physical threat) is provided by the social and cultural context or matrix of evaluation.[5]

PERSONALISTIC VARIATIONS
IN VULNERABILITY TO THREAT

In spite of, and in addition to, the strong degree to which threat is a matter of what is claimed to be such for a given category, account must be taken also of the extent to which Actors can vary in their personal propensity to define events as threatening. Such variations seem to center on Actor's sense of secure attachment to the categories and meanings that compose the self. An Actor who sees himself as an instance of some category or categories but has doubt about how good a representative of it or them he may be seems to be highly vulnerable to defining a large number of occurrences as very threatening. He may have, as is said, "low self-esteem" (Coopersmith, 1967; and Rosenberg, 1965), and such low (or high) self-esteem may be generated by initial family experiences.

Beyond the simple facilitative character of conventionally threatening events, it is further facilitative, then, to have such events happen to Actors with a weak or attenuated sense of their social worth. Thus it appears that Actors engaged in what Lemert has called "naïve check forgery" (isolated and amateur bad check passing) tend to be people who have precarious claims to conventional categories of identity. And Actors who come eventually to die by their own hands tend to be persons who see themselves as socially worthless in terms of available categories of identity and the meaning—action possibilities—provided by these categories (Breed, 1967; and Kobler and Stotland, 1964).

Enduring variations in Actor's sense of self-esteem and social worth are, of course, hinged upon a course of biographical events, which are, in turn, a function of larger configurations of social organization. Among amateur bad check writers, we find that

> . . . such contingencies as unemployment, business failure, gambling losses, dishonorable discharge and desertion from the armed forces, alcoholic sprees, family and marital conflict and separation and divorce all figure predominantly in [their] . . . case histories. (Lemert, 1953:301.)

These sorts of contingencies serve to make more problematic Actor's sense of firm self-esteem, not only in terms of these categories but of whatever categories of identity may become problematic in given face-to-face situations. Likewise, Actors situated in categories of identity that render them of less than

[5] See, in addition, the "unique" or "inexplicable" as a further source and/or intensifier of threat, pp. 54–55, Chap. 3 and pp. 178–87, Chap. 8.

full social worth—that provide for them a tenuous basis of social and self-esteem
—have higher suicide rates.

> The high [suicide] rate among widows, widowers and divorcees has been
> long and repeatedly noted. Older persons, especially those who have
> been separated from their families, have a high rate [of suicide]. . . .
> (Kobler and Stotland, 1964:13.)

SOCIAL ORGANIZATIONAL
SOURCES

Given the social character of threat (and noting personalistic variations in
vulnerability), the question is then raised as to the kinds of factors upon which
variations in social definition of threat may depend. We may ask, for example,
in what kind of a society will there grow up a belief that an Actor can make a
foolish investment for which he should feel shameful and threatened, as is the
case with many persons who later embezzle? What kind of society is it in
which some persons can come to hinge their selves on the use of heroin or on
the integrity of public territories which can be so easily violated by Others?
Answers to questions such as these link the psychosociological concern with
objects and events defined as prideful or shameful with the analysis of social
organization per se. Psychological biases notwithstanding, subjective matters
of threat and self-esteem are not very personal or private. They are related,
rather, to such public matters as the social conditions under which investment
as a concept is something over which humans can feel anything at all, much
less feel foolish over a bad one. The fact that there have been societies with
little or no concept of investment (much less notions of foolish or wise invest-
ments) tells us that the occurrence of such a threat is a very local matter—local
in the sense of being built up and maintained only under a specific set of circumstances.

Definitions of heroin use and of violation of the integrity of what is, in fact,
public territory must be treated in a similar manner. How is it that the self-
conceptions of persons may come to be intimately bound up with such matters?
In the case of heroin, it would seem to depend, in part, upon the ghettoization
—the isolation, confinement and stigmatization—of large numbers of publicly
identifiable (because of race, as in the above case, ethnicity, culture, etc.) persons for whom life, compared with that of the majority who create and maintain
the ghetto, is mean and squalid (Chein *et al.*, 1964). In the case of territory,
such definitions seem likely to arise under conditions of high-density, low-
income, and intraghetto separation into firmly defined age and sex grades.
Where residences and public establishments are already claimed and dominated by other age grades (older women and older men), young males have
little territory left to them upon which they can lay claim. Public territory is

left over, and they place a precarious claim upon it (Suttles, 1968). In turn, questions may be asked about the conditions under which high density and low income will come to be the situation of a sector of a society's population. Attention is directed to the society at large, and issues are raised regarding how the larger population defines a subject category and treats it, in terms of access to housing, education and employment.

A general point about threat, then, is this: the subjective character of constructs like threat, or some equivalent notion, should not be taken to imply that deviant acts are individual, private or secret matters. Even the most shameful and hidden topics are public and social in the sense that they are viewed as shameful, etc., only in response to social definition and configurations of social organization. Actors subjected to threat and Actors with an enduring and precarious sense of self-esteem are so only because they are enmeshed in a social order in which whatever is at issue *can be* at issue. As others have said, biography, the self, and on-going experience are interpenetrated with society and history.

ENCAPSULATION

The occurrence of a sense of threat only facilitates the eventual commission of a deviant act; it is not in and of itself sufficient for such an occurrence. In order further to ensure this outcome, it is facilitative for the Actor to enter a state of psychosocial encapsulation.

THE CHARACTER OF ENCAPSULATION

Under conditions of threat and of a consequent high anxiety level, Actor may come to have a kind of fixation upon the threat itself, wherein he desires to remove or render harmless as quickly as possible that which is threatening. A state of intense focus upon the threat, in the midst of increasing anxiety, appears *sometimes* to lead to a constriction of the range of perceptible action alternatives and a foreshortening of the time span to which Actor refers his conduct in order to judge its propriety. Modes of dealing with the threat which are long term, multistepped and indirect become more difficult to contemplate and view as viable in the face of the pressing character of the threat itself. The Actor appears to become, rather, relatively open and responsive to threat-reducing management efforts which have the character of being short-term, simple and close at hand or proximate.

Phenomenologically, the state of encapsulation is experienced by the Actor as a rather qualitatively different state of mind. In his study of embezzlers or trust violators, Cressey quotes expressions such as these:

. . . I didn't think. When you are in one of those [situations] you don't think; you are in another world. Or you don't think like other people. You are devoid of proper thinking. You put a puzzle together like a jig-saw puzzle and see that things have to be done and you can't get the puzzle together and then you see the solution and use it. You go on and on . . . .

                ❖   ❖   ❖

The only thing I can say is that I just went nuts, that's the only way I can figure it.

                ❖   ❖   ❖

I was sitting there at the desk and I saw it, so I said, "Well, I might try it." The first thing I thought was "How long can I avoid being caught?" You've got to reach a place where something like that has no moral bear-ing for you. (Cressey, 1953:48–49, 53, 90.)

Phrases like "I didn't think," "went nuts," "has no moral bearing" seem to be various ways of saying that one had reached a state where considerations of long-term effects and consequences had become attenuated.

Speaking generally, Cressey observes of trust violators that

. . . at the time of their own peculation they did not look into the future to try to determine the ultimate consequences of their "borrowing" but in-stead merely thought that it would somehow be repaid. In prison, trust violators often said that if they "had stopped to think" for a few minutes they would have known they could not return the funds, and therefore they would not have used them. Also, they pointed out that their reason-ing that they were "borrowing" the money seemed "phony" in retrospect, that they must have been "kidding themselves" into thinking that they would or could repay. They carefully distinguished between their type of thinking in the past and in the present and indicated that at the beginning they had the genuine belief that they were going to repay the money even if, from a more objective view, it would have been impossible. (Cressey, 1953:118.)

Such a state, wherein Actor is primarily attuned to the immediate management of proximate threat and is largely unencumbered by considerations of long-term consequences, is suggested also in the coming-to experiences of some trust violators.

Various violators reported that it occurred to them that they were "in too deep" when they added up the total amount taken, read an article in a newspaper about an embezzlement case, observed another embezzlement case in their own company, observed that it was physically impossible to return the money without detection or in some other way became con-cerned with the facts of the defalcation. One violator claimed that he was in bed when it suddenly occurred to him that he had not been borrowing but embezzling instead, and he described the process as being similar to awakening from a dream. (Cressey, 1953:120.)

The same sort of encapsulation experience is suggested for naïve or amateur check forgers. Lemert suggests that there occurs

> . . . a real, albeit ephemeral, suspension, abeyance or distortion of the internal aspects of social communication. It led in our forgery cases to an attenuation of what Mead called the "inner forum of thought" and lowered sensitivity to the "generalized others" which might otherwise have produced a rejection or inhibition of the criminal alternative of forgery. The evidence for this came out in strong feelings of unpleasantness immediately following first forgeries, in the tendency for naïve check forgers to give themselves up to the police, in great feelings of relief on being arrested, in desires to "pay their debts to society," in extreme puzzlement as to how they "ever could have done it" and in personality dissociations attributing the behavior to "another me" or to a "Dr. Jekyll-Mr. Hyde" complex. (Lemert, 1953:306.)

Put another way, by foreshortening the time span of contemplatable consequences, the state of encapsulation renders Actors less sensitive to possible future sanctions and punishment for an entertained deviant act. The fear of punishment at some indefinite time in the future that might otherwise inhibit the performance of a deviant act comes to be of less or of no concern or topic of consciousness relative to the perceived seriousness and threatening character of the immediate circumstances.[6]

---

[6] Unfortunately, there appears to be only a limited amount of material available on the phenomenology of the state of encapsulation. And even the few close-up and directly relevant studies tend to be primarily interested in the investigator's own abstract construction of the Actor's most immediate and proximate perceptual field. Among these, see Short and Strodtbeck (1965:Chap. 11) on the shooting of a pedestrian on a public street by a gang leader; Westley (1953:38–39) on the illegitimate use of violence by the police; Kobler and Stotland (1964:123, 134) especially on the final phenomenology of people who commit suicide; Ward and Kassebaum (1964, 1965:74–79) on homosexual and other acts among imprisoned women as strategic defenses against depersonalization.

Happily, at least one investigator in a closely allied specialty—that of collective behavior—has independently isolated a phenomenon and developed a conception remarkably similar to encapsulation. Indeed, his explanatory construct for the analysis of collective disturbance is quite parallel in logic and substance to the one used here in depicting deviant acts. See Max Heirich, *Conflict on Campus: Demonstrations at Berkeley, 1964–1965* (forthcoming).

Hopefully, such a convergence points to the possibility of a theory which will surmount historically accidental specializations and will permit truly generic and general analytic classes of social facts. Aspects of the more or less common-sense rubrics, "collective behavior" and "deviance" may someday be subsumed to a single class of conceptual concerns; namely, the character and occurrence of non-routine social acts, individual or collective. This is a sense in which "deviance," "riots," "demonstrations" and "war" are analytically identical, a primary difference being merely their popular labels. (See, further, Lofland, 1968:especially 140–43.)

ENCAPSULATION AND
DEVIANT ACTS

The state of psychosocial encapsulation is facilitative of an eventual deviant act not because of the characteristics of this state itself but rather because of the *congruence between* some features of encapsulation and some features of a few types of social acts, deviant ones in particular. Encapsulation, in response to threat, heightens Actor's sensitivity to, and proclivity to engage in, acts that are short-term or quick, simple and close at hand or proximate. There are many possible social acts in American civilization that have these features. We can contemplate the possibility, however, that, of the total class of actions with these features, acts defined as deviant are *overrepresented*. Deviant acts may be, with disproportionate frequency, the quickest, most effective, most efficient responses to proximate threats, at least in the short run.

One way to view the task of self-control and social control is as an effort to convince or coerce Actors *not* to employ what are, in fact, the most effective short-term means of coping with situational pressures. The effort is, rather, to convince or coerce them into using an indirect, mediated, long-term, multi-stepped *set of actions* in coping with immediate problems. When insulted or injured or cheated, Actor is required to call the police, his lawyer or some other third party who will initiate a drawn-out, frequently unsuccessful process of coping with the threat. It is surely more effective and efficient in the proximate sense to deal with the threat on the spot and with dispatch. When in debt or otherwise in need of money, moral and legal precepts counsel Actor to engage in the long-term process of negotiating a loan with a lending institution or negotiating bankruptcy in a court of law. It is surely more efficient and effective, again in the proximate sense, to scheme for the immediate and direct gain of funds from whatever sources are most proximate, be these sources the bank or other organization where the Actor is employed or the corner drugstore over in the next neighborhood. In order for college students, who find themselves unprepared, to earn a passing or high grade in a course organized so that cheating is possible, it is surely more effective and efficient to cheat on an exam than to undergo post-test negotiations with the instructor, make up work, etc.

In a state of encapsulation, Actor becomes sensitive to deviant acts, perhaps not so much because he has a proclivity for such acts but because of his sensitivity to *any* simple, short-term, quick and close-at-hand or proximate acts. What might be called his vulnerability to deviance during encapsulation may not be a vulnerability to deviance itself but rather a propensity to select from a *class* of acts which, in American civilization, happens to consist in high proportion of deviant ones. It should additionally be observed that there appears to be no a priori reason why deviant acts are so frequently the most efficient and effective short-term manner of responding to immediate threats. It is perhaps one of the grand paradoxes and ironies of organized social life that one of its tasks must be to struggle to conduce Actors to act in ways that are, in short-run terms, least effective and efficient in managing their problems. Conformity is, in this sense, irrational. If deviant acts are so frequently effective and, in the short term, rational, explaining their occurrence may be less a question of understanding why they sometimes occur than of understanding why they do not occur more often. After all, deviant acts are often in compliance with two of American civilization's most cherished values: short-term efficiency and short-term effectiveness.

Put in briefest form, then, encapsulation is a heightened sensitivity to simple solutions. Simple solutions tend to be deviant acts. Therefore encapsulation heightens sensitivity to deviant acts.

FACILITANTS OF ENCAPSULATION

Threat does not in and of itself lead to encapsulation. Indeed, it does not considerably more often than it does. We may ask, then, what conditions facilitate the occurrence of encapsulation? Beyond Actor's pre-existing social and personal vulnerability to threat, two additional variables appear to be of primary importance: (1) the extent of Actor's previous experience with the given occurrence; and (2) the degree of active social support for mediated responsive actions.

Threat is not only a matter of what is defined culturally as such, but also of accumulated experience in managing occurrences of a given variety, culturally defined as threatening or not. Culturally defined and anticipated possible threats have associated with them devices for defining and responding to them. Infrequent or unique occurrences, not well defined and anticipated, can be, from the point of view of Actor, intensely threatening. Under circumstances of the new and the inexplicable, humans can become paralyzed, flee in panic or strike out in a fury of rage and aggression (Hebb, 1953). Such states are rare only because each Actor in everyday life goes to great lengths to ensure that the multitude of events that can be productive of ambiguity, fear and anxiety do not occur. Social life is a highly elaborate protective arrangement, structured and contrived to ensure that each person will be accorded reasonably protective treatment in face-to-face contacts.

The protective masking of social life is so thorough as to be deceptive, and one must look to situations of nonprotection, of the occurrence of unique events, in order fully to appreciate the circumstances most highly facilitative of encapsulating threat. Such a circumstance appears to have obtained, for example, for the *first* groups of American military personnel to be incarcerated in Chinese brainwashing camps before information was forthcoming as to the kind of social games played therein. Through the application of what were to these

humans unique devices for systematically withdrawing the supports to their social selves and for undermining the social bases of self-esteem, the Chinese
Communists were able to extract from a high proportion of their prisoners what
could be viewed as deviant acts (e.g., signing false confessions, informing on
their own people, making propaganda broadcasts). The uniqueness of the
threat increased its intensity and appears to have led to something like states
of encapsulation, in which the Actors were highly oriented to whatever kind of
immediate and proximate acts promised to bring an end to the seen-to-be-
unendurable discomfort.[7]   More recent efforts by the U.S. military to put
troops through brainwashing simulations are intended to reduce the uniqueness
of such circumstances and to provide devices for managing this kind of threat.
Although such anticipation may not altogether remove the potentially threatening character of the brainwashing situation, it is intended to lessen it.

Indeed, all efforts under the label of training or education or preparation
may be viewed as efforts to reduce the possibility of threat being provoked by
reason of the mere uniqueness or strangeness of circumstances.   Nonetheless,
neither participants nor planners can perfectly foretell and prepare for the
future.   The unique continues to occur.   To the degree that it does, it can be
expected that at least some Actors will experience intense threat and will be
set up, so to speak, as candidates for states of encapsulation.

It is possible for relatively unique occurrences of a threatening variety to
take place in the presence of an Other or Others for whom the event is either
not unique or not threatening or less threatening than to Actor because it is not
happening to them.   If such Others are present and are actively involved with
Actor, they may intervene in ways that conduce him to orient himself to longer-
term considerations and to a wider range of action alternatives than he might
do if he faced the threat alone.   Actively involved Others are likely to remind
or cajole Actor, perhaps with phrases such as these:

Jesus Christ, if you do that, X will . . . .

Look, man, they'll catch you because of . . . and put your ass in jail or . . . .

Think about X, what will (he or she) think of you if you . . . .

Now what in the hell is that going to get you . . . ?

Now come on, let's think this thing over . . . .

Look, why don't we look at it this way . . . ?

No, I don't think you should do that. Why don't we instead . . . .

Come on, forget that asshole. Let's get out of here . . . .

Shit, man, it's not that important. Think about . . . .

Why don't you and me . . . and handle it like that?

Why don't we just say, "fuck the whole thing," and bug out by . . . .

You could just tell them (him, her) about it and see what happens. You do have
    . . . going for you.

[7] See, Schein, 1956, 1957, 1961. See also Lifton, 1963.

I know how you feel, but . . . is just going to make more trouble for you and
  everybody else.
Why don't you let me help you to . . . instead of . . . ?
I'll get hold of . . . and see if we can't . . . instead of you going out and . . . .

Although the phraseology and content may differ slightly across categories of
sex, education and income, statements of these sorts from involved Others may
function to retard Actor's entrance into a state of encapsulation. If such statements are supported by *activity* on the part of Others that serves to reduce the
threat by some mediated and acceptable means, then the likelihood of a deviant
act is further reduced.

It is reported that a significant difference between Actors who attempt and
threaten to commit suicide but never do so and those who threaten and attempt
and eventually succeed resides in the differential responses of Others to Actors'
expressions of intent and actual attempts. Summarizing research on the matter, Kobler and Stotland report the following:

> Attempted suicide is a loud cry for help—and almost invariably people
> hear and respond. Stengel and Cook (1958) report that the attempts often
> lead to significant changes in the person's life through the intervention of
> other people, such as would come through medical and psychiatric care,
> as well as to changes in the relationship with X "a special person." Ruben-
> stein *et al.* (1958) report that in 34 of 44 cases of attempted suicide "de-
> sired effects" were clearly brought about through the attempt. They
> add: "We regard these 34 attempts as successful in the sense that desired
> changes in the life situation of the patients occurred as a consequence of
> the attempt . . . ." Moss and Hamilton (1957) stated, in evaluating
> factors in recovery after suicide attempts:

>> Success in recovered cases was most often attributable to the therapist's
>> active intervention in the patient's home environment . . . . We found
>> consistently that recovery requires a major change in life situation. Only
>> three recovered patients returned to the same environment in which the
>> illness arose without fundamental changes in the employment situation
>> or personal relationships.

>> The most common changes, in order of frequency, were (a) changes in
>> occupation or retirement; (b) significant improvement in the marital rela-
>> tionship; (c) emancipation from domineering and restricting parents; (d)
>> breaking of unsuitable engagements; (e) changes in psychosexual orienta-
>> tion . . . ; (f) divorce of immature and sadistic mates . . . and marriage
>> . . . ; (g) significant widening of social contacts, recreations and hobbies.
>> (Kobler and Stotland, 1964:7.)

Active intervention in these cases appears to have had the effect of keeping
wide the temporal and social span to which Actor could meaningfully refer his
possible courses of conduct. The initial promise or live possibility of removing
the threat retards Actor's entrance into encapsulation where suicide can appear

to be (and objectively is) a highly effective, efficient and proximate way to deal with an overwhelming threat to self. Through what is referred to above as "significant changes in the person's life," the threat is removed in actuality, not just in subjective possibility.

If, on the other hand, intense threat occurs in the presence of Others who cannot or will not support and aid Actor in keeping wide the temporal and social span relating to a meaningful future, encapsulation is facilitated. This facilitative possibility, relative to suicide, is dramatically illustrated by the well-known case of Ellen West:

> Mrs. West was hospitalized, at age 33, after much treatment and four sui-cide attempts. In the hospital, suicide preoccupation and threats con-tinued. At the hospital, the feeling was that release meant certain suicide. There were consultations, what [Carl] Rogers . . . called the "comic-tragic argument over her diagnosis." ". . . then comes the last, final, incredible decision. She is suicidal, schizophrenic and hopeless for treat-ment. Therefore we will discharge her and let her commit suicide." Binswanger (1958) wrote that he and his renowned consultants all agreed "that no definitely reliable therapy is possible. We therefore resolved to give in to the patient's demands for discharge." Ellen West, who had said, "I scream but they do not hear me," went home and, on her third day at home, killed herself. In Ellen West's case, actual suicide did not take place until total hopelessness was made explicit and definite. While hope existed—and treatment went on for many years—although the apparent desire for suicide existed in Ellen West, actual suicide did not occur.[8]

In some cases, absence of active support and intervention may take the form of Others' knowing about Actor's difficulties but feeling helpless to do anything about them. According to Kobler and Stotland, this is fairly common in con-nection with eventual suicide. Indeed, they argue that expression of the in-ability to do anything about what is threatening Actor is a positive condition promoting suicide, or, in the terms used here, a facilitant of encapsulation, which, in turn, renders suicide a viable defense against threat (Kobler and Stotland, 1964: especially Chaps. 1 and 9).

Absence of active intervention which retards encapsulation may also be a product of Actor's shame or guilt or fear over having gotten himself into the current difficulty. Others may not be able to intervene because Actor is secre-tive about the sources and character of his proximate problem. It is this kind of secretiveness, leading to encapsulation, that Cressey seems to denote with the concept of the nonsharable problem.

[8] Kobler and Stotland, 1964:264–65. The moral judgment made by Kobler and Stotland must be kept separate from a judgment of how suicide can be facilitated. Kobler and Stotland are evidently against suicide, but Ellen West's therapists apparently felt, from a more existentialist perspective, that the taking of one's own life was a morally ambiguous and private act. One can conclude that this latter stance facilitates the occurrence of sui-cide without necessarily condemning the position on moral grounds.

> In all cases of trust violation encountered, the violator considered that a financial problem which confronted him could not be shared with persons who, from a more objective point of view, probably could have aided in the solution of the problem. Criteria of an objective nature in regard to the degree of "sharability" which various types of problems have in our culture were not set up, but instead the subject's definition of situations were used as data. Thus a man could lose considerable money at the race track daily, but the loss, even if it constituted a problem for the individual, might not constitute a nonsharable problem for him. Another man might define the problem as one which must be kept secret and private, that is, as one which is nonsharable. (Cressey, 1953:34–35.)

Nonsharable problems are themselves connected with threat and, in trust violation, particularly, with the loss of proper public reputation. As Cressey puts it: "All situations producing problems considered as nonsharable by the subjects were concerned with status-seeking or status-maintaining activities . . ." (Cressey, 1953:36).

In the case of naïve or amateur check forgery, absence of support for a mediated act appears to be associated not only with the more general condition of identity precariousness mentioned above but also with the immediate situation—with what Lemert calls "certain dialectical forms of social behavior, dialectical in the sense that the person became progressively involved in them" (Lemert, 1953:303).

> It was our . . . impression that many of the type situations more specifically leading to forgeries—gambling, borrowing and "kiting" to meet debts and business obligations, desertion, and escaping authorities, and being the *bon vivant*—tended to be dialectical, self-enclosed systems of behavior in the sense that the initial behaviors called for "more of the same." While making the possession of money critically necessary, they also reinforced or increased the social isolation of the indulgee; many forgers admitted that at the time such behavior was perceived as having a "false structure" to it. (Lemert, 1953:304.)

The terms "dialectical, self-enclosed systems" calling for more of the same refer to situations of this variety:

> . . . A man away from home who falls in with a small group of persons who have embarked upon a two- or three-day or even a week's period of drinking and carousing . . . tends to have the impetus to continue the pattern which gets mutually reinforced by [the] interaction of the participants, and [the pattern] tends to have an accelerated beginning, a climax and a terminus. If midway through a spree a participant runs out of money, the pressures immediately become critical to take such measures as are necessary to preserve the behavior sequence. A similar behavior sequence is perceived in that of the alcoholic who reaches a "high

point" in his drinking and runs out of money. He might go home and get clothes to pawn or go and borrow money from a friend or even apply for public relief, but these alternatives become irrelevant because of the immediacy of his need for alcohol. (Lemert, 1953:303.)

The Actor may be physically alone and caught up in a behavior sequence with a logic of its own, calling for completion which creates the threatening press into encapsulation; or he may simply be with a set of Others to whom stopping now is an immediate social defacement. Although not so dramatic and glamorous as the difficulties of persons in positions of trust who may have debts due to mistresses, high living or large stock-speculating losses, the immediate situation of needing money to continue a drinking spree with others, to finish an evening's entertaining of a young lady in high style or to continue in an all-night gambling session can appear to be, at least at the moment, equally momentous. Because such Others expect Actor to continue in whatever social game is being played, and because he fears they will think ill of him if he stops before it is over, Actor's view of the situation is in terms of its most immediate and proximate demands. The already tenuous sense of social worth of such Actors makes them extremely vulnerable and sensitive to these immediate demands. Their precarious self-esteem functions in the immediate context to make them even less willing to risk the possible and proximate shame of not fulfilling the expectations of Others.

Although it is not, at present, clearly the case, encapsulation seems seldom to occur in a climax fashion. Available materials suggest, rather, that it is rather slowly built up, sometimes over hours, as in such acts as naïve check forgery; sometimes over weeks, as in the case of suicide. In either case, there seems to be involved more of a gradual narrowing of perceptually viable alternatives than a dramatic or traumatic constriction of perception. Such gradualness of onset may, however, be an artifact of the immediacy of need for action. Persons with nonsharable financial problems have considerable "stall time," as it were, and naïve check forgers usually have at least a few hours in which to contemplate their problems. The stall time in these cases, of course, stands in considerable contrast to that available to Actors being attacked with knives or bricks. A general point to consider, therefore, is that the greater the available time in which to stall, the less the likelihood of encapsulation, since there is a correspondingly longer time in which an Other can intervene. Thus, to facilitate a deviant act, the threat induced should permit only a very short period of time for considering responsive actions. Ideally the threat should require immediate defensive action, as appears to be the case in many episodes of homicide (Wolfgang, 1958).

In the same way that threat does not in and of itself lead to encapsulation, encapsulation does not in and of itself produce closure on a *deviant* act. Having brought Actor to a more than usual openness to the class of proximate, simple and effective acts which are responsive to a situation of threat, there remains the question of the conditions under which Actor will select a deviant act from among this class. What conditions, in other words, facilitate closure on a deviant act?

In turning to the conditions (or facilitants) of closure on a deviant act, it is possible to discriminate a set of elements of the concept of conditions, along the line of what Actor is likely to view as phenomenologically problematic topics. These elements are the availability, amenability and capability of: (1) a set of physical *places,* (2) a complement of relatively mobile nonhuman objects or *hardware,* (3) a set of human *Others,* and (4) *Actor* himself. The general statements which can be made concerning each of these elements call for, again and in turn, a separate analysis of conditions which facilitate the facilitative states of the elements. That is, the facilitative states of what are initially independent variables must themselves be made problematic and thus converted to dependent variables which vary as a function of less proximate classes of concerns, namely, wider and more abstract units of social organization and more remote events of individual biography.

THE CLASS OF AVAILABLE ACTS: DEVIANT AND NORMAL

The general suggested principle regarding closure is this: Among the class of proximate and relatively immediately available social acts, the act which is most proximate and performable in terms of the facilitative states of places, hardware, Others and Actor himself will be the act chosen. This is to say that the responsive act *may or may not* be a *deviant* social act, depending on the relative standing of all more or less proximately and immediately performable social acts. An implication of this conception is that equally or more important than any of Actor's dispositions, tendencies, etc., toward deviant acts are the range and character of the set of acts from which he can make some sort of selection.

An analysis of closure, then, requires knowledge not only of proximately available *deviant* acts, but of *all proximately available acts as a general class.* It must be said, sadly, that even among that small number of investigators who have bothered to look at deviant acts in the close-up manner promoted here, such a depiction has not been a prominent concern. Although a limited amount of mostly case materials can be presented, this general proposition cannot be pursued in detail and will remain here more of an orientation to the materials than a suggestion for which there is a fair degree of supporting empirical evidence.

EMPHASIS ON UNREMARKABLE
ARRANGEMENTS

Further, as a small corrective to existing tendencies, I want to couch the above orientation within a more general issue involving a somewhat selective emphasis upon facilitants of closure on a deviant act. The focus thus far upon the concepts of threat and encapsulation and the associated notions of fear and anxiety conduce to the image of the defensive deviant act as a very dramatic and soul-rendering affair. And it may be, at least to Actor. Such a feature should not, however, mislead us into believing that the deviant act has a non-routine, peculiar and dramatic quality all the way along the line. The subjective states to which I have referred must now be recognized as frequently occurring in a social context which, although disturbing to Actor, appears for the most part and from the point of view of Others to have a rather undramatic, routine and orderly character. The fact that Actor has some sort of problem in a rather immediate sense provides no necessary warrant for the assumption that the entire social field has become thoroughly problematic to all its participants. One can be most impressed, rather, with the way in which everyday life frequently appears to be going forth in a business-as-usual fashion around Actor and all his fears and threat (*or* enchantment and adventure) and state of encapsulation. Although this is not necessarily and always the case, the social context is of this nature often enough to justify an emphasis upon the ways in which normal, unnoticed and unremarkable arrangements, skills, beliefs and relationships appear to be facilitative of closure on deviant acts by rendering such acts the most proximate of available responses.

THE ORDERING OF ELEMENTS

To emphasize the *situational* character of deviant acts, we will begin the analysis of closure with a consideration of how routine features of *places* can be facilitative, move to a discussion of available physical objects or *hardware* and then turn to analyzing the facilitative significance of *Others* and, finally, of *Actor*.

FACILITATING PLACES

Given the typically clandestine character of many, if not most, deviant acts and given the fact that all acts have to be performed somewhere, one may ask what sorts of places are most highly facilitative of such acts.

PROTECTIVENESS

Places, as bounded physical sites, appear to vary in the amount of protection which they afford from Others who might have an interest in interfering with the performance of the act. A protected place is one in which (1) possibly interfering Others are excluded by reason of physical barriers (like walls); (2) possibly interfering Others are regularly- absent, even if there are few or no obstacles to vision and action; (3) possibly interfering Others are excluded by virtue of legal rules about place entry; or (4) the possible intervention of Others is neutralized by their compromising entanglements with Actor.

THE HOME

In American civilization the institution known as the home is, without doubt, the most protected of places in the above senses. Bounded by walls, by elaborate legal rules and by entanglements that the inhabitants have with one another, it should be expected that the home would be a highly favored site for deviant acts (and even for deviance generally as a role phenomenon). Of course, its features as a specialized social place will inherently limit what can go on; but within such constraints, one can expect deviance to blossom. Among sex offenses, for example, incest occurs overwhelmingly in the home. Indeed, for sex offenses generally, "homes predominate as offense locations in the majority of offense types" (Gebhard *et al.*, 1965:763). They are, in particular, the "favored locale" for homosexual offenses and heterosexual acts not involving force (Gebhard *et al.*, 1965:763–64, 815).

Various kinds of other conflicts appear also to have an affinity for the home. The Reiss tabulations of places in which violent altercations occur, relative to selected categories of race and sex, reveal the following types of relations (in the city of Chicago):

Negro men and women most commonly victimize one another in an offense with a gun when they are in a private residence.

※   ※   ※

White and Negro women are most commonly victimized in assaults with a knife by White and Negro men in a residence . . . .

※   ※   ※

When men are victimized by women of their own race in assaults with cutting instruments . . . they are more commonly victimized in a residence than on a street or in some other setting.

※   ※   ※

The most common place where Negro women are victimized by a male in assaults without a dangerous weapon is the private residence.

*   *   *

When women are victimized by a man or woman of their own race, the most common place of occurrence of the offense against the person is the residence. (Reiss, 1967:112, 114, 115, 122, 127; italics omitted.)

Reiss comments on these relations:

Men and women of the same race meet one another most frequently in the domestic setting of the private residence, or at least in meetings that potentially lead to conflict. Conflict is endemic to the domestic relationship; quite commonly the police are called to deal with "domestic disturbance." Observation of these domestic disturbances discloses that in a substantial proportion of them there is a high potential for violence. It is not surprising, therefore, that assault or battery involving men and women of the same race arises most commonly in the domestic setting of the private residence. (Reiss, 1967:129; see also Wolfgang, 1958:Chap. 7.)

Among "crimes without victims" (in any clear sense), it is found that users of illegal substances such as marijuana, LSD and heroin have a certain partiality for private dwelling places in which shades can be drawn and doors locked and where toilets are available for flushing away evidence. And, persons desiring to kill themselves can find it advantageous to do so either in their own homes or in the temporary homes provided by hotel rooms.

PROTECTIVE PUBLIC PLACES

It is not the home per se, as a common-sense place designation, but rather its analytic features as a highly protected place that make it a hotbed of deviance. Any place that displays such features will facilitate deviance. The more protective features it has, the more deviance therein is facilitated. It is reasonable, therefore, to scrutinize places as a category, especially those commonly thought of as public, in terms of the degree to which they are, analytically speaking, protective. For it is in terms of protectiveness that the class of places called public assumes considerable interest. In common sense and in law, a "public place" refers to "any region in a community freely accessible to members of that community" (Goffman, 1963b:9). Or, in legal language, "public" denotes "any street, alley, park, public building, any place of business or assembly open to or frequented by the public, or any other place which is open to public view or to which the public has access" (City of Ann Arbor, Michigan, 1957:Chap. 108, paragraph 9:61).

It happens that public places vary considerably in the degree to which they embody features protective of deviant acts. Indeed, in the history of American civilization there was a period in which the term "criminal underworld" referred not only to a class of persons oriented in a particular way and engaged in illegal activities, but to a set of public (and private) places within urban settlements as well. These areas were underworlds precisely because they were highly protective of deviant acts. Crime took place on the streets and within public and private buildings with impunity because the main class of possibly interfering Others, the police, hardly dared to penetrate such areas. (Asbury, 1927. On the parallel British phenomenon of "rookeries" see Tobias, 1967:24–29, 131–47.) Subsequent and continuing struggles for a policed society and safe streets can be viewed as an effort to make public places minimally protective of deviant acts. However, although underworlds in the territorial sense have all but disappeared, many features of more contemporary public territories continue to facilitate deviant acts.

Public places are, by definition, unprotected, since possibly interfering Others cannot be legally excluded. Protectiveness is often created, nonetheless, by a variety of de facto circumstances. Pedestrian and vehicular traffic patterns can develop such that some places are virtually abandoned during large portions of a typical day. In urban settlements a variety of alleys, lots and even entire streets or blocks can come to be highly protective because of their sparse or nonexistent use. Despite the population density of such areas as New York's Harlem, many alleys and apartment house hallways and rooftops apparently remain sufficiently unused for many persons to feel safe in appropriating them as temporary private places where drugs may be taken. Similarly, the sparse evening use of many center cities appears to convert very large territories into inviting sites for muggings, burglaries, holdups and the like. In rural areas there can develop the ironically well-known back country roads. Places of this kind not only justly earn reputations as lovers' lanes but also sometimes achieve more dubious distinctions as sites of suicides, homicides, holdups, kidnappings and "sexual perversions." Their reasonable protectiveness makes them attractive also for glue sniffing or for the quickie use of drugs such as marijuana and heroin.

Further, the daily cycle of light and dark has facilitative consequences for the protectiveness of many places, a fact which may account for the association between the higher rates of many deviant acts and the dark or night portion of the day (Johnson, 1964:66–68). Darkness reduces the distance from which Actor can visually be sighted in the public place, and darkness is associated with the movement of population from streets and places of business to homes and areas of residence. A Detroit filling-station operator who neglected to light his station, even though it was located in a relatively night-deserted area, unsurprisingly had his establishment burglarized eleven times within eighteen months (Detroit News, October 21, 1966). It is perhaps difficult for modern man, accustomed as he is to an abundance of electrically lighted public places, to appreciate fully the extent to which darkness facilitates many kinds of deviant acts. To see the enormous hardship that lighting imposes upon the possi-

bilities for such acts, one has to contrast the modern public place with urban
public places prior to the invention (and wildfire diffusion) of gas lighting. As
one scholar concluded about 19th-century American cities: "Gas began to light
the city streets; and a whole medieval world, in which all streets at night were
more dangerous than a jungle path, disappeared from man's consciousness"
(Fitch, 1966:115. On the parallel British experience, see Tobias, 1967:38–39,
189–90).

Places surrounded by objects which function as barriers to long-distance
viewing and which are honeycombed with pathways and niches also facilitate
deviant acts by making escape (for those acts requiring it) quite easy and
thereby rendering the act more attractive. The visual barriers, pathways and
niches may, of course, be on the scale of foot, automobile or even aircraft transportation. Pedestrians and stores, surrounded by a maze of alleyways and
apartment house basements and hallways, and banks, surrounded by a complex
of streets and parkways, facilitate the work of an Actor or Actors who would
encounter them in ways that would be defined as deviant. Los Angeles banks
which locate their branches at freeway entrances and exists for the convenience
of their customers find that their locations are also convenient for amateur acts
of robbery.

A pattern of sparse traffic combined with low levels of light and combined
further with a variety of barriers to vision add up to a kind of place that is
highly facilitative of a variety of deviant acts. Concern over safety at night in
New York's Central Park arose out of just such a combination of facilitants.
The sparse traffic and dim illumination of that territory, together with the
wooded and broken terrain, created a most auspicious setting for a variety of
acts that would be less than safe to perform in Times Square. More recent
efforts to light up certain sections of that park and to hold very large nighttime
gatherings there concomitantly attenuated its protective features.

A public place is not necessarily a territory at ground level. Modern means
of construction have made possible all manner of public places in the sky,
namely the corridors of high-rise housing, especially public housing. In the
words of Jane Jacobs,

> The elevators and corridors of public housing projects are, in a sense,
> streets. They are streets piled up in the sky in order to eliminate streets
> on the ground and permit the ground to become deserted . . . . Not only
> are these interior parts of the buildings streets in the sense that they serve
> the comings and goings of residents, most of whom may not know each
> other or recognize, necessarily, who is a resident and who is not. They
> are streets also in the sense of being accessible to the public. They have
> been designed in an imitation of upper-class standards for apartment liv-
> ing without upper-class cash for doormen and elevator men. Anyone at
> all can go into these buildings, unquestioned, and use the traveling street
> of the elevator and the sidewalks that are the corridors. These interior
> streets, although completely accessible to public use, are closed to public

view and they thus lack the checks and inhibitions exerted by eye-policed city streets. (Jacobs, 1963:42–43.)

The public but protective character of such places, as is well known, has for some years been associated with a high rate of deviant acts therein (Suttles, 1968). According to Jane Jacobs, such a problem led the New York City Housing Authority to experiment, at one point, with "corridors open to public view" in a Brooklyn project she refers to as Blenheim Houses.

Because the buildings of Blenheim Houses are sixteen stories high, and because their height permits generous expanses of shunned ground area, surveillance of the open corridors from the ground or from other buildings offers little more than psychological effect. But this psychological openness to view does appear effective to some degree. More important and effective, the corridors are well designed to induce surveillance from within the buildings themselves. Uses other than plain circulation were built into them. They were equipped with play space, and made sufficiently generous to act as narrow porches, as well as passageways. This all turned out to be so lively and interesting that the tenants added still another use and much the favorite: picnic grounds—this in spite of continual pleas and threats from the management which did not *plan* that the balcony–corridors should serve as picnic grounds. (The plan should anticipate everything and then permit no changes.) The tenants are devoted to the balcony–corridors; and as a result of being intensively used the balconies are under intense surveillance. There has been no problem of crime in these particular corridors, nor of vandalism either. Not even light bulbs are stolen or broken, although in projects of similar size with blind-eyed corridors, light bulb replacements solely because of theft or vandalism customarily run into the thousands each month.
  So far so good.
  A striking demonstration of the direct connection between city surveillance and city safety!
  Nonetheless, Blenheim Houses has a fearsome problem of vandalism and scandalous behavior. The lighted balconies which are, as the manager puts it, "the brightest and most attractive scene in sight," draw strangers, especially teen-agers, from all over Brooklyn. But these strangers, lured by the magnet of the publicly visible corridors, do not halt at the visible corridors. They go into other "streets" of the buildings, streets that lack surveillance. These include the elevators and, more important in this case, the fire stairs and their landings. The housing police run up and down after the malefactors—who behave barbariously and viciously in the blind-eyed sixteen-story-high stairways—and the malefactors elude them. It is easy to run the elevators up to a high floor, jam the doors so the elevators cannot be brought down, and then play hell with the building and anyone you can catch. So serious is the problem and apparently so uncontrollable, that the advantage of the safe corridors is all but canceled—at least in the harried manager's eyes.

What happens at Blenheim Houses is somewhat the same as what happens in dull gray areas of cities. The gray areas' pitifully few and thinly spaced patches of brightness and life are like the visible corridors at Blenheim Houses. They do attract strangers. But the relatively deserted, dull, blind streets leading from these places are like the fire stairs at Blenheim Houses. These are not equipped to handle strangers, and the presence of strangers in them is an automatic menace. (Jacobs, 1963:43–44.)

SOCIAL ORGANIZATIONAL SOURCES

If one views the degree to which a place is protected as an item that itself requires explanation, one can note the connection between the high protection accorded the home and the value placed on privacy and the "sanctity of the home." The strong historical emphasis in the Western world on private, unmonitored and wallbounded spaces into which human beings can withdraw and remain unbothered (unless there is a very dramatic reason to intrude) creates the cultural and structural foundation for a considerable amount of deviance. The cherished belief, buttressed by all manner of laws, in the inviolate nature of the private place creates a basic facilitant for the growth of incestuous relations, illegal homosexual and heterosexual acts and practices and intense and unaudited interpersonal conflicts. In a similar fashion, some conceptions of the "city beautiful" or at least the "city practical" sponsored in the past and at present by some city planners and architects appear, inadvertently, to create public territories with features that are highly protective of deviant acts. The engineered introduction of low-use streets (and entire center cities) and high-rise public housing with deserted halls, and the effort to destroy street life and acquaintance in public places more generally, conduce to circumstances that virtually invite deviant acts (Jacobs, 1963:especially Part X).

One of the most effective ways in which to reduce the rate of deviant acts would doubtless be continuously to monitor all homes, perhaps by means of omnipresent and inescapable television cameras, after the manner of Orwell's depiction of 1984. Specialists in social control do, indeed, from time to time recommend practices that move in this direction. Such recommendations typically encounter strong resistance among those who strongly value the private place. Objections on grounds of values must nonetheless be kept separate from judgments based on considerations of technical effectiveness. The peoples of Western societies quite clearly place a higher value on the privacy of the home than on lower rates of the kinds of deviant acts facilitated by such privacy. Further, the occurrence of deviant acts in public places could be inhibited through intensive *state* monitoring of the civilian population and strong regulations regarding who can be abroad at what hours for what purposes in what sorts of establishments. In the five days after Michigan Governor George Romney declared an "early preventive state of emergency" in the Detroit area following the assassination of Dr. Martin Luther King, Jr., "the rate of the usual kinds of crime declined [by about half] in the city" (*Ann Arbor News,* April 10, 1968). Mandatory closing of many classes of public establishments, banishing citizens from the street at night, prohibition of assembly of more than three persons and constant patrolling by military units does indeed make for a very quiet and orderly—albeit totalitarian—society. The usual kinds of crimes are one of the costs of a somewhat free society.

Under conditions of some degree of threat and encapsulation, where closure has become problematic, the range of available places construed in terms of their comparative degree of *proximity* and *protectiveness* is likely to be crucial in determining which act, from among all more or less available acts, Actor will select. It can well happen that, among all proximately available acts, otherwise available deviant ones are ruled out because protected sites are not accessible for their performance.

FACILITATING HARDWARE

If the term "hardware" denotes reasonably transportable nonhuman physical objects, it can be said that, under conditions of necessity to select from among a range of proximately available alternatives, those acts requiring *no* such items are most highly facilitated. *Deviant* acts requiring no hardware are, on that account, highly facilitated. Acts of exhibitionism, disturbing the peace, homosexuality, adultery, public brawling, casual prostitution, child beating and the like are distinguished by the lack of necessity for any kind of hardware for their perpetration. (There are, of course, elaborated forms of these acts in which hardware might be used; it is simply not technically necessary.) But even those requiring no hardware are not necessarily easy to accomplish. There remains the typical necessity for one or more Others and some sort of reasonably protected and conducive place in which to perform the acts.

EVERYDAY OBJECTS

Many deviant acts do, of course, require some kind of physical artifacts for their commission, but such hardware often seems to be rather widely and routinely present. Routine and proximate availability thereby heightens the possibility that Actors will close on the deviant acts made feasible by such hardware. Various kinds of violent assaults, some of which eventuate in homicide, often involve quite prosaic household implements and other common objects, among which are knives, bottles, meat cleavers, hammers, bricks, decorative statuary, etc. (Wolfgang, 1958:Chap. 5). That assault upon the self called suicide is nicely facilitated by substances freely available from any drugstore or hardware store, such as sleeping pills and rope, by the gas manufactured by automobile engines and the like. Until the very recent past, naïve check forgery was facilitated by the wide availability of counterchecks, a piece of hardware now being constricted by the advent of automatic data processing. The almost universal convention in American civilization of wearing clothes creates the hardware necessary for the more elementary forms of shoplifting, requiring as they do some means of protective concealment such as pockets, purses, bulky sweaters or overcoats. It is reported (perhaps in jest) that, for a time, sexual intercourse among unmarried adolescent persons was highly facilitated by the purported discovery that a kitchen product called Saran Wrap could serve as a reasonably effective contraceptive device.[1] Theft of mail from apartment houses is facilitated through installation of cheaply constructed multiple mailboxes whose master panels lack recessed edges and close-tolerance locks and which are made of soft metal, making the front easy to grasp and simple to pull open.

On a somewhat different level, the marked modern increase in the sheer *amount* of portable property, brought about by mass production, increases the number of things that can possibly be stolen, vandalized, pilfered or otherwise trifled with (Tobias, 1967:43). Stanton Wheeler thus observes that "probably the best predictor of the auto-theft rate (usually a youth crime) is not some characteristic of the youths in question, but, instead, the number of available automobiles in an area" (1967:643; see also Wilkins, 1965).

SPECIALIZED OBJECTS

Where the deviant act necessitates hardware of a rather specialized or even esoteric nature, in the sense that it is not routinely available to the average man, it is often found that, from the point of view and situation of the particular Actor, the hardware is highly proximate and routine. Whereas the Others and places, as well as the hardware, for embezzlement are highly remote and inaccessible for most Actors, they are, for those Actors who close on this act, highly proximate. According to Cressey:

> Persons violating positions of trust do not depart from their ordinary occupational routines, the routines in which they are skilled, in order to perpetrate their crimes. Accountants use checks which they have been entrusted to dispose of, salesclerks withhold receipts, bankers manipulate seldom-used accounts or withhold deposits, real estate men use deposits entrusted to them and so on. (Cressey, 1953:84.)

[1] It is said later to have declined in popularity because of the reported association with a vaginal irritation called "Saran Wrap rash." Although reliably reported, the entire affair may, of course, be apocryphal.

So, too, certain currently illegal drugs, such as marijuana, LSD or heroin, although inaccessible to many, circulate rather freely within certain social milieux or territories (Lindesmith, 1968:172–74). And, it should be recognized that to be a medical doctor is automatically to possess the hardware necessary to conduct a variety of illegal activities, especially the acts of abortion and personal drug use (Winick, 1961).

Superficial or casual acquaintance with the situation of deviant acts involving esoteric and specialized hardware can sometimes lead outside observers to conclude that a high degree of effort and very strong, probably perverse, motivation were surely involved for Actor to have come by particular pieces of hardware to perform such an act. But closer inspection often reveals that the proximity of hardware for a particular deviant act has less to do with Actor's efforts to possess it for a deviant purpose than with the conjoining of situations, due to forces outside his will and intentions, that simply have the *effect* of bringing Actor and hardware into proximity.

SOCIAL ORGANIZATIONAL
SOURCES

Social scientists have shown a strong tendency to underplay matters of hardware and places in accounts of deviant acts and of deviance generally. A concern with hardware and place is traditionally identified with the police and other categories of persons—such as political conservatives[2]—who are devalued and scorned in the social scientist's typically liberal world view. (Left only with Actor and Other, social scientists have shown an additional partiality for Actor rather than Other, at least until recent years.) Liberal ideology aside, and viewing the matter on grounds of simple technical efficacy, the constriction of availability of hardware, for those acts requiring any, seems reasonably to inhibit the possibility of their occurrence.

The irony, however, resides in the specific kinds of hardware that would have to be controlled in order to make many kinds of deviant acts remote and therefore less likely to be closed upon. Although it might be feasible eventually to restrict the possession of firearms—an item not defined as necessary to daily living—that item is trivial compared to the much more empirically frequent sorts of physical objects involved in deviant acts.[3] The kinds of hardware more typically used in deviant acts are bound up and inextricably intertwined with the most conventional and laudable purposes of American civilization. The social sources of hardware for many deviant acts are the *same* as the social

[2] The political conservative's traditional concerns with the control of hardware has not, peculiarly, included the control of firearms. An interesting instance of a social scientist's enthusiastic discovery of hardware (and places) is presented in Etzioni, 1968b.

[3] Firearms do, however, seem rather massively to facilitate the commission of one sort of deviant act rather than another; i.e. what might otherwise have been simple assault becomes murder.

sources of hardware for the conduct of normal activity. Assault, homicide, suicide, shoplifting, sexual intercourse among adolescents, abortions and embezzlement might well be reduced by making it very difficult to possess kitchen
knives, meat cleavers, automobiles, sleeping pills, purses, overcoats, Saran
Wrap, medical instruments and entrusted funds, but such restrictions would
massively interfere with conventional acts. Such restrictions are not of course,
impossible; but their enactment would seem to be a matter of how much people
are willing to pay to reduce the incidence of deviant acts. It may well be that
there is a preference for concentrating on controlling Actor per se—his personality, his dispositions and the like—precisely because focus on *him* least dis-
rupts or interferes with ongoing social life. Confinement and manipulation of
Actor is the easiest thing to do, for, relative to attempts at manipulating other
elements, the public is least inconvenienced by it.

FACILITATING OTHERS

EVERYDAY ROUTINES

In turning to Others and their facilitative significance, let us first examine
some ways in which their everyday routines can render a deviant act the most
proximate and effective of immediately feasible responses. Once Actor has
begun to code or be sensitive to his situation in terms of ways in which to manage some current stress (or perhaps aroused sense of adventure), he can sometimes discover that the normal activities of the world at work have certain
built-in (but usually unnoticed) vulnerabilities. He may find that the normal
routines of Others dovetail with the more current of his felt needs. Persons
working in banks who become so newly sensitive can thus discover, perhaps to
their genuine surprise, that there are Others in the world who rarely use the
funds in their checking or savings accounts, permitting the possibility of "borrowing" such funds. Or, an Actor might become aware that certain of his
business customers regularly buy large amounts of goods for cash rather than
on credit, making it possible for him to pocket a large portion of the money
from these unwritten exchanges (Jaspan and Black, 1960:41–45). Persons not
in positions of financial trust who need immediate money can become sensitive
to the features of the check-cashing policies of various business organizations
and discover, in the words of Lemert, that "forgery (excluding actually imitat-
ing other people's signatures) is very simple to perform; it is probably
the easiest major crime to commit that we have" (Lemert, 1953:305). Aside
from characteristics of hardware that have made check forgery easy (at least
until recently), the rather routine attitudes of at least some Others in at least
some places are highly facilitative of such an act. And, people who feel in
need of someone else's car can discover many with keys left in the ignition

(about half of those stolen were so left) and with the doors left unlocked (about three-quarters of those stolen were left unlocked) (*New York Times,* July 30, 1967).

It might be said that many acts of white-collar crime, especially, are very strongly a function of routine features of the social order that in some sense invite use by those who can be brought to this kind of sensitivity about that order. As Sutherland documented in his classic work on *White Collar Crime,* the wide variety of crimes found in business, politics and medicine are intimately facilitated by astute and not very difficult manipulations of the world as it stands. Restraint of trade and rebates; violations of patents, trademarks and copyrights; misrepresentation in advertising; and the like have been, at least in the past, marvelously facilitated through the dovetailing of the interest of given Actors and the standing arrangements of Others (see also Clinard, 1952). White-collar crime, as Sutherland has said, "flourishes at points where powerful business and professional men come in contact with persons who are weak. In this respect, it is similar to stealing candy from a baby" (Sutherland, 1940:9).

Although it may be easy to steal candy from an Other who happens also to be an infant, that easiness must first be identified by Actor. The identification by the Actor of the ways in which Others can unknowingly and routinely facilitate his commission of a deviant act is suggestive of a rather high degree of creative discernment. Creativity of this sort is rather similar to the capacity for creating other recombinations of elements, usually defined as more socially acceptable and sometimes even rewarded. The more conventional sort of creativity and the present type also occur under similar circumstances: a stressful situation which demands a reconceiving of the cognitive field in order to achieve a solution. At least some normals who commit some kinds of deviant acts are, in a sense, creative social pioneers in structuring an image of how everyday life operates and in thus being able to see previously undiscovered possibilities for action. (See, for example, the case materials in Cressey, 1953; Jaspan and Black, 1960; Sutherland, 1949; Geis, 1968.) And, as with other discoveries of new possibilities for action or meaning, once they are known, Others are likely to say, "it is so obvious" or "it was so easy."

PERSONAL ENTANGLEMENTS

Built-in vulnerabilities in the standing social arrangements of Others that can be creatively discovered under stress is but one way in which the routine activities of Others can facilitate a deviant act. Another is for Others routinely to act in a manner which presumes that Actor has an interest in going along with or even actively supporting some developing situation of face-to-face interaction. Such a presumption centered on the commission of a deviant act makes that act, for Actor, the course of least resistance—the proximately easiest thing to do in the immediate circumstance. According to Chein *et al.*, the first act of heroin use for many young Harlem males

> came about in a simple, casual way. About a third of the boys were offered a "shot" or a "snort" by a youthful friend, and, in about another third, the opportunity developed in a group setting and at the initiative of the group. Very few actively sought the first opportunity, and a few others were offered drugs by members of their families or unrelated adults. In most cases, the heroin was obtained easily and without cost. (Chein *et al.*, 1964:150.)

Situations of the following variety can develop in what Chein *et al.*, describe as an "easy and 'natural' manner":

> I was at a party. Everybody was having a good time. I wanted to be one of the crowd. I thought, if it didn't hurt them it wouldn't hurt me. That started the ball rolling. They were sniffing at that time. Two or three pulled out a few caps: said, "Here, if you want to try." I accepted. They weren't trying to addict me; they just gave it to me.

❉   ❉   ❉

> Some of us was in a car. We was going to town one night, so one of the guys said, "Let's take off [use drugs] before we start." I said, "Not me; I don't want any." But one of the guys owed me $2, so he said: "Come on, I'll give you four pills, and we'll call it even." So I tried. That was just skin-popping. The next day I was with this same guy, and he was main-lining. Wanted me to try it. I tried two pills at once that time. (Chein *et al.*, 1964:151–52.)

An Actor who happens, for whatever reason, to be involved with Others who engage in one or another deviant act may find that it is "just a matter of time until a situation arises"[4] such that the presumptions that Others make about him will render a deviant act his course of least resistance, creating a miniature or temporarily collapsed sequence of threat, encapsulation and closure. Concerning a first act of marijuana use, Becker quotes this situation:

> I was with these guys that I knew from school, and one had some, so they went to get high and they just figured that I did too. They never asked me, so I didn't want to be no wallflower or nothin', so I didn't say nothin' and went in back of this place with them. They were doing up a couple of cigarettes. (Becker, 1963:62.)

Having begun to circulate in some circle, Actor may subsequently become aware that his engagement in deviance is more than simply possible or likely: he may perceive such activity to be more or less mandatory.

---

[4] H. S. Becker, 1963:62.

I didn't know much about heroin in those days. I knew everybody was doing it and it was just a socially accepted thing. More than that, you just *had* to. It was just the next natural step for anyone to take, after joining that group. (H. Hughes, 1961:109.)

The connection of deviant acts to a routine world begins to point also to some more immediate kinds of relations that Actor can have to Others in his world, routine or not. Among relations, we can see how those of trust and intimacy can have a facilitative significance. In the above examples of heroin and marijuana use, there is evidently the presumption that Actor is deserving of being with these Others, that he can in some sense be counted on, that he can be trusted not to inform to authorities and, perhaps, even that he is pleasant and likable or at least tolerable company. Trust and intimacy are not, then, exclusively the prerogatives of "good citizens" who are publicly believed to refrain from deviance indulgence.

Studies of what is sometimes considered to be among the most serious of deviant acts, homicide, suggest that even this act is frequently predicated upon, and made more possible by, the existence of trust and a degree of intimacy between Actor and Other. The bulk of homicides occur between persons who are at least acquainted with each other prior to the act, and a significant proportion occur in the abodes of males and females who are living together. So, too, sex offenses by males against females not involving physical force occur between parties who are strangers far less often than between those who are at least acquainted with each other (Gebhard *et al.*, 1965:774; Amir, 1967). Incest in particular is, of course, by definition, a family affair.

Actor might also be fortunate (or unfortunate) enough to have friends who point out to him possibilities for a deviant act and actively encourage him to commit it, as with the following young man who, charged with the task of taking his employer's daily receipts to the bank for deposit, was coaxed by two friends into simulating having been robbed.

A couple of friends suggested that it would be a good idea. If it hadn't been for the coaxing and reminding I don't think I would have done it; I would have just forgot it if it was left up to me. I didn't want to do it myself. I really don't want to say I was influenced because I have a mind of my own, but I know I wouldn't have attempted it alone 'cause I thought a lot of my employer. I had considered it before but had never thought about how to get it or anything, so it didn't take much talking or persuasion. Maybe my resistance was low because of my greed or something. It sounded so easy, and he explained it so clearly that there wouldn't be much chance involved. I would be much better off. They presented it to me in such a form that it would be just like a gift. It was there. I knew it was a possibility and could be done. And then when I told X he wondered why I hadn't done it long before that. (Cressey, 1953:97–98; italics omitted.)

Because of the circumstances of its typical consummation, suicide is sometimes viewed as the loneliest of deviant acts. In many other respects, however, it is an intensively interactional or social, if not sociable, matter. Having looked closely at the interaction process leading to suicide (and not leading to suicide), Kobler and Stotland have argued that Actor's actual closure on the act of suicide is crucially a function of how the proximate and significant Others in his field align themselves vis-à-vis his expressions of being intensely threatened and his announcements that he is contemplating suicide as a way to reduce that threat. If such proximate and significant Others respond with firm action to bring about changes in Actor's life and to reduce his sense of what Kobler and Stotland call "hopelessness"—the sense that things will always be intolerable —then suicide is unlikely. If, on the other hand, proximate and significant Others respond to Actor with their own sense of "helplessness and hopelessness," suicide becomes likely. These investigators report the following in the cases studied by them.

The behavior of the disturbed individuals was influenced powerfully by the atmosphere in the field. This is not to say that atmosphere is all—that the individual does not bring his own predispositions into the field. Clearly he does. But the predisposition to suicide is only one among many.

                                *   *   *

Selection from among . . . predispositions is a function of the social field. And the more acute the disturbance, the more intense the anxiety, the more severe the need, then the more vulnerable the person to influence by those significant people in the field. (Kobler and Stotland, 1964:261.)

The question, then, is how Others can conduct themselves to facilitate Actor's selecting from among the range of available acts the act of suicide as the most proximate and effective manner in which to deal with threat. Put simply, it is highly facilitative for Others to join together in the expectation that, no matter what they do, Actor is probably going to commit suicide. That is, they can unanimously impute to Actor the active expectation that he *will* commit suicide and to themselves a helplessness to do anything about it. In discussing a report by two clinicians, Moss and Hamilton (1957), Kobler and Stotland observe that the pair

viewed their patients—people who had attempted suicide—with the expectation they would actually commit suicide unless they received therapy specifically directed to the elimination of the suicidal drive. They state: "Since in our series [of cases] only seriously suicidal patients were selected, therapy was often lifesaving." While treating their patients with intensive psychotherapy, they expected a recurrence of suicidal impulses. "The reactivation phase must be anticipated. The patient and his relatives must be adequately warned and prepared for a return of suicidal urges and symptoms." Thus, their expectations were explicit. Their results were as follows. "Fifty per cent of our cases were considered recovered and 20 per cent much improved. . . . Four patients remained unimproved and permanently hospitalized. Eleven died by suicide." That is, 22 per cent of their total group actually committed suicide, a figure strikingly higher than any other report on follow-up of persons hospitalized as a consequence of suicidal attempts.

Our view is that the expectation of suicide and feelings of hopelessness and helplessness are facilitative of actual suicide. The expectations of Moss and Hamilton, as they appear in their statements, were clear; the relatives were warned of the suicidal danger. It is noteworthy here that "four-fifths of all reactivations occurred while the patient was on a day or overnight visit." Further, "The characteristic reactivation of the suicidal drive in over 90 per cent of the patients . . . occurred when the patient was considered markedly improved and had the opportunity to come into contact once more with the environment in which the illness began." We suggest that the families, faced with the warning that their relatives were intense suicidal risks, felt hopeless and helpless and expected suicide to occur. The relatively high suicide rate in Moss and Hamilton's group may be a consequence of the communication of the therapists' fears and expectations. (Kobler and Stotland, 1964:11–12.)

Kobler and Stotland themselves became involved in the study of suicide because of their puzzlement over a mental hospital of their knowledge which, after a long suicide-free period, experienced four cases within six months— what they called an "epidemic of suicide." The eventual suicides entered the hospital with the expectation of being helped but

At the time these patients were admitted . . . the staff's self-confidence was slowly deteriorating due to certain drawnout organizational conflicts over policy and styles of treatment. The hospital and its personnel in this situation were incapable of providing the disturbed individuals with new goals, new social roles, new identities. In their hopeless and helpless state, and finding no meaning in life, the patients struggled still more desperately for purpose . . . . What was offered in the environment of the hospital—in the disintegrating social atmosphere—was the expectation, the fear, of suicide. The patients grasped at it as an identity. (Kobler and Stotland, 1964:16.)

A sense of staff fears and their incapacity to act effectively is conveyed in the following letter from the director of another hospital. (The patient had been transferred from "Crest," the establishment studied by Kobler and Stotland, when his relatives perceived that he was getting worse.)

[Joe, the patient] stated, for instance, that when he came to Crest, everyone seemed to be quite worried about him and to "expect the worst." He said that they would not allow him to get a haircut for weeks after he came there. He was impressed by the fact that when he came here and stated that he wanted to get a haircut, he was taken downtown to a barbershop to get a haircut the first day that he was here. He mentioned that a number of things that were done at Crest seemed to him to be encouraging him to think of himself as more depressed and sicker than he was. He mentioned being left alone in virtual isolation for the first day and a half that he was at the hospital. He contrasted this to the fact that here he spent several hours talking with the doctors and was involved in activities with nurses and aides almost from the very minute he arrived.

He mentioned, in addition to that, that many of the security measures adopted concerning him at Crest seemed to him to reflect a lack of logic on the part of the people there which made him feel a general lack of confidence in them. He mentioned, for instance, that his glasses were taken away from him because of fear that he might break them and use the glass to cut himself. He stated that this idea had never occurred to him and it was particularly worrisome to him because at times he was restrained in bed and would not have been able to use the glass anyway. He mentioned also having his shoestrings taken out of his shoes as something that both puzzled him and also filled him with dismay. Although all of this sounds quite impressive and the patient assured me that he could go on for hours telling me other contrasting experiences, I do think it quite probable that at the time that he came here he was out of the depths of the depression and one might take some of these statements with a "grain of salt." (Kobler and Stotland, 1964:95–96.)

It was in such a social situation that a person could behave in the following fashion toward a doctor and have it make no difference. As told by the doctor:

> I talked to her on . . . Sunday and found that she was very distraught
> . . . . She was pouring out her hopelessness—pleading for electric shock or amytol or anything. I then went down the hall to see someone else again, before I left the ward. Came back and she was crawling on the floor; she was throwing herself up against the door; she was saying in essence, "do something," in such a way that it was just like tearing with claws at everybody who was within hearing range. (Kobler and Stotland, 1964:200–1.)

The good doctor then put this human being on "suicide precautions"—the furniture was removed from her room, "wrist restraint" was applied and the door to her room was locked—and left the scene. A few hours later one of the ward nurses made this entry into the "ward log":

> Sally and I were sitting there in the office talking about [the above human being]. Just about that time I said how much I disliked her, that somehow this woman really got me, and that I honestly wondered if she shouldn't have ECT. It seemed to me that what we were doing wasn't working; what else could we do for her? . . . If she got out of treatment

[with a different doctor from the one above] I honestly felt, "What's left for this woman but dying, really?" So anyway, [the woman] made this funny noise, and Sally went into her room to look at her; and Sally said she was just lying still. I said something about, was she facing the window or facing the door? I was concerned about her committing suicide at that time. And Sally, just having come back, said—I think she was facing the door. And I at that moment thought [to myself]: "You really ought to take a look yourself." And I didn't. (Kobler and Stotland, 1964:202–3.)

This person was later found with a "piece of sheet tied twice around her neck." Revival efforts were not successful.

A situation of high stress and precarious or low self-esteem renders human beings highly open to the suggestions, definitions and imputations of Others. If, under such a circumstance, Actor is imputed the identity of the suicidee, he may well accept that identification and play it out.

If the potential suicide is responded to with an expectation that he will commit suicide, his suicide will be facilitated. He grasps at the suicidal identity, and achieves a kind of equanimity and stability of behavior. [On these grounds, one might account for the fact that] many clinicians have noted that patients act in an organized fashion, seem to be getting better, seem to be calmed, prior to a suicidal act.[5]

It might be said, more generally, that a costly but effective way for Actor to protect himself or herself against being a victim or perpetrator of many deviant acts is to avoid becoming more than casually acquainted with anyone. Getting close to people may lead to psychic and other pleasures, but it concomitantly creates a basic condition facilitating at least some kinds of deviant acts.

STRANGERSHIP

There are, of course, in contrast, a variety of deviant acts which often involve persons not so preexistingly entangled with one another. Among these are such sex offenses as male window peeping, exhibitionist acts, some sexual aggression against females and nonaggressive homosexual contact (Gebhard

[5] Kobler and Stotland, 1964:14. Considered at a more detailed and microscopic level, acts of suicide may involve a miniature or temporally collapsed version of the processes of "social and personal identification" and "escalation" to be discussed in Part II, especially Chaps. 6 and 7. If suicide were not so immediately and permanently self-terminating, and therefore, socially terminating, there would be considerable justification for treating it as a deviant identity. The character of suicide itself, however, inherently limits possibilities for role behavior, making analysis of it as an act seem at least reasonable. Nonetheless, the case for treating it as a deviant identity is not without merit.

et al., 1965:Chap. 34).   One study of the victims of delinquent acts suggests
that, although low-income male youths tend to perpetrate their indiscretions
within their own neighborhoods, the victimized Others tend to be nonresident
strangers and other outsiders.

> Most often the victims are either nonresidents in the Addams area (30
> per cent) or a corporate personality such as a school or large business
> establishment which is owned and operated by nonresidents (34 per cent).
> Most of the remaining victims (20 per cent) differed from the local of-
> fenders on one or both of the following criteria: (1) they were of different
> ethnicity and/or (2) they lived in different [ethnic] sections of the
> Addams area.   Only about 12 per cent of all victims belonged to the same
> ethnic group as the offender [closest to whose home the offense was com-
> mitted] and lived in his section of the neighborhood. . . .   The com-
> plainants follow almost the same pattern.   Thus, while the boys commit
> most of their offenses within the neighborhood, it is mostly outsiders they
> offend.   All of this tends to follow the local view that outsiders "have no
> business here."   (Suttles, 1968:210.)

It may be that deviant acts have something of a "bimodal" distribution.   The
involved parties tend either to have a rather considerable involvement with one
another or not to know one another very much at all.   In the case of the general
class of sex offenses the most offended against sorts of persons are either relatives, friends or complete strangers.   Being an "acquaintance"—someone
known but not known well—appears to be the safest distance from other human
beings (Gebhard *et al.*, 1965:817, Table 146).

   Viewed in terms of facilitative significance, it can be said that stranger-
Others might well serve to increase the frequency of deviant acts if they more
frequently penetrated low-income sections of urban settlements, especially
during hours of darkness.   So, too, acts of peeping tomism could be increased
if more adult females would choose to expose themselves before windows
(Gebhard *et al.*, 1965:375).   Aggressive sexual offenses against adult females,
sometimes called "rape," as well as homosexual offenses against males, appear
to be facilitated by the person later defined as a victim acting in a manner
which encourages Actor to interpret Other as interested but appropriately resistant and *demurring* (or even as frankly interested).

> In most rapes there are moments when the offender's eyes and genitalia
> could easily be damaged. . . .   The aggressors we have interviewed
> emerged from their rapes either unscathed or with only scratches.   They
> were seldom even bitten.   The ineffectual resistance put up by most vic-
> tims is sometimes taken as an indication that they have a conscious or
> unconscious desire to submit.   This is undoubtedly true in some undeter-
> mined number of cases, but we feel such cases constitute a definite
> minority.   It is more probable that the ineffectuality results from fright or

from a realistic appraisal of the danger involved in making a determined resistance. (Gebhard *et al.*, 1965:196.)

While Others who are raped seem only ambiguously interested—their passivity permitting Actor's imputation of interest—contact between adult males and strange males for homosexual purposes appears to have a considerably less ambiguous character. Males arrested for this offense appear more often to underestimate the zealousness of the police than to misinterpret the dispositions of the approached stranger. In one study of arrests resulting from such contact, the official record and the offender agreed overwhelmingly (93 per cent) that "the solicited male was encouraging or at least passive" (Gebhard *et al.*, 1965:354).

SOCIAL ORGANIZATIONAL SOURCES

The facilitating activities of Others are themselves functions of variables lying just beyond the proximate relation of Actor and Other. Viewing these activities as dependent variables, there can be concern with, for example, technological and social constraints which conduce to the existence of overlooked vulnerabilities to many sorts of deviant acts. Likewise, friendship, trust and kindred emotional entanglements as general phenomena become states which require explanation. Given the tendency of homicides to occur between persons who are married to each other, it is perhaps necessary to consider the possibility that the socially required and sanctioned institution of marriage contributes, at least analytically, to the homicide rate. And, the condition of strangership that figures in other kinds of deviant acts requires some understanding of the kind of social order in which it is possible for persons to be physically proximate but personally unknown. If an urban, technological social order characterized by high rates of geographical mobility makes impersonal proximity possible, then it must be said that such an order contributes to the occurrence of acts of homosexuality, rape and window peeping between strangers.

FACILITATING ACTOR

Even after Actor has traversed the sequence of the perception of threat and encapsulation (or adventure and enchantment), and has come into proximity with facilitating places, hardware and Others, there still remains a final proximate moment of selection from among available acts. This selection appears to be a function of at least two features which Actor brings to the situation: (1) the kind and amount of his knowledge and skills and (2) the degree of subjective availability of all proximately available acts.

KNOWLEDGE AND SKILLS

By "kind and amount of knowledge and skills" is meant the character of Actor's preexisting motor habits and stockpile of cognitions. These range from the capacity to walk and talk to the more esoteric types of physical and mental manipulations such as those involved in the juggling of account books. Knowledge and skills can be roughly divided into those sorts of things that everyone knows and everybody can do, on the one hand, and other sorts of things that only persons in specialized social locations are likely to know and are likely to know how to do. The former may be referred to as *civil* knowledge and skills and the latter as *technical* knowledge and skills.

To the degree that Actor is in possession of a typical complement of a society's civil knowledge and skills and a deviant act involving only such skills has become proximate, closure on that deviant act is facilitated. Although this point may seem rather obvious, it assumes more interest when we compare rates of deviant acts between those who do and those who do not possess selected civil knowledge and skills. So it is that the crippled, the blind, the mute, the seriously intellectually retarded, even the mentally ill and others are rather massively underrepresented among known perpetrators of deviant *acts* of many kinds (Lemert, 1951; Scheff, 1966). It might be said that being normal in the sense of knowing and doing what everybody knows and does increases the range of deviant acts available to an Actor and thereby increases the likelihood that he will become involved in deviant acts. Although the price is very high, public policy aimed at the reduction of deviant acts could be based upon a variety of measures which would reduce civil knowledge and skills. Indeed, some societies have at times attempted to move in that direction, as in the reported practices within a few countries of cutting off one or both hands of persons apprehended for theft or of administering frontal lobotomies to persons who make interaction problematic or of castrating persons who are likely to project undesired sexual relations.

A society in which the participants are trained to perform a wide variety of tasks and to know about a wide variety of objects and possibilities would seem to be a society that not only increases the range of conforming acts, but, at the same time, increases the range of possible deviant acts. To erect and to advertise the presence of public toilets and to provide knowledge in how to use them (especially those with booths and doors) is to create knowledge and skills that facilitate homosexuality, at least among males. To manufacture, advertise, retail and teach the use of knives, scissors, firearms and other such instruments is to create knowledge and skills that facilitate assault and homicide. To manufacture and train in the use of automobiles and widely to advertise the dangers of carbon monoxide in closed places is to create knowledge and skills that facilitate suicide. To train females in the wiles of femininity is to provide skills that facilitate acts of prostitution. To adopt a monetary system based heavily upon the check and to train in its use is to create knowledge and skills that facilitate forgery.

> Most people in their everyday transactions have occasions to cash personal or payroll checks and hence encounter all the precautions business uses to prevent the making and uttering of bad checks.

❋   ❋   ❋

> A college class of 25 students [upon being asked] to write brief accounts of how they would obtain and pass a bad check if circumstances forced them to do so [described] . . . about the same class of techniques . . . as those actually employed by the forgers in our sample. Only one female was unable to devise a workable scheme. Sources of the ideas in a few cases were listed as radio programs and crime fiction, but most students simply put down "experience with checking account," "experience in retail stores," or "just imagination." (Lemert, 1953:305.)

A proposition of this order is equally applicable to knowledge and skills of a technical kind. Relative to the frequently quite technical act of embezzlement, Cressey notes that (in many cases)

> Persons trained to carry out the routine duties of a position have at the same time been trained in whatever skills are necessary for the violation of that position, and the technical skill necessary to trust violation is simply the technical skill necessary to holding the position in the first place. (Cressey, 1953:82.)

Likewise, to train persons in the esoteric arts of medicine is to train them in the arts of abortion. To train persons in the mysteries of locksmithy is to create a strata uniquely capable of theft from banks and residential units. To train persons as printers and engravers is to train possible counterfeiters. To train persons as jewelers is to train in the skills of fencing for jewel thieves. To train as a photographer is to train in the skills of a pornographer (although recent advances in technology make that, of late, more of a civil skill. See Leigh, 1963). Training in business, of course, provides skills for many kinds of white-collar crime (Clinard, 1952; Sutherland, 1949). Indeed, there seem to be few skilled occupations that do not simultaneously provide the technical knowledge and skills necessary both for the occupational task and for one or another kind of deviant act. Aside from possible ventures into pornographic writing, the poor academician appears to be among those few occupations that are rather disadvantaged in their special access to deviance.

All of this is to say that much conventional socialization is at the same time an *inverse education* for deviant acts. When asked how he learned the things necessary to bring off an embezzlement, an Actor convicted of this crime can tell us:

I would have to say that I learned all of it in school and in my ordinary accounting experience. In school they teach you in your advanced years how to detect embezzlements, and you sort of absorb it. . . . It is just like a doctor performing abortions. In his medical training he must learn to conduct the abortion because many abortions are necessary for the health of the mother. Maybe he will perform a few legitimate abortions, and then an illegitimate one. He has learned to conduct the illegitimate one in his ordinary medical training, but he could not identify the point at which he learned that, because he would have to include all of his courses in physiology, anatomy and everything else, as well as the specific technique. In my case, I did not use any technique which any ordinary accountant in my position could not have used; they are known to all accountants, just as the abortion technique is known by all doctors. (Cressey, 1953:82.)

To construct a society is at the same time to build in, widely and deeply throughout the social order, the potential for deviance. On this account alone, deviance, at least in the form of isolated or episodic acts, is likely always to be with us.

SUBJECTIVE AVAILABILITY

Thus far in connection with closure I have tried to emphasize variations of an external or hard sort, namely, contingencies posed by the degree of facilitative presence of places, hardware, Others, and Actor's knowledge and skills. *The general point is that even under conditions of threat and encapsulation, mundane matters of who is present where, in the presence of what sorts of material objects, and possessing what kind of skills, must be seen as crucial determinants of what act (deviant or not) is finally closed upon.* It must be recognized that the occurrence of any social act (including a deviant act) may be as much a function of these mundane matters as of any ways in which Actor is himself in some personal way differentiated from the total population.

Having said this, it must be added that closure on a given act will also be a function of subjective states, for Actors vary in their definitions of the availability of those acts which are proximately accessible in other objective regards. By variations in definitions of accessibility, I refer to Actor's *subjective* conception of the morality and objective consequences of various social acts. Actors are likely to conceive of a wide range of acts as entirely moral (and conventional) and as having consequences that either are entirely good or beneficial or are at least neutral. And, they are likely also to conceive of a range of acts as somewhat or highly immoral in and of themselves and/or as immoral because they have deleterious consequences for Others and/or themselves. Acts which Actor feels to be moral or neutral may be referred to as *subjectively available.* Acts defined as immoral, or of dubious morality, may be referred to as *subjectively unavailable* or inaccessible. This is, of course, an overly strong distinction between classes of acts, drawn merely for clarity. In empirical cases, subjective availability is likely to be a matter of degree, ranging from some acts strongly considered immoral, through acts about which the Actor is not sure of the morality, to acts about which Actor is convinced of their high morality. Acts vary in the degree of their subjective availability, and Actors may vary through time in the moral assessment they make of one or another act.

Generalizing on the basis of theory and data now existing, it appears to be the case that Actors are unlikely to perform acts that they personally believe to be unequivocally wrong; that is, they are unlikely to perform acts which are, in the terms used here, subjectively unavailable. If the above is true, then, for a deviant act to be closed upon, an Actor must be able to render such an act subjectively available. As will be detailed below, acts which Others may later view as deviant come to be viewed by Actor either as moral or *conventional or* as wrong in some abstract sense but *justified* in the instant case at hand and under the circumstances.

IGNORANCE OR DISBELIEF

It is, of course, entirely possible that Actor could bring to the situation a definition of an act as positively moral, but that Others would later, and at the public level, define the act of deviant. This possibility is referred to in criminology under the rubric of culture conflict. The oft-quoted example given by Thornstein Sellin is that of "a Sicilian father in New Jersey [who] killed the sixteen-year-old seducer of his daughter [and expressed] surprise at his arrest since he had merely defended his family honor in a traditional way" (Sellin, 1938:68). (See also, Clinard, 1952, on wartime black markets.) Although such circumstances of culture conflict were doubtless rather common in American civilization during the era of immigration, moral rulings have likely diffused such that most Actors today will at least have some qualms and prospective guilt over a wide variety of acts publicly defined as deviant. They will, at least, not be surprised at the definition of the act as deviant, as was the Sicilian father.

Nonetheless, if Actor has already defined as moral an act which is publicly defined as deviant, then closure upon it can easily follow. In American civilization such private definitions which run counter to public policy tend to exist, especially with regard to drug use, abortion, gambling, white-collar crime and certain homosexual and heterosexual practices. A definition of an act as positively moral is especially easy to construct when all relevant parties consent to involvement in the act. Under such circumstances the act can more easily be construed as a private affair and of no legitimate concern to outsiders. Even in the absence of a definition as positively moral, the claimed private character of an act can render it morally neutral, perceptually removing it from the legitimate concern of uninvolved persons, especially governmental agents. Although acts of suicide or prostitution, for example, may not be viewed as the most laudable of activities, they can be seen as being no one's business but my own. Labeling this last variation "the denial of injury," Sykes and Matza suggest likewise that "gang fighting may be seen as a private quarrel, an agreed-upon dual between two willing parties, and thus of no concern to the community at large" (Sykes and Matza, 1957:667).

Although enormously more public in character, many acts in American civilization captioned civil disobedience are founded on a similar stable belief that a given ruling is simply wrong (or invalid) and ought willfully and publicly to be violated. Some such violations have, indeed, subsequently been endorsed by the U.S. Supreme Court as proper because the local laws at issue (laws perpetrating segregation in public schools and in public transportation) were ruled to be in violation of the U.S. Constitution. Other willful and public violations have not been so endorsed but involve a similar belief in the unjust or unwise character of a particular law itself. Such instances have included refusal to participate in civil defense drills because they are unwise and refusal to register for the military draft in the belief that conscription and/or war is immoral (American Civil Liberties Union, 1968; Dworkin, 1968).

Of much more interest are the ways in which acts defined by Actor as clearly immoral or dubiously moral can be rendered, at least for a time, as not clearly immoral or even as positively moral. Such a transformation appears to be accomplished by means of one or another of at least two mental strategies or mechanisms: conventionalization and special justification.

CONVENTIONALIZATION

By "conventionalization" is meant the practice of continuing to believe that the general class of deviant act in question is wrong and subjectively unavailable, but managing to avoid defining the actual act as an instance of the subjectively unavailable class. Although perhaps rare relative to all deviant acts, the strategy of conventionalization appears to be reasonably common among those Actors who commit embezzlement and other white-collar crimes. For example, the structure of much business practice is such that Actor can come to see his peculation(s) not as embezzlement but as *borrowing*.

A real estate dealer who converted a large number of deposits by putting them into his business did so only after . . . convincing himself that he was only borrowing the money temporarily. Since he was going to lose all of his money if he did not "borrow" the deposits until he was "able to get on his feet," and since "the people would all get the money back when the deal was completed," the ends justified the means. He did not consider, even while in prison, that his behavior was criminal. (Cressey, 1953:104.)

Interviewed in prison, another embezzler could say: "I have been strictly honest all my life. I have had to work for everything I have, but every cent of it was secured honestly. There was nothing dishonest in what I did" (Cressey, 1953:106). In addition, it is apparently possible for some businessmen to believe that other people's money is really their own anyway, giving them a moral right to use it:

> Trust violators claim that it is usual business practice to accept deposits on goods and then, before the goods actually are delivered, to use part of the money deposited, on the assumption that before the delivery date enough money for the purchase of the goods will be secured elsewhere. In solving a nonsharable problem they . . . used the deposited money for themselves, on the assumption that it need not be accounted for—i.e., that it "belonged to" them. (Cressey, 1953:108.)

Or, conventionalization might be achieved through the more difficult and fuzzy tactic of distinguishing between the letter and the spirit of the law. In the General Electric antitrust episode of the fifties, at least one businessman was able "to persuade himself that what he was doing in defiance of the letter of the antitrust directive was not done in defiance of its spirit" (Smith, 1963:105). Conventionalization, then, renders a deviant act available through defining it as an instance of a conventional category, or at least on the margin between deviance and conventionality.

An Aside on Social Organizational Sources. As a definitional device, conventionalization appears to go hand in glove with types of social organization involving considerable *ambiguity* over the deviant or normal meaning of acts. That is, conventionalization is facilitated by the kind of ambiguity that prevails in American business culture and the legal tradition. It was not entirely cynical for someone once to have observed that one does not know who is the brilliant, progressive and sharp businessman and who is the criminal until after the courts have spoken. Although at a very general level there appear to be rather clear conceptions of what is deviant, the intrigues of business and other practices make it difficult to know whether to code instant acts into categories of conventionality or deviance. So it is that Cressey can report:

> In most instances the rationalization that the conversion of deposits would merely amount to "borrowing" the deposits for a short time was an easy and logical step to make, since the ordinary practice of the businessmen interviewed was similar to such borrowing. (Cressey, 1953:103.)

It should be recognized, in general, that the *legally* deviant character of many acts is quite indeterminate prior to court decisions (Dworkin, 1968). Other acts, because public moral opinion is yet unformed as to their threatening character, are neither clearly deviant nor clearly conventional. And, a society can be highly divided as to the conventional or deviant character of particular acts. Such ambiguities of legality, of moral opinion and of divided definition form a context within which Actors can more easily exercise their own discretion. They can more easily define an otherwise problematic act as conventional—as in fact falling into the category of convention rather than deviance.[6]

SPECIAL JUSTIFICATION

Situations of ambiguity which make possible the practice of conventionalization seem considerably less common than situations which permit the virtually rampant practice of special or circumstantial justification. In special justification, Actor views his prospective or current act as an instance of some category of deviant act but renders it subjectively available through defining it as being not entirely wrong due to particular circumstances. Although holding that the act is immoral in the general case, a special set of conditions in this case make the act in question not wrong even if it is not unambiguously right or moral. The act becomes available for performance by the Actor through the claim that some particular set of facts or some other moral rule pressed upon him such that while his conduct may not represent a paradigm of virtue, neither is it unambiguously immoral.

The detailed specification of particular forms of special justification has been of considerable fascination to sociologists in recent years. Delineated forms have included the claims (a) that any victim justly deserved his victimization; (b) that he, Actor, was not a responsible person; and (c) that transcending moral commitments overrode prohibitions against a particular act.[7]

Deserving Victims. If injury to an Other is an anticipated outcome of a deviant act, the act can be rendered available through defining the prospective victim as a morally disreputable sort of person who deserves what he is projected to get. The projected victim may be viewed as morally disreputable because of widely known and long-standing definitions of his social category or because of some proximate and personal injury perceived by Actor as emanating from a particular Other toward him. Among social categories which are

---

[6] Indeed, the achievement of a wide range of freedom under law may require the continual exercise of such conventionalization. Given the ambiguity that so often exists, if actors always assumed that an ambiguous act was deviant and thus refrained from its commission, the range of the permissible would quite quickly constrict. See Dworkin, 1968: 16–17.

[7] Apparently sensitive to the lead provided by Sutherland concerning "definitions favorable to violation of law" (Sutherland and Cressey, 1966:81), Gresham Sykes and David Matza have been among those most vigorously specifying the character of such definitions. I here adopt their formulation and attempt to expand upon it. See Sykes and Matza, 1957; Matza and Sykes, 1961; Matza, 1961 and 1964. See further the review by Cressey, 1965: 51–54 and the generalized statement by Scott and Lyman, 1968.

rather consensually viewed as morally reprehensible, one may refer to Communists, homosexuals, prostitutes and ethnic minorities. These and other categories stand as ready targets of deserved victimization because "everybody knows what they are." In more territorially localized and parochial settings, certain only locally defined categories may come to be seen as undeserving of sympathy and meriting any harm that might befall them. In Black ghettos certain classes of commercial establishments, such as furniture stores, may achieve a local but consensual definition as rightfully recipient of any misfortune that happens upon any one of them. Conversations with persons who looted during the Detroit civil disorder of 1967 elicited these explicit claims about local institutions:

> We were in the Packer store on Trumbull and Grand River. Man, there was everybody in there, hillbillies and soul brothers and everybody just takin' all the shit they could get their hands on and everybody was saying "this motherfuckin' Packer store done robbed everybody for so long we just gonna clean the store out . . . ." (Quoted in *The Fifth Estate*, August, 1967.)

> [Commenting on her taking of three portable television sets, a woman says:] That ain't looting. That's just getting back what they done got from me. I was glad to see that man's store burn. He never did treat black folks nice, always rushing you to make up your mind. And he never wanted to sell you the cheap stuff. Always talking about how another one was better, but it always cost more money. (*Detroit Free Press*, July 31, 1967.)

With regard to indiscretions of a more routine kind, Sykes and Matza provide this miniportrait of what they call "denial of the victim" among youth:

> By a subtle alchemy the delinquent moves himself into the position of an avenger, and the victim is transformed into a wrongdoer. Assaults on homosexuals or suspected homosexuals, attacks on members of minority groups who are said to have "gotten out of place," vandalism as revenge on an unfair teacher or school official, thefts from a "crooked" store owner —all may be hurts inflicted on a transgressor, in the eyes of the delinquent. (Sykes and Matza, 1957:668.)

Stigmatized categories and localized institutions are widely known deserving victims, but one cannot slight the possibility that, for some Actors at least, the most general, venerable and public of respectable social categories and organizations will be similarly defined. There are thus some people who feel that businessmen, the police, or doctors deserve whatever misfortunes befall them. Definitions such as these can be part of the rhetoric of motives by means of which particular Actors victimize instances of these categories. A middle-class professional, who episodically shoplifted in concert with a friend, apparently as a leisure activity, could define "society" and the victimized institutions in these terms:

> Knowledge of high price markups of merchandising helped us to feel that we were paying about the right price in taking one or two items "on the house." Anger at the law for issuing parking or speeding fines made us want to find a way to hit out at them and "get our money back." Annoyance at being kept waiting to pay for something an inordinate time, or the rudeness or indifference of the clerks, would facilitate immensely the temptation to take something "from under their noses."[8]

And deserved victimization can arise out of a history of very personal and intimate exchanges between two persons who act toward each other in their capacities as persons rather than as instances of widely recognized social categories, a circumstance that appears to obtain in much homicide.

Lack of Personal Control. Current renderings of human acts and and persons as determined by psychological or sociological forces are merely the latest formulations of the age-old human propensity to view oneself and others as passive victims or beneficiaries of uncontrollable forces. To some degree such forces are believed to make one not responsible for what one is and what one does. Whether the force be fate, witches, stars, evil spirits, body chemistry, body shape, childhood trauma, family interaction, area of residence, cultural deprivation, organizational commitments or whatever, humans can come to believe that what they have done, do or plan to do is in some sense beyond their personal will to decide. Actors who possess such a belief and who activate it under a given set of circumstances thereby make possible and probable exactly that outcome forecast by the belief.

In a biological vein, one can note the belief that apparently existed (and continues to exist, to some degree, today) among early Italian immigrants that the men of that nationality possess sexual appetites which become uncontrollable when they are alone with females.

> What the men fear is their own ability at self-control. This attitude, strongest among young unmarried people, often carries over into adulthood. The traditional Italian belief—that sexual intercourse is unavoidable when a man and a woman are by themselves—is maintained intact among second-generation [Italians], and continues even when sexual interest itself is on the wane. For example, I was told of an older woman whose apartment was adjacent to that of an unmarried male relative. Although they had lived in the same building for almost twenty years and saw each other almost every day, she had never once been in his apart-

---

[8] Quotes from persons committing deviant acts which are not otherwise cited are drawn from anonymously written accounts by students in a course on deviant behavior (University of Michigan, Summer, 1965).

ment because of this belief. (Quoted from Gans, 1962, in Scott and Lyman, 1968:49.)

Of course, when males and females happen to be alone, this kind of preexisting
belief functions to facilitate the occurrence of sexual intercourse. And in the
same biological vein, it is possible to see how homosexual impulses are facilitatively converted into homosexual acts when Actor conceives such an impulse
in these terms: "It's part of nature. You can't alter it, no matter how many in-
jections and pills they give you" (Westwood, 1960, quoted in Scott and Lyman,
1968:50).

Although persistent, facilitating beliefs of a biological character are probably less prevalent than special justifications based upon defective personal or
social character. For Actor to believe that he is trapped by the implications of
his toilet training, his unloving parents, his frigid wife, prejudiced police, di-
lapidated housing or organizational position is for the deviant acts stereotyp-
ically associated with such misfortune to become more subjectively available.
Referring to this general device as "the denial of responsibility," Sykes and
Matza note the possibility of the development of a "billiard ball" conception of
self on the part of youth called delinquent, "in which [the delinquent] sees
himself as helplessly propelled into new situations" (Sykes and Matza, 1957:
667). (See, further, Cressey's instructive discussion [1962] of compulsive
crimes.)

   Transcending Commitments. The claim of transcending commitments is by
far the most interesting and important of special justifications. Throughout
history this has been a prominent mode of rendering subjectively available
those acts considered to be deviant within some social system. The claim of
transcending commitments is the most positive and moralized of special justifications in the sense that it is most likely to be presented publicly as justification
after a deviant act.

   Justification by transcending commitment grants the legitimacy of a prohibition against a given act at the level of the appropriateness of generalized rulings.
The issue is, rather, the ordering of priorities in obedience to such acknowledged generalized rulings *in specific cases.* Thus an Actor can subscribe to the
general notion that he should not kill others, but in specific circumstances he
can come to believe that his personal survival takes precedence over the general
rule against homicide. Because deviance as here construed focuses upon Actor's commitment and orientation to rulings emanating from the nation-state
or jurisdictions therein, transcendence primarily involves questions of ordering
priorities between the state and (a) Actor as a person, (b) Actor's intimates or
community, and (c) humanity, history, or the highest of man's moral ideals.

   Beyond the very limited situations in which Actor can legitimately and legally act in self-defense, there are a wide range of circumstances in which he
can come to feel that his honor or personal integrity or reputation have come into
question such that he must take swift and decisive action to defend or uphold

them. It happens to be the case in contemporary American civilization that
only very limited and mild measures are permitted in defense of personal integrity.[9] Verbal repartee and court action exhaust, for all practical personal
purposes, legitimate means of redress under most circumstances of assault upon
dignity. Duels and other physical altercations are illegal. Court rulings even
specifically counsel Actors to be unmanly and to be cowards:

> Before a man can use force and violence under the law for his protection
> . . . he must be situated, he must be in such a position that he cannot
> safely retreat. . . . We may not feel always like retreating in the face of
> an attack; it may not seem manly to us; but it is the law that if a man can
> safely retreat . . . he must do so even though it may not seem dignified
> and manly. (*People* vs. *Tomlins*, quoted in Matza, 1964:78–79.)

The state's claim to a virtual monopoly upon settling affronts to dignity (and
personal safety) can, nonetheless, appear to civil Actors to violate the primordial right of a human being to stand up and act in defense of himself. That is,
it can be felt that one's commitment to himself transcends commitment to the
state. In some social circles, the feeling can become public and socially standardized, being converted thereby into a virtual obligation. Among some of the
more ghettoized portions of the population,

> A male is usually expected to defend the name and honor of his mother,
> the virtue of womanhood (even though his female companion for the eve-
> ning may be an entirely new acquaintance and/or prostitute) and to ac-
> cept no derogation about his race (even from a member of his own race), his
> age or his masculinity. Quick resort to physical combat as a measure of
> daring, courage or defense of status appears to be a cultural expectation
> for lower socioeconomic class males of both races. When such a culture
> norm response is elicited from an individual engaged in social interplay
> with others who harbor the same response mechanism, physical assaults,
> altercations and violent domestic quarrels that result in homicide are
> likely to be relatively common.[10]

In addition, as seen in the above quotation, an Actor's commitments to the
state and to his intimates—his parents, relatives, peers and other friends—can
come under conflicting priority demands. To be loyal to one is to be disloyal
to the others. He, as is said, "can't win for losing." When Actor encounters
circumstances where he is going to lose no matter what he does, it should be no
surprise if, at least on occasion, he puts himself and his intimates or other reference group ahead of the state. This is what some corporation executives appar-

[9] There are a highly limited number of exceptions to this, of course. The slaying of one's
wife and her lover when caught *in flagrante* is not always viewed by the courts as unjustified.
[10] Wolfgang, 1958:188–89. It should be remembered that the use of violence in the defense of "honor" has successfully been defined as deviant in America only in relatively recent
times. Alexander Hamilton was killed in a duel, and Andrew Jackson participated in a
number of them.

ently have done in altruistically fixing prices in order to "make enough to keep our plant and our employees" (Geis, 1967:144), or what youth called delinquent do when they "appeal to higher loyalties" (Sykes and Matza, 1957:669). It is on such occasions that people can ask, "After all, what's the Constitution between friends?"

Historically, the most famous and socially important special justifications have involved references not to self or to intimates, but to the most generalized of moral referents: humanity, history, man's highest ideals and the like. The general rule to be violated continues to be viewed as legitimate, but violation of it is considered trivial compared to the moral harm that is rendered if it is *not* violated. Thus some of the acts lately coded as civil disobedience involving violation of trespass and other rules of civil order have not involved attempts to challenge the laws intentionally violated but are, rather, acknowledged violations, justified in terms of moral commitments that are said to transcend or override rules made by particular nation-states or lesser governmental units. Often such violations are performed as a means of calling attention to some purported evil. Such has been the case when:

> access of materials to a construction site is blocked by persons lying down in the path of trucks in order to protest discriminatory employment practices by the general contractor or labor union involved. Or garbage may be dumped into a government office building to protest inadequate sanitary facilities in a slum area or the failure of the municipality to take corrective action. (American Civil Liberties Union, 1968.)

SOURCES OF SUBJECTIVE AVAILABILITY

If the above types of definitions constitute some ways in which deviant acts can be rendered subjectively available, then we can inquire, in turn, into elements of situations, of biography and of social organization that facilitate the availability and possible use of these definitions. A first and primary feature of note is that *at the most abstract level each of these definitions is a legitimized public platitude.* Everybody believes and thinks obvious the propositions that people should be allowed to do anything they wish so long as it does not hurt others; that persons who transgress others and are generally offensive should be punished or penalized; that human behavior is in some sense and to some degree determined by forces outside immediate control; and that people should have integrity, be loyal to their intimates and live in compliance with high moral ideals. At this level, the beliefs that facilitate the subjective availability of deviant acts are the same beliefs that facilitate conforming action. Such beliefs belong to the common pool of shared moral sentiments or values.

If we want to explain how people who commit deviant acts can come to believe such things, we must refer to the processes through which a population at large comes commonly to believe in propositions of these kinds. These processes are only the most common of socialization procedures explicated more generally in sociology and social science and, as such, need not be considered problematic vis-à-vis a more limited and technical conception of the sociology of deviance. What must be pursued, rather, is how such common beliefs can come to be employed in rendering deviant acts subjectively available. The issue between Actor and Other when Actor commits a deviant act is defined less in terms of the merit of general platitudes, such as those above, than in terms of the legitimacy of using a general platitude to justify a given act. What sorts of conditions facilitate Actor viewing a given general platitude as specially justifying his deviant act?

SITUATIONAL

In terms of proximate conditions, it must be recalled that Actor's facilitating state of threat and encapsulation creates considerable impetus to construe or discover *nonroutine* and *novel* relations between acts and abstract generalizations. Among such construals can well be a newly discovered connection to the effect that indeed, after all, what he projects is moral, conventional or specially justified under one or another of the above definitional devices.

BIOGRAPHICAL

But even under threat and encapsulation it can be presumed that Actor will not be pressed or released such that he can justify simply anything in any terms whatsoever. The construals he will be able to accomplish are likely to remain, at least in part, constrained and structured by typical moral construals he has made and seen others make in the past. It can thus happen, for example, that people who lack experience in, and exposure to, construing violence as a specially justified means of dealing with encapsulating threats will never even have it occur to them that a violent act might be a highly reasonable selection. Middle-class, sedate types, exposed only to a world of behind-the-back abuse and other indirect connivance, become thereby selectively sensitive to moral construals that hinge upon secret manipulation rather than violence.[11]

[11] Conversely, people who do have experience in, and exposure to, violence can more readily construe it as a specially justified means of dealing with encapsulating threats. Wolfgang (1958:Chap. 9) thus found that people arrested for homicide tend disproportionately to have been previously arrested, especially for assault. Such a ready construal of violent action as specially justified has, of course, its own *social organizational* as well as biographical sources. It seems located especially in populations where, over a long period of time, civil authorities or the polity have not attempted to impose third party intervention or arbitration on personal disputes. This seems to have been the case in the American South, among Whites and Blacks alike. Officials often defined disputes, injustices, violence and murder as private affairs of little concern to the state. In the absence of state avenues for redressing problems and punishing violence, it is not surprising that "taking the law into one's own hands" would become a tradition. Southern migrants to Northern cities, of course, still make such construals, aided and abetted in large measure by exclusionary treatment that has differed little from the indifference shown by Southern governments. (See Wolfgang and Ferracuti, 1967; and C. Brown, 1965:278.)

Accountants, bankers, business executives and independent businessmen [who were convicted of embezzlement] all reported that the possibility of stealing or robbing to obtain needed funds never occurred to them, although many objective opportunities for such crimes were present. Even a man who had been convicted of fraud or embezzlement as many as three times stated that crime of any other kind is repulsive. Many other persons expressed this same opinion by saying, "Well, at least I didn't hurt anybody," or "I could never steal under any circumstances; it is against my nature." (Cressey, 1953:140.)

Even if more direct and possibly violent moral construal does occur in middle-class people, their training in physical cowardice may lead them to immediate rejection of this class of violent possibilities. As with naïve check forgers, they may experience "a distaste or sense of repugnance toward forms of crime other than forgery. In case after case came the unsolicited, 'I could never hurt anyone,' or 'I wouldn't have the nerve (or guts) to rob anyone or to steal'" (Lemert, 1953:299).

Stated more generally, it seems probable that for most Actors there are at least a few acts which, due to a course of biographical experience and resulting sense of moral revulsion, are unlikely ever to be rendered subjectively available. One can, nonetheless, overemphasize the number of deviant acts that are unlikely ever to become subjectively available. It seems more likely that most deviant acts can become subjectively available for most Actors under sufficiently pressing conditions of threat and encapsulation.

SOCIAL ORGANIZATIONAL

The possibility of the commitment of almost any sort of deviant act by almost any Actor is connected to normal—in the sense of typical—features of American civilization.[12] These normal features have to do with the situation of there existing in the society at large contradictory assertions about, and conceptions of, exactly what acts are legitimate in terms of what general platitudes. That is, there exists not only an issue about the legitimacy of Actor's specific justification of his particular deviant act in terms of one or another of the mentioned definitions. Such conflicts exist, as well, throughout the society and are a by-product of the play of power among various more or less organized groups, each in pursuit of its respective interests. Conflict over the legitimacy of acts in terms of what abstract principles is precisely what organized social life is most prominently about. A democratic and pluralistic society is that kind of society in which organized and public pursuit of private interests is given special homage. A society structured to allow—indeed to promote—open and vig-

---

[12] The observations made in this section are informed in part by the line of thought formulated by, among others, Sellin, 1938:Chap. 4; Vold, 1958:Chap. 11; Taft and England, 1964:Chaps. 2, 3, 16. See also Sutherland and Cressey, 1966:101–6, 118–19; Matza, 1964:Chaps. 2–5; Clinard, 1968:214–24.

orous prosecution of moral preferences and of concrete programs must, in the nature of the case, be a society of competing and conflicting moral standards. It will be a society which, from the point of view of the individual, engenders ambiguity over what is right or just and, even, over what is deviant and what is conforming. Various strata or sectors of the society will promote competing and perhaps antithetical conceptions of the real, the moral and the possible. Abstract social values—consensual moral platitudes—will receive widely different concrete operationalizations. Although such conflicting definitions are most frequently thought of as residing within the political or economic realms, they extend as well to items thought of as deviant. In this light, deviance becomes highly political, in the sense of involving publicly promoted expressions of disagreement. Definitions which might *privately* render deviant acts subjectively available to Actors form part of the *public rhetoric* about many such acts.

a. Moralization or neutralization of acts on the ground of their not hurting others is a public and widely disseminated view. It frequently emanates from the public media with regard to such acts as homosexuality, abortion, drug use and suicide. The legality of homosexuality between consenting adults in Illinois and its imminent legality in Britain serve to undercut any attempts unambiguously to define it otherwise. The rather different rules of abortion in some European countries serve to render such action ambiguously immoral. Intranational exceptions to drug use (among certain American Indians) and different (or lack of) rules in other countries serve to make such substances morally ambiguous. International variations in the public definition of suicide render that act less than wholly immoral. Direct statements to this effect are promoted within American civilization by partisans, who engage in public debate over the moral meaning and consequences of this or that act involving a claim of no harm to others.[13] There has now even come to be something of a sloganed caption providing public legitimacy to this private claim. There are now "crimes without victims" (Schur, 1965).

b. So, too, in a pluralistic society there is considerable difference of opinion over who should get what sort of punishment in what manner over what kind of transgression. The economic boycott, the strike, the sit-in, the dismissal, the enacted law are almost never unanimously supported, and there seem frequently to be Actors on the receiving end of punishment who feel they do not deserve it.[14] They may feel, in fact, that those who have managed to secure

---

[13] Cf. the continual musing in the columns of a magazine such as *Playboy* over the moral character of pornography, wife swapping, premarital sexual intercourse and the like.

[14] If auto-safety critic Ralph Nader and certain Congressmen had had their way, this would have been the case for the automobile industry relative to safety legislation. Although Senator Vance Hartke wanted to "provide criminal penalties up to $50,000 fine and a year in jail for 'knowing and willful violation,'" most other Senators were content with providing the consumer with civil rather than criminal redress. Given the financial burden thus placed upon the private citizen (a deterrent to instigating any civil action), it is perhaps not surprising that automobile people were happy with the potential punishment thus accomplished against them. Relative to questions of social power and who will get defined in what way,

the power to punish are the persons who should actually, if the facts were known, be the true objects of punishment. And, through various means, any group being punished seems able to find ways—not infrequently, extralegal ways—in which to inflict counterpunishment upon their persecutors, almost always in the name of self-defense. Southern states find ways in which to subvert court orders. Large corporations finds ways in which to lighten or vitiate regulatory legislation and to subvert accomplished law.

Both parties to conflicts tend to think of themselves as victims or as acting in the interests of other parties who are believed to be victims. Southern states and corporations may believe themselves to be victims of the federal government, permitting, therefore, extralegal action. The federal government sometimes acts on behalf of what are felt to be victimized nations and on the basis of claims that various shortcuts are necessary and specially justified because of pressing circumstances. Thus those persons responsible for the Central Intelligence Agency can feel that various kinds of spying, subversion and support of political regimes is necessary. Of course, others in all these cases take strong exception to such action and engage in what is believed to be justified counter-victimizations.

The principle that there exists a set of morally reprehensible Others toward whom one's dubiously moral actions are specially justified is, then, a central principle of American civilization. And, the of course, twin theme of that principle is that still Others will not agree with that particular interpretation of the abstract mandate and are likely to victimize the victimizers, often in an extralegal fashion.[15]

c. Actors in everyday life find it easy to take unto themselves the conception that they are not in some sense responsible for themselves. This is possible in significant part because powerful and vigorous sectors of the larger society are in the routine business of making the same claim about deviance in particular and action in general. One of the more publicized aspects of the psychiatric, psychological and sociological conceptions of man is the assertion of his brute determination by deep-lying psychic forces that impel him or massively implicating social forces that corrupt him. Professional discourse and popular ideology abound with notions of strange compulsions, deficient super-egos, undersocialized personalities, emotional disturbances, cultural deprivation and the effects of being led astray by bad friends. Although there may not

---

it is further of interest that Congressmen were loath to think of auto makers as capable of "criminal" acts and as conceivably meriting punishment. As one Senator put it: "We're not dealing with mobsters or gangsters. . . . We are dealing with an industry that is the pride of the world . . ." (*Detroit Free Press*, June 25, 1966).

[15] Considered at a more fundamental level, the mere fact of social differentiation—the splitting of mankind into social categories—itself tends to create distance, exploitation, fear and distrust. Such practices and feelings are conducive, in turn, to a belief in "deserving victims" and the redressing of perceived injustices already wrought on one's own category. Social differentiation or social life itself is, in this sense, productive of deviant acts (or, more generally, of conflict, some of which is defined as deviant).

really be any such thing as a bad boy, boys and others can have a good deal drastically wrong with them. Psychic ills, in particular, can be such that persons committing criminal acts can be declared not responsible for them and remanded to a mental hospital instead of a prison. Such much-publicized remanding involves a public definition of Actor as really beyond his own control such that punishment would be inappropriate. In whatever sense, the person could not help what he did.

The publicly legitimate definition of Actors in such a way and the wide public proclamation of that view over many years should not make it surprising to find that Actors can come to believe the highly paid and regarded authorities who make these definitions and to take them seriously in formulating motives upon which to predicate action (Cf. Cressey, 1962, on compulsive crimes). One must indeed be appreciative of the irony.

> A number of observers have wryly noted that many delinquents seem to show a surprising awareness of sociological and psychological explanations for their behavior and are quick to point out the causal role of their poor environment. (Sykes and Matza, 1957:667, footnote 8.)

d. The question of what kind of basis upon which to give priority to what kind of loyalty is among the most ancient of dilemmas posed for human beings in social organization. To the degree that a society is differentiated into various realms (the separation of work, family, religion and politics) and into many levels (immediate face-to-face groups, organizations, communities, the national state, a world society or humanity), to that degree, one supposes, the *potential* for conflict of loyalties—conflicts of priorities—is intensified. This potential can become all the more acute and realized in a democratic-pluralistic society as distinct from a totalitarian nation-state. In the latter the state itself clearly and forcefully claims to transcend all other commitments.

As stated, a first and primary feature of a democratic-pluralistic society is precisely the freedom of various strata to promote their own particular conceptions of what commitments should transcend what other commitments. Within a few limits (namely, a prohibition against advocating violent subversion of the state) there come to be a plethora of publicly expressed competing and contradictory conceptions of what is morally prior to what. That is, there is *conflict among priority schemes.*

Second, a society of high differentiation, high complexity and rapid social change confronts its participants with a succession of novel situations about which some sort of principle of moral priority must necessarily be constructed. A fluid and kaleidoscopic situation induces to a sense that moral priorities invoked yesterday may be inappropriate today in the face of a similar but somehow different situation. Yesterday's decision may give one kind of priority, but today's somehow requires another; and the participants may well wonder if yesterday's action was morally consistent with today's. *There can be intra-scheme priority confusion.*

Third, priority schemes can contain *contrary moral mandates.* They can provide principles that internally compete, in contradictory directions, for priority of application. Although such contradictions are elusive and difficult to grasp because we are so close to them, an attempt to do so by Robert S. Lynd points to the following kinds of dilemmas:

> Everyone should try to be successful.
> *But:* The kind of person you are is more important than how successful you are.

> The family is our basic institution and the sacred core of our national life.
> *But:* Business is our most important institution, and, since national welfare depends upon it, other institutions must conform to its needs.

> Religion and "the finer things of life" are our ultimate values and the things all of us are really working for.
> *But:* A man owes it to himself and to his family to make as much money as he can.

> Honesty is the best policy.
> *But:* Business is business, and a businessman would be a fool if he didn't cover his hand.

> Education is a fine thing.
> *But:* It is the practical man who gets things done. (Lynd, 1939:60–61.)

Other leading explicators of simultaneously held but contradictory principles also point to the less than publicly articulated and defended moral principles that compete for priority. Dubbing such principles "subterranean values," Matza and Sykes have noted, in particular, competing mandates regarding the use of violence:

> The crucial idea of aggression as a proof of toughness and masculinity is widely accepted at many points in the social system. The ability to take it and hand it out, to defend one's right and one's reputation with force, to prove one's manhood by hardiness and physical courage—all are widespread in American culture. They cannot be dismissed by noting the equally valid observation that many people will declare that "nice children do not fight." The use of aggression to demonstrate masculinity is, of course, restricted by numerous prohibitions against instigating violence, "dirty" fighting, bullying, blustering and so on. Yet, even if the show of violence is carefully hedged in by both children and adults throughout our society, there is a persistent support for aggression which manifests itself in the derogatory connotations of labels such as "sissy" or "fag." (Matza and Sykes, 1961:717.)

Without lamenting (or advocating), one can agree with the Jeremiahs who warn us of moral confusion and moral chaos. Conflict between advocates of differing systems of priority and contradiction between the tenets contained within a particular system of advocacy make possible a relatively widespread sense of ambiguity over what *is moral* action. Ideological conflict and inconsistency, the hallmarks of a free society, may force upon Actors so exposed a realization of the contingent, tentative and even arbitrary character of all definitions of action. It may also force upon them the realization that no matter what they do—what priorities they adopt—they may have to abandon their decision in the future or defend it against competing conceptions of what should come before what. The principle learned by George Orwell is a principle learned by many. "This was the great abiding lesson of my boyhood: that I was in a world where it was *not possible* for me to be good" (Quoted in Linder, 1961:28).

Conflict, confusion, contradiction and ambiguity of moral priorities give rise to the possibility that Actors will be afforded considerable flexibility or even freedom in choosing which moral priorities to invoke in dealing with concretely problematic situations. Where there exists a variety of conceptions of what moral principles are to be given compliance priority, and where some of these principles even contradict one another, there can be a very wide range of *personal discretion* in ranking *moral* priorities and acting on them. That is, a very wide variety of *deviant* acts can be viewed—at least temporarily—as, in some sense, moral, in a society of the sort just sketched.

Conditions of threat and encapsulation are especially likely to make Actors more sensitive to conflicts, confusions, contradictions and ambiguities and more in need of exploiting such features in order to render previously unavailable acts subjectively available. One might say, indeed, that a society of this sort makes it relatively easy to justify almost anything in the name of almost anything. Under such conditions almost anybody can see almost anything as morally right, at least for a time. In such a society almost anything is possible. And, as stated at the outset, exactly who or what is deviant can be quite unclear. The deviance of yesterday can be the politics of today and the convention of tomorrow.

All of the foregoing goes to the point that what people can find possible is a function of what moral justifications for what kind of activity are available to them. Action is in part a function of the scope and character of the rhetoric and motive-justifications supplied to Actors by the encompassing culture. The crucial proposition is that, in a society of the complexity and diversity of the American one, there are available moral justifications for almost anything.[16] Given stressful circumstances, people might even be surprised to observe what they have suddenly discovered to be perfectly justifiable.

[16] Further detailed discussions and illustrations are presented in Clinard and Quinney, 1967:30–31, 92–93, 136–37, 183–85.

This view of justifications and their availability is founded on the still more general proposition that such motives are not so much spurs to action as they are releasers of action. If it is assumed that humans are always acting, are always in motion, the question is not what makes them act but rather what *permits* them to act in *this* rather than in *that* way. One component of acting this and not that way is the selective force of the pool of available justifications or motives. A complex, diverse culture, providing a plurality of approved moral motives, supports and makes possible, therefore, not merely conforming, creative and heroic acts but also deviant acts.

THE CONJUNCTION OF SUBJECTIVE AND OBJECTIVE AVAILABILITY

Even though all acts here defined as relevant are more or less proximate, the acts of such a class are still likely to vary in the exact degree of their proximity. On the *objective* side, necessary places, hardware and Others of all proximate acts are unlikely to be equally close in the physical and temporal sense. The places, hardware or Others for one act may be two seconds, two minutes or two feet away; those for another act may be many minutes or hours or miles away. On the *subjective* side, some proximate acts may be very highly available, to the degree of being defined by Actor as merely conventional or conforming acts. Other acts may pose some slight moral qualms which require moral redefinition, and still other acts may require a great deal of definitional work to render them really conventional or specially justified.

The various possible conjunctions between degrees of objective proximity and degrees of subjective availability of all proximate acts seem likely to pose a real decision problem for Actor, even within all the constraints and possibilities heretofore sketched. Even if he perceives a choice between only two proximate acts, degrees of objective proximity and subjective availability can well combine to make none of the possibilities particularly pleasant prospects. An act that is objectively proximate may be subjectively less available than a less objectively proximate but more subjectively available alternative. If one act among available acts is grossly more objectively proximate and subjectively available than all other possibilities, that, of course, would seem to be the likely candidate for closure.

Situations of confounded conjunction between objective proximity and subjective availability seem likely, further, to be situations of shifting and unstable objective proximity and subjective availability. As Actor wrestles with such confounding, and perhaps goes through rather random search and resolution movements, his relations to both objective possibilities and subjective availability are likely to be in flux. If he moves about while thinking the problem over, the objective proximity of places, hardware and Others will shift from moment to moment as a function of his travel. Likewise, his train of thought is likely to be responsive to his changing external field which can cue off new and changing ways in which to view his problem, possible acts and the morality of various lines of action. Even if he remains more or less physically stationary, his attention can roam over objects present and he can happen to overlook others, conducing to one or another rather chancelike stream of consciousness about his troubles. As a function of momentary presence of physical objects, of people and of events, Actor may have a rapidly shifting conception of what is real, what is moral and what is possible.

As the felt necessity to act increases, there may come a point where he senses that he must do *something* or even *anything* about what threatens him. Such a point of desperation will coincide with one or another of his changing assessments of objective proximity and subjective availability. In desperation, Actor may close on whatever act is most available at that moment, even though an hour before he might have had a different objective proximity to that act and a different sense of its subjective availability. And, an hour later, Actor's still-shifting conception of subjective availability may make it possible for him to wonder, "How could I ever do it?" or "Why did I ever do it?" and to lament, "Oh, if I only hadn't done it" or "I wish I hadn't done it" or "I must have been crazy to do such a thing."[17]

Through all of this and here at the end, one cannot neglect the possibility that the most objectively and subjectively available act under conditions of threat and encapsulation will be a conventional, conforming or heroic act. After all, human beings are threatened rather regularly during their lives, and a state something like encapsulation is also probably not uncommon. The processes involved in achieving a deviant act are not unlike the processes involved in conducing people to engage in any sort of routine or nonroutine action. The difference in outcome mainly resides, objectively, in what happens to be around in the way of places, hardware, Others and skills as materials on the basis of which to construct action and, subjectively, in what can be defined at a given moment as moral in a given circumstance.

If it is necessary to think about how people who have committed a deviant act are different from people who have not performed the act, it may be just as important to keep in mind the more mundane and proximate differences as to focus on the broad and deep differences. Let us never forget that, at the last moment, someone could have started deeply to care about and help that would-be suicide; at the last moment that would-be embezzler could have received a phone call telling of a large inheritance; at the last moment that would-be check forger could have found that the all-night restaurant didn't cash checks; at the last moment the would-be murderer's spouse could have

---

[17] Cf. the portrayals provided by Matza, 1964:Chap. 6; Briar and Piliavin, 1965; and the excellent close study of juvenile vandalism by Wade, 1967, especially pp. 106–8. Additional relevant materials are conveniently chronicled in Rodman and Grams, 1967:201–2, "Containment and Control Theories."

simply fled from the dwelling. The perpetration of many deviant acts seems in many ways as fragile, tentative, delicate, disruptable and indeterminate as the perpetration of many conforming acts. And, in the end, that is not surprising. No matter how acts are divided and labeled, they are all human acts. And they are, therefore, often the fragile and groping, pitiful and fleeting attempts of a threatenable creature in search of safety.

———————

There is, then, a sense in which deviant acts are facilitated by providing Actors with the knowledge of what everybody knows, and training them in what everybody can do, as well as by various efforts to inculcate them with more technical knowledge and skills. And deviant acts are facilitated by providing Actors with quite conventional moral justifications of their actions. When such provision of moral motives is performed in a society in which there is public conflict and contradiction over the morality of almost all action, those acts that might be called deviant can more easily take on a morally justified character. They can become subjectively available by means of the same moral renderings or definitions used by even the most famous of conventional Others in defending the morality of the most public and mainstream of actions.

Having paid homage, in Chapters 3 and 4, to the more dreary and dismal emotions and phenomenologies that can sometimes be associated with deviant acts, it is time now to redress the imbalance thus created. The next chapter will stress the more positive, exhilarating and *adventurous* personal states that can accompany deviant acts.

CHAPTER 5
THE ADVENTUROUS DEVIANT ACT

Up until now I have, in many ways, played into the hands of the conventionally sentimental. There has been emphasis on the ways in which unpleasant acts are preceded by unpleasant experiences. Isolation of something called "the defensive deviant act" and the tracing of its facilitants is in some ways another version of the postulate "evil follows evil." The empirical materials suggest, however, that it has not been unreasonable to do this. Evil does seem often to follow evil, in the sense that strongly felt unpleasant experiences are sometimes associated with deviant acts (and with many *conforming* acts). To acknowledge and to deal with an association between evils does not, however, commit one to the proposition of a perfect or unitary association. We can conceive the additional possibility that deviant acts can result from sequences of experiences of a much less negative character. We can entertain the notion that human beings are also capable of a positive sense of adventure, of excitement and of enchantment and that such experiences can be associated with, or even generated by, acts of deviance.

OPTIMUM LEVEL OF EXCITATION

Such a possibility is founded not merely on facts about some deviant acts or even about human beings, but on some qualities of vertebrates in general and of mammals and primates in particular. A considerable body of material on comparative animal studies suggests the viability of the proposition that, at least among mammals, there exist optimum levels of excitation. Mammals, including Homo sapiens, are those sorts of creatures which act so as to reduce possible and existing threat and unpredictability in their environment should it rise above a certain level *and* to *increase* existing and possible threat and unpredictability in their environment should it fall below a certain level. Summarizing studies of this phenomenon, Hebb and Thompson observe that

> . . . it appears empirically that for any one animal there is an optimal level of fear or frustration. First, the evidence concerning fear: strange surroundings tend to produce emotional disturbance in the rat, but Montgomery . . . and Thompson . . . have shown experimentally that the rat which has the choice of familiar and unfamiliar territory will tend to move toward the unfamiliar—the well-known exploratory drive. Whiting and Mowrer . . . and Berlyne . . . have suggested a connection between fear and investigative tendencies. The dog that is frightened by a

strange object is nevertheless apt to return to look at it again, balanced between closer approach and flight. . . . The same thing can be observed in chimpanzees, and Woodworth . . . and Valentine . . . have described the behavior of young children who ask to be shown again—at a safe distance—the object that has frightened them. Secondly, concerning frustration: Harlow, Harlow and Meyer . . . have demonstrated the monkey's willingness to expose itself repeatedly to the frustrations inherent in problem solving, without extrinsic reward. Mahut, working in the McGill laboratory, has shown that the rat, when offered two routes to food, one short and direct, the other via a maze problem, will choose the problem on 20 to 40 per cent of the runs. Some of the time even a rat prefers to work for his living.

Such phenomena are, of course, well known in man: in the liking for dangerous sports or roller coasters, where fear is deliberately courted, and in the addiction to bridge or golf or solitaire, vices whose very existence depends on the difficulty of the problems presented and an optimal level of frustration. Once more, when we find such attitudes toward fear and frustration in animals, we have a better basis for supposing that we are dealing with something fundamental if a man prefers skis to the less dangerous snowshoes, or when we observe an unashamed love of work (problem solving and frustration included) in the scientist, or in the businessman who cannot retire. Such behavior in man is usually accounted for as a search for prestige, but the animal data make this untenable. It seems much more likely that solving problems and running mild risks are inherently rewarding, or, in more general terms, that the animal will always act so as to produce an optimal level of excitation. (Hebb and Thompson, 1968:759.)

Uncertainty, unpredictability, threat, fear, frustration, anxiety and the like, when felt to be manageable—felt to contain little possibility of overwhelming the organism—appear to be labeled by human beings as excitement, challenge, fun or adventure. In managed and manageable measures, experiences of fear, anxiety, etc., are felt to be pleasantly fearful, pleasantly anxious, pleasantly uncertain, pleasantly frustrating. Circumstances providing too little of such experience are said to be boring, dull, gray, or spiritless.

THE PLEASANTLY FEARFUL IN EVERYDAY LIFE

There may be said to be a rather powerful demand for the pleasantly fearful among humans. Pleasant fearfulness thus comes to be socially institutionalized (in the sense of being planned, formally organized, publicly recognized and culturally legitimized), usually in the form of *contests* which focus on the staged competition of parties in "making the most points." On the purely game or unserious side, there arise sets of professional competitors, whose fans ex-

perience pleasant fear over their fortunes.   Professional athletics of all varieties
are prominent among such fear producers, but amateur endeavors centering on
university campuses should also be included.   The activities of such professional pleasant-fear producers are paralleled by an infinity of localized leagues
of pleasant fear and frustration, including baseball ("little" and "adult"), bowling, golf, bridge and even chess.   On what is called the real-life or serious side,
social life abounds in contests over initiating an enterprise, being hired, getting
promoted, getting a raise, getting a contract, making a sale or meeting a self-
set standard of performance.   It is noteworthy that one concern sometimes
raised about the serious and unserious contests of social life is that the competition may get so rough, or one party may win so much, that occasions of engagement are no longer fun or exciting.   They can become merely threatening
or merely fearful or merely dull, because outcomes are too highly determinate
or too highly indeterminate.

Pleasant fear can also be derived from unserious profaning of the sacred, as
in skits and humor (at which some people can come to make a living); from
geographical forays, in which people try their luck in new territories for a
period of time (lately institutionalized under the rubric "tourism"); and from
changes of social membership such as occur in getting a new job, getting married, joining a new group or quitting any of these.   *It may be suggested, further, that deviant acts can be one more way in which the pleasantly fearful is
produced.*

PLEASANT FEARFULNESS
AND DEVIANT ACTS

1. The pleasant fearfulness produced by the commission of a deviant act
does not necessarily derive from the violation of a *moral* prohibition.   Rather,
from the point of view of the participants, it may derive from involvement in
one of the contests of social life.   This is especially likely to be the case among
those who are more aware of contests than of moral prohibitions, namely
among those very small and young humans called children.   The classic account of this possibility is provided by one Sidney, who recollects "How I
Learned To Lie and Steal" at age four.   Of Joseph, his somewhat older friend,
Sidney says:

> One day while we were passing a fruit store [Joseph] picked up an apple
> while no one was looking and continued to walk past the store with the
> apple in his hand.   He performed for me in like manner quite a few times,
> and nothing would do but that he must teach me to do the same thing.
> That was the first time I ever stole anything.
>
> This fruit store had baskets, barrels and boxes containing fruit and
> vegetables setting out in front of it, as the weather was still quite warm.
> He, that is, Joseph, started to walk past the fruit store and, as he came to a

box of fruit, he took some fruit and walked on. He motioned me to do the same thing.

I would walk behind him and, as soon as he would pick up a piece of fruit, I was supposed to do likewise. It took lots of practice, and he had to set many examples before I could at last gain enough courage to follow suit.

Never a thought occurred to me as to whether it was right or wrong— it was merely an interesting game. The apple or orange didn't make as much difference as the getting of them. It was the taking them that I enjoyed.

On subsequent afternoons we made it our habit to pass the fruit store many times and steal various things. I found as much fun and enjoyment in grabbing a potato or an onion as to grab anything else. The proprietor soon discovered what was going on and, in his endeavor to curtail further depredations on his stock, began to keep a sharp lookout for our approach and to watch us closely as we passed. This only made the game more interesting, and it began to require real skill to get away with anything. Often after this he would chase us for a block or two in order to teach us a lesson, but he never did. This is when it started to get real good, and you couldn't keep us away after that. *The chases added spice to our little game.* (Shaw, 1931:58; italics added.)

The not infrequently encountered plea among children of many ages that "we were just having fun" or "we were just fooling around" or "we were just playing" is possibly often a correct accounting, in the sense that, in the absence of strong and repeated enunciations of moral prohibitions, humans will engage in a variety of contest activities that are pleasantly fearful but which are likely to be defined by moralized Others as deviant. Investigating what can be labeled "juvenile vandalism," Wade finds that such acts are "sometimes the inadvertent result of ordinary play activity." (Wade, 1967:100.)

2. Possibilities of a more interesting character arise when Actor is fully apprised of the fact that an act or activity is considered deviant by Others. To create a prohibition is to create the possibility of deriving pleasant fear from violating that prohibition. The process of violation and the chance of "getting away with it" can assume the same contest character as the legitimated contests of conventional social life. Associated with this there can be the pleasantly fearful experience of making an excursion into the forbidden. The very fact of being out there, on the other side of the rule, can become a matter of excitement, of adventure, of feeling oneself to be daring and game.[1] A very conventional youth can thus relate this kind of experience of theft from a jewelry store:

---

[1] The extent to which Actor shares in a belief in the wrongfulness of an act is an empirical question for which there are little data. However, it seems likely that, at least at the moment of commission, he does not believe the act to be unequivocally wrong. Mechanisms similar to those operating in the defensive act render the act subjectively available. Especially where acts are ambiguously immoral, it would not be difficult to see adventure as having higher priority than conformity. The sense of adventure probably derives, in part, from the knowledge that *Others* define the act as wrong, not from unequivocally believing so oneself.

I was fifteen at the time. B. and I went to M.'s Jewelry Store to look at some ID chains. The store's sole salesman was showing some Ronson lighters to a potential customer. While waiting, we browsed around looking at watches and chains through the showcase glass panels. The customer, being *merely* potential, could not make up his mind; as a result, he caused quite a number of lighters to be brought out and scattered on the counter-top during his deliberation. When he did select one, he paid for it in the exact amount, slipped it into his pocket and left. The salesman moved to the back counter to register the sale; his back was to me. I moved to the counter to look over the lighters. I took out a cigarette, picked up a lighter—naïvely thinking at the time that the lighter would be fueled. At the moment the salesman returned to the counter; he smiled and asked if I was out of fluid and whether I needed a light. *To this time, it had not occurred to me ever to steal the lighter.* It was in conjunction with his remark that it occurred to me *I could* steal the lighter and that I *could get away* with it. I said I needed a light and slipped the lighter *into my pocket.* The salesman gave me a light. We then priced some chains and left. B. was not aware that I had just executed what I thought to be a *"beautiful case"* of stealing. *I could hardly wait to get out of the store to tell him.*

And the same person could, after the act, be "overcome by feelings of remorse and fear" and even say, "I hid the lighter and was afraid to use it till a long time afterwards." The subsequent onset of unpleasant fear in this case does not rule out the possibility that persons can continue to feel prideful over indiscretions. Of being caught sneaking into an amusement center without paying, a person can report that "I felt a thrill doing it . . . . I enjoyed the naughty act." Or before first using an illegal substance, a person can feel: "I was quite fascinated by the aura of 'sin' which surrounded the use of marijuana." A middle-class person who engaged in several episodes of shoplifting with a friend relates:

> For us the only wrong aspect of shoplifting was the possibility of getting caught, no matter how careful. The greater the risk involved, or the more exquisite the article being taken, the more heightened our excitement, sense of accomplishment and pride at making off with it. We never suffered a moment's guilt, before, during or after. We are still keenly proud of all we accomplished. We always took things we would have bought. However, we have stopped completely; we are professional people and have our careers to keep in mind.

We can suspect the operation of the same adventurous impulse when we find people who have no evident instrumental need to cheat on examinations in an educational system working out elaborate systems to do so as a self-imposed challenge. Inducted into the military service, a young man with a college degree in electrical engineering found himself in a two-week army course on electricity. Not surprisingly, he received the highest class grades; yet he nonetheless purchased black market answers to the final examination and devised a system to make them available during the final.

> All during the course my notebook cover had been used as a scratch pad—it was covered with several mathematical problems I had solved. My plan was simply to add one more insignificant problem to the notebook—an inconspicuous long division problem. The dividend was to contain the number of all problems in which the "a" alternative was correct; the divisor included the numbers of all the "b" alternatives; the "c's" were represented in the quotient; the "d's" were missing. The unopened notebook was placed as usual on the floor next to my desk.
>   Looking back at my feelings at the time of the act, I guess I knew the behavior was wrong. I had to scheme, hide the act, make the behavior as inconspicuous as possible, etc. On the other hand, I did not consider the cheating qua cheating since my orientation was toward accepting the challenge of beating the system. I knew the material cold, probably better than the instructor. I was in no way defending my intellectual prestige, since I was already the class leader in this field. I undoubtedly could have done just as well if not better without the cheating as with.
>   . . . My motivation appeared to be just to see if I could get away with beating the system.

To create categories of sin and the aura of sin is to create the possibility of people finding fearful pleasantry in being at least a little bit sinful or occasionally sinful. Tenderloin districts of cities and tenderloin cities of nations are, after all, economically dependent upon, and economically impossible without, a large encompassing population that is serviced by the forms of pleasant fearfulness they provide.

3. At least some kinds of prohibited activities are claimed by some parts of the population to be *in themselves* fun, exciting and adventurous. More than simply deriving pleasant fearfulness from violating the prohibition per se, there can exist claims that the prohibited activity *itself* produces a pleasant level of excitation. In American civilization such claims have centered, of late, on a variety of types of drugs and sexual relations. The host of counterclaims to the real harmfulness of various drugs and sexual relations are simply testimony to the existence of conflicting counterdefinitions of these and other activities.

Organized and public arguments for the extraordinary merits of, for example, marijuana, LSD, gambling, homosexuality and more unconventional heterosexuality serve to create widespread interest in these forms of claimed adventure in a manner not unsimilar to the interest created by arguments for the extraordinary excitement of athletic contests or the claims for zestful living made by military posters. That others will say a particular form of deviance is really a drag or really too dangerous or really sick is but nomal—in the sense of typical—because partisans of athletics and other occupations must cope with exactly the same counterclaims about their respective conventional activities. While there are those who view an activity with horror (whether it be playing football, being in the military, making war toys, gambling at the track or with a bookie, having homosexual relations or taking LSD), there are others who view the same activity as a form of rhapsody. Of taking LSD on only one occasion, a conventional young lady tells us:

> I would gladly do it again if I had a chance and am not afraid to tell about my very interesting and good experience with it when I hear people "moralizing" against it. (Sometimes I feel like going on an absolute proselytizing campaign.) With my social science orientation, I am a bit hesitant in using the traditional language of morality; but for me (now and at the time of my act), taking LSD lies in the same class of positively valued, exhilarating, self-stretching experiences as climbing a mountain, reading a wonderful book or discovering a soul-mate.

One supposes that the exciting lure of deviance is all the stronger when the prohibition is not against the activity per se but against engagement in it by particular categories of persons. Thus sexual contacts are publicly touted as a very fine thing, *except* between what are defined as underage humans; humans not married to each other, and humans of the same sex. Operating automobiles is fine, except by those humans who are not licensed. Imbibing alcoholic beverages is acceptable and even widely expected, except among humans who are not "of age." These and other activities are defined as exciting and as gratifying but hedged in so as to disqualify many humans from engaging in them. It should come as no surprise when such disqualified humans act, if the occasion arises, in a manner that will let them in on the otherwise legitimate excitements of social life.

Account must be taken, then, of the likelihood that deviance can be fun, or, in the current vernacular, it can be kicks. Such kicks can derive from a conventional contest orientation apart from moral considerations, from violating the prohibition itself and from defining the deviance as inherently exciting or adventurous. If many kinds of deviant acts are simply more fun than considerable portions of conventionality, the widespread popularity of them would appear no more mysterious than the popularity of conventional adventures. If deviance could not be fun, it would hardly be necessary to preach against the joys of sin. (And, if crime did not pay, it would hardly be necessary so adamantly to argue otherwise and so strenuously to attempt its control.)

AVAILABILITY AND SOCIAL ORGANIZATIONAL SETTINGS

Occasions of engagement in adventurous deviant acts will, as with defensive deviant acts, be a function of combinations of subjective availability and objective proximity. And, in the same way that closure on a defensive deviant act can be highly fortuitous, relative to Actor's enduring orientation, engagement in adventurous acts can often be aleatory or random, relative to Actor's intentions. Adventurous acts (as well as some defensive acts) often seem to be spontaneous, unplanned, unsought occurrences in the sense that objective proximity and subjective availability combine to conduce specific behavior outcomes not previously structured by Actor as a certain and concretely desired specific course of action. He can have generalized and vague dispositions to adventure (or defense) that eventuate in a specific adventure (or defense) that neither he himself nor anyone else could or would have predicted a few hours earlier. Paralleling the processes of threat and encapsulation in defensive acts, there can perhaps be processes of activating an adventurous orientation and processes of activating a temporary state of *enchantment* with adventure. And, after the circumstances inducing such possible enchantment have terminated, Actor can also feel guilt, remorse and shame or pride and elation.

Actors themselves are likely to differ in their capacities for an adventurous orientation and in what they can find to be enchanting. There may well be some truth in the folk belief that those Actors with the *most* strictly programmed lives without opportunity for conventional adventure *and* those Actors with the *least* strictly programmed lives with the most opportunity for adventure are Actors who will have the greatest capacity for adventurous orientations and enchantments in general. Not only may it be true that an "idle mind is the devil's workshop," but the overly occupied dreg of a mundane existence may be as well. It is with regard to this latter possibility that one can best understand the adventures of an otherwise quite sedate young lady who, in a single evening, penetrated the recesses of a deviant subculture, smoked marijuana, engaged in interracial sexual relations and got pregnant (leading to the defensive deviant act of abortion). As she tells it:

I was living in New York . . . and I was lonely for the first time in my life, although I was kept busy by my studying. I . . . had a friend with whom I felt comfortable and we rented an apartment together. [One] evening . . . my friend and I had dates, and we dressed up in as sophisticated style as possible and went to the Round Table. Our dates did not turn out to be very sharp, and neither could dance at all. That night, after we got home, she and I decided that Saturday night we would go down to the Village to a particular bar we'd been told about and meet people and "really live it up." So Saturday evening we dressed up in mild versions of beatniks and went to the Village. Offbeat musicians generally went to this place, so we managed to meet some and off we went to a party—very pleased with ourselves.

I was attracted to a very good-looking six-foot-six Negro (I am white) who everybody seemed to know. He played several instruments and was a good dancer. We danced. He took me to another party. We drank and talked—I liked him. Then we went to someone's apartment, smoked marijuana and then went to a bedroom.

Put more generally, in the words of Hebb and Thompson:

> The plain fact is that the primate is only too ready to become a trouble-maker when things are dull, and we had better stop comforting ourselves with the accurate but insufficient statement that man has no instinct to make war.

> ❃   ❃   ❃

> Poker and bridge and pennant races, and bowling alleys and detective stories, may have more to do with our social stability than we think. Even today, an economically successful society may require circuses, in some form, as well as bread.   (Hebb and Thompson, 1968:759–60.)

In different terms, numerous observers have pointed to the very high level of reasoned, planned and coordinated action required of players of many life-plots in American civilization.   Such observers have lamented what they feel to be the lack of role possibilities for "spontaneity" and "emotional catharsis" because of the need to maximize complex cognitive and technical skills.[2]   Leaving aside moral evaluations of such a role emphasis, it may well be the case that many social roles are so well planned, so certain, so—let us be plain—dull, that they generate considerable impetus for adventurous activity should the opportunity for such arise.   It is perhaps not fortuitous that automobile production workers drive with extreme recklessness upon release from eight hours of assembly-line confinement.   It is perhaps not fortuitous that middle-class bureaucratic types can develop a taste for the adventures of wife swapping or, if they are more affluent, for the fancy sex provided by call-girl circles or for the personal mysteries of LSD.   Under slightly different conditions of objective proximity and subjective availability, persons involved in the above sorts of activities might as easily be found among the partisans of the claimed joys of amateur politics, the United Fund, the bowling league or the local church, and vice versa.   One suspects, however, that these latter forms of legitimate adventure are rather hard put to compete with the former illegitimate excitements. It could well be that many people do their "bit" in the legitimate realms of adventure and, to an extent greater than is publicly recognized, "have something going" in deviant forms of excitement as well.[3]

Actors whose lives are very loosely programmed, in the sense that they have a very wide range of discretion over what to do when and very few "whats" which they feel have to be done "when," are in a generically similar position to the very strictly programmed.   The virtual absence of events that mark out

[2] E.g., among recent works, Keniston, 1965:Chap. 12, "The Dictatorship of the Ego"; Leeper and Madison, 1959:Chap. 9, "Emotional Richness and Emotional Poverty."

[3] Among studies of the hidden adventures of normals, see Leigh (1963) and Laud Humphreys (1967) on various sorts of unconventional sex; Blum and Associates (1964) and Suchman (1968) on LSD and other drugs.   For all their subsequent sense of threat and "nonsharable problems," the embezzlers studied by Cressey (1953) seem, in significant proportion, to have generated a threat for themselves out of adventurous (sometimes deviant) acts that went astray.

time can produce a sense of dullness, a sense of oppressiveness, a sense of nothing happening and thereby open Actor to suggestions for activities that have an exciting and adventurous character. This seems to be, in particular, the situation of young males living in low-income areas. The fundamental insight concerning such young humans was provided by Frederic Thrasher more than forty years ago.

> How to break the humdrum of routine existence—this is a problem for the boy. It is the problem of life generally, and a great deal of human energy is expended in the flight from monotony and the pursuit of thrill.
>
> ❋   ❋   ❋
>
> Behavior in the gang often takes the form of movement without much purpose or direction. Almost anything which possesses novelty suffices— until its newness wears off. Activity may lead in the direction of delinquency or anywhere else, so long as it keeps the gang boy "going."
>
> ❋   ❋   ❋
>
> The fundamental fact about the gang is that it finds in the boys who become its members a fund of energy that is undirected, undisciplined and uncontrolled by any socially desirable pattern, and it gives to that energy an opportunity for expression in the freest, most spontaneous and elemental manner possible. (Thrasher, 1927:82, 85, 101.)

Almost forty years later another analyst, observing the progeny of some of the boys studied by Thrasher, provided this depiction of the unprogrammed character of everyday life for this category of young males.

> When some of the boys arrive at their hangout during the afternoon there is seldom any previous agreement about what they are going to do. Generally, the practice is simply to "come on the scene" and ask "what's happening." From then on, joint activities emerge crescively as situations present themselves. Probably the most frequent activity is gossiping about people in the neighborhood. If it is Friday (payday) some of the older boys may "chip in" for some beer or wine. Periodically they may start "rapping" or insulting one another. Sometimes they pitch pennies for an hour or two. During weekends there may be a local dance or social, and some of them may go there. Often someone in the older groups will own a car, and all the guys will "pile in" and go for a ride around the neighborhood, yelling and waving at girls and other boys they know. Occasionally all those present will arise and go to the nearby beefstand, the Tastee Freeze, and Good Humor truck or a hot dog stand. If there is a fight, a fire or wreck, everybody—adults and adolescents— runs to see it. Sometimes there are games: "babies," "ringoliva," "war" and so on. During the summer, ball games attract a sizable audience. A policeman stops someone and everyone gathers to see what will happen. Three or four boys may wander over to where one of their girl friends lives and sit with her on the front steps. A few times each week their

social worker will drop by and take them for a ride or get them to hold a meeting. Peddlers come by and sell a nickel's worth of peanuts or pistachios. For a week the Italians' carnival draws many boys to the "rides," dart games and improvised roulette wheel. The Mexicans' fiesta and parade last a day each. In early 1964, glue sniffing became popular, but by the next summer it was almost out of fashion. Card playing in doorways, roughhousing and record playing are more enduring activities.

Interspersed among all these little episodes is a continuing line of conversation that is bawdy, irreverent and earthy. Often they talk about each other, and there is a good deal of boasting along with insulting anecdotes. Among the Negro and Mexican boys, when this becomes highly stylized, it is called "signifying." When other people in the neighborhood come up for discussion, they are treated in much the same way.

As the boys move from one ad hoc activity to another, it becomes obvious that they have nothing like a daily agenda or even clearly defined set of group "values" toward which they are feeling their way.[4]

Also interspersed among "all these little episodes," as Suttles terms them, are deviant acts, some of which have the character of defending the honor of self, group or neighborhood, but some of which are simply adventurous. Focusing on this latter possibility, Carl Werthman provides these insightful materials on how events can be created among low-income Black males in San Francisco. Among such males,

. . . joy-riding is viewed as an abundant source of the anxiety, excitement and tension that accompanies the taking of risk for its own sake, a complex of emotions often referred to as "kicks."

(Did you guys do much joy-riding?) Yeah. When I was about thirteen, I didn't do nothing but steal cars. The guy that I always stole with, both of us liked to drive so we'd steal a car. And then he'd steal another car and we'd chase each other. Like there would be two in our car, two in the other car, and we'd drive by and stick out our hands, and if you touch them then they have to chase you. Or we'd steal an old car, you know, that have the running boards on it. We'd stand on that and kick the car going past. We used to have a ball when we'd do that other game with the hands though. (Werthman, 1967:156.)

Assiduously prosecuted, acts of theft apparently can get to be very safe affairs, so that if a sense of adventure is to be produced, they must be pursued under conditions of intentionally contrived detection risks. Choosing daylight hours on a Saturday, the younger boys observed by Werthman

[4] Suttles, 1968: 184–85. On the social organizational sources of release from the social order among youth in industrial societies, see Toby, 1967, on "Affluence and Adolescent Crime"; Vaz, ed., 1967; Downes, 1966. See further Lerman, 1968; Feldman, 1968; Reiss, 1951.

would delight in trying to steal hubcaps from a packed parking lot next to a local supermarket, and on special occasions, they enjoyed breaking into gum and candy machines located in a crowded amusement park. In the parking lot the challenge consisted of making away with the hubcaps without being seen, while in the equally crowded amusement park, the essence of the enterprise consisted of darting through the customers away from the police after making sure that the theft itself had been observed. (Werthman, 1967:156.)

Deviant acts can serve to make things happen, or they can be the things that are happening. They can, for the loosely as well as the strictly programmed, create new kinds of contests, and they can be viewed as inherently enjoyable engrossments.[5]

It is perhaps the loosely programmed who are most likely to experience the greatest number of what they will code as adventures—as episodes of pleasant fear. Through the repetition and hence routinization of adventures, such repeated activities can cease to produce a level of excitation and can lose their quality of pleasant fear. Ever new episodes can be required to produce a previous level of felt adventure. It is conceivable that the experience of a great deal of adventure can lead to "a taste for 'adventure,'" as Hebb and Thompson put it, rendering a wider and wider span of acts and activities game for engagement. In the absence of control exerted otherwise, there can perhaps come to be adventurers who merely climb mountains, explore Antarctica or test jet aircraft, but there can also come to be adventurers who engage in what will be labeled horrendous deviant activities.[6] As Thrasher put it about young males in unprogrammed togetherness:

[5] Along these lines, see further the commentary on excitement and risk provided by Goffman, 1967:149–270; Feldman, 1968; and the reviews by Fowler, 1965; Fiske and Maddi, 1961; Klausner, ed., 1968. These types of materials, conjoined with those on threat, hopefully provide a solution to some difficulties pointed up by Cohen and Short (1958:30) concerning delinquency or deviance and the issue of whether it can be "assumed to be a potentiality of human nature which automatically erupts when the lid is off." See also Matza, 1964:181–83.

[6] See, e.g., the Roebuck and Cadwallader (1961) study of the "Negro Armed Robber as a Criminal Type"; Williamson's (1965) case study of a hustler; Thompson's (1967:Chap. 8) portrayal of "motorcycle outlaws"; and the studies in Klausner, ed. (1968) of mountain climbers, sports parachutists and other adventurers. Commenting on the findings of Sheldon and Eleanor Glueck (1950), Wolfgang observes:

> The delinquent boys were characterized as hedonistic, distrustful, aggressive, hostile and, as boys who felt they could manage their own lives, were socially assertive and defied authority. The nondelinquents were more banal, conformistic, neurotic, felt unloved, insecure and anxiety-ridden. The attributes associated with the delinquents sound similar to the description of the Renaissance man who defied the authority and static orthodoxy of the Middle Ages, who was also aggressive, richly assertive, this-world rather than other-world centered, and was less banal, more innovative, than his medieval predecessors. The Glueck delinquents also sound much like our 19th-century captains of industry [and] our 20th-century political leaders and corporation executives. (Wolfgang, 1967:152.)

The gang stimulates the boy to an even greater craving for excitement. His adolescent interest in that which thrills becomes reinforced by habit; ordinary business and pleasure seem tame and dull in comparison with the adventures of the gang. Habituation to this type of life in adolescence goes a long way toward explaining behavior in the young-adult gangs and even of the hardened gangster. (Thrasher, 1927:82–83.)

CONCLUDING REMARKS ON DEVIANT ACTS

Persons concerned with the control of deviant acts are led, quite reasonably, to focus on aspects and conditions of human action that are capable of rather direct manipulation. Through control and manipulation by means of, typically, a bureaucratically organized program, it is hoped that the incidence of a particular act will be reduced, if not entirely eliminated. Although such a focus and its correlative perspective and procedures may be socially necessary and useful, it does not follow that the point of view thus generated is sufficiently broad so as to be synonymous with criteria of an adequate sociological account. The business of controlling deviance is not the same as the business of analyzing it as an aspect of human dealings. We should expect, therefore, that accounts useful or illuminating to the one will not necessarily be useful or illuminating to the other.

In viewing deviance simply as an aspect of human dealings—as a topic of analysis in the sociology business—it thus became relevant and reasonable to consider how deviant acts are connected to social organization in ways which are not immediately or feasibly manipulable (as well as in ways which are). When seen simply as a form of human activity, it is possible also to see ways in which essential conditions or facilitants of deviance are embedded deeply and fundamentally in conventional society. Deviant acts, as other acts, are connected to matters of self-esteem, threat and adventure; to conventional patterns of social organization and participation; to mundane matters of hardware and places; and to conventional topics of morality. Age-old persistent attempts and age-old persistent failures at control and elimination are perhaps best explained by these broader and underlying connections between deviant acts and social organization. Given the seeming pervasiveness of such connections, it might accurately be observed that the typical and mundane features of human societies themselves are the most fundamental facilitants of deviant acts. Anyone seeking to ensure their occurrence would be well advised to organize social life in very much the same manner as it is now organized.[7]

On a more methodological plane, note should again be made of the relative

---

[7] However, on the likely character of a deviance-free social order, see Taft and England, 1964:534–35.

imbalance in the amount of attention devoted above to features of Actor relative to features of Others, places and hardware. Note should be made also of the imbalance of attention given to Actor and Other relative to that given places and hardware. The rather scant attention accorded the latter two elements reflects what has been, in my opinion, the massively skewed attention of sociologists of deviance. It does not reflect any strong personal preference on my part for subjective matters. If most has been said about Actor, somewhat less about his Others and relatively little about hardware and places, it is because this has been the ordering of attention priorities among sociologists. The present attempt to draw sociological materials together unsurprisingly reflects this more general imbalance. The redressing of this imbalance is hopefully furthered by its identification.

Thus far the focus has been upon those deviant acts that are either a first commission for Actor or performed by him with sufficient infrequence that each engagement has a novel, unroutine, isolated or episodic character. Deviant acts of this sort represent the most amateur kinds of deviance. We turn now, in Part II, to considering facilitative circumstances under which amateur deviance may be worked up or transformed or processed into a stable pattern of conduct. That is, we will consider the circumstances that facilitate the assumption of a deviant identity.

THE ASSUMPTION
OF DEVIANT IDENTITY

The people we meet are the playwrights and the stage managers of our lives; they cast us in a role, and we play it whether we will or not. It is not so much the example of others we imitate as the reflection of ourselves in their eyes and the echo of ourselves in their words.

ERIC HOFFER

Eric Hoffer, *The Passionate State of Mind,* p. 81.

In order to discuss the assumption of deviant identity or roles, we must be particularly concerned with Others and the imputations they make of Actor. My focus on Others adopts—assumes to be true—a general principle, one that underlies almost all the literature on socialization as a general phenomenon. This principle asserts that, other things being equal, the greater the *consistency*, *duration* and *intensity* with which a definition is promoted by Others about an Actor, the greater the likelihood that an Actor will embrace that definition as truly applicable to himself.[1] Since we are concerned here with specific implications of this general principle for the

CHAPTER 6
SOCIAL IDENTIFICATION AS PIVOTALLY DEVIANT

analysis of the assumption of deviant roles, we will first examine social identification, focusing on some conditions that facilitate imputation of Actor as deviant; and second, escalation, focusing on some specific arrangements that facilitate or promote consistency, duration and intensity of definitions of an Actor as a pivotally deviant type of person.

However, before beginning these tasks, it will be necessary to introduce the reader to some basic facts and features of human social life. This is essential because the dynamics involved in the assumption of deviant identity represent merely one specific manifestation of some general features of the ways in which human beings organize their dealings with one another. This is also essential, and more importantly so, because a perspective of *distance* from human social life is necessary for an adequate understanding of all that follows. The basic features of human life must be wrenched from the submerged background of our out-of-awareness understandings and must be made consciously problematic. It is necessary that we—the reader and writer alike—achieve a wider bracketing of social life than is usual in our everyday dealings. We must achieve a socioanthropological perspective, as distinct from a societal or participant perspective. The uncustomary terms and concepts which follow in the section on identity are intended to provoke such distance—to provoke a long and broad view of the kind of business in which humans are engaged.

---

[1] Cf., in criminology, Sutherland and Cressey, 1966:Chap. 4, especially p. 82; and, regarding socialization generally, Goslin, ed., 1968; Brim and Wheeler, 1966; Clausen *et al.*, 1968; Kinch, 1963. As a socialization model, what follows here and in Part III is more applicable to social deviance of an "achieved" sort than to deviance that is more physically based, such as being blind or crippled. See, however, Lemert, 1951:Chap. 5, especially 111–30, on social identification, escalation and the social selves of the blind.

IDENTITY

SOCIAL CATEGORIES

We begin with the observation that there exists a most peculiar species of animal whose most distinctive characteristics include, among other things, the following: it walks on its hind legs, uses symbols and is extraordinarily sensitive to what the other animals of its kind think and feel about it. This animal is further distinguished by the assiduousness with which it feels a need linguistically to designate objects in the world. So it is that this creature has a category with which it designates its general kind of object and with which it sets itself off from all other objects in the world. The more esoterically inclined of these animals label the general category "Homo sapiens"; the more mundane dub the category merely "mankind," "human beings," "people" or—that vestige of male supremacy—"man."

This peculiar animal is not satisfied, however, with simply setting itself off from all the other kinds of objects in the world. Nor is it satisfied with the enterprise of making fine distinctions among and between all the objects that fall outside its own general category. This animal which calls itself man, or mankind, engages also in making distinctions *within* the category of its most general kind. One of the more popular subdivisions is based on differential contributions to what is identified as the reproductive process. The dimension of sex is thus divined, and there arises a division between the categories of "male" and "female." A second very widespread division identifies the amount of time human objects have existed and divides mankind on the dimension of age. Thus there are categories such as "child," "adolescent," "adult," etc:, the specific terms depending upon who is doing the discriminating and designating. Because it is possible for selected combinations of people to produce other people and to cooperate in managing their joint young products, and because it is possible for these same combinations of people to cooperate in the task of sheer survival, there exists yet another basis for further division, this time along the dimension of biological relationships of one to another. Thus there are categories of family or kin position.

Many units of kin occupying adjacent ground may come to see that particular territory as reasonably and legitimately theirs, setting it off (at least symbolically) from all other pieces of ground on the planet. As some kin groups come to dominate other kin groups, the claimed area may grow quite large, relative to the total space on the planet. Or, even if it is quite small, it may be seen as equally crucial (as, for example, with units such as neighborhood or even city blocks). Our animal may even get to feel that the location of one's residence on the planet is a crucially important dimension and come to distinguish categories of territorial habitation. Such a territorial category of mankind, settled in a place for a long period of time, may even come to feel that it has some special way of life that distinguishes "my kind of people" from all the rest of the people in the world. There can thus arise various categories of a dimension called "culture." As this animal moves about on the planet, differences in specific definitions of sex, age, kinship and territory may be seen as associated with differences in the color or form of the surface casing of the animal, and another dimension along which to divide kinds of people in the world appears, one sometimes called "race" or "ethnicity."

The process of extracting sustenance from the surface of the planet (or from other people) may place these two-legged animals in relation to one another such that it is felt reasonable to divide the general category yet again, this time along the dimension of how the materials necessary for physical survival are assembled. Such designations may be called jobs or occupations and in some societies may run into thousands upon thousands of distinctive categories. Such categories themselves have differential capacity to assemble resources. Some seem able to command the obedience of many of the other animals. Thus there can grow up another dimension of difference, designated by this animal with categories such as the more wealthy and the less wealthy, or the rich and the poor.

This species of animal, then, is the sort of creature that is constantly dividing itself into categories of "kinds of people" along dimensions such as sex, age, kin, territory, culture, race, work and material resources. In this context, the dimension of deviance or crime can be seen as similar to the dimensions just mentioned, and the categories of this dimension are equivalent to the categories of the more conventional dimensions. In the same way that people can be concerned with "male" and "female," they can also be concerned with other common-sense categories such as prostitute, mentally ill person, homosexual, murderer and the like. All categories of mankind are phenomenological constructs employed by the members of mankind.

CATEGORICAL CLUSTERING

Having complicated its world by discriminating all these and other dimensions and designating numerous categories along them, humans then try to simplify the world again through the process of creating, both perceptually and empirically, a *clustering* of selected categories of some dimensions. So it is that a significant proportion of the species feels, for example, that animals of a certain category of the dimension of race should reside in certain categories of the dimension of territory and should assemble sustenance by occupying themselves with certain categories of the dimension of work. More concretely, some of the species feel that what are called "whites" should reside in "nice" neighborhoods and make a living from some of the "cleaner" kinds of work; correspondingly, other categories of race have their appropriate other places and other categories of work. Or, some of the species may feel that certain categories of age are most appropriately clustered with certain kinship categories and with certain occupational categories. When these presumed proprieties of clustering are breached, comment and perhaps punishment are undertaken as means of forcing these erroneously clustered instances of the species back into a proper or acceptable cluster of displayed categories. We see such a concern on those occasions when for example, newspapers deem as newsworthy the fact that two married 16-year-olds are publishers-editors of a town newspaper;[2] or when it is deemed newsworthy—even to the extent of requiring an accompanying picture—when a 16-year-old girl marries a 62-year-old man, thereby becoming "stepmother to five, grandmother to another five and a great-grandmother."[3] These and numerous other occurrences are seen as news and as worthy and in need of reporting and comment because they violate shared conceptions of appropriate categorical clustering. Such cluster violations are also, of course, objects of many kinds of punishment—the reason, I suspect, that the 62-year-old husband just mentioned felt it necessary to tell reporters, "We'll make a go of it if they leave us alone."

If categories begin to cluster—both perceptually *and* empirically—we can conceive the possibility that a very large number of categories along the most fundamental dimensions can pile upon one another, as it were. Thus in an exaggerated case the human animals in the category of immigrant (on the dimension nativity) can be almost exclusively of a particular category of race or ethnicity and also almost exclusively of low education. They can be also almost exclusively those who occupy certain territories (say, inner-city areas); almost exclusively those who work in low-paid, unskilled jobs or who are unemployed; and almost exclusively those who practice a given category of religion and/or culture.

Pivotal Categories and Consistency

When the categories of a set of dimensions begin, empirically, to pile upon one another—that is, to cluster—this peculiar animal not only perceives and comes to expect the clustering, but it introduces a further simplification. For public purposes and on occasion of face-to-face engagement, *one* of the clustered categories is singled out and treated as the most important and significant feature of the person or persons being dealt with. It is seen as defining the character of those animals whose categories are so clustered. That is, there comes to be a *pivotal category* that defines "who this person is" or "who those people are."

[2] Sudomier, 1965.
[3] Associated Press wire release, *Detroit Free Press,* July 21, 1965, p. 2.

CONSISTENCY OF SOCIAL
CATEGORIES

Having taken the step of allowing one category to be primarily definitive of "who" or "what" an Actor is in a defined situation, there can then begin the reverse game of scrutinizing Actor for the degree to which his other categories are appropriately consistent with the category taken to be pivotal. It can thus be believed that doctors are appropriately white, male and middle-aged and that they reside in upper-income neighborhoods. Should a doctor in America be female or Black or very young or live in a slum, some witnessing sectors of mankind may take this as a sign of something being amiss. They may feel that all is not right with this person who claims to be a doctor. He is, in some sense, an impostor.

Further, should an Actor, knowing that such consistency will be assessed, be desirous of receiving a particular pivotal imputation, he may undertake to manipulate categorical occupancy to achieve consistency. Where consistency exists, there can even be concerted attempts to announce that fact. It is no trivial matter, for example, that aspirants to public office take great pains to inform the other animals of their record of creditable public service and (to point up the consistency) of their properly married state. Their claim to fatherhood must also be announced and the names and ages of their legitimate children made public. Sometimes photographs of these offspring are also produced, possibly as testimony to the claimed paternal facts. Although marriage and children are not prima-facie necessities for assuming the category of public officeholder, politicians and the public alike are well aware that they are often a package deal.

CONSISTENCY OF PERSONAL
QUALITIES

Pivotal categories and their appropriately correlative categories carry with them, in addition, a cluster of what are thought of as properly consistent "personal qualities." Produced typically as adjectives, there come to be imputations of typical "physical and personality features" associated with pivotal categories such as male and female, child and adult, father and mother, Harlemite and Greenwich Villager, Black and White, doctor and lawyer.[4] All such labels evoke a range of adjectival designations of "what they are like." It is on this basis

[4] Although surprisingly unattended to by scholars of deviance, the processes explicated here have been intensively (if not extensively) pursued by social psychologists under such rubrics as social perception, person perception and stereotyping. For recent summaries see McCall and Simmons, 1966:Chap. 5; R. Brown, 1965:Chaps. 4 and 12; Newcomb, Turner and Converse, 1965:Chap. 6; Secord and Backman, 1964:Chap. 2; Tagiuri and Petrullo, 1958. The best sociologically grounded discussion of these phenomena is still to be found in E. C. Hughes, 1945, 1949. Relative to deviance, good beginning investigations have been performed by Sudnow, 1965; Simmons, 1965; Scheff, 1966; Kitsuse, 1962.

that a Hollywood violation of such typification can be seen as humorous and worthy of note.

> "East Berlin?" asks sweet and innocent research assistant Julie Andrews in [the motion picture] *Torn Curtain,* upon discovery that her fiance, virile and presumably patriotic nuclear physicist Paul Newman is furtively planning to fly there from a scientists' convention in Copenhagen. "But . . ." (quiver of lips, flutter of eyelids), "that's behind the iron curtain."
> Right! Miss Andrews knows her geopolitics. East Berlin *is* behind the iron curtain; and Newman, his cortex crammed with America's plans for an antimissile missile, may well be the most dastardly defector in cold-war history. But then again he may not be. Defectors do not have neon blue eyes or strong chins. Defectors are sneaks. Defectors are defectives. (*Newsweek,* August 8, 1966.)

Of course, the obvious inconsistency between Mr. Newman and the "known" personal characteristics associated with the pivotal category of defector provides a clue to later developments. Mr. Newman, it turns out, is a heroic counterspy, a pivotal category much more appropriate to his personal (and physical) features.

CONSISTENCY SPECIALISTS

In societies where social and personal categories have become rather complex, there tend to arise specialists in discerning and communicating correlations among such categories. These specialists, sometimes called "behavioral scientists," compute correlations when it is possible and guess at and impute correlations when it is not. There can thus come to be books with such titles as *Social Characteristics of American Negroes* or *Sexual Behavior and Personality Characteristics,* the latter of which could be described in advertising blurbs as "correlating personality characteristics with sexual behavior, explaining *what kinds* of people participate in lesbian and homosexual acts, in masturbation, sado-masochism, extramarital sex acts, and the meaning of different positions during intercourse." By the same sort of alchemy, simple statistical descriptions of the incidence of *deviant acts* slip easily into descriptions of deviant people. Consider this excerpt from a leading text on criminology:

> Generally the daily incidence of serious crime was highest during the hours from 8 P.M. to midnight when approximately 70 per cent of the daily offenses were cleared by the police. . . . These are the hours when muggers, rapists, holdup men, automobile thieves and burglars are active under cover of darkness. (Johnson, 1964:66.)

Acts of mugging, rape, robbery, automobile theft and burglary here become more than acts: they are perpetrated by *people who are* "muggers, rapists, holdup men, automobile thieves and burglars."

AMBIGUITY AND CONSISTENCY

It is possible to imagine a society wherein all possible social categories combine *randomly* and are *perceived* as likely to present themselves in any individual in a random fashion. Thus participants in civil society would not, for example, presume that doctors are male, that male children of low-income families are delinquent, that females are nonintellectual, that "Negroes" are lazy and the like. Knowing one category would not provide a basis upon which a perceiver could feel it possible to guess or predict, with some propriety or certainty, *other* categories of a given individual. This would be a society without categorical clustering, for no given category would be seen as usually or frequently or properly combining with any other given category (E. C. Hughes, 1945). In fact, no such society exists or is likely to exist, probably because lack of actual or perceptual association among categories creates a condition of very *low predictability* in dealing with other persons. It creates excessive ambiguity. Given a lack of association, knowing only one or a few categories of other persons would provide little guide for activating a sufficiently broad repertoire of interaction devices for managing these other persons. A state of excessive ambiguity approaches something like a Durkheimian state of anomie and is accompanied by anxiety which is both too intense and too prolonged (Suttles, 1968). Such a state is personally and socially intolerable for the human organism.

Given knowledge of one or a few categories, humans want to be able to *predict*, with reasonable accuracy, what the people they encounter will be like in terms of other categories and in terms of personal qualities. Concern over clustering is such a fundamental feature of the social order that we find it built into such mundane matters as employment questionnaires or vitaes, newspaper stories and social scientific research instruments. In the absence of some specific detailing of categorical clusters, would-be perceivers of a person feel uninformed. The person becomes an *ambiguous* object; how he should be treated becomes problematic. The communication of some combination or constellation of categories allows others to build up an "image" of the person. They can activate a repertoire of ways in which to treat this Other and develop expectations of how the Other will act. To know that a human being is female, sixty and a maid activates a considerably different treatment repertoire than knowing that the human is male, forty and a Ford executive.

PIVOTAL CATEGORIES AND ESSENTIAL NATURE

"HE REALLY *is*. . . ."

The phenomenon of humans adopting a category as pivotal and scrutinizing all other categories in terms of their consistency with it, implies, in practice, that whatever is taken as pivotal *is* Actor—*is* his essential nature or core being.

If a human's correlative categories are discerned to be inconsistent with his presumed essential nature, then investigation and manipulation must be undertaken to determine what kind of person he is—"really." Sometimes it may be possible to define such discrepancies as especially excusable, "actually" irrelevant, "really" unimportant or justified as the exception which proves the rule. When such strategies fail, however, it becomes necessary to assign Actor to a different pivotal category with which his complement of categorical placements is more practically, if not ideally, consistent. This is the case because, as noted, pivotal categories and their consistent correlatives appear to be viewed by humans not simply as convenient and frequently erroneous simplifications indulged in for the purposes of maintaining a workable social order, but, rather, as depictions of what people "really" and "in fact" are. "He tries very hard but he is really only a B student." "Despite what he says, he is in fact a thief and a murderer." "I know she seems OK, but she's actually a whore." Such statements make the assumption that, in the case of personal claims to some other pivotal category or in the case of conduct that would suggest definition as some other kind of social object, there is actually (or after all or really or in fact) a something, a core, a category that the person *is* despite any indications to the contrary. There is an underlying or even hidden consistency that is at least potentially discernible; there is a *special* core being, as it were, that will and does manifest itself. This core being is not simply common humanity but some much more restricted category that differentiates the person from others. Discovery of the person's "actual" core or pivotal category, his true essentiality, may require, especially in modern times, a detailed life history and even a battery of psychological tests, but it can be found. Witch trials with dunking tests and psychiatric examinations with psychological tests are alike in their assumption that, although very esoteric and complicated detection devices may sometimes be required to turn up personal essentiality, it can, nonetheless, be discovered, and assignment to a "true" pivotal category can be made.[5]

Pivotal categories and their correlative features provide *models* of the characteristics which are to be attended to when encountering other humans. The available range of such models will typically permit humans to assign their fellows to the appropriate ones and to operate in everyday interaction in terms of these assignments. Pivotal categories and their correlative features provide models in the sense that they specify relatively abstract sets of characteristics in terms of which an instant human body can be assessed and appropriately assigned.

---

[5] Professional discerners of essentiality can, of course, also become inventors of *new* kinds of core being. Such inventions are, in turn, employed by their creators in discerning the "true nature" of encountered humans. Cesare Lombroso and Sigmund Freud were among the early modern giants in an inventive tradition that continues unabated, although the substance of the essentialities discerned have shifted somewhat. (See, e.g., materials cited, footnote 9, Chap. 2.) It is peculiarly appropriate that these early inventors of identity were historical contemporaries of the giants among mechanical inventors, namely Thomas Edison, Orville and Wilbur Wright and Henry Ford.

SOCIAL AND PERSONAL IDENTIFICATION

When a human's features "map on to"—show a correspondence to—an operative pivotal category and its correlative features, the human so successfully assessed may be said to have been *socially identified*. That is, social identification has occurred in the sense that those making the assignment have at least tentatively concluded that this instant human is *an instance of* the more abstract model. Such placement is likely, however, to be more than a judgment that the instant body is similar to or "practically equivalent" to a model. As noted, it is likely to be a judgment that Actor *is* the pivotal category to which he has been assigned. Thus it is said that someone "*is* a juvenile delinquent," "*is* mentally ill," "*is* an alcoholic," "*is* a prostitute."

But humans assess not only the bodies they encounter for correspondence to models of pivotal categories; they also assess themselves. They assign themselves as instances of, or as being, one or another kind of social object. This subjective process may be referred to as *personal identification* (Cf., Strauss, 1959; Foote, 1951; Kuhn and McPartland, 1954; Berger, 1966; Dennis, 1960).

PROSAIC IMMEDIACY

Models of pivotal categories and their consistent categories are not simply, or only, abstract and rather inarticulate imageries used vaguely by people in general at the most abstract levels of society. They are part of the intimate and moment-to-moment assumptions about the nature of persons that guide even the seemingly most trivial of interactions. The stranger on the street who asks for a match and provokes by his presence and request an experience of fear has generated that fear out of the other's instant and out of awareness assumptions about him. Sex, age, dress, grooming and a host of gestures are assessed in lightning manner and rapidly compared with a repertoire of stereotypic pivotal categories, and within a second a response is produced.

Nor are such models merely "carried in the head," as it were. They receive organizational expression through being built into the physical structures of a society and through embodiment in social rules. Every set of social rules and ecological arrangements presumes a theory of the *character* or essentiality of the persons being ruled and arranged. Constellations of ecological arrangements and socially constructed rules build in a more or less explicit conception of the holistic nature of the humans dealt with. Thus, for example, one might read the typical social control arrangements of many college settings to discern the presumed character of those who use such settings, i.e., students. In-class, monitored examinations presume that students are *dishonest* and will cheat if not watched like hawks. Lecture courses in which Actors sit quietly while a stranger rambles on presume that the listeners are *passive* and lacking in independence and "free spirit." The felt necessity to examine on course reading to ensure that the reading is performed presumes that these Actors are *untrustworthy*. Assignment of "secondary literature" and "interesting material" with the knowledge that this is not actually the "best" material presumes a *disinterested* and relatively unscholarly clientele.

That is, social control practices involve not merely rules and ecological arrangements but something broader. They are not merely elements of a "participation contract" but "a definition of the participant's nature" (Goffman, 1961a:179).

> Built right into the social arrangements of an organization . . . is a thoroughly embracing conception of the member—and not merely a conception of him qua member, but behind this a conception of him qua human being. (Goffman, 1961a:179–80.)

> A self . . . virtually awaits the individual entering a position; he need only conform to the pressures on him and he will find a *me* ready-made for him. In the language of Kenneth Burke, doing is being. (Goffman, 1961b:87–88.)

This is perhaps most easily seen in those instances where Actors feel themselves to be drastically different kinds of people than the organization defines them as being. As Goffman notes, a pacifist's refusal to register for the draft and an imprisoned conscientious objector's refusal of yard privileges or art materials are refusals to accept the pivotal category accorded them and the correlative features implied by it. Since cooperation, in these cases, is a correlative feature of the organization's definition of "C.O." or "prisoner," to be cooperative is to communicate a level of acceptance of the organization's view of the type of people with which it deals. In the same manner, the human animals pivotally defined as students who "play the game" in some measure assent to the correlative attributions assigned them as passive, disinterested and untrustworthy cheats.

The way in which a full range of social and personal imputations is engineered into the organization of social life is seen also in those rare instances in which social standing and social worlds cut across one another. The following account of Teamster chief Jimmy Hoffa's entrance to a federal prison conveys, by its acute incongruity, a strong sense of what is believed to be the character of "typical prisoners."

> He will be confined for five to seven days in "A&O"—admission and orientation . . . . [A part of] the briefing will cover educational opportunities.
>   Jimmy Hoffa, who dropped out of school after the ninth grade, can earn a high school diploma at Lewisburg [prison] if he wants to.
>   There are also college level courses, but these can't be built toward a degree.

Hoffa, the nation's leading practicing expert on the trucking industry, even can take a course in traffic management.

Successful completion of the course would qualify Hoffa for work at the terminal near Lewisburg of "one of the nation's largest motor carriers" under Lewisburg's work-release program.

The Teamster boss, who has expressed contempt for testing programs for employees, will be tested heavily in the next few days.

In addition to the aptitude tests Hoffa has objected to, there will be batteries of psychological tests designed to elicit hints about a wrongdoer's compulsions.

A social worker will interview him and compile the story of his life. If the tests and interviews indicate therapy, Hoffa will be sent to see the prison psychiatrist.

"All of his old habits are washed out. It helps to make a new routine," the warden said [of the A&O period]. (*Detroit Free Press*, March 8, 1967.)

This set of activities quite explicitly defines its human objects as probably defective in a variety of ways. It performs the prosaically immediate work of identifying exactly how the bodies subjected to it are consistent with the pivotal imputation of prisoner or criminal.

SOCIAL IDENTIFICATION AS PIVOTALLY DEVIANT

Against the background of the foregoing conceptions of how humans deal with one another, we may now turn to the more specific topic of pivotally deviant categories. Within a conception of a socialization model which assumes that acceptance of a personal identity by Actor is facilitated when Others impute it, the factors upon which the initiation of that imputation depends become centrally problematic. We want to inquire, then, into the circumstances that will increase the probability that an imputation of pivotal deviance will be made by anyone at all and, if made, into the circumstances which will promote the acceptance of it by yet other persons in Actor's milieu.

KNOWLEDGE

HISTORICAL VARIABILITY

An obvious but fundamental first circumstance is that, whatever the pivotal deviant category, it must appear among the repertoire of types of possible persons possessed by a possibly imputing set of Others. If possibly imputing Others do not *know* of the pivotal category, they can hardly interpret experience in terms of it. Thus, for example, part of the reason for past differences in rural-urban rates of delinquency may have to do with the failure of rural people to employ the pivotal category of juvenile delinquent in coding juvenile misconduct. If rural folk tend to view such misconduct as merely an expression of normal youthful exuberance, and if they are unaware that the same acts could be viewed as indicative of a pivotal category called "juvenile delinquent," then rates of official delinquency and the number of "delinquent boys" will be low in rural areas. Recent increases in rates of rural delinquency may as well reflect an increasing awareness of the pivotal category of juvenile delinquent as a way to identify those involved in youthful misconduct, as much as a change in the true rate of offenses.

In a modern society characterized by almost universal state education and by exposure of the population to mass communication, the number of such universally known deviant pivotal categories may be increasing. Local pockets of ignorance and provincialism, both urban and rural, crumble under the penetrative power of large organizations of all kinds. It becomes possible under these circumstances to create (or abolish) deviant (and other) identities in relatively short periods of time. At the same time that the pivotal category "witch" is disappearing and "Negro" is under assault, other types are swiftly being created and disseminated. Most recently the pivotal categories of "high school dropout," "bigot," "hippy" and "Hell's Angel" (Thompson, 1967) have entered the popular lexicon of disapproved types of persons. Further, the psychiatric establishment and its allies vigorously disseminate conceptions of certain acts as criteria of various kinds of mental illnesses, categories of mental illness being themselves of relatively recent vintage, although of growing currency. Surveys taken between 1950 and the early sixties, in which people were invited to impute mental illness to fictitious portraits of "juvenile character disorder," "anxiety character neurotic," "alcoholic," "simple schizophrenic" and others have demonstrated a rather marked increase in "the public's readiness to see . . . behavior [in the presented sketches] as mentally ill" (Dohrenwend and Chin-Shong, 1967:422).

Social organizational sources

If categories of deviance can come and go in public awareness, the question is raised of the conditions under which these changes take place. Such changes will bear upon the probability of Actor's identification as an instance of some kind of deviant person. One of the most important implications of the seemingly banal observation that what is deviant is relative to a defined system is that, for most existing categories of deviance within a society, one is likely to be able to find in the society's history a time when the category did not exist, or, if it did, when its use was confined to parochial social groupings. Toward the end of the last century in America, for example, the juvenile delinquent did not exist. There were at that time conceptions only of criminals. To the degree that this pivotally deviant category was alive at all, it was nurtured only in the minds of social reformers who wanted to create a specialized legal apparatus to deal with certain children as kinds of people who were different from adults. And they were quite successful, for, as the new century began, many states in quick succession passed laws creating special courts to handle what came to be officially considered juvenile delinquents.

Prior to the advent of a category in public consciousness, there is, sociologically speaking, no deviance (in the sense of deviant identities) of the particular kind. That is, it does not exist when it has not been "worked up" or articulated such that it is possible to identify human bodies as instances of it. One of the more interesting facets of the sociology of deviance is the concern with historical circumstances and processes by which a category enters the coding scheme of the participants in a society. Although still scattered, a number of works have attempted to trace the development of such categories as drug addict, marijuana user, vagrant, mentally ill and thief.[6] One key pattern highlighted in such sociohistorical studies has been that of social enterprise or *moral entrepreneurship*, wherein some people come to feel that there is "X" deviant in the world and set about vigorously propagandizing others as to his existence and evil character and as to the necessity to do something about him. That is, categories of deviants do not just appear naturally. Social action has to be mobilized and zealously prosecuted if a new conception is to be foisted upon the larger mass of indifferent and otherwise preoccupied members of the body politic (H. S. Becker, 1963:Chaps. 7 and 8; Erikson, 1966).

As should be the case with all reasonably construed analytic fields, at some point the chain of casual links leads to a different level of concepts and questions. Thus when we begin to focus upon the work of conventional Others in promoting acceptance of new categories of deviants, we move somewhat out of the field of deviance per se and into the traditional concerns of sociological specialties dealing with social movements, social trends and macrosociology more generally. I will not push further along this causal chain, save to note one additional key topic at the level of concern with social movements. This is the question of the larger macrosocial conditions under which such movements are themselves generated. Why, for example, at the turn of the 20th century in America did there come to be an organized concern with treating children under a special set of legal rules and with viewing them as different kinds of creatures under the law? Or, what were the social conditions in the first two decades in the 20th century in America that could spawn so many movements concerned with imbibing alcoholic fluids and with promoting an effort to outlaw such fluids?

Appropriate answers to these kinds of questions involve reference to the organization of the economy, the family, the distribution of ethnic and religious

---

[6] See H. S. Becker, 1963:Chap. 7; Chambliss, 1964; Hall, 1939; K. Davis, 1938; Gursslin, Hunt and Roach, 1959–60; Foucault, 1967; Szasz, 1961:Part I; Sutherland, 1950; Dickson, 1968; Lindesmith and Strauss, 1968:401–5; Lindesmith, 1968:Part II; Cohen, 1966:31–36; Erikson, 1966. See also, the description provided by Thompson (1967) of how the mass media were able in 1964–65 to create the category "motorcycle outlaw" or Hell's Angel.

groups, the rate of urbanization and the like—the range of variables conventionally identified as the central subject matter of sociology.   Thus with reference to the questions posed, it has been argued that a belief in the special nature and treatment of children arises under conditions of their progressive exclusion from the economic process under the impact of increasing complexity of technology and in response to the coming of labor unions (which had to worry more about fathers working steadily for a living wage than about the employment of sons).   The label "juvenile delinquent" arose in the context of the introduction of a wide range of "child welfare" legislation which, among other things, excluded children from many kinds of gainful employment and forced them to attend public schools.   Not having access to the former and disinclined to the latter, children were set free like an army upon the land. Juvenile delinquency labels and laws were one formal way to attempt to control this newly created under-enmeshed stratum.   (Cf., the discussion in Chap. 2 of fear, power, organization and the name of the conflict.)

With reference to the coming of legal restrictions on alcohol, some sociologists have suggested that Prohibition was a by-product or symbolic expression of larger shifts in power taking place in America in the early part of the century.   While 19th-century America was dominated by the rural, Protestant, northern European agrarian sectors of the country, the influx of Catholic and southern European immigrants at the turn of the century and afterward began a shift of power to the urban industrial sectors.   The Catholic and southern European immigrants happened to have somewhat different attitudes toward alcoholic beverages than did the rural Protestants.   In the power struggles that ensued (and still furtively survive), the rural elements came to define the use of alcohol as epitomizing what they saw as the debilitating and dissolute characteristics of the urban population.   Thus there arose organized expressions of such moral sentiments in such famous movements as the Anti-Saloon League and the Women's Christian Temperance Union (Gusfield, 1963, 1967).

Sociologists who have undertaken analyses of this type have been particularly fond of noting that moral entrepreneurs often have a narrower and more self-interested concern with the deviants they seek to create than they are willing to acknowledge.   Moral enterprise often predicates its legitimacy on a concern for "problem people" who are doing harm to themselves or others or who are being victimized or harmed by someone else.   Scrutinizing the social interests of those who proclaim this about others, more cynical sociologists have suggested that a weighty element of self-interest often underlies this altruism (H. S. Becker, 1963:147–52).   So it can be suggested that moral concern over the welfare of children among unionists was conveniently congruent with union interest in cutting down the labor supply, thereby forcing up the level of wages and the availability of jobs.   Moral concern among rural Protestants over the "self-destructive" doings of urban Catholics was conveniently congruent with reasserting and maintaining the dominance of Protestant small-town America (Gusfield, 1963).

Reasonableness

It is possible, however, to know of a given pivotal category but still not to believe that it is "real" or "reasonable" or ever relevant for purposes of identifying known others. The classic category of "witch" is thus well known but has of late lost its "reasonableness" (cf., the period of its popularity reviewed by Erikson, 1966). As is perhaps most evident in contemporary America, some persons who have knowledge of psychiatric pivotal categories do not accept them as reasonable constructions of "kinds of people." It is necessary, therefore, for those who know a category to have a certain amount of faith in it, or, at least, if they are not personally taken with its validity, to be cynical enough to use it to manipulate others. So it is that some hypercynical sophisticates who spurn psychiatric categories may nevertheless use them in the presence of believing Others to discredit a third party. It is perhaps more typical for "knowers," especially lay knowers, to be rather ambivalent about the reasonableness of a category of deviance. They may alternate between thinking that there really is such a thing and wondering if it is not, in some sense, an "artificial" construction. However, under the press of managing the Actors of their world, such Others seem likely to squelch such doubts in favor of the social control gains derived from having a firm faith in a category.

A belief among a population at large in the "reality" or "reasonableness" of a category seems best fostered under circumstances of the adoption and promotion of the category by well-financed elite groups, especially elite groups which control the means of mass communication. Such elites speak, in some sense, with authority. It well behooves the recipients of their messages to accept these messages as true facts about the world. The degree to which special groups, promoting one or another conception of what is deviant, complain about the difficulties in getting their messages across should not detract attention from the rather major successes they have enjoyed. The rather widespread beliefs that there are obviously mentally ill persons and that there are obviously juvenile delinquents are among their more recent successes in making constructions seem reasonable.[7]

Prevalent Sensitivity

The collective bearers of a category or categories of deviance are likely to vary in the degree to which they are disposed to find instances of even that which everyone knows about and feels to be reasonable. In a complex society, social differentiation by occupation and other pursuits may result in segments

---

[7] See further, Clinard's (1968:702–14) review of general public education.

of the population being rather insensitive in their everyday lives to discovering instances of those deviant categories they know about and feel to be reasonable. They can be "turned off" for coding, such that much escapes their attention. The greater the number of Others in a society who are not "turned off"—who are sensitively disposed to coding—and the larger the portion of their days they are so disposed, the greater the probability that Actor will be identified as an instance of a deviant category.

IMPUTATIONAL SPECIALISTS:
NUMBERS

It would appear dubiously facilitative to rely completely on everyday citizens for imputations of pivotal deviance. They appear too ready to code potentially "deviant" emissions as simple variants of normality (e.g., Yarrow *et al.*, 1955). Immersed in conventional pursuits, the man on the street has too little time or interest to be a fully effective coder, except, perhaps, during periods of "crackdown" on some form of deviance (cf., Erikson, 1966). In all of social life, a high probability for the occurrence of a set of activities is best ensured by giving a set of Others some interest in, and pay-off for, performing them. In the same way that profit in industrial manufacture ensures a flow of goods, the flow of imputations of pivotal deviance can be facilitated by paying people to spend a major portion of their time making them. As the number of *imputational specialists* increases in a society, it is likely that the number of people imputed as deviant will also increase. A study of juvenile justice in two southern California communities thus found that although

> one of the two communities . . . (Community A) had both a slightly larger population and a higher adult crime rate . . . [it] had . . . 3200 current cases of juveniles suspected or confirmed to be offenders . . . [while] Community B, on the other hand, had approximately 8000 current suspected or confirmed juvenile cases. Community A has two juvenile officers on its staff, while Community B has five juvenile officers. (Kitsuse and Cicourel, 1963:138.)

The growing army of social workers, psychologists, psychiatrists, police, etc., constitutes a stratum with a precise interest in ensuring a flow of persons defined as deviant. The training undergone by such specialists creates a stratum whose aim it is to discover "out there" in the empirical world those sorts of people they have been trained to see.[8] As more of them become better trained

---

[8] And, ironically, at least some imputational specialists become so sensitive and so zealous that they code well beyond their occupational obligation to do so—as with those social workers and psychiatrists who impute their friends and spouses in addition to the humans presented professionally. An obligation is thus translated into a mandate. In so doing, they exercise the mantle bequeathed by Sigmund Freud, the modern initiator of promiscuous imputation. His talent has been delightfully epitomized in this account of the young Gordon Allport's encounter with him in 1920.

and organized—that is, more professional—their sensitivity could well increase. This possibility is suggested by a study of two police systems which varied in whether or not they had developed specialized juvenile bureaus.

> The department whose juvenile officers had more advanced and professional training (and thus were more prepared to consider delinquents as problem children) . . . had much higher rates of arrest for juveniles than a department in which these conditions did not hold true. (Wheeler, 1967:662; Wilson, 1968.)

IMPUTATIONAL SPECIALISTS:
STRATEGIC DISPERSION

In addition to their sheer numbers, the facilitative significance of sensitive specialists is increased by their institutional and territorial dispersion. The psychiatrist in the factory and the social worker (or even policeman) in the school, by their penetration of new institutional spheres, increase the visibility of the conduct of a larger number of Actors. They thereby collectively increase the number and range of Actors who are likely to be imputed. Such a dispersion of specialists gives rise, in turn, to opportunities for collaboration and cooperation among them, even further increasing the possibilities for imputation. Recent research on police vice-squad operations in two cities thus discovered an interesting pattern of cooperation in one of the cities between the police and the welfare office in connection with cases of statutory rape.

> Despite the fact that Mountain City's population outnumbers Westville's by more than two to one, during 1961 there were forty fewer cases of statutory rape reported to the Mountain City police. The Mountain City family support division does not systematically report violations it discovers while taking welfare applications, and it is largely to this difference

---

With a callow forwardness characteristic of age twenty-two, I wrote to Freud announcing that I was in Vienna and implied that no doubt he would be glad to make my acquaintance. I received a kind reply in his own handwriting inviting me to come to his office at a certain time. Soon after I had entered the famous red burlap room with pictures of dreams on the wall, he summoned me to his inner office. He did not speak to me but sat in an expectant silence, for me to state my mission. I was not prepared for silence and had to think fast to find a suitable conversation gambit. I told him of an episode on the tram car on my way to his office. A small boy about four years of age had displayed a conspicuous dirt phobia. He kept saying to his mother, "I don't want to sit there . . . don't let that dirty man sit beside me." To him everything was *schmutzig*. His mother was a well-starched *Hausfrau*, so dominant and purposive looking that I thought the cause and effect apparent.

When I finished my story, Freud fixed his kindly therapeutic eyes upon me and said, "And was that little boy you?" Flabbergasted and feeling a bit guilty, I contrived to change the subject. While Freud's misunderstanding of my motivation was amusing, it also started a deep train of thought. I realized that he was accustomed to neurotic defenses and that my manifest motivation (a sort of rude curiosity and youthful ambition) escaped him. For therapeutic progress he would have to cut through my defenses, but it so happened that therapeutic progress was not here an issue. (Allport, 1968:383–84.)

in policy that the different outcome is attributable. (Skolnick and Wood-worth, 1967:133.)

Institutional dispersion and collaboration are associated with patterns of terri-torial dispersion. Surveillance for deviant types tends to be highly uneven within human settlements, concentrating in areas of high residential density and use and declining in more sparsely employed zones. Public more than private territories come under surveillance for "things amiss" and "suspicious persons." To the degree that sensitivity is territorially skewed, the likelihood of imputa-tion is correspondingly altered. On the basis of observing two groups of young males, whom he calls the Saints and the Roughnecks, William Chambliss con-cludes that each group engaged in much the same sort of indiscretions, an im-portant difference between them residing in the circumstances of surveillance in which they performed their escapades. Despite relative similarity in behav-ior, the members of one group were imputed to be delinquent types, whereas the others were seen as forming the youthful backbone of the community.

> The single most important factor determining the differential treatment of the two gangs was that one gang was infinitely more *visible* than the other. This differential visibility, in turn, was a direct function of the eco-nomic standing of the families of the two groups. The Saints had access to automobiles and would, as a result, remove themselves from the sight of the community when they engaged in their recreation. In even so commonplace a decision as where to go and have a milk shake after school, the Saints stayed away from the mainstream of community life. Their favorite hangout was a small cafe on the north side of town. The Roughnecks, on the other hand, could not make it to the edge of town. . . . The center of town was the only practical place for them to meet since their homes were scattered throughout the town and any noncen-trally located meeting place put an undue hardship on some of the mem-bers. It was therefore only reasonable for the Roughnecks to congregate in an area that was crowded, where everyone in the community passed frequently, including teachers and law enforcement officers. They could easily see the Roughnecks hanging around the drugstore. Or, since the drugstore owner did not like their hanging around inside, they were even more visible standing along the wall outside the drugstore . . . .
>   The Roughnecks, of course, made themselves even more visible by making remarks to passers-by and by occasionally getting into fights on the corner. Meanwhile, just as regularly, the Saints were either at the cafe on the edge of town or in the pool hall at the other edge of the town. Without any particular realization that they were thereby making them-selves less conspicuous, the Saints, in effect, were able to hide their wast-ing of time. Not only were they removed from the mainstream of traffic, but they were almost always inside a building. The cafe owner did not particularly like having them around since they did cause disruptions to his business. But neither was he willing to throw them out since they

represented a substantial expenditure of money on food and drink in this place. The pool hall owner, of course, was thoroughly pleased to have them as often as they wanted.

Then, on their escapades, the Saints once again were relatively invisible, since they recreated in a large urban center. And here, too, they were mobile, roaming the city, rarely going into the same area twice. The Roughnecks could not so easily manage a trip to the big city, and consequently, they engaged in their activities under the eyes of an already suspicious and suspecting set of community members, including, of course, the police. (Chambliss, 1967a:30–32.)

A pattern such as this one explicated by Chambliss suggests that imputations of pivotal deviance might be increased by a more even distribution of territorial surveillance, perhaps to the point of monitoring not only public but also private places. Any effort to increase the prevalence of imputational specialists would, of course, have to deal with interest groups in whose behalf the dispersion of such specialists is already protectively skewed. The sorts of deviance which are rampant among higher-income families and occupations could provide a rich field for imputing pivotal deviance, but the better-off classes are unlikely to abide any extension of imputational activity that might make them significant objects of concern. And, of course, coding everyone all the time might well produce much more deviance than anyone could possibly want or need.

SIMPLE INDICATORS

As schemes for the identification of human bodies, pivotal categories and their correlative features may be viewed as a set of instructions for the coding of the raw emissions of persons. Similar to coding schemes of other sorts, they can vary as to the number of qualitative features of the information necessary to accomplish a given placement. Given this variance, it can be asked, what organization of indicators most increases the likelihood that human bodies will be coded as instances of a widely known and believed in category? Phrased generally, imputation of pivotal deviance is most facilitated under conditions of minimal indicators, minimal here being used in two senses.

SMALL NUMBER REQUIRED

First, imputation is facilitated through having a very small number of necessary indicators. The ideal number is perhaps zero, but, of course, that would lead to such unpredictability as to be unworkable (cf., the problems experienced by the Puritans in identifying witches, Erikson, 1966). More practical is the use of only one or a few indicators as sufficient for making a pivotal imputation. The following coding practice, said to have existed among some ethnic groups at one time, seems rather well constructed for the facilitation of the imputation of "prostitute."

> In some . . . ethnic groups, such as the Italian, a rigid dichotomy was culturally drawn between "good" girls and "bad" girls. Parents customarily refused to forgive a single misstep, even assuming that if a girl stayed away from home overnight she was guilty of illicit sex behavior. The behavior consequently was unequivocally reflected in the parental reaction as that of the "bad" girl or the folk equivalent of the prostitute. (Lemert, 1951:269.)

In some American cities there have existed Youth Referral Programs wherein the police release information on encountered juveniles to helping organizations. In a program of this kind in Philadelphia, the fact of a child's apprehension was released to members of a "volunteer visitor" program who would then visit the home of the child in order to "do good." As part of their cooperation, the police filled out referral forms on the children, apparently without regard for degree of the child's asserted guilt or seriousness of his alleged deviant act of delinquency. As described by the director of the Philadelphia American Liberties Union (ACLU), the forms so released to volunteer visitors and to school authorities were designed such that there was

> only a single line of about two and a half inches to describe the "reason for referral." If the child was discharged at the police station, the word, "Remedial" is checked, and the 1½ [inch] space labeled "Disposition" is left blank. If the child is taken to the Youth Study Center, the word "Arrest" is checked . . . and the word "Adjusted" is entered under "Disposition." Thus the recipient of the form has no clue as to what actually has happened. There will be no indication, for example, that the wrong child may have been picked up in connection with the "reason for referral." Several instances of just this have come to our attention: that a completely blameless child was referred in connection with a rather serious offense and that the volunteer visitor had absolutely no knowledge of this innocence. (Coxe, 1964.)

By means of such minimal numbers of indicators the probability of a given Actor being identified as deviant is increased. Objecting to the use of such a small number of indicators, the Philadelphia ACLU argued:

> The form . . . creates the inescapable presumption of guilt, or at least wrongdoing. An official police form is on file with the school authorities and with the neighbors [the volunteer visitors], linking the child with "assault and battery," "intoxication" or some other crime.

✿   ✿   ✿

Some parents have complained [that] . . . well-meaning visitors have stopped in, under the impression that their children are delinquents or bad or incorrigible or in need of help. (Coxe, 1964.)

Leaving aside the moral merits of the practice about which organizations like the ACLU are so concerned, it can be appreciated that requiring a large number of indicators (e.g., in the case above, requiring the filling in of detailed forms) is likely to reduce the probability of any given Actor being defined as deviant.

LARGE NUMBER ALTERNATIVELY SUFFICIENT

Second, coding as deviant is facilitated if there are available for use in small numbers a large number of alternatively sufficient indicators. One of the most effective features of some psychiatric coding schemes is their ability to use only a few of a very large number of alternative indicators in order to code Actors as pivotally deviant. In reporting on psychiatric screening examinations for mental hospitalization, Scheff details a case in which

. . . one of the patients, when asked, "In what ways are a banana, an orange and apple alike?" answered, "They are all something to eat." This answer was used by the examiner in explaining his recommendation to commit. The observer had noted that the patient's behavior and responses seemed appropriate and asked why the recommendation to commit had been made. The doctor stated that her behavior had been bizarre (possibly referring to her alleged promiscuity), her affect inappropriate ("When she talked about being pregnant, it was without feeling") and with regard to the question above: "She wasn't able to say a banana and an orange were fruit. She couldn't take it one step further; she had to say it was something to eat." In other words, this psychiatrist was suggesting that in her thinking the patient manifested concreteness, which is held to be a symptom of mental illness. Yet in her other answers to classification questions, and to proverb interpretations, concreteness was not apparent, suggesting that the examiner's application of this test was arbitrary. In another case, the physician stated that he thought the patient was suspicious and distrustful, because he had asked about the possibility of being represented by counsel at the judicial hearing. The observer felt that these and other similar interpretations might possibly be correct, but that further investigation of the supposedly incorrect responses would be needed to establish that they were manifestations of disorientation. (Scheff, 1964b:409.)

Likewise, in totalitarian societies, a wide range of political revisionisms may be coded as "treason" and their espousers as "enemies of the people," thus increasing the number of persons classified as beyond the pale. Writing in the late forties, Lemert described contrasting coding schemes for the pivotally deviant category of "radical."

> In democratic societies such as the United States and England a person does not necessarily have to join a radical party in order to voice his criticisms and express antagonisms to established institutions. One may become a lone professional agitator—as in England—or a labor organizer, a labor lawyer, or join a group fighting for civil liberties, or in politics becoming a "fighting liberal." The individualistic ethos of our culture, indeed, ideologically imposes a responsibility upon the citizen to participate in a critical decision-making process. Furthermore, a person may join a radical organization or become the ally of radicals without necessarily identifying himself as a radical. The symbolic environment of radicalism in American culture is blurred and contains numerous alternative definitions for what would be absolutely defined as radicalism in a society like Russia. (Lemert, 1951:215.)

And it is presumably on a similar basis that George Wallace and his partisans and sympathizers can perform the following codings:

> "Alabama taxi drivers knew Fidel Castro of Cuba was a Communist before *The New York Times* and some college professors did." The man in the street, the ordinary person, can spot a Communist or a wrong guy instinctively, Wallace reassures his audiences. (Vestal, 1967.)

SOCIAL ORGANIZATIONAL SOURCES

It can be suggested that coding schemes relying heavily upon a small number of necessary indicators, with a large number of alternatively sufficient indicators, are likely to predominate in social orders where a high proportion of the population are in necessary contact but are relative strangers to one another. Under conditions of rapid social change and territorial mobility, there is created a situation in which persons have little information about one another, yet need to deal with and manage each other (L. H. Lofland, 1966). A reasonable, at least short-run, adaptation to this situation is to squeeze from meager amounts of available information a large amount of "indicativeness" (giving rise, perhaps, to a popular concern with managing impressions, a concern most poignantly explored by David Riesman et al., [1950] and Erving Goffman [1957]). When some doubt is raised as to the standing of a given Actor under conditions of anonymity and, therefore, under conditions of a measure of distrust and fear, the safest course is quickly to presume the worst, that is, to code for pivotal deviance using a large number of alternatively sufficient indicators in small numbers. (Such action is the safest course because it activates, subsequently, practices that presume Actor's deviant character.) Anonymity, combined with cultural and class heterogeneity and an orientation to routine imputations under the press of developing and processing the day's cases, serves to expand even further the range of possibly imputed Actors. The following case of a Navaho male initially imputed to be psychotic but later released as having been wrongly diagnosed need not be seen as indicative of "coding error." Rather, it is suggestive of the character of indicators that must be utilized whenever bodies are processed on a mass basis.

> Bill managed to raise a little money doing odd jobs about the section camp near Barstow, and then returned to San Bernardino on the first lap of his return to Phoenix and home. It occurred to him that if he could get to a hospital, the officials there would send him to a reservation hospital, from whence he would be sent home. This was logical thinking: on the reservations, the hospitals, schools, and trading posts are the major source of assistance in all sorts of troubles.
>
> As this idea occurred to Bill, he noted a woman dressed in white whom he took to be a nurse. He approached her and endeavored to explain that he was sick, but his endeavors were misinterpreted and he was taken to jail.
>
> At the county jail Bill was apparently mistaken for a Mexican since a Mexican interpreter had tried to interview him. When the interview failed he was transferred to the psychopathic ward. Interviewed by the medical examiner there, he reportedly demonstrated an anguished appearance and repeated, "Me sick." He was diagnosed as Schizophrenia, Catatonic Type, and delivered to the state mental hospital.
>
> Upon admission to the hospital, Bill was first taken to be a Filipino. The psychiatric admission note indicated that he was, ". . . confused, dull and preoccupied. He has a look of anguish and appears to be hallucinating . . . . He repeats, 'I don't know.'" He was diagnosed as Dementia Praecox, which was later specified as Heberphrenic Type.
>
> Several months later the psychiatrist on Bill's cottage tested him for *cerea flexibilitas* (waxy flexibility) and, finding it to be present, altered the diagnosis to Catatonic Type.
>
> Eight months after his admittance he was discovered by the writer.[9]

Conditions of anonymity, distrust and fear create a demand for simple and direct characterizations of types of persons, a demand catered to in no small measure by those who call themselves medical and social scientists. It is their mission to come up with "essential findings" and essential correlates and features or indicators, the better and easier to identify various sets of "them" toward whom one should be on guard. At one extreme there emerge people such as Sheldon and Eleanor Glueck, who attempt to provide, by means of a

[9] Jewell, 1960:112–13. See also Scheff's systematic observations of mental hospital intake interviews (1964b) and his comparison of indicators used in rural and urban commitment proceedings (1964a). Further, more general discussion and illustration are provided in Lemert, 1967b:94; Szasz, 1963 and 1965; Katz, Goldstein and Dershotwitz, eds., 1967; Wilde, 1968.

jiffy five-item interview, a means for identifying delinquents at the age of five (Craig and Glick, 1964. See, further, Lemert, 1967b:92–94).

DIFFERENTIAL VULNERABILITY TO IMPUTATION AS DEVIANT

As almost everyone wants to believe, items that can be indicative of pivotal deviance are probably not evenly or even randomly distributed throughout the population of a society. Models of deviant categories are founded precisely upon the assumption that particular classes of people are more likely to perform deviant acts and to be particular types of deviant persons. I have tried in the above to hold in abeyance that proposition in order to point up the possibility that imputation of Actors as deviant can have as much or more to do with who is coding with what category under what circumstances than with simple discernment of specially differentiated deviant persons. But, as is popularly believed, some Actors are, to a degree, likely to be specially differentiated from the general population in their acts and activities in a way that makes it more likely that they will be imputed. Others have probed this possibility so thoroughly[10] that I need not pursue it here. I will, in the next chapter, note only that information known about Actors tends to be highly selective relative to the total amount that can be known. This fact poses the question of the extent to which almost anyone might be "informationally sampled" so as to effect identification as some type of pivotal deviant.

The initiation of an imputation is but the beginning of the possibility that Actor might eventually identify himself as that deviant he is tenuously imputed

[10] Aside from the theories of psychiatry, psychology and sociology precisely intended to discover the underlying or correlative features of "deviant people," attention has been called to matters such as (1) the Actor's demeanor during contact with imputation specialists (Black, 1968; Goldman, 1963:106; Piliavin and Briar, 1964); (2) the degree of his previous contact with authorities (Cicourel, 1968; Werthman, 1967:167); (3) the degree of incongruity of a current act against the background of a given biography, especially social-class biography (Werthman and Piliavin, 1967; Cicourel, 1968; Erikson, 1966:141–53; President's Commission, . . . Assessment . . . , 1967:106–9); (4) the existence of a "segmental or checkered pattern" of "interpersonal difficulties" (Lemert, 1962:7–8); (5) the circumstance of Actor being situationally disoriented (Scheff, 1966:39–54; Chap. 8 of this volume) and (6) the fact of being male rather than female (e.g., Johnson, 1964:76–81) as affecting ease with which pivotal deviance will be imputed, that is, the degree to which Actor is vulnerable to imputation. These and other factors relevant to the general topic of social identification have been placed in appropriate general perspective by Erikson (1966). The organization of his analysis of witches around issues of their "functional necessity" among the Puritans of the Massachusetts Bay Colony should not detract attention from the potential usefulness of the historical materials in answering other kinds of questions. See also Reckless' helpful conception of "categoric risks" (1961:Chap. 3).

to be. To facilitate a deviant *personal* identification, the imputation should spread and become unanimous among Others in Actor's world. This spread and unanimity should occur in conjunction with certain other processes and practices to which we now turn.

CHAPTER 7

ESCALATION TO DEVIANT IDENTITY: OTHERS AND PLACES

ESCALATION

Initiated imputation, as a phase in the assumption of deviant identity, has been viewed in terms that are relatively independent of specific features of Actor. We must now introduce Actor as an active participant in the process and focus upon his perceptions and responses. This focus, however, cannot be exclusively on Actor. Concern with him must be incorporated into a joint consideration of the reciprocal dependence through time of the actions of Others and Actor. By reciprocal dependence I mean an interactional process of the following formal character. Others undertake action O; Actor perceives O and responds with action A; Others perceive A and use it as part of the basis for responding with new action P; Actor perceives action P and incorporates it as part of his basis for undertaking action B. Each action of each party is in some measure dependent upon the previous action of the other party. The outcome of such an *interaction process* is a joint product of *both* parties, each party having supplied, as it were, a share of the material out of which the process is elaborated. Interaction processes of this character are, of course, a ubiquitous feature of social life and are to be found in the highest levels of international relations and in the fleeting encounters of the office hallway.

Escalation and Interaction

There are many types of such interaction processes, but we are here concerned only with *spiraling* or *escalation* processes. Many interaction processes involve only well-known routines wherein an initiated sequence runs a predictable and expected course, arriving at an expected and unremarkable terminus, with the status quo quite undisturbed. Each party to the interaction is able to anticipate and, in a relatively unreflective way, take account of the other party's action. Such processes may be said to be in stable equilibrium. They maintain and confirm preexisting arrangements and identities (Goffman, 1956). On the other hand, parties may become involved in interaction in which they feel and are perceived as feeling that the Other's response is of such a character that previously exercised responses are not sufficient. The present response must be, in some way, stronger, more firm or more drastic. If both parties come to feel and act this way about each other's actions, there exists a spiraling or escalation process.[1]

[1] Participation in escalating interaction may or may not be a routine matter for Others. There are, of course, professional escalators.

This latter type of interaction process appears to be prominently involved in the building of personal identification with many categories of identity, including deviant ones.[2] As an inherently unstable process, escalation cannot continue indefinitely. One way in which equilibrium is eventually achieved is through Actor's accepting the identity embodied in the escalating actions of Others. This acceptance of the proffered identity is, of course, only one among many ways in which escalation can terminate. Others include one or both parties physically destroying the other or one or both parties leaving the field (including, literally, running away).

At this time very little of a detailed character is known about the dynamics of the escalation process per se. We have some knowledge of what to feed into the black box to get out a deviant identification of self, but we have meager knowledge of its contents. That is, we are in a position similar to that of the little old lady who knows what to feed into her automobile to get out movement but has only a vague conception of what is under the hood. Although I will explicate something of what we know about the contents of the black box —and make some additional guesses—the primary focus will be on elements that may be fed in.[3]

ESCALATION AND DEVIANT IDENTITY

If the escalation process has the *formal* structure detailed above, what might be its more specific and substantive features? Although Actor and Other are enmeshed in a process of mutual contingency, some general features of their respective lines of action appear to be of the following kind.

OTHERS

During escalation, Others experience both increasing doubts that Actor can reasonably be imputed a normal pivotal identity and increasing faith in the imputation of his pivotal deviance. Initiated imputation can be a fragile, tentative or even reluctant act. As an identity possibility, it can be important in the sense that Others take strong account of it, but, like a hypothesis, it awaits confirmation. However, the identity hypotheses of everyday life structure the degree to which Others act in a self-protective manner. Even though the imputation as deviant may be tentative, the very fact that suspicion has been

---

[2] Escalating interaction is, of course, not confined to matters of personal identity. The term, as is evident, is drawn from the modern analysis of war and conflict.

[3] Speculation in addition to that which follows, some of which informs the present statement, may be found in Parsons, 1951:Chap. 7; Cohen, 1955 and 1959; and, most important, Lemert, 1951:Chap. 4, especially pp. 76–78, and 1967a:Chap. 3. See also the empirical materials in Werthman, 1967; Schafer and Polk, 1967; and the principles of "covert communication" in interaction summarized by Abrahamson, 1966:Chaps. 3 and 16; Halmos, 1966:90–105.

aroused is likely to conduce action which takes account of that suspicion and attempts to protect Others against the worst that Actor might do.

Such subtle and tentative shifting of the ground of perception begins a process whereby Others double-code Actor's emissions, scrutinizing him for indications of pivotal normality and pivotal deviance. And, because of certain features of human activity which I will discuss momentarily, confirmation of the tentative imputation is likely to begin to occur, leading to increasing certainty on the part of Others that Actor should definitely be coded as an instance of a deviant type. Such growing confirmation may attain a critical mass of informational input, precipitating a gestalt switch in the perception of Actor. In discussing the escalation process in paranoia, Lemert puts it this way:

> At some point in the chain of interactions, a new configuration takes place in the perceptions others have of the individual, with shifts in figure-ground relations. The individual, as we have already indicated, is an ambiguous figure, comparable to textbook figures of stairs or outlined cubes which reverse themselves when studied intently. From a normal variant, the person becomes "unreliable," "untrustworthy," "dangerous" or someone with whom others "do not wish to be involved." (Lemert, 1962:8.)

Throughout escalation, there can occur some general perceptual processes which have the character of feeding upon themselves as well as feeding upon the possibly changing emissions of Actor. These processes involve the shedding of new light on (1) Actor's current acts and (2) his biography.

Redefinition of Current Acts. First, a wide range of Actor's current activity that was previously not defined as indicative might now be so defined. Although Actor may be emitting the same acts, they can take on different meanings. Instead of having imagination, he may now be a wild visionary. Instead of being optimistic, he may now be gullible. Instead of having a philosophy of life, he may now be blindly following dogma. Instead of engaging in a debate or spat, he may now be prone to quarrels and fights. Instead of failing by oversight, he may now fail by negligence. Instead of being stoic or stolid, he may now be apathetic. Instead of having naughty sexual interests, he is now interested in pornography and is perverted. Instead of engaging in escapades or indiscretions, he may now have tawdry affairs. Instead of giving due consideration, he may now be stalling. Instead of being enterprising, he may now be opportunistic. Instead of voicing a legitimate complaint, he may now be a chronic malcontent. Instead of being merely determined, he may now be pigheaded. Instead of being prudent, he may be timid. Instead of dressing casually, he may be seen as sloppy. Instead of showing a good deal of hopefulness, he may now be seen as living in a fool's paradise. Instead of being diplomatic, he is now two-faced. Instead of having engaged in a harmless prank, he has now perpetrated vandalism. Instead of being shy, he is aloof and a loner. Instead of displaying irony, he is now sarcastic and nasty. Instead of being trusting, he is naïve. Rather than being circumspect, he is now suspicious and distrusting.[4]

Because of the threatening image that is therein created, such redefinition serves to magnify the visibility of Actor, making it all the more likely that ever more qualities will additionally be noticed. In escalation to what is labeled paranoia, this redefinition is concomitant with magnification of acts, and even of Actor's physical qualities. There can occur

> distortions of his image, most pronounced in the inner coterie of exclusionists. His size, physical strength, cunning and anecdotes of his outrages are exaggerated, with a central thematic emphasis on the fact that he is dangerous. Some individuals give cause for such beliefs in that previously they have engaged in violence or threats; others do not. One encounters characteristic contradictions in interviews on this point, such as: "No, he has never struck anyone around here—just fought with the policeman at the State Capitol," or, "No, I am not afraid of him, but one of these days he will explode." (Lemert, 1962:13.)

This is not to say that such redefinition of Actor's emissions, bringing them in harmony with already suspected deviance, violates the empirical facts of Actor's conduct in any important way. It is quite easy to engage in this sort of recoding because the acts and character of persons are *in fact ambiguous*. People and their acts do not have "unequivocally stable meanings," to quote Egon Bittner (1963). As a long tradition of social psychological experimentation suggests, ambiguous situations are open to the imputation of meaning. Once imputation as a deviant begins, the inherent ambiguity of action makes possible redefinition of a wide range of Actor's conduct. This redefinition involves little or no empirical contradiction, since the empirical materials provided by persons are almost never very clear.

Reconstruction of Biography. Second, there can begin a process of biographical reconstruction. Whatever may have been the preexisting selection of facts from the Actor's life line that supported a view by Others of him as a pivotal normal, there now begins a reexamination of that life line to discover if these selected biographical events are consistent with the prospective reclassi-

---

[4] Kudos to columnist Sidney Harris (1965, 1966, 1967) for his apprehension of the ambiguity of human action from which I have here borrowed. See further Strauss, 1959:Chap. 4; Kitsuse, 1962; Ward and Kassebaum, 1965:85–88; Erikson, 1966; Lindesmith, 1968:188–89. By way of preview, empirical demonstration of the relation between negative imputation and the self (at least among male sixth-grade children imputed by teachers to be headed for contact with legal officials) is presented in Reckless, Dinitz and Kay, 1957; Dinitz, Scarpetti and Reckless, 1962. See also the D. B. Harris (1968) and Toby (1968) interpretation of how a delinquency prevention program increased, under some conditions, the number of youth officially imputed as delinquent by legal authorities. The moral valence of such imputations can, of course, operate in the opposite direction, as, for instance, in Rosenthal and Jacobson's (1966) demonstration of the relation between teachers' beliefs and pupils' IQ gains.

fication. Efforts are made to render the known facts consistent, either through discounting (or redefining the significance of) what is known or through undertaking to discover additional facts that support the new imputation.

It is in such biographical reconstructions that we see most clearly the social need of Others to render Actors as consistent objects. As mentioned previously, one of the most broadly and deeply held of human beliefs in recent Western societies is that an Actor must have some consistent and special history that explains the current social object that he is seen as being. It is believed that a person's acts must arise from or be a manifestation of an imputed social character. Personal history cannot simply involve the universal experience of being human and being subjected to human society; there must be a *special* history that *specially* explains current imputed identity. Relative to deviance, the *present evil* of current character must be related to *past evil* that can be discovered in biography.

These premises are most clearly played out by specialists in biographical reconstruction, most prominently by those involved in the "professions" of psychology and psychiatry. Their work is, however, merely a more elaborate and detailed version (as one might expect from persons who do it for a living) of a well-nigh universal practice. Acts in his past that were once viewed in a certain way are reinterpreted. Other acts, which had gone unnoticed or had seemed irrelevant, are brought forth and considered central, for they help Others to understand that Actor was that way all along.

This biographical reconstruction is also clearly seen at the public level, in the efforts that newspapers make relative to persons who commit widely publicized crimes. In July, 1966, eight student nurses were murdered in a Chicago apartment, and some days later one Richard Speck was apprehended and charged with these acts. Wire services and local newspapers went into a frenzy of research to find out about Richard Speck. The initial material published on his biography seemed unsatisfactory (at least to the *Detroit Free Press*, in which I followed the story), for interviews with people who liked and defined Speck as an intelligent, gentle and sensitive young man were buried in the back pages. However, four days after his apprehension enough appropriate material was available to credibly present the "right" biography on the front page. Under the headline "Richard Speck's Twisted Path," the rite of consistency could begin:

> Charged with the brutal slaying of eight student nurses, Richard Speck was trapped by the tattoo that bore his credo: Born to Raise Hell. Here is a special report on the man accused of mass murder, a report on the twisted path that led to tragedy. (*Detroit Free Press*, July 24, 1966:1.)

And, of course, the facts presented were consistent. He was a "murder suspect" in another case who "had been hating for a long time," and "had been arrested 36 times." In his youth he was already "a reckless tough . . . with the leather jacket crowd" who "would drink anything." "A high school drop-out" who was "divorced," he had served three years for burglary and was "woman crazy."

This consistent biographical construction was considerably easier to accomplish than that required when another well-publicized set of acts occurred in August of the same year. Charles Whitman's shooting of fourteen people from atop a tower at the University of Texas required rather more strenuous efforts, because the most public facts of his biography were less amenable to reconstruction than were Speck's. Whitman's Eagle Scout boyhood in Texas, unexceptional service in the Marines, and superior grades in college were first defined as a puzzle in connection with his act and finally seen as unrelated. Other events had to be discovered, and it took the newspapers an entire week to produce the first version of a biography supportive of a mad murderer identity. Buried in the third section of the *Detroit Free Press*, a *New York Times* story headlined: "Friends and the Record Dispute Sniper's All-American Image."

> Charles J. Whitman . . . has been described as an all-American boy. But according to his friends, he has gambled with criminals, poached deer, written bad checks, kept illegal guns and tried to sell pornography. (*Detroit Free Press*, August 19, 1966.)

Interestingly enough, the concrete acts that are then spelled out in the story seem less malevolent than the abstract characterization of them given above. This is perhaps why the *Detroit Free Press* felt the story merited only page three of section three for that day. The problems posed in the effort to reconstruct consistently Whitman's biography possibly explains the later popularity of attributing his acts to an alleged brain tumor. When social and psychological explanations fail, one can always try biological or physiological ones. Regardless of the character of the account, Actor must be accounted for.

Note that Whitman's all-American image had to be *disputed,* but one could as well suggest that his acts were very much related to his all-American properties. As some wags have observed, being a Texan, a Boy Scout and a Marine would seem to be ideal training for a disposition toward and skills in the use of violence.

Perhaps more commonly, exactly the opposite kind of biographical rendering also occurs at the public level. Almost daily the mass media, as well as private persons, carry stories of meritorious promotion or transfer, stories which also contain a rehearsal of biographical events that in some sense support the current change and lend credence to the consistency and orderly character of persons (Scheff, 1963:445). Employment forms demand such consistency, too, even to the point of inquiring for arrests and mental disorders, the clear implication being that, if one wants to be hired, these lines should be left blank.

Paralleling the ambiguity of current action permitting coding as a deviant type, the concrete events of biography are also ambiguous, permitting the same items to be variously defined. More important, it is likely the case that the life lines of almost all Actors contain enough events of a discrediting kind to support a wide variety of deviant identities. When people can relate their biographies with assured anonymity, one finds that discrediting episodes are reported with enormous frequency.[5] Since existing studies of the evil episodes populating the biographies of normals have focused on only a few delimited aspects of a sample's life line, one wonders if a *full census* of deviant episodes for almost any individual might not yield up more than enough evidence to convince others that the individual was, indeed, really the sort of person to have done this—almost regardless of how heinous the "this" in question. (One can, of course, also show for most individuals enough good biographical events to make him good enough to have been able to do something wonderful, heroic or exceptionally meritorious.)

No actual biographical rendering of an individual is exhaustive. What is called biography is of necessity an extremely short and highly *selective* list of events drawn from the totality of an individual's past. This must be so if for no other reason than that a *total* rendering would require the same amount of time in rendition as the individual has already existed, doubling the Actor's biography-to-be-told in the very process of working on a total telling of it. The fact of enormous selectivity, without benefit of a sampling frame or random selection procedures, means that the biographies available on Actors are likely to be highly distorted (in the probability sense), for what is known is unlikely to depict accurately the essential features of the vast amount that is unknown.[6] The reported biography of an Actor will, then, be very much a function of how much control he has over concealing his past, of the access that Others have to it and of what they are attuned to detect and report.

These forms of evidential coding are accompanied by an increasing intensity in the actual treatment of Actor as a deviant person. Actor may become increasingly implicated in surveillance, concern, patronization, put-downs and other abuses which communicate to him the nature of his true character. In addition, deviants of his imputed kind may begin to treat him with increasing solicitude. The following kinds of cumulating differential treatments are reported by Lemert as characterizing the process of escalation to an identity clinically labeled "paranoid."

> In an office research team . . . staff members huddled around a water
> cooler to discuss the unwanted associate. They also used office tele-
> phones to arrange coffee breaks without him and employed symbolic cues

[5] See the references given in note 12 of Chap. 2.

[6] Indeed, biographies composed of a true random sampling of events might be so contradictory that it would be very difficult for persons to impute identities to one another. If humans were fully informed about one another, they might, as Gerald Suttles has suggested, hesitate forever in a pit of ambivalence (Suttles, personal communication).

in his presence, such as humming the *Dragnet* theme song when he approached the group. An office rule against extraneous conversation was introduced with the collusion of supervisors, ostensibly for everyone, actually to restrict the behavior of the isolated worker. In another case an interview schedule designed by a researcher was changed at a conference arranged without him. When he sought an explanation at a subsequent conference, his associates pretended to have no knowledge of the changes.

❀   ❀   ❀

Concern about secrecy in . . . groups [excluding the imputed person] is revealed by such things as carefully closing doors and lowering of voices when ego is brought under discussion. Meeting places and times may be varied from normal procedures; documents may be filed in unusual places and certain telephones may not be used during a paranoid crisis.

The visibility of the individual's behavior is greatly magnified during this period; often he is the main topic of conversation among the exclusionists, while rumors of the difficulties spread to other groups, which in some cases may be drawn into the controversy. At a certain juncture steps taken to keep the members of the ingroup continually informed of the individual's movements and, if possible, of his plans. In effect, if not in form, this amounts to spying. Members of one embattled group, for example, hired an outside person unknown to their accuser to take notes on a speech he delivered to enlist a community organization on his side. In another case, a person having an office opening onto that of a department head was persuaded to act as an informant for the nucleus of persons working to depose the head from his position of authority. This group also seriously debated placing an all-night watch in front of their perceived malefactor's house. (Lemert, 1962:12–13.)

ACTOR

Actor is unlikely to be oblivious to the beginning and subsequent development of this new coding, and he finds himself confronting a rather perplexing range of alternative responses. He can act as if nothing were amiss; that is, he can strive to act normally. But by doing so, since he then takes no overt action explicitly to deny what is suspected, his behavior may be taken as indicating insensitivity, evasiveness or even assent to what is suspected. He can seek to counter the suspicions through denials and counterdefinitions of himself, but such a response is easily read as protesting too much or being too defensive and as confirmation of Others' doubts about his normalcy. Or, he can act in compliance with the identity imputed to him. The irony is, of course, that, once begun, the practices of Others toward Actor operate to confirm what is suspected, almost irrespective of what Actor does. This is especially true if the imputations arouse in Actor a new level of anxiety and concern over what seems to be believed about him, thereby altering his orientation to the situation (see pp. 184–86).

None of this should be taken as necessarily implying that Actor dislikes the deviant identity tentatively proffered to him. He may well wish to reinforce the imputed identity or, at least, not be wholly adverse to the possibility of his pivotal deviance. For example, after spending eighteen months in a federal prison for refusing the Vietnam draft, a young man could feel that the experience was "worth it because it defined the kind of person I am, it defined my beliefs for me" (cf. Lorber, 1967). Nor is it necessarily the case that Actor and Others are agreed as to the concrete sort of deviant of which he is an instance. For successful escalation it need only be agreed that Actor is *deviant*. Within this agreement there may be continuing negotiation over the specific type. In the paranoia cases quoted above, some of the Actors apparently saw themselves as embattled social reformers, a self-identity nicely compatible, at the practical level of treatment, with the label of paranoia eventually applied to them. The treatment accorded people who come to believe they are Jesus Christ or some other such figure is not strongly incompatible with the way in which Jesus Christ *et al.* might expect to be treated in the modern world (Rokeach, 1964).

Assuming that the above characterization of the black box interaction process is at least minimally accurate, I want to specify what the successful conditions—or facilitants—of escalation might be. What kinds of arrangements increase the likelihood that escalation will continue through time and will eventually terminate in Actor identifying himself as deviant or, at least, organizing his life in a deviant fashion in response to the knowledge that Others define him as such? An answer to this question may be formulated around the same abstract elements employed in analyzing the deviant act, namely, places, hardware, Others and Actor. Here, however, a slight rearrangement of emphasis must be effected. The more situationally bound and episodic character of the deviant act made it appropriate to emphasize a progression from physical matters of places and hardware to more social matters of Others and Actor. But the initially social character of identity and the significance of Others in the construction of identity make it necessary now to begin with *Others* and subsequently to consider how *places* and *hardware* can be supportive of the activities of Others, in combination, finally, with features of *Actor*.

FACILITANTS OF
ESCALATION: OTHERS

Taking as a point of reference an Actor living out a daily round of encounters with typical Others and their definitions, we may distinguish among sets of these Others on the basis of (1) the degree to which they are in agreement regarding Actor's deviant identity, and (2) the ways in which Others are themselves distributed between normal and deviant public identities.

UNANIMOUS OTHERS

DEGREE OF UNANIMITY

Considered generically and in a simplified way, Actor might confront any one of these collective definitional situations among Others:

a. unanimous agreement that he is a pivotal deviant;
b. a split over his deviance, some imputing, the rest ignorant of any issue and defining Actor as normal;
c. a split over his deviance, some imputing, some ignorant and some who know there is an issue about his normalcy but who challenge the imputation of pivotal deviance;
d. a split over his deviance between those who impute and those who challenge the imputation.

Other things being equal, the most facilitative arrangement is unanimity among Others, a situation which undercuts any possibility of Actor's taking refuge among ignorant normals or among those who know of the imputation but who fight to defend a conception of him as normal (cf. Backman, 1963; J. Davis, 1963). Any disagreement among Others can only serve to confuse Actor as to who he is.

FORGING UNANIMITY

If this is the case, the technical question is raised as to how unanimity might be brought about and confounding counterdefinitions avoided. Among relevant considerations are the degree of preexisting consensus on the indicators of deviant identity used by those who have initiated the definition, the social position of those who initiate the imputation and the manner in which the imputation is prosecuted.

Even when a category is widely known and believed reasonable, unanimity can be retarded if there is disagreement on exactly what must be present before identification as deviant is justified. The widespread use of simple indicators increases the probability of imputations of deviance being initiated. But unless these simple indicators are a matter of consensus, conflict is likely to ensue, interrupting the escalation process and transforming it into a political struggle over the protection of the would-be deviant. A few years ago retired Army General Edwin Walker was the focus of an attempt at escalation which was transformed into a political struggle. Alleging that he had incited a riot on a university campus, government officials defined him as mentally ill and whisked him off to a mental hospital. (Clearly these officials must have had available a large number of alternative indicators which could be used in small numbers.) However, General Walker's actions were defined as insufficiently

indicative of mental illness by other political interests, and, in the subsequent
maneuvering, the federal government relented in its definition (Szasz, 1965:
Chap. 6). If such disagreement and activation of political interests existed in
every instance of initiated imputation, there would be no social deviants, only
self-righteous participants in political struggles (cf. conflicts over who is a
witch, Erikson, 1966:149–53).

It nonetheless seems possible to forge a kind of consensus under conditions
in which those who initiate the imputation are seen as having *special expertise*
or power in discerning deviants. Imputational specialists are among those so
viewed, and the work they do seems highly facilitative in forging unanimity in
Actor's world. Their command over resources endows their work with a gravity and bathes it with a degree of publicity far beyond anything the mere
layman can achieve. Often garbed in a distinctive manner, imputational specialists can be mobilized in a coordinated manner to use distinctive vehicles of
transport to carry them to and about a variety of places and buildings designed
and maintained for their exclusive use. Within such places of imputation (e.g.,
police interrogation offices, courtrooms, psychiatric clinics) there can be
mobilized a chain of impugning forms and files, agents and aids. As they write
and code in official documents, their judgments of the moment become solid
and permanent records—far more powerful for purposes of escalation than the
laymen's transitory gossip. Attention accorded them by the mass media serves
not only to publicize their work but continually to reinforce its legitimacy.
Actors and Others can hardly be expected to disregard or take lightly the kind
of imputational dramas which such specialists can produce. As Tannenbaum
has suggested, they act in a manner that suggests their being about the gravest
of affairs. In the case of youthful misconduct there can

> . . . suddenly appear the police, the patrol wagon, the police station, the
> other delinquents and criminals found in the police lock-ups, the courts
> with all its agencies such as bailiffs, clerks, bondsmen, lawyers, probation
> officers. There are bars, cells, handcuffs, criminals. He is questioned,
> examined, tested, investigated. His history is gone into; his family is
> brought into court. (Tannenbaum, 1938:19.)

Given the imagery of gravity and expertise which surrounds such specialists, it
is not surprising that the mere fact of their codings can be sufficient for others
to grant them credence and that the mere fact of their having coded Actor as
deviant is sufficient to pre-sell this coding to a multitude of Others. In addition, their propensity to incorporate their judgments into official records can
give these judgments a kind of immortality, extending belief in their validity
far into the future, sometimes beyond the life spans of the Actors of whom they
were made.

The faith which employers can place in the police records of prospective employees is testimony to the power of the written word. In a study of the effect of a police record on employment as a dishwasher in a resort area, Schwartz and Skolnick, posing as employment agents, presented fictional portraits of possible employees to prospective employers. There were four variations of the portraits, each variant being shown to twenty-five potential employers. Except for the variations, which were based on the extent of the potential employee's involvement with law enforcement specialists, the portraits were identical. The four versions were: (1) the prospective employee had no police record; (2) he had been charged with armed robbery but acquitted with a letter from the judge; (3) he had been charged with this crime and acquitted but without a letter; (4) he had been convicted of the crime. The percentage of employers who said they could ever possibly employ as a dishwasher the person presented in the portrait declined as involvement with imputational specialists increased. Of the twenty-five presented with the portrait of a man with no record, 36 per cent indicated that they might ever have a use for the person. But among the employers presented with the prospect convicted of the crime, only 4 per cent made such an indication (Schwartz and Skolnick, 1962:110).

Likewise, a study presenting to laymen verbal depictions of persons with various types of mental illnesses and of a normal, happy person found that the rate of impugning rejection increased sharply when the portrayals involved the person being associated with imputational specialists (Phillips, 1963). Of special interest is the degree to which suspicion was aroused by such association even toward the normal who was described in this fashion:

> Here is a description of a man. Imagine he is a respectable person living in your neighborhood. He is happy and cheerful, has a good enough job and is fairly well satisfied with it. He is always busy and has quite a few friends who think he is easy to get along with most of the time. Within the next few months, he plans to marry a nice young woman he is engaged to. (Phillips, 1963:996.)

There was almost no unwillingness on the part of respondents to have such a person marry their children, rent a room in their homes, work on the same job, belong to the same club or be a neighbor. However, the identical portrait affixed with the statement

> He has been going to see his psychiatrist regularly about the way he is getting along
> or
> He has been in a mental hospital because of the way he was getting along

decreased willingness to associate with this person in the same contexts.

In a more personal and positive vein, a sociologist, posing as a skid row resident, found that the degree to which other skid row residents were disposed to view him as one of their own kind was greatly facilitated by his being officially imputed to be a skid row type by specialists. "The public label of deviance . . . adds to the credentials . . . [the apprentice] needs for admission into the in-group of skid row."

> When I returned to the Lower Loop [skid row], I saw many of my former jail and workhouse inmates. Although we may not have talked to each other during our confinement, they now greeted me and were much more friendly than before I had been arrested and jailed. Several introduced me to their friends, often remarking that we had just returned from a "rest in the country." One asked me if I wanted some "pot" [marijuana], another wanted to share his woman with me and a third wanted me to go with him to L.A. (Wallace, 1965:175.)

Specialists, of course, vary in the degree to which they publicize their imputations and, associated with this, the degree to which their imputations are dramatized. Other things being equal, highly public, publicized and dramatic *denunciation ceremonies* seem best calculated to promote unanimity of imputation. Nonroutine and visible denunciations by state authorities and/or similar acclamations by members of the relevant deviant category increase the circle of persons who will respond to Actor as being "that kind" or "our kind." When such denunciations are accompanied by branding of the flesh, excisement of appendages, ingestion of feces or kindred ordeals, Actors themselves, in addition to Others, are likely to be deeply impressed that character has truly been revealed.[7] Recent tendencies to issue a summons instead of making an arrest for certain crimes can but serve to curtail publicity, unanimity and even initial imputation as deviant. There is little escalation mileage to be gained in something like New York's project VERA, which accords this treatment to the perpetrator of an act of shoplifting:

> The whole check-out [and release] process had taken 40 minutes. Alice had experienced no personal indignity; she was not searched like a common criminal; she did not go into a cell; she was not taken by police wagon to Night Court. She was put on her honor to show up in court. (Samuels, 1964:24.)

---

[7] Cf. a practice recounted in Sutherland and Cressy (1966:319):

> An English statute of 1698 which provided for branding on the left cheek was repealed after eight years with the explanation that this penalty
> > . . . had not its desired effect of deterring offenders from further committing crimes . . . but, on the contrary, such offenders being rendered thereby unfit to be entrusted in any service or employment to get their livelihood in any honest and lawful way, become the more desperate. [Pike, 1873–1876, Vol. II:280.]

See further the classic and more general explication by Garfinkel, 1956; and the analysis by Goffman, 1961a. See also Schafer and Polk, 1967:251–57; Sutherland and Cressey, 1966: Chap. 14; Erikson, 1966; and Young's (1965) general study of status dramatization.

NORMALS AND DEVIANTS PRESENT

WHO IS PRESENT

In a set of simple cases, the public identities of Others in Actor's world might be: (1) split between persons defined as normal and persons defined as deviant, (2) exclusively persons who are seen as deviant or (3) exclusively persons who are seen as normal. Considering only these possibilities, it is most facilitative for normals and deviants both to be present, rather than simply deviants or normals alone. Irrespective of the imputations they are undertaking, if they agree, each serves to ratify the judgment of the others. In spite of their different social positions, their agreement strongly supports whatever reality they are foisting upon Actor as to his essential deviance. If only normals or only deviants are typically encountered, concern can more easily be aroused over what the physically absent but mentally present category would construe Actor to be. Unanimous presence rules out the possibility of such doubt, at least to the extent that Actor cannot wonder what *some* or *any* representatives of either absent category would impute to him. (No matter who is present, there can always be, of course, a concern over what other people of any variety, not personally known, might think about him.)

Although probably less effective than a mixed situation, the condition of deviants only seems more facilitative than one of normals only. A primary basis for this ordering is that deviants can and do offer concrete models upon which, and in terms of which, Actor can mold his own conduct. The models of possible being are more clearly specified. Tutoring in how to perform the role and in the tricks of the trade can be carried on. The satisfactions that can be derived from occupying the category can more easily be communicated. And such entanglements can more quickly form the basis of *commitment* (H. S. Becker, 1960). In contrast, the situation of normals only imputing a deviant category can only present to Actor the *reciprocal* or role-other part of the interaction game since normals do not provide positive models to be imitated. Only by carefully reading the implications for his own behavior present in the acts of normals can Actor piece together a model of appropriate conduct.

This is not, however, to rule out completely the possibility of an Actor's coming to see himself as a deviant of a given category in the presence of normals only. This would appear to take place through a process of what might be called prosaic enmeshment, similar to the unspectacular development of identification with an occupation that sometimes takes place among more conventional persons. Lemert reports, for example, that

> . . . a girl [may] more or less come to a conclusion on her own that she is a prostitute, growing out of a long series of quasiprostituting sex experi-

ences, the implications of which become inescapable. A waitress who has been taken on dates by customers of the restaurant where she works and given entertainment or gifts in return for sexual favors may suddenly perceive the bargaining features of the relationships and decide to formalize them through a prostitute's role in order to improve what frequently is a bad bargain from her point of view. The new role materializes from the sexual exploitation implicit in her former role. Retrospective insight is sometimes verbalized thus: "I suddenly realized I had been giving thousands of dollars worth of it away for free." (Lemert, 1951:270.)

CONJOINT OPERATION

Considering these two simplified dimensions in combination, it is possible to specify some crude types of daily round interaction fields that seem related to the success of escalation and personal identification. Despite a lack of information of this close variety, looking at Chart 7.1, "Some Variations in Who Is Imputing What to Actor: Deviant Identity," it is possible to postulate that escalation to a deviant identity is most strongly facilitated under the conditions of situation 1A and that facilitation declines as we proceed across and down through the progressively split situations. At least on the basis of the tales that are told, it would appear that only very few ignorant or challenging definitions are required in order seriously to retard the Actor's escalation toward identification of himself as thoroughly deviant. In autobiographies and case records, we encounter again and again stories of the unusually loyal friend, of the chance meeting containing imputations which confounded those otherwise prevailing or of the faithful relative, sibling or spouse (see, e.g., C. Brown, 1965: 82–89).

Situation 1A might be said to be the escalation situation par excellence. In it, the two main kinds of people in Actor's world are agreed that he is one of whatever deviant kind of being they are making him out to be. Daily (or almost daily), his essential nature can be communicated to him by both major categories of role definers. While the normals are excluding him from conventional social life, thereby escalating his alienation from it, the deviants of his imputed kind are teaching him that life within his candidate category has joys of its own and can be endured and perhaps even triumphantly conquered and savored. Other situations, in which normals and deviants are both present and display some combination of ignorance (that is, treat him as a given category of normal) or challenge to the deviant definition laid on by some, can only serve to confuse and raise doubts in the Actor as to the nature of his true identity. Even the deviants may be divided on how to define the Actor: some may think that he is a true and exemplary candidate to be "one of us," and others may think the Actor can never under any circumstances be one, insisting that he belongs to some other deviant category or is simply and irrevocably an instance of some kind of a normal.

CHART 7.1.   *SOME VARIATIONS IN WHO IS IMPUTING WHAT TO ACTOR: DEVIANT IDENTITY*

Some Combinations of What Is Imputed	Some Combinations of Who Is Imputing		
	A. Normals and deviants are both typically encountered.	B. Only deviants are typically encountered.	C. Only normals are typically encountered.
1. Unanimous imputations of pivotal deviance.	1A	1B	1C
2. Some impute as deviant; some are ignorant and impute as normal.	2A	2B	2C
3. Some impute as deviant; some are ignorant; some challenge an imputation of deviance.	3A	3B	3C
4. Some impute as deviant; others challenge imputation of deviance.	4A	4B	4C

These other combinations of imputations under conditions of normals and deviants both present can become quite complex. When Actor encounters some variety of them, escalation can be a very nip-and-tuck process, building or withering, depending upon particular exposures to what kinds of definitions in the daily round. If there is to be successful escalation to deviant roles, then one is well advised to accomplish and maintain the 1A situation. All others too easily compromise the budding identity; they provide the Actor with the possibility of thinking of himself as something different than deviants and/or normals treat him as being.

The variables of degree of unanimity and who is present do not exhaust ways in which we should be concerned with facilitative arrangements and activities of Others. At least two additional distinct and important elements must also be addressed. But for reasons of expository clarity, introduction and discussion of them must be postponed until after facilitative features of Actor have been explicated. The degree to which Others provide a comprehensive, articulate and moralized ideology, as well as technical knowledge and skill, will then be taken up.

FACILITANTS OF
ESCALATION: PLACES

Integrated Place Round

PLACE ROUNDS: INTEGRATED
AND SEGREGATED

In the course of his typical day, Actor may move through a number of physically distinct sites or places. Each of these places will typically contain a more or less stable set of Others for whom Actor's conduct is a subject of observation. The total complement of these typically entered places during his typical day may be referred to as Actor's *place round*, an analytic component of his daily round, more generally conceived.

Holding constant the number of physically distinct places in an Actor's place round, we find that they differ in the degree to which the Others who populate them carry on cross-place communication among one another. At one extreme we may find that the Others of an Actor's place round never, or hardly ever, encounter one another. Communication may be low because of simple physical distance between the complement of Others in the places of Actor's round; because the Others of his respective places do not know that Actor frequents given other places; or because social distances are felt to be large and communication inappropriate even though place Others may know of one another's existence. Social distance due to class, race, marital status and religion is particularly effective in holding down the level of interplace communication among Others. A place round tending toward the separation pole may be called a *segregated place round*.[8] This is to be distinguished from its polar opposite where communication among place Others is relatively frequent and intensive. A high level of communication may be typically associated with small physical distances among places, full knowledge of all the places frequented by Actor and little or nonexistent social distance between the Others of Actor's places. This pattern is appropriately referred to as an *integrated place round*.

This distinction is important in considering the escalation of Actor to the embracement of a deviant identity because the amount of communication among place Others is not simply a matter of general information flow but is, in signifi-

---

[8] I draw here and below upon Goffman, 1956; 1959:Chap. 3; and 1961a:35–43.

cant measure, a matter of a *flow of information about Actor*. Integrated place rounds lay down the conditions for all manner of reciprocating circuits of information exchange about Actor.

Placing this in the context of normal and deviant Others, both of whom are present and unanimous in their imputations (situation 1A, Chart 7.1), it can be seen that the intensity of imputation is greatly facilitated by the continuous and reciprocal feedback on Actor made possible in an integrated round of places. Continuing definition of Actor's ambiguous acts as further evidence of his essential deviant character assumes more importance because new evidence of his infamy is less likely to be confined to a single place and less likely to reinforce merely local conceptions. New information and episodes can do double or triple duty, so to speak, by virtue of tales about them being circulated among the full complement of place Others. Circulated incidents of infamy, combined with the store of Actor's perceived indiscretions within any place, lead nicely to a formidable and increasingly negative apperceptive mass against which Actor's current activities are judged.

The populace of *segregated* rounds, on the other hand, have available to them only local happenings in terms of which to make imputations of Actor, more easily permitting the possibility of normals or deviants having second thoughts about the deviant identity being imputed.

TOTAL INSTITUTIONS AS
INTEGRATED PLACE ROUNDS

Among the variety of ways in which integrated place rounds can be contrived, mental hospitals are of special interest, for they create one of the most integrated of rounds that an Actor can confront. Whereas in some integrated rounds, information is circulated only by word of mouth and is dependent upon the memory and zeal of information circulators, many mental hospitals reach a higher level of efficiency by maintaining a running log (commonly called "ward notes") and a dossier (into which are entered all manner of items felt to be relevant to the case) on each inmate. The possession of *written* evidence of Actor's indiscretions avoids the problems of human forgetfulness and of the ignorance of new personnel. Written evidence provides continuing and new Others with a compact and permanent record on Actor on the basis of which they can make judgments about him. And, given the propensity of such records disproportionately to note negative items, they serve to support the pivotally deviant category initially imputed. The assiduousness with which such records are maintained and circulated also serves to keep information flowing about very current and on-going matters. As Erving Goffman has observed:

> In total institutions, spheres of life are desegregated, so that an inmate's conduct in one scene of activity is thrown up to him by staff as a comment and check upon his conduct in another context. A mental patient's effort

to present himself in a well-oriented, unantagonistic manner during a
diagnostic or treatment conference may be directly embarrassed by evidence introduced concerning his apathy during recreation or the bitter
comments he made in a letter to a sibling—a letter which the recipient has
forwarded to the hospital administrator, to be added to the patient's dossier and brought along to the conference. (Goffman, 1961a:36–37.)

Places like mental hospitals, or total institutions more generally, are of special interest, in addition, because of the special constraints and imperatives
posed by their high integration of the place rounds of a *large number* of Actors.
Total institutions (e.g., prisons, mental hospitals, monasteries, military posts)
are engaged in the business of moving through the day large batches of relatively "untrustworthy" persons in an *orderly* manner. The accomplishment of
such orderly routing is felt to require *simultaneousness* of action. So that the
institution itself can reasonably get through its organizational day, all the Actors must get up, groom themselves, eat, work, take their recreation, etc., at
pretty much the same time. The organization thus introduces a high level of
discipline of impulse and reduces the range of discretion that Actor may exercise over his personal action. To quote Goffman again, in segregated place
rounds, or, in his terms, in "civil society,"

. . . many actions will be defined as matters of personal taste, with choice
from a range of possibilities specifically allowed. For much activity the
judgment and action of authority are held off and one is on one's own.
Under such circumstances, one can with over-all profit schedule one's activities to fit into one another—a kind of "personal economy of action," as
when an individual postpones eating for a few minutes in order to finish a
task, or lays aside a task a little early in order to join a friend for dinner.
In a total institution, however, minute segments of a person's line of activity may be subjected to regulations and judgments by staff; the inmate's
life is penetrated by constant sanctioning interaction from above, especially
during the initial period of stay before the inmate accepts the regulations
unthinkingly. Each specification robs the individual of an opportunity to
balance his needs and objectives in a personally efficient way and opens
up his line of action to sanctions. The autonomy of the act itself is violated. (Goffman, 1961a:38.)

The introduction of sanctioning about matters that are properly objects of personal discretion in civil society produces a moralization of minutiae. That is,
the range of items that take on a *moral significance* is increased. The actual
increase in the number of matters about which he can daily be deviant makes
Actor even more vulnerable to imputations of pivotal deviance. Upon entry
into a place of confinement for delinquents (known to the author), a youth
may find himself presented with a list of "rules and regulations" such as the
following (presented, one can note, in a rather unfriendly tone):

All smoking is done under supervision and is limited to one cigarette after each meal and during visits.

✿   ✿   ✿

Keep your hands off other boys and don't intentionally irritate others. Do not handle anything on the Wing Supervisor's desk and don't block his view of the Wing.

✿   ✿   ✿

Cursing and swearing or name calling is not tolerated.

✿   ✿   ✿

Loud talking is not permitted when you are part of a group watching TV. You are *not* permitted to select your own TV programs, so there is no need to play with the channel selector.

✿   ✿   ✿

Boys are not permitted in each other's rooms.

✿   ✿   ✿

You are expected to eat everything you take. You are not permitted to give your food to another boy at the table.[9]

QUASI-INTEGRATED PLACE ROUNDS

Total institutions represent an extreme instance of the integrated place round. One step over on the continuum of integration-segregation, we find the more empirically frequent quasi-integrated or quasi-total place rounds. These are less self-consciously constructed, in the sense that no central administrative authority with coercive power maintains them. For many Actors, certain sections of the city or certain complements of places spread throughout the city may come to have a highly integrated character. Relative to the former, it is possible that a territory populated primarily by low-income representatives of a single ethnic or racial minority can, for some Actors, come to have a quasi-integrated or even integrated character wherein imputations of their deviance are generated and reinforced. Thus it appears that an area populated primarily by Italians along Taylor Street in Chicago once had such a potential for some of its residents in connection with more or less organized crime (Suttles, 1968). The Harlem area of New York City could likewise form a quasi-total or integrated round for the imputation of deviance to Black youth. (C. Brown, 1965. See also Tobias' [1967:131–47] descriptions of 19th-century English "rookeries" and ease of socialization to a criminal identity therein.)

The above possibilities involve single patches of territory, but it is possible that a similar effect can be achieved in places that are not territorially adjacent but among which the Actor is routed and his Others circulate such that his

---

[9] Additional facilitative features of the social organization of total institutions are usefully summarized in Gibbons, 1965:Chap. 5; Cressey, ed., 1961; Belknap, 1956; Weinberg, ed., 1967:Part IV; Ward and Kassebaum, 1965:Chaps. 1–3; Sutherland and Cressey, 1966:Chap. 23; Ullmann, 1967; Street, Vinter and Perrow, 1966.

daily round is still rather integrated. Prime instances include the homosexual underworld, some types of criminal underworlds (see, e.g., Maurer, 1962; Sutherland, 1937) and some deviant religious enclaves in urban settlements. Relative to this last, Father Divine's Kingdom in its heyday was rather spread out across Harlem—work, worship and residence being territorially separated—but candidates (and believers) could be nonetheless effectively encapsulated within it and could participate in an integrated round. (Sarah Harris, 1953.) The homosexual world of Los Angeles is reported to have a similar ecology, tending perhaps, in certain sections, even to territorial dominance.

> Although homosexuals as a total group do not have a bounded territorial base, they are, nevertheless, not randomly distributed throughout the city, nor are the facilities of institutions which provide needed services and function as focal gathering places. Mapping the residences of persons known to us, or known to subjects who have supplied us with their addresses, and noting the residential areas in the city described by them as having heavy concentrations of homosexuals—the "swish Alps"—results in large cluster formations. In these sections, apartment houses on particular streets may be owned by, and rented exclusively to, homosexuals. Single streets of individual dwellings may have only one or two nonhomosexual families. The concentrated character of these areas is not publicly known except in the homosexual community, and in some instances by the police.

❀   ❀   ❀

The most important of these community gathering places is the "gay" bar ("gay" is a synonym for homosexual as used by many members of that community), but there are also steam baths catering almost exclusively to homosexuals, "gay" streets, parks, public toilets, beaches, gyms, coffee houses and restaurants. Newsstands, bookstores, record shops, clothing stores, barbershops, grocery stores and launderettes may become preferred establishments for service or for a rendezvous.[10]

In some cases, the accomplishment of a quasi-total integrated round may be quite fortuitous and exist only temporarily, although long enough to accomplish escalation to deviant identity. In a religious cult studied by the author and others, it was found that the person attempting to escalate five candidate Actors into believership and total commitment to a millenarian cause was not able to do so until the six of them were gathered together in close physical proximity for some four months. Four of the candidates lived in relatively adjacent houses in an isolated rural area, and one of them happened to have an

---

[10] Hooker, 1961:43–44, 45. On the rise of similar worlds in Edwardian England, see Annan, 1968:8–9. Such "worlds which transcend space" (Strauss, ed., 1968:522) unfortunately continue to elude analytic sociological delineation. Deviant identities (and identity more generally) will likely be better understood once the structural features of such amorphous units are more precisely specified. Good beginnings may be found in the neglected essays by Hollingshead (1939) and Katz (1958).

extra empty house into which their future leader and the fifth candidate moved. In contrast to the previous six months of acquaintance with their future leader, when she lived some miles away, this arrangement

> resulted in daily exposure of the [five candidates]to Miss Lee's [the leader's] total conversion, which produced their increasing engrossment in the [belief system] until they came to give it their entire personal and material resources.

❋   ❋   ❋

> In the multitude of days and nights that Lee was able to spend with her charges, a feeling of new and special group identity could be built. She could handily mold notions of what the world was about from their daily grievances. Without such physical proximity, the tenets of the [cult doctrines] could not have been kept so constantly before them or made so directly meaningful as a system. (J. Lofland, 1966:58, 61.)

It is evident from the above instances of quasi-integrated place rounds in civil society that the additional items that can be subject to sanctioning, and therefore additionally indicative of deviance, are not necessarily defined negatively by imputing Others. The items are deviant only from the point of view of the total society and may well be occurring in the presence of Others by whom this additional evidence is welcomed and considered a positive accomplishment. Outsiders may look with horror at the new evidence so produced, as among homosexuals and religious cultists, but deviant Others can view the same evidence with joy and rejoicing.

ATTENUATED SITUATIONS

I have assumed thus far a condition of *normal and deviant* Others, relatively *united* on their imputations of Actor within an *integrated* place round. Let me now refer briefly to possible consequences of more attentuated situations. First, it is possible for Actor to be enmeshed in an integrated round within which his Others are divided in one or another way on whether a deviant category should be imputed to him. Such a situation would seem to be an inherently unstable one and tend eventually to result in unanimity. The direction in which the imputations are likely to move is a function of the power and attributed expertise of those backing whichever category. To facilitate unity (and therefore escalation), the more powerful and expert definers should be promoting the deviant pivotal category.

Second, the situation of united imputations in a segregated round seems to be an unlikely occurrence (and rather ineffective if it does occur). The fact of segregation inhibits the flow of information across places, and, more important, within a segregated round there is more likelihood that Actor will encounter ever new people who are not aware of imputations already made of him and thus will impute to him some variety of normality. Segregated rounds are considerably less powerful in general because of the inherently greater range of discretion that the Actor has over what places he will enter without his full complement of place Others knowing of or monitoring his place participation.

Third, a situation of imputationally divided Others in a segregated round seems most common in a modern society and rather marginal as an effective escalation arrangement. Typical instances are the outpatient who visits his therapist, the parolee, the welfare recipient and the homosexual who limits his participation in the homosexual underground. In all such situations there is the possibility for Actor to segregate imputations of deviance to one or a few sets of place Others, while at the same time participating in places where such imputations are unknown and not made. (See, e.g., Meyer and Borgotta, 1965.) There is, of course, a tendency for knowledge of imputations of deviance to leak through to all the places of an Actor's round, in no small measure due to his own announcements. Nevertheless, place segregation, which divides the imputations of Others, makes possible the reinforcement of attributions of normality.

DEVIANT PLACES

PLACE IMPUTATION

Places themselves vary in the definitions accorded them by the public at large. Just as human bodies are the kinds of objects to which deviant and normal imputations can be made, so too are physical territories or places. Thus human beings speak of "good places" and "bad places," "nice places" and "crummy places," "clean places" and "dirty places." Human beings can impute to territories, somewhat independently of people, a character or identity. In this sense, pieces of land and people are much the same kinds of objects.

Imputations to places imply some conception of an appropriate (even if immoral) clientele felt typically to inhabit or to frequent them. Nice places are frequented by that kind of people; crummy places are frequented by their kind of people. And, some places come to be defined in public consciousness as the kinds of physical territories in which one finds one or another kind of deviant person. Mental hospitals, jails, prisons, psychiatric clinics, welfare offices and crowded, unkempt parts of a city have attributed to them a populace of suspect personal character. These are to be contrasted with places whose populaces are not presumptively suspect, such as most work settings, homes, churches, schools, business organizations, stores and manufacturing plants. The places into which humans have divided the world, then, are distinguishable in terms of their presumptive *habitation or frequence by deviants or normals*.

Those places presumably inhabited by deviants are in turn distinguishable in terms of whether this presumption is *formal* or *informal*. Some are formally so designated even to the extent of being written into the budget of a government

under titles such as "State Prison," "State Mental Hospital" and "Boys' Re-
formatory." Signs may be erected on public frontage declaring to the passerby
that these are places for deviants. (Of course, the ironic euphemisms adopted
of late serve only to amuse the public without changing the definition, e.g., a
boys' prison being called a "conservation camp" or a private mental hospital
being called a "rest home.") Entire sections of cities may even be formally declared as occupied by deviants, although the euphemistic treatment of these
formal efforts under the rubric of "urban renewal" slightly obscures the definition. Many other places presumptively occupied by deviants may not have
had their use so formally acknowledged, but the definition may still be a matter
of more or less common knowledge. These *informal* places include criminal
and homosexual bars or entire sets of service institutions catering to deviant
clienteles. Bars and other such informally designated sites become known,
especially to taxi drivers and tourists and to locals who often derive an evening's entertainment from moving among them.[11]

FORMAL DEVIANT PLACES

Assuming that the strongest conditions enumerated thus far exist for Actor,
it can be suggested that escalation is additionally facilitated if all places in the
Actor's round are *formally* defined as occupied by *deviants*. Formal definition
of Actor's places as territories for devients serves to impress upon him, in a
quite literal fashion, his "place" in the world. He derives his very character
from the territory within which he resides. Part of his essential nature is generated by the territory he occupies. Character can be embodied in the very
architecture and in the physical arrangements which bear the stamp: deviants
live here. The following description of a mental hospital ward for the elderly
provides some sense of facilitative ways in which places for deviants can be
designed.

> The patient sleeps in a dormitory with 40 elderly persons, eats in the din-
> ing room with a like number and sits with them in an enormous day room.
> Privacy or a place for belongings is hard to come by. Most of the single
> and double rooms are already occupied by the tractable long-stay patients
> who comprise the working force of the hospital.
>
> ❋   ❋   ❋
>
> The newly admitted patient . . . has probably never lived in such a large
> area or been so close to so many people. (Sommer, 1959:589.)

Referring to a state mental hospital, a reporter provides a further sense of how
places for deviants might by their very features facilitate communication of
Actor's special character:

[11] In its own way, such slumming by normals is the functional equivalent of the tours
through loony bins taken for amusement by aristocrats of a former era.

A prison-like atmosphere permeates most of the wards—where there are locks on the elevators, bars on the windows, bolts on the doors and even locks on the light switches.

There is one shower to serve a ward of 70 men. (McDonald, 1965.)

Traditional prisons are, of course, the most explicit and straightforward regarding the character of their clientele.

Mechanical security measures . . . includ[e] . . . the building of high walls or fences around prisons, construction of gun towers, the searching of inmates as they pass through certain checkpoints, pass systems to account for inmate movement and counts at regular intervals. (President's Commission, . . . *Corrections*, 1967:46.)

At the level of immediate social interaction within a place *formally defined* for *deviants*, a number of practices on the part of normals also promote escalation. Of primary importance, and resting upon the normal's presumption of deviant character, is the practice of *role distance denial*. By "role distance" is meant the "margin of face-saving reactive expression—sullenness, failure to offer usual signs of deference, *sotto voce* profaning asides or fugitive expressions of contempt, irony and derision"—that an individual engages in when he "must accept circumstances and commands that affront his conception of self" (Goffman, 1961a:36). Life among normals in civil society abounds in small expressions by persons of their incomplete acceptance of the arrangements in which they are enmeshed. Role distance is normal in the sense that those who engage in it and those who observe it take it as a typical and to-be-expected reaction under a variety of even mildly vexing circumstances. Indulged in with sufficient moderation and selectivity, expressions of role distance seem even to be obligatory if witnessing Others are to feel that a witnessed Actor is a good guy. Persons who seem to embrace the vexations of circumstance too happily are themselves slightly suspect.

However, in places formally defined as populated by deviants, a different kind of interaction game is played. The normal caretakers of these places typically define expressions of role distance by those defined as deviant not as normal griping but as revealingly symptomatic of deviant character. Deviants in total institutions formally defined as being for them may find that they have considerably less freedom to act normally in this regard than they would have had in normal places. Much more is likely to be made of their expressions of dislike of the place itself and of the staff who runs it than, let us say, similar expressions in a total institution such as the U.S. Army, where those who do *not* express role distance may be objects of suspicion. There is a tendency, then, to *deny* to participants a measure of normal role distance. It is made, rather, an object of concern and is defined as a manifestation of deviant character and/or as a type of expression best suppressed through punishment. Ironically, there is a significant sense in which those with the worst lot are expected to be most accepting of it.

ATTENUATED SITUATIONS

Although the place round situation of an Actor participating only in *formally* designated *deviant* places appears to be the strongest condition,[12] escalation can also occur (usually with less frequency and effectiveness) under more attenuated circumstances. Participation in a place round of *informally* designated *deviant* places is one such attenuated situation. Underlying or highly correlated with the formal-informal distinction is the dimension of the degree to which the Others have the *power* to force candidate Actor to sustain his participation. Others who manage places formally designated for deviants typically have the police powers of some political unit at their disposal. The Others of informal places must, in contrast, rely upon persuasion and the evocation of attractiveness to Actor. Since his presence there is more or less voluntary, Actor may simply go away or fail to come back. Even under circumstances of united Others in an integrated round, escalation in informal worlds (such as deviant religious milieux, homosexual undergrounds or hippy culture) is a very tenuous affair. Escalation becomes even more problematic when the degree of integration of the place round is also decreased. When unanimity of imputation and the proportion of even informally defined deviant places in Actor's place round are also attenuated, it is a wonder that any new personnel are taken on at all—and worlds characterized by these conditions do indeed have personnel problems.

It is for these sorts of reasons that normative, emotional ties to Others who already wear the deviant label become particularly important in place rounds made up of at least some informal deviant places. (See pp. 187–91.) The institution and success of escalation seem sometimes to rest heavily upon the availability of informal sites that make possible rather powerful emotive attractions and attachments in a relatively short amount of time. It may be, for example, that the particular and peculiar characteristics of homosexual bars as a *type of place* are instrumental in the success of the homosexual milieu in populating its places. Hooker reports that such

> bars also serve as induction and training and integration centers for the community. These functions are difficult to separate. The young man who may have had a few isolated homosexual experiences in adolescence, or indeed none at all, and who is taken to a "gay" bar by a group of friends whose homosexuality is only vaguely suspected or unknown to him, may find the excitement and opportunities for sexual gratification appealing

---

[12] Cf. McKay, 1967:113: "The greater the participation of the young person in the institutions for treatment of the juvenile offender [in Chicago, Cook County and the State of Illinois], the greater is his probability of acquiring a record of adult criminality."

and thus begin active participation in the community life. Very often, the debut, referred to by homosexuals as "coming out," of a person who believes himself to be homosexual but who has struggled against it, will occur in a bar when he, for the first time, identifies himself publicly as a homosexual in the presence of other homosexuals by his appearance in the situation. If he has thought of himself as unique, or has thought of homosexuals as a strange and unusual lot, he may be agreeably astonished to discover large numbers of men who are physically attractive, personable and "masculine" appearing, so that his hesitancy in identifying himself as a homosexual is greatly reduced. Since he may meet a complete cross-section of occupational and socioeconomic levels in the bar, he becomes convinced that far from being a small minority, the "gay" population is very extensive indeed. (Hooker, 1961:52.)

Informal deviant milieux whose participants feel that they have a recruitment problem might well benefit from adopting the practices of the homosexual milieu, at least as it is organized in Los Angeles, the setting of the above description.

Another attenuated situation, that of a place round composed exclusively of sites formally and/or informally designated for normals, seems not to preclude escalation but to be marginally facilitative. Of more interest are place rounds composed of a mixed variety of sites, some defined (formally or informally) as for deviants and some defined as territories for normals. Within or across such a mixture of sites, normal and deviant Others may be divided on their imputations of Actor, and in addition the Actor himself may move in a relatively segregated round. This is one of the more complicated of possible place rounds, and it is probably among the empirically most common. In it, escalation is problematic. The Actor who regularly frequents his social work agency, his outpatient clinic, his parole office, his Students for Democratic Society headquarters or his homosexual bar but is at other times in sites where very different kinds of imputations will be made of him will less easily come to embrace (and maintain) any deviant identity. Although Others in these places surely engage in the denial of role distance, the moralization of minutiae, the reconstruction of current activity and of biography and all the rest, their location in such a complex and varied place round weakens their ability to prosecute their inclinations vis-à-vis Actor. Not only can their definitions be contradicted, but the time and effort they can devote to their efforts are severely limited.[13]

---

[13] Although I will not pursue them here, each of the foregoing (and subsequent) maximally facilitative states have, in turn, their respective social organizational sources. The varying strengths that any given element can assume may themselves be made the objects of analysis. Thus, for example, one can ask under what conditions there will (or will not) arise in a society places formally defined as specific resorts for people believed to be deviant sorts

The assumption of a personal identity, deviant or otherwise, is facilitated not only by particular arrangements of Others and places but also by certain manipulations of hardware and by certain states of our central figure himself, Actor. These latter elements are discussed in the next chapter.

---

of persons. (Cf. Eaton and Weil's report [1955:Chap. 11] of a case where they have not arisen.) Under what conditions will such places, once occurring, manifest a distinctively impugning design and physical facilities far less comfortable than those prevailing in the culture at large? Such third level questions (see pp. 29–31) direct our attention again to the encompassing social order, to its history, to the current interests of, and conflicts among, the major institutions and to the dominant groups' conceptions of what is proper and practical. Relative to the occurrence (and persistence) of distinctively impugning formal deviant places, for example, there can arise particular interest in how state and federal legislators come to make decisions to support such places and to support them at a given financial level. (A provisional answer to this specific question is provided in Grob's [1966] excellent historical analysis of the Worcester State Hospital in Massachusetts, 1830–1920. See also Nelson, 1967.)

CHAPTER 8

ESCALATION TO DEVIANT IDENTITY: HARDWARE AND ACTOR

HARDWARE

CHARACTER AND COMPONENTS OF HARDWARE

What humans believe themselves and others to be rests, in part, upon the physical items surrounding and structuring the representations they can make to one another. There is a significant sense in which clothes, most generally construed, not only *make* the man but *are* the man. The props on the stages of social life provide the physical underpinnings which help make possible the belief among humans that they are really and certainly what they believe themselves to be. Sufficiently large and weighty supplies of such props, imbued with a degree of positive emotional value, serve quite literally to hold down their human possessors. Should humans come to doubt that they are really what their physical artifacts construe them to be, anticipation of the effort required to dispose of these artifacts may give such doubters second thoughts and conduce a return to that identity communicated by their hardware.[1]

The term "hardware" is intended to denote both those physical objects that can be attached or affixed to the body of an Actor and those that can be picked up or manipulated. The term is limited to items which can be moved with relative ease by one or, at most, a few Actors. Hardware may be as light as false eyelashes or as heavy or heavier than an automobile. To retrieve this term from the submerged background of common-sense, unproblematic affairs, let me briefly explicate some of its main categories, thereby enabling us to see some of the ways in which available hardware can vary and to note the identity implications of such variance.

There are, first, items of physical attire, typically, although far from exclusively, constructed of cloth. Second, there may be a stock of apparel-maintenance devices, such as shoeshine equipment, washing machines, irons, coat hangers and the like. Third, Actors may possess a range of body-grooming equipment composed of such simple items as combs, deodorants and soaps and of somewhat more elaborate devices such as hairdriers, electric razors and various cosmetics. Fourth, Actors are likely to have feeding and sleeping equipment (excluding the actual site where such equipment is stored), including eating utensils, food, pots, pans, beds, lamps, etc. Fifth, affluent Actors can

---

[1] About a million Americans a year are reported, however, still to find it possible to skip out on their assembly of hardware (largely because they owe a great deal of money on it) and to take up residence under some different category in some other place. See "Vanishing Americans," *Newsweek,* February 24, 1964.

embroider their existence with elaborate place furnishings. Sixth, some Actors are to be found possessing occupational equipment (used here in the narrow sense of items employed directly in the task of making some sort of living). Seventh—and of some prominence in suburban America—is a range of recreational equipment, sometimes including special types of motorized vehicles but more typically involving television sets, radio receivers, outdoor grills and the like. Finally, there are the ideological artifacts (used here in the limited sense of physical embodiments defined by Actors as expressions either of the most general principles by which they live or of the most significant events of their lives). Among these there may be special books (such as Bibles and scrapbooks), mementos, trophies, diplomas or accouterments thought of as art. The Actors of the world, of course, differ enormously in the number, variety, quality, state of repair and stylishness of the items within and across these categories which they possess. Some Actors may have a large number in all of these and in other categories; others may possess none or very few items in every category.

NORMAL HARDWARE WITHDRAWN, DEVIANT HARDWARE SUPPLIED

Holding constant the number and variety of items possessed, we may consider two general principles applicable to the manipulation of hardware for purposes of facilitating escalation. First, in order to precipitate and escalate doubt on the part of Actor (and Others) that he is an instance of some normal category, all hardware conventionally associated with a normal identity should be *withdrawn* from his possession. Reciprocally, in order to facilitate Actor's personal identification (and to facilitate Others' continued imputations of him), hardware conventionally identified with a given deviant category should be *supplied*.

Withdrawal of normal hardware decreases the possibility of Actor's thinking of himself as that kind of person. At the level of concrete arrangements, total institutions of many kinds perform this withdrawal in a prototypically facilitative way. Entry into some prisons and mental hospitals (and convents and military institutions) is often accompanied by a shearing off of almost all the hardware enumerated in the above list and conventionally associated with living under the label, normal. Actors are even stripped of their "identity kits," to use Goffman's phrase; that is, their grooming equipment and maintenance devices are confiscated. (Goffman, 1961a.) Of entry into a reform school, a young man can thus relate:

> I was still attired in a good suit and would not have looked out of place at a high school prom as we stepped inside [the juvenile "reform" school]. Twenty minutes later I had stripped, taken a shower and been marched

through a tray of smelly disinfectant. I was issued one of the rough uniforms and, as a final indignity, my head was shaved. I was a reform
school inmate. (Sands, 1964:23.)

The same person's account of hardware stripping upon entry into San Quentin
is considerably more graphic and appreciative of the identity implications of
dress.

Then came the grey—my prison uniform. Across the back pockets of grey
pants, over the left breast pocket of grey shirt, across the back of the shirt,
on the back and the inside of the grey prison jacket was a number: 66836.
    I was 66836. There was no longer an entity called Wilber Power
Sewell or Bill or Sewell. I was to answer as "six-six-eight-three-six." That
was "who" I was. Shaved head, grey uniform, a number. (Sands,
1964:36.)

To the degree that more modern institutions abolish this practice, as some are
now doing, destruction of existing identification as some kind of normal is inhibited.

Correspondingly, escalation is facilitated by providing Actor with a wide
range of new hardware that is publicly defined as the physical expression of
the deviant category in question. Again, many total institutions for deviants
perform this with some effectiveness, as suggested in the above quote, by providing uniforms, handbooks of rules and other paraphernalia applicable to the
deviant category. It should be noted, however, that the range and variety
of hardware provided in public total institutions are rather meager when one
considers the range and variety that are possible. Although inmates of prisons
and mental hospitals may have available to them (but do not own) a few items
in each of the enumerated categories, their total supply tends to be rather
sparse and spartan. Perhaps for budgetary reasons, keepers of such institutions
have not exploited the rich possibilities for providing hardware specially identified with the categories of convict and mental patient.

Humans already living under a deviant label, who are actively interested in
recruiting additional Actors, sometimes seem more aggressive in sponsoring a
rich repertoire of hardware particular to their category. Thus organizations
such as the American Nazi Party, the Ku Klux Klan or the Hell's Angels, or
loose worlds such as the current hippy milieu, seem to display a broader and
richer range of distinctive physical artifacts, including formal or informal uniforms and feeding, sleeping, occupational and recreational equipment. However, organizations and milieux of these sorts do not have the coercive power to
strip the Actor of his existing hardware or to enforce the use of a new set. Unlike state-sponsored institutions, these more voluntary affiliations are likely to
find escalation more tenuous and subject to breakdown partly because of their
rather low control over hardware. In addition, meagerness of resources with

which to assemble distinctive hardware is also likely to be a feature of deviant groups at large in civil society. Many categories of deviants are unlikely to have the funds necessary to work up a truly distinctive complement of physical artifacts. Often they are forced to accord this matter rather low priority in their hierarchy of ways in which resources should be expended. This is most poignantly the case for deviant categories whose occupants are drawn from low-income sectors of the population. In cults and other bizarre religions, for example, we find that some small lapel pin or headpiece (as is largely the case in the Black Muslims) may be as far as a category will feel it can go.

That is, I am suggesting that, in contemporary America, even those deviants operating outside state institutions who are proud of their deviant identification seem not to have exploited possibilities for distinctive hardware nearly to the extent that deviants have in other times and other places. Even so aggressively self-righteous a category as the Black Muslims content themselves, in large measure, with the distinctiveness of white middle-class hardware. There is a sense in which the utopian communities of the 19th century were more nearly on the right track in elaborating the entire range of hardware, even to the point of growing their own special varieties of foods and of manufacturing distinctive sleeping, eating and occupational equipment (Kanter, 1967). It may be that the hippy movement and the Hell's Angels organizations of the late sixties have been the objects of particular note by normal Others primarily because of their utilization of distinctive hardware—especially distinctive when compared with the pallid outfitting characteristic of many, if not most, deviant categories.

It can be suggested, then, that escalation is facilitated when candidate-identifiers with a deviant category are provided with a full supply of hardware items distinctive to that category.

ACTOR

Giving those inclined to psychologistic interpretations their due, it is clear that not all Actors subjected to even the strongest conditions suggested to this point are equally vulnerable to eventually identifying themselves with a deviant category. As with Others, places and hardware, some arrangements of Actor himself are more facilitative of escalation than are others. By "arrangements" of Actor, I refer to (1) the degree to which he is oriented; (2) the character of his attachments to normals and to deviants; and (3) the congruence between his cognitive field or set of coding categories and those presented. Each of these elements may vary. Depending on the values of their joint combination, Actor is rendered more or less vulnerable to, or, in previous terms, more or less facilitative of, the escalation process. In addition, there are variations in the work of Others (particularly deviant Others) which have facilitative signifi-cance. These are, as previously mentioned, (1) the character of the ideology and (2) the degree of tutoring in technical knowledge and skills which they offer to Actor. As was noted in Chap. 7, these matters belong logically in the earlier discussion of Others, but for expository reasons they are considered here.

DISORIENTATION

ORIENTATION AND DISORIENTATION

The term "disorientation" denotes Actor's phenomenological state of high anxiety, fear and ambiguity over how to cope with or manage his proximate life situation. States of disorientation are not untypically coded by Actors with such terms as bewilderment, consternation, confusion, shock, trauma, astonishment, being at loose ends or at the end of one's rope, immobilization, having one's back against the wall, being at the bottom of the abyss, paralyzation, etc. Situations or states of affairs are coded as having gotten out of hand, become unmanageable, or, even fallen into disorganization. A phenomenological state of orientation, in contrast, entails the absence of such experiences, at least to any significant degree. An Actor who is oriented is finding his established categories for defining raw reality to be quite adequate and is activating with reasonable success his repertoire of strategies for coping with and managing events and Others. Disorientation is precipitated by the occurrence of events that fall outside or between Actor's existing cognitive categories for rendering reality coherent and understandable. The occurrence of events that are uncodable (even as a residual "other") means that Actor is unable to activate strategies for coping behaviorally or linguistically with the circumstance. Such occurrences lack meaning; that is, they lack possibilities for action (E. Becker, 1962).

VULNERABILITY TO DISORIENTATION

Vulnerability to, and the occurrence of, disorientation is not randomly distributed throughout a population but is connected to, among other things, (1) the character of Actor's extant cognitive system and (2) the character of circumstances he encounters.

Strength of Orientation, Education and Age. Actors' extant cognitive systems vary in terms of the degree to which they are complex, articulated and self-consciously justified. Actors with the most complex, articulate and self-consciously justified schemes for coding reality may be referred to as *strongly oriented*. Actors with the least complex, articulate and self-consciously justified schemes may be referred to as *weakly oriented*. (It is of course recognized that, empirically, Actors are ranged widely along such a continuum. I have here dichotomized the variable for purposes of straightforward explication.)

Other things being equal, it can be suggested that the more strongly oriented the Actor, the less vulnerable he is to disorientation and therefore the less facilitative he is of escalation.   To be strongly oriented is to have a strong sense and awareness of the category or categories one *is* and to have a self-conscious justification of *why* one is and why one *should remain* an instance of the category or categories.   That is, to the degree that orientation of the cognitive field is accompanied by *moralization,* Actors are resistant material in escalation. They will have less doubt about themselves in response to negative imputation by Others.   They will more actively seek out Others who support their categorical identifications.   They may even seek to mobilize sympathetic Others against the negative imputations and, by so doing, transform an initiated issue of deviance into a purely political struggle.   (See the interesting case of General Edwin Walker reported in Szasz, 1965:Chap. 6; and on p. 155 of this text.)

On the other hand, Actors who are more weakly oriented (who have a less firm sense of their personal identity), can more easily doubt whatever categories they vaguely ascribe to themselves and more easily believe that the imputations made by Others (especially expert and unanimous Others) are reasonable, realistic and factual, even if grim, undesired, discrediting and socially devastating.

It can be suggested that strength of orientation is highly associated with amount and quality of either formal education or other exposure to the range and variety of human categories and their accompanying justifications.   We should expect, therefore, that more highly educated people, for this reason alone (as well as others), are less likely to be escalated to deviant roles. Should such a process begin, they are more able, by virtue of their ideologization, to talk their way out of it.   This is to say that because they are able to give more complex and articulate accounts of themselves, they are more likely to convince any imputors of the reasonableness or real (i.e., harmless, nonsymptomatic) meaning of their actions.   And, since they are likely to share in the universe of understandings and cultural ideology of expert imputors, they are more likely to be aware of what kinds of reasons or explanations such imputors will buy.[2]   The more educated know the proper motives and accounts to offer.   The less educated, being less strongly oriented and less likely to share a universe of cultural understanding (including acceptable accounts of self) with imputors, are more vulnerable.   Vulnerability is increased by their lack of skill in the production of acceptable accounts or by their lack of knowledge as to what constitutes a salable account.   The well-known differentials among the social classes in rates of *officially recorded* apprehension and conviction or commitment can be at least partially understood in these terms.

I do not wish, however, to overemphasize the role of education per se in fostering a strong orientation.   Although it may be an important one in this regard, a more complete picture of the relationship requires, in addition, a consideration of what it means in American civilization for one to be highly educated.   In large measure, education is training for social survival in, and

[2] See further Mills, 1940; Scott and Lyman, 1968; and Erikson's discussion of persons vulnerable to imputation as witches (1966:141–53).

mastery of, those situations frequently confronted by Actors in a society of large-scale bureaucratic organizations. Survival in such a society depends upon knowledge and understanding of formalized rules, of slow, step-by-step, procedures and of reading and writing. It depends additionally on Actors being connected with Others who can explain and manipulate those segments of social life with which they are unfamiliar (e.g., having a competent attorney and other connections). Education is orientation in how to play the bureaucratic social game, and it should therefore not be surprising that, within the context of American civilization, bureaucratized as it is, the highly educated are most strongly oriented. In addition, because it is the highly educated who make and administer the rules and procedures and structure the character of the social game generally, their skill as players is hardly problematic. *They are playing their own game.* People who have less education are only weakly oriented *relative to* the game played by, let me be plain, White, middle- and upper-class America. People with less education may be quite strongly oriented *relative to* the social games played outside bureaucratic society. But at those points where less educated persons must *intersect* with bureaucratic society, they are likely to appear and to become weakly oriented. The strong orientation of the more educated may be, then, merely an illusion, an artifact of their position in the dominant sector of American civilization. The more educated are less likely to encounter situations for which they are undereducated or unoriented and, on that account alone, are less likely to experience disorientation.

One might wonder what would happen if the current dominant and subordinate sectors were to be reversed. It seems likely that the masters in the reversed situation might well become concerned over the inability of the more educated to cope effectively and over their apparent vulnerability to disorientation. Even in the absence of such a reversal, one might wonder how strongly and persistently oriented college graduates and Ph.D.'s would remain if they had to survive in certain Black ghettos, coping with ghetto life on its own terms. Their fellow residents might well come to be concerned over the incompetence and disorientation of such usually stellar players in this different social game. It is not, then, only, or even primarily, education per se that provides the educated with their strong orientation, but the meaning of education relative to, or in the context of, the dominant social game in American civilization.[3]

Other gross demographic attributes are also correlated with orientational strength. Of some importance is *age*. In contemporary society a weak orientation appears to be characteristic of both the very old and the very young. In part because of physical deterioration, the old are less able or less inclined to defend their actions in terms of their cognitive categories (and, ironically, have less worthwhile categories of identity to defend), and they are, consequently, more vulnerable to imputors (Miller and Schwartz, 1966). And the young have

---

[3] For a different view see Roach's (1967) recent compilation of materials on "lower-class" behavior.

not been around long enough to learn the ideologization of social categories. Their responses to the voiced suspicions of Others regarding their actions are more likely to involve simple verbal or physical assaults than complex verbal accounts. Such responses are easily read by would-be or actual imputors as further indications of suspected pivotal deviance. It is in this context of the typically weak orientations among the young that we can better understand the attention paid to, and amazement expressed over, ten-year-olds who do graduate work in universities and who talk meaningfully (i.e., in adult terms) about who they are and to what they aspire.

When low education and youth or old age are combined in the same Actor, producing a person with a particularly low degree of orientation, it seems apparent that he becomes especially vulnerable to escalation. It may be for this reason, as well as others, that public institutions for pivotal deviants tend to contain high proportions of the poorly educated young and old.

Disorienting Circumstances. It has been quite popular in social science to emphasize early socialization climates as crucial elements in the production of weak orientations. Although the impact of early training, especially within the family, can be granted,[4] such an emphasis seems terribly narrow relative to the wide range of empirically demonstrable *contemporaneous* sources of disorientation. All human lives are subject to a variety of crises. Among the more typical are: marital disputes and dissolution through conflict; death or other loss of a beloved spouse, parent, child or friend; loss of a fondly embraced job; severe physical deprivation, such as starvation; disruption of life due to a natural disaster, such as a flood or tornado; collapse of a life style because of war or invasion or conquest; drastic shift in life situation due to military induction, combat or imprisonment; contraction of a severe illness; change of life because of migration or menopause; exposure to a highly monotonous environment; or even traumatic incarceration in a prison or mental hospital.[5] In these and in many other ways, people can be exposed to *disorienting circumstances.*

Under such circumstances, orientation can be weakened, not only among those who are already weakly oriented but, of more interest, among those who have been the most strongly oriented as well. Even persons with the firmest and most articulated identities can, under certain conditions, be forced to wonder about the meaning, efficacy and reality of the categories in which they have heretofore conceived themselves. The range of justifications and routine

[4] See especially the materials relating to the development of strong self-esteem as a buffer against immediate influence and possible disorientation: Coopersmith, 1967; Rosenberg, 1965; Weinberg, ed., 1967:Part III; and the materials in note 5 below.

[5] Extended discussions of the character, causes and consequences of disorientation may be found in: Brownfield, 1965; Tyhurst, 1957; Bennis *et al.*, 1964; Farberow, 1967; Scheff, 1966:40–54; Schein, 1956, 1957, 1961; Appley and Trumbull, 1967; Bettelheim, 1943; Solomon *et al.*, eds., 1961. Especially relevant are materials suggesting ways in which Actors can be convinced of unfactual or highly ambiguous "facts." See Festinger and Carlsmith, 1959; Janis, 1955; Zimbardo, 1967; Bem, 1967; Aronson and Mills, 1959; J. Davis, 1963.

modes of action connected to their categories may no longer have the same meaning and relevance because they now exist within a different context. This context may be one of *ambiguity,* wherein few people, if any, are certain as to what kinds of categories are applicable and upon what bases action should be organized. For example, a situation of ambiguity appears to result from out-side military attacks or natural disasters when no provisions have been made for such eventualities—that is, when no set of categories for acting have been specified, when no bodies have been designated to act in terms of the categories and when no action routines have been practiced. Or, the new context may involve the imposition of a *new scheme* of categories. In this case the problem is not so much one of ambiguity over what the categories might be within which to conceive oneself and in terms of which to act, but one of being able, phys-ically and psychologically, to make the transition to the new scheme and to find a category into which one can fit. In either event, old schemes of action are brought into doubt and identity crises are created. Regardless of previously existing strength of orientation, almost every Actor so subjected becomes more vulnerable to identifying himself with imputations—deviant or otherwise—that may be made by Others. Even those referred to as the most mature, stable or adjusted of adults can, under sufficiently disorienting circumstances, be made to doubt the adequacy of their schemes for organizing the world.

Conceiving what has been said thus far in more general terms, capacity for, or vulnerability to, disorientation is a function of what categories exist within an Actor's cognitive system. An occurrence is disorienting only if the Actor has no category with which effectively to designate the occurrence and no as-sociated repertoire of coping responses which he can activate. No concrete occurrence in the above list of disorienting experiences is, in itself, necessarily disorienting for any given Actor. It is possible to compile such a list only be-cause human animals have, in fact, frequently found one or another of such experiences to be so. The foregoing points up a crucial factor in effecting vulnerability to disorientation. The larger the number of possible occurrences that have been designated and categorized by Actor and the larger the range of associated routines that have been worked out for managing them, the less the likelihood that Actor will become disoriented and encounter an identity crisis. However, it is unlikely that any Actor has a cognitive system so complex and articulated that no possible occurrence can fall outside the range of what he is already able to designate and manage. In this sense all Actors are, in one way or another, to one degree or another, vulnerable to disorientation.

We see again the relevance of education, for the number of categories possessed for the designation of occurrences is likely to be correlated with extent of education, or at least, with general breadth of experience (and, up to a point, with age). To be educated is to possess a broad range of categories for designating occurrences and at least some vague notion of how to manage them. Poorly educated, isolated and parochial persons are simply more likely to encounter events which to them are inexplicable, baffling, bewildering, incomprehensible and the like. They are thus more vulnerable to escalation than their more "sophisticated" fellows, for the simple reason that, in the face of the incomprehensible, Actors *seek out* definitions of events from Others. The underlying and more general principle has been stated by Blake and Mouton:

> An individual requires a stable framework, including salient and firm reference points, in order to orient himself and to regulate his interactions with others. This framework consists of external and internal anchorages available to the individual whether he is aware of them or not. With an acceptable framework he can resist giving or accepting information that is inconsistent with that framework or that requires him to relinquish it. In the absence of a stable framework he actively seeks to establish one through his own strivings by making use of significant and relevant information provided within the context of interaction. By controlling the amount and kind of information available for orientation, he can be led to embrace conforming attitudes which are entirely foreign to his earlier ways of thinking.[6]

EXCURSUS ON DISORIENTING
INNER EMANATIONS

Among occurrences that can fall outside an Actor's cognitive categories, of special interest are those events which appear to Actors to *emanate from within themselves* and which may give them reason to wonder about their sanity or stability. Events of this character, such as hallucinations, loss of muscle control, blackouts and the like, can arise for a variety of reasons. Not unimportant are purely physical causes such as Parkinson's disease, multiple sclerosis, physical deprivation, long exposure to a monotonous environment or long subjection to a highly stressful situation such as military combat. It has apparently been the case in the past, and still is today, that events arising under these circumstances are sometimes baffling to the involved Actors. That is, they do not directly define them as the normal, to-be-expected results of their situations. As a result, some of these Actors begin at once to categorize the events as indicators, instances or symptoms of broader psychological categories, maladies or pathologies. Other Actors simply do not know what to "make of" them and seek out those who are presumed capable of offering valid categorizations. In American civilization those sought out are likely to be medical doctors; elsewhere they might be witch doctors or priests. Recalling an earlier

---

[6] Blake and Mouton, 1961, quoted in Scheff, 1963:444, footnote 19. It should be noted more generally that these extreme matters of orientation and disorientation are in no way alien to the more everyday aspects of social life. All efforts to disseminate information are efforts to define the character of objects and of events and to stabilize responses. We see this stabilizing function most clearly in those programs intended to deal with highly extraordinary occurrences. Civil defense organizations and natural disaster teams are overtly designed to forestall and prevent disorientation under circumstances that would be disorganizing for almost everyone if preparations were not made.

discussion, it can be seen that whatever the category of the person sought, what these Others say to Actor under these circumstances is of crucial importance. With Actor open to definition, indeed, actively seeking it, what he is told becomes fundamentally significant for what he will make of himself as a type of person. In the case of what is called "battle neurosis," for example, "the incipient state . . . is described as 'amorphous and unstructured.' In this phase it is exceedingly difficult to draw any sharp lines between normal and abnormal combat fatigue, fear, anxiety, 'jumpiness,' and sleep disturbances" (Lemert, 1951:429).

> Importantly, the transition from an incipient to an acute phase in which the soldier "surrendered to his neurosis" *was found to vary closely with the way in which the soldier was handled.* Oversympathetic battle surgeons and evacuation out of the battle zones were discovered to be dynamic factors in converting the amorphous symptoms of the incipient stage into definitive neurotic form. Conversely, the absence of any rear area for evacuation, a "tough" attitude by battle surgeons and direct discipline on the battlefield often were means by which badly disturbed soldiers bore up with their roles.[7]

"The way in which the soldier was handled" refers here to whether he was designated, under these circumstances, as an instance of a pivotally deviant type, such as a schizophrenic, or whether he continued to receive imputations of normality.

Ironically, the very act of designating an Actor who is disturbed by inner emanations as a pivotal deviant sometimes produces *additional anxiety.* Actor not only labors under the anxiety and fear provoked by the disturbing inner emanations, but he now experiences that provoked by the meaning and implications of being what he is imputed to be. And, this additional anxiety can, in turn, be taken by Others as yet further evidence for their imputation and for the need to prosecute more intensive treatment. Finding himself subjected to the resulting more intensive treatment, Actor can become even more anxious over the possibility that he may be worse off than he had thought. This response, in turn, feeds back to Others, and the cycle of escalation starts again.

Under these circumstances an additional and important self-fulfilling process can be begun by Actor himself (and fed back to Others). Increasing levels of anxiety and fear serve to make Actor more intensively sensitive to, and more acutely aware of, all his feelings and actions. The most mundane of these can come to be scrutinized for their actual meaning vis-à-vis his new deviant category. What he (and Others) previously discounted, overlooked or did not perceive can now be grist for the mill of his pivotal deviant identity. As Goffman has put it, the deviant category can become a "coat rack" upon which are hung

---

[7] Lemert, 1951:429; italics added. See also Coleman, 1967; Scheff, 1966:80–101.

all manner of minor failings, disturbing feelings and inappropriate acts. That is, under conditions of doubt, anxiety and fear, a variety of new things are coded by Actor himself as indicators of his deviant category. What may have formerly been defined by Actor (and Others) as normal fear, normal anger, normal frustration, normal temper, normal criticism or normal depression may now be defined as abnormal (i.e., as evidentially indicative of the validity of the imputation).[8]

If the category of self into which the Actor is coding his feelings and actions is a psychiatric one, there is likely to be an even greater number of feelings and acts that are taken to be symptomatic. As it is often operationally implemented, psychiatric theory promotes the belief among Actors that their problems include the *inability to control their feelings and actions*. If an Actor believes, as some psychiatric specialists would have him believe, that he is the sort of person who lacks control, then it is reasonable for him to demonstrate this lack whenever, in some immediate circumstance, self-control becomes problematic. He is, after all, one of those persons who suffer from this type of defect. Peculiar and disturbing experiences which Actors view as emanating from themselves can be defined, of course, in other than psychiatric terms. One can wonder, however, how many persons residing in mental hospitals were escalated to a category of mental illness from an initial transitory disorienting experience which was transformed in the manner just sketched and which came, therefore, to have a dynamic of its own (see Scheff, 1966).

One can also wonder how many people who think of themselves as mentally ill began with, and still experience, symptoms arising from a purely physical base. There are numerous physical illnesses which produce disturbing inner emanations that might easily be defined as indicative of a type of mental illness. It is known, for example, that multiple sclerosis, a neurologically degenerative disease of young adults, produces perceptual distortion, exhaustion, forgetfulness, speech difficulties and, in varying degrees, loss of motor control. Only a handful of medical persons are capable of diagnosing it in its early stages or in its milder forms. One might wonder how many low-income, low-education young persons actually suffering from this disease have never come to the attention of medical specialists who could make the diagnosis but have, instead, been processed as mentally ill.[9]

Some people, disoriented by disturbing inner emanations, may bypass the psychiatric establishment altogether and take up a label other than that of mentally ill. Such Actors remain, however, particularly vulnerable to the possi-

[8] This process is, of course, formally similar to that spelled out regarding the activities of Others in identifying and escalating Actor (pp. 147–53 above).

[9] Therefore the reported association between multiple sclerosis and relative affluence may be an artifact of affluent persons having the symbolic and material resources necessary to bring themselves to the attention of those medical people operating with a broad range of diagnostic categories.

bility of assuming a *deviant* identity, even if not a mentally ill deviant one. Although in some societies, nonroutine, nonempirical, even personally disturbing inner emanations are categorized as indicative of a special and highly valued relation to a supernatural world, most natives of American civilizations are skeptical of such a possibility. As is well known, Actors who announce supernatural experiences are usually segregated into special communities for the disturbed. Despite this majority attitude, there still exist numerous pockets of sympathetic persons where Actors are protected from the usual results of making known their experiences. Within such protective surroundings, Actors may impute a religious superempirical character to their inner emanations. When religiously defined emanations are experienced on a wide enough scale and in respectable enough circumstances (i.e., by people with strongly normal pivotal identities in settings strongly defined as frequented by normals), such emanations may even be defined by nonsympathetic Others as only weakly or not at all indicative of deviant character. This seems to have been the case when a rash of tongues speaking broke out among congregations of respectable denominations on the West Coast in the early sixties (Bess, 1963). However, the same kind of religiously defined inner emanations, occurring less in respect - able circumstances (i.e., among people with low-prestige pivotal identities and in places defined as frequented by deviants or at least by some suspect sorts of people), are more likely to result in escalation to deviant, although not psychiatrically deviant, roles. A possible pattern of this kind is suggested by the sequence of experiences and involvements found among a number of Actors (studied by the author) who came eventually to identify themselves as the elect of God, faced with the task of preparing for the worldly millenium. Many of them had experienced hallucinations for which they "lacked any successful definition" (J. Lofland, 1966:34). These Actors were relatively uninformed about conventional psychiatric categories in terms of which they could define their problematic experiences. Although unaffiliated with any organized religion, they came from backgrounds that accustomed them to define events in a religious way, and they were in search of a specific religious meaning to impose upon their problematic inner emanations. Although these Actors remained undiscovered by Others who had the power or inclination to process them as instances of psychiatric types (although some made such imputations), they did come into contact with Others who imputed to them the identity of specially prepared persons whose destiny it was to save the world. Their problematic inner emanations were defined as spirit manifestations, the spirits having prepared them to be able to see the truth: that they were members of a cadre who would save the world and be honored forever. Acceptance of the category offered brings an end to the Actor's disorientation. For the cult converts, the newly attributed and accepted category of world saver was

> grandly teleological and [offered] a minute and lawful explanation of the whole of human history. [The doctrines of the category] systematically

revealed and defined the hidden meaning of individual lives that had lacked coherence and purpose. (J. Lofland, 1966:48.)

I have digressed somewhat in the discussion of disorientation in order to suggest more clearly the interrelations of the separately explicated processes. The main point remains, however, that Actor is most amenable or vulnerable to (or facilitative of) escalation when he, for whatever reason, is disoriented, his disorientation being produced through the induction of highly unfamiliar and stressful circumstances. Not the least of such circumstances is the experience of being processed by agents of the social control establishment.

AFFECTIVE BONDS

AFFECT AND SOCIAL TRUTH

A long tradition of social psychological theory and experimentation suggests the viability of the proposition that what human beings believe to be true, real, moral and possible is intimately a function of the emotional ties they have to other human Actors. Human animals tend to accept as true what is said by people to whom they have positive emotive attachments and to disbelieve or doubt what is said by people they dislike or distrust. Shibutani summarizes the materials suggesting this proposition in this fashion:

> Although the exact character of the connection is not clear, there is some kind of relationship between one person's sentiment toward another and the extent to which they share a common outlook. It is apparently not possible to accept another person and at the same time reject his values. As unlikely as it may sound, the manner in which a person experiences "reality" is somehow related to his intimate ties with other people. (Shibutani, 1961:588.)

Positive Affect for Both Normals and Deviants. Under conditions of unanimous imputation to Actor of a pivotally deviant category where both normals and deviants are present, escalation would appear most facilitated if Actor has positive emotive ties to at least some Others in the categories of *both* normals and deviants. The empirical infrequency of this situation does not gainsay its facilitative superiority for escalation. (Cf. the continuity between the stance of parents of young radicals and young radicals themselves, Keniston, 1968: 111–25.)

Imputing normals usually tend to be rejecting of Actor, thereby reducing or destroying his positive feelings toward them. Sometimes, however, normals assume a stance that might be called "sympathetic imputation." While believing that Actor is pivotally deviant, they at the same time express sympathetic concern over his plight and are desirous of "helping" him understand the true nature of his condition as a first step in the "recovery process." By playing upon the ties that Actor has to them, these sympathetic imputors are in a very effective position to convince Actor that he is a pivotal deviant. Such a stance is often promoted by persons in what are called the mental health professions, and one supposes that, to the degree that these specialists can train themselves to adopt it, they will be more successful in escalating Actors to think of themselves as centrally deviant.

If while sympathetic imputation is progressing, we also introduce supportive and appropriately deviant Others toward whom Actor can feel positively, then escalation is even further facilitated. Supportive deviants can undertake to teach Actor the tricks of the category's trade and can serve as direct exemplars after whom Actor can model his conduct.

The power of sympathetic imputation (by normals or deviants) has been most clearly recognized and exploited by those Chinese Communist types who have directed what are called, in this country, brainwashing camps (to be sharply distinguished from concentration camps). A central feature of the "program" in such places is the definition of incarcerated Actors as unfortunate dupes of a false (capitalistic) belief system. Such poor unfortunates must be more or less gently brought to see the errors of their ways. Through sympathizing with Actor over his having been so badly misled by capitalist Others, and by rewarding him for seeing who he really is (and through the institution of other conditions, somewhat approaching the strongest ones explicated here) an effort is made to escalate Actors to Communist identities (Lifton, 1963).

Positive Affect for Deviants Only. However, because the pivotally deviant category being imputed is itself usually so strongly disapproved, the empirically more frequent response of normals appears to be *unsympathetic* imputations to Actor. There seems to be some tendency to avoid, patronize, lecture or cajole him or to tut tut over his imputed character failings. Indeed, normals sometimes physically assault the Actor, beating, strapping, branding, starving, mutilating or otherwise abusing the flesh-and-bone container of the self imputed to him. Such behavior, as well as normals' involvement in ceremonies of denunciation, serve well to lower Actor's attachment to them (Matza, 1964; Garfinkel, 1956). For this reason, the condition of having normals present, making unsympathetic imputations to Actor, ranks only second in effectiveness.

Nevertheless, this arrangement can serve reasonably well if, at the same time that normal Others are rejecting him, we introduce Actor to sympathetic deviant Others of the type imputed. Punishment by normals impresses upon Actor the grim reality of who he is, while the sympathy and support of his imputed own kind make it possible for him to conceive of the possibility of living under the label. If the deviants are actively helpful, if they provide physical and emotional shelter and a rhetoric of defense and new possibilities for positive action, then identification with them and of self as one of them appears likely.

ATTENUATED SITUATIONS

The circumstances of only deviants or only normals present to whom Actor has positive emotional ties has a somewhat unclear potential for escalation. The circumstance of only deviants present would appear, however, for reasons already suggested above, the more facilitative of the two. Of course, whoever is present, Actor's loyalties may be divided. He can, for example, hate some normals and love others and hate some deviants and love others. Such divisions probably make escalation highly problematic, or even unpredictable, depending upon whose imputations Actor finally considers most important (J. Lofland, 1966:54–57). This is further complicated in empirical cases by the possibility that Others may be divided, rather than unanimous, in their imputations of Actor, while Actor's emotional ties may be variously distributed within or among each division.

If we simultaneously consider only (1) what categories of persons are present (normals and deviants, deviants only, etc.); (2) what combination of imputations Others are making (unanimous, some ignorant or challenging, etc.); and (3) the distribution of Actor's emotional attachments, it can be seen that there are a very large number of possible, if attenuated, escalation paths. Stated differently, Actor's emotional attachments can be variously distributed within the variety of ways in which (1) various categories of Others can be present and (2) imputations can be distributed. Because these more attenuated paths are probably also empirically the *most frequent,* the empirical study of how deviant identities are assumed becomes, indeed, highly complex. Instead of being puzzled over why so many people think of themselves as deviant and live such a role, we might more fruitfully wonder how it is that any Actor is ever escalated to a deviant identity. We should expect to find, as we indeed do, that only a small proportion of Actors who live under some deviant label actually believe they are "really" an instance of the imputed type. Apparently few youths regarded as juvenile delinquents by many Others conceive of themselves in those terms, and a high proportion of both children and adults defined as mentally retarded are reported to deny their "true" character. (Edgerton, 1967.)

VARIATIONS IN AFFECTIVE
RECEPTIVITY BY DEVIANTS
PRESENT

Because the situation of disaffection from normal Others (or even the absence of normals) and affection for deviant Others is probably the most frequent circumstance, it is reasonable to explore somewhat further the factors associated with, or influencing, the existence of disaffection, neutrality and

affection.   The disaffecting practices of normals have been rather well documented in a variety of places.[10]   We need simply note the tendency of normals
to kill, expel or drum out Actor or (if he is allowed to remain in their presence),
to render him an isolated or marginal participant.   It is more relevant to refer
to how *deviants* present in Actor's round may vary in their willingness to accept
him as one of their own and therefore to be supportive of and affectionate
toward him, making possible his reciprocation of affection.

Viewing the full range of deviant labels, we find the people living under
them varying with regard to their willingness or propensity to make own-kind
imputations to new and candidate Actors.   Some kinds of professional criminals, for example, have appeared quite hesitant to take on new members (impute their category) at least until after a period of testing (Sutherland, 1937;
Tobias, 1967:117).   Others impute categorical membership on the basis of the
slightest possible indication.   Among the latter, male and female homosexuals
are especially aggressive, even appearing to feel that the whole of mankind is
really homosexual.   These more promiscuously imputing categories tend also
quickly to embrace their social young with warm, emotive regard and with intensive training in the trade.   Such a propensity for encompassment would
appear to be highly productive of reciprocal affection—far more productive
than those situations in which the fledgling must largely fend for himself and
catch on to the game as best he can.   Of special note, as the grand masters of
promiscuous imputation and intensive support, are small deviant religions and
cults.   Many of these tend to engage in very strong envelopment of candidate
Actors with expressions of sympathy over problems involved in the new label
and instructions on how to cope with "our kind of life."

The variation among categories in the extent to which they are supportive
and affectionate seems to depend, in part, upon the degree to which the ideology
associated with the label is self-consciously moralizing, that is, emphasizes that
to be one of us is to be morally superior.   Deviant categories armed with some
variety of this theme may even take it as a positive duty to bring others into the
fold.   (Cf. Keniston, 1968:135–40 regarding this theme, affect and role models
among young radicals.)   It is possible, nonetheless, for a category to be rather
careful about making imputations of newly encountered Actors and to feel no
need for moral justification, but to engage in warm embracement once an imputation is made.   Thus Black hustlers are apparently rather discriminating
about imputing their own kind to others, but, if a new body displays one of
their rather rare indicators, aggressive embracement quickly takes place.   On
arriving in Roxesbury, the bright young man whom the world would later know
as Malcolm X encountered Shorty, a hustler, to whom Malcolm X was a "home
boy"—a person from the same rural home town.   Malcolm X relates:

> I mentioned the names of Lansing people and places, he remembered
> many, and pretty soon we sounded as if we had been raised in the same

[10] E.g., Goffman, 1961a, and the literature cited therein.

block. I could sense Shorty's genuine gladness, and I don't have to say how lucky I felt to find a friend as hip as he obviously was.

"Man, this is a swinging town if you dig it," Shorty said. "You're my homeboy—I'm going to school you to the happenings." I stood there and grinned like a fool. (Malcolm X, 1966:44.)

Shorty and Malcolm X met in a poolroom, the first one the latter had ever entered, and the day of this meeting was Malcolm X's first exposure to the urban Black ghetto. With this meeting, however, this training—his escalation—began:

All afternoon, between [Shorty's] trips up front to rack balls, Shorty talked to me out of the corner of his mouth: which hustlers—standing around, or playing at this or that table—sold "reefers," or had just come out of the prison, or were "second-story men."

Throughout the afternoon, Shorty introduced me to players and loungers. (Malcolm X, 1966:45.)

Under rather strong conditions facilitative of escalation, Malcolm X, fourteen years old and possessed of a brilliant school record from Lansing, Michigan, was, after only a few months, an adept and prominent hustler in the underworld of Boston.

Malcolm X's positive affective regard for the imputations made of him should not imply that support for entrance into a deviant category is always positively defined by Actor; it may be only grimly appreciated. This is especially likely to be the case in less supportive and affectively embracing settings where the Actor is not positively buying the category imputed to him but nonetheless comes to grips, through Others, with the grim reality of his situation and of his social kind.

Cognitive Congruence

Content of cognitive systems

The earlier analysis of Actor's orientation involved reference to the formal structure of his cognitive system in terms of its complexity, self-conscious articulation and the like. This formal structure is to be distinguished from the character of the *substantive* content of the cognitive system. It is this latter's relation to escalation that concerns us here. The proposition to be propounded is that, to the degree that the cognitive categories already used by Actor are congruent with—similar to—those composing the identity being attributed to him by Others, escalation is facilitated. The notion of congruence calls attention to the similarity or dissimilarity between Actor and Other relative to the fundamental assumptions of their meaning systems in terms of which personal, interpersonal and more remote events are categorized and acted toward.

Types of content

At the most general level, meaning systems, or systems of cognitive categories, may be distinguished in terms of the content type of the system of categories typically evoked in the categorization of experience. By content type I mean the category's system of reference, the most basic aspect of reality to which it purports to refer; i.e., to a realm of *personal* experience, a realm of *interpersonal* experience or a realm of *superpersonal* experience.

Meaning systems centered on the realm of *personal* experience are composed of component categories which seek to make distinctions between persons and events primarily on the basis of the psychic states and enduring dispositions of individuals qua personalities or some similar concept. Human action is explained by reference to Actor's being an instance of some person-based category. Having spawned many categories of personality types, character types, personality disorders and so on, bearers of a personalistic world view then explain human behavior in terms of such categories. All human behavior, that of famous political leaders and that of obscure grocery clerks, is conceived and explained in such terms as pathological functioning, sadomasochistic tendencies, latent homosexuality, asocial personality, etc. From distinguishing among Actors on the basis of their personal experiences and explaining their acts in terms of personal categories, interest logically extends to the individual's personal past. Many additional categories are developed for the purpose of making distinctions within that past, as, for example, the terms employed to denote various phases of development. The quest for categories within the personalistic realm reaches its quintessence among specialists who call themselves personality theorists.

Given their operating orientation, participants in the *personalistic perspective* or meaning system tend, quite logically, to advocate the manipulation of personality systems as a route to the control and change of persons. The personalistic categories of the personalistic past must be worked through, resolved or manipulated by some such conception of personalistic solutions. What is here called the personalistic perspective is, of course, very well known under more familiar labels, among which are psychiatry, psychology and counseling. In the recent history of American civilization, the personalistic perspective has been one of the more popular ways in which to conceive experience. Of special relevance, this perspective has been particularly widespread among those specialists who deal with those Actors suspected of being or defined as being some kind of deviant. But it has also been rather widely utilized by laymen as a perspective within which to regard problematic persons.

The *interpersonal perspective,* in contrast, is centered upon categories that make distinctions between and among persons on the basis of their relations to one another. In so distinguishing, interest logically extends to the bases for the various kinds of relations, and categories are spawned which point to the differential allocation of material resources and the differences in structural location of persons qua participants in a web of relationships. This quest for categories in the interpersonal realm has its quintessence in those social analysts who would explain all action in terms of categories of material interest, as, for example, in Marxist accounts of economic and political life. More generally, participants in the interpersonalistic perspective presume that the behavior of famous political leaders and obscure grocery clerks alike arises out of their relations to others. Categories such as social class, power, the constraints of office, system needs, organizational strain, etc., figure prominently in their explanatory accounts.

Issues of changing persons—themselves or others—become issues of manipulating relations. Rather than reconstituting personality systems, the interpersonalists would reconstitute systems of relations or social systems. Interpersonalists are rather well known under such labels as politician, political scientist, political radical and, in some cases, sociologist. The present work, indeed, represents one variant of the interpersonalistic perspective. And it appears to be the case, whether for better or for worse, that, in American civilization, the interpersonalistic perspective is providing an increasingly popular basic set of presumptions or categories for the conceptualization of experience.

Finally, and in terms of recent popularity in the Western world, of least importance, there is the *superpersonalistic perspective*, which seeks to make distinctions between persons on the basis of their relation to a supernatural, superempirical realm. In distinguishing among Actors on the basis of their relation to this realm, interest logically extends to making distinctions within the supernatural realm itself. Thus bearers of this perspective concern themselves with how many superempirical entities there are, what their characteristics, disposition and plans might be, how they might be communicated with and what Actor's relations to them might be. This particular quest reaches its quintessence in those religious devotees who develop and live by a very elaborate set of supernatural categories which have an immediate, intimate and continuing relevance for human Actors. (J. Lofland, 1966.) Once these categories are spawned, the action of human beings is then described—categorized—and explained in their terms. Actors can, for example, be right with, or wrong with, God; Actors can be invaded by, or resistant to, the evil or good spirits that immediately surround them. From the broadest matters of international relations and the actions of political leaders to the most anonymous and obscure acts, the behavior of people is to be understood in terms of superempirical categories.

The relevance of the above for escalation to a deviant identity resides in the fact that Actors tend to use one or another of these broad perspectives rather exclusively. Although any given Actor may participate in and occasionally use more than one or even all three, there would seem to be a tendency for one perspective to dominate. Some more strongly oriented Actors (or, in popular jargon, more ideological Actors) may even see these perspectives as mutually exclusive and imcompatible modes of conceiving experience (e.g., Stark, 1963). Actors operating within one of these tend to view the categories of the others (if they view them at all) as unrealistic, foreign, inexplicable, improbable or even as false, ridiculous or shallow. Perspectives other than his own may not be familiar to an Actor, with the result that when presented with isolated categories out of them, the terms and the empirical reality they designate may seem vague, distant and easily forgotten. Because these foreign categories are viewed outside the context of their containing perspective (within which they take on a fuller meaning), such particulars fail to make sense or to have much relevance.

CONGRUENCE OF CONTENT

The fact that Actors tend to be constrained to a single perspective within which experience easily and immediately makes sense, leads us, finally, to a direct consideration of the relation between Actor and Other and the congruence of their respective perspectives. By congruence I mean that Actor and Other use more or less the same perspective—personalistic, interpersonalistic or superpersonalistic—in coding experience. (This is represented in Chart 8.1

CHART 8.1. *RELATIONS OF ACTORS' AND OTHERS' GENERAL PERSPECTIVES*

Actors' General Perspective

		Personalistic	Inter personalistic	Super personalistic
	Personalistic	*1A*	*1B*	*1C*
Others' General Perspective	Inter personalistic	*2A*	*2B*	*2C*
	Super personalistic	*3A*	*3B*	*3C*

along the diagonal cells 1A, 2B, 3C.) When congruence exists, escalation is facilitated. Put in more everyday terms, and with reference to deviance, we expect to and do find that Actors with a psychological or psychiatric perspective tend (under all other enumerated conditions) more easily to think of themselves as psychiatric cases; Actors with a political perspective tend more easily to be escalated to the deviant role of political radical (e.g., Keniston, 1968:111–20); Actors with a religious perspective tend more easily to be escalated to the deviant role of religious fanatic or cultist (e.g., J. Lofland, 1966:41–49). Given congruence, it can be suggested, additionally and more specifically, that the greater the similarity between the categories of Actor's and Other's specific formulations and between the contents of their categories, the more escalation is facilitated.

CHANGES OF PERSPECTIVE

The facilitative character of preexisting congruence does not rule out the possibility that Actors will *change their general perspectives* for coding reality. Although it seems relatively rare, under circumstances of extreme disorientation and strain, Actors sometimes do begin to doubt the basic *realm* of categories they have been employing to designate objects. Thus strong Catholics do sometimes become Communists or psychiatric espousers; political radicals do sometimes become religious adepts or psychological analysts; psychiatric devotees do sometimes become religious fanatics or purely political partisans. However, those who would attempt to escalate an Actor to a category of a general perspective other than his own face a massive task, and success would seem possible only if *all other* conditions promoting escalation were simultaneously activated in very strong form and sustained for a rather long period of time. As sustained activation of all the conditions is rarely accomplished, Actors typically make smaller switches between the more specific formulations of one of the three general perspectives.

MEETINGS AMONG INCONGRUENT PERSPECTIVES

Perhaps only within modern societies, given their enormous complexity, can there be produced those grimly humorous dramas of encounters between persons with fundamentally different perspectives and of their ensuing struggles to negotiate a definition of the situation. Indeed, such incongruous occurrences, especially involving strongly oriented persons, have become an important literary theme, as for example in Kesey's *One Flew Over the Cuckoo's Nest* (1962) and Tarsis' *Ward 7: An Autobiographical Note* (1965). The latter, as an account of how the Soviet Union has more recently managed its political dissenters (i.e., deviants), is especially instructive. Dissenters are officially defined as psychologically aberrant and in need of psychological rehabilitation and are remanded to the appropriate facilities. However, only those into whose custody the dissenters are placed appear to have much faith in the personalistic imputations made of them. The patients (Tarsis among them) employ, rather, a political perspective, both in understanding their own fate and in counterdefining their custodians, and this leads to all manner of intriguing conflicts over the meaning of events. It does not, however, at least in this case, lead to the deviants' coming to define themselves in the terms of their imputors. Such treatment is to be contrasted with that employed in the early days of the Communist regime in Russia when political deviation was seen as exactly that and deviationists were sent to prison or executed.   Then the official definition of dissenters was a part of the same general perspective employed by the dissenters themselves.   And, ironically, it was this congruence which formed part of the basis upon which even the mildest of reformers, once incarcerated, could come finally to view themselves as radicals (Lemert, 1951:214–17).

Modern Russia is not the only place where the perspectives of imputed and imputor may diverge.   In American mental hospitals we find strongly oriented persons who define themselves in religious terms, perhaps very grand religious terms (e.g., who think of themselves as Jesus Christ), for whom a personalistic perspective seems only so much nonsense (e.g., Rokeach, 1964).   It is quite possible for some Actors to be defined as deviant, to travel through the escalation process and to come to live out a deviant role, yet, in spite of all that, to conceive of themselves as a different kind of deviant—or special kind of person—than the type that is imputed.   Those persons whom Others may code as paranoid, for example, are especially likely to conceive of themselves in different terms.   In many of these cases the Actor comes only to feel that he is a special figure whose political enemies have temporarily outmaneuvered him by having him hospitalized.   And, as Lemert has shown, there is a significant sense in which this is, in fact, the case.[11]

FURTHER FACILITANTS
AND OTHERS

Reality is always more complex and "messy" than the analyst of it might prefer.   The discerning reader will already have noted that in the discussion of the facilitative states of Actor—disorientation, positive affect for imputing Others and a cognitive system congruent with that being offered—Others, both deviant and normal, are prominent.   They are important, too, in connection with the facilitative arrangements of places and hardware.   That is, whatever the analytic unit being considered, the ubiquitous Others in Actor's world are, at least indirectly, involved.   I want now, however, to look at two further *direct* contributions which Others, particularly deviant Others, can make to the escalation of Actor to personal identification as deviant.   As was noted earlier, this discussion logically belongs in the previous chapter.   But since an understanding of it is at least partially dependent on the reader's having been introduced to matters of orientation and disorientation, for expository purposes it has been postponed until now.   We turn, then, to a consideration of the character of the ideology and the degree of tutoring in technical knowledge and skills which Others offer to Actor.

---

[11] Lemert, 1962.   Usefully read in the context of changes in general perspective is Mills' essay on the relation of "private troubles and public issues."   (Mills, 1963 and 1959:8–13.) On the social organizational contexts of such changes, see Stark, 1964.

COMPREHENSIVE,
ARTICULATE AND
MORALIZED IDEOLOGY

FUNCTIONS OF COGNITIVE SYSTEMS

Cognitive systems or ideologies perform at least two fundamental functions for the humans who espouse them, and they vary in the degree to which they are structured to perform these functions. First, to one or another degree, they define events and provide a range of strategies for coping with occurrences. Systems which provide definitions and management devices for a very wide range of occurrences and which render them understandable, explicable, surmountable and manageable may be said to be *comprehensive*. In addition, to the degree that such definitions are worked up—ideally written down and systematically communicated—a comprehensive ideology may be said to be *articulate*. Comprehensive, articulate ideologies function to protect adherent and prospective espousers from ambiguity, from stalled action, from situations where one can only shrug one's shoulders and ask, "What can I do?" or, worse, "What does it mean?" Less comprehensive and articulated ideologies have less capacity to deal with raw reality, and their prospective and actual adherents can more easily encounter ideologically unmanageable difficulties. Such difficulties may, and not unreasonably, precipitate questioning of the scheme itself as a viable system for the management of everyday life. That is to say, with less comprehensive and articulated ideologies, disorientation is more easily precipitated.

Second, it is the function of ideologies morally to justify the actions of humans, to provide them with a sense that what they are about is a correct, proper and right thing. Humans appear to be the sorts of creatures who demand to believe that what they do on a continuing basis (as distinct from their isolated acts) has some moral validity or is at least morally neutral. And ideologies differ in the degree to which they are *moralized*.

VARIATIONS IN COGNITIVE SYSTEMS
AND MAKING DO

Surveying the range of ideologies—of cognitive systems—associated with deviant identities, we find that they differ greatly along these dimensions. Many appear quite primitive, in the limited sense of overlapping with everyday perspectives and of being uncomplicated, inarticulate and only sporadically and unsystematically moralized. These features of ideologies are important because identities appear not to be accepted by Actors on a wholesale basis or all at once. Rather, they are tried on and tried out. They are tested for their capacities to get Actors through the day in a reasonable fashion. Even under the strongest of escalation conditions, if the ideology of the identity being imputed to Actor is primitive, then difficulties may be encountered in its use. These difficulties can but retard his acceptance of the identity as a way in which to conceive himself. That is, escalation will be hindered if the Others of Actor's candidate category have not succeeded in developing a relatively comprehensive, articulate and moralized ideology which they can offer him.

Nonetheless, if other facilitants are in force, the capacities of even relatively primitive ideologies to allow Actors to make do should not be underestimated. Personal identification may be less likely and more fragile, but it is still possible. Some degree of moralization seems especially important in allowing Actors to make do. Students of prostitution, for example, have repeatedly remarked that this oldest of professions, at least as it has been practiced in more recent years, seems to have a rather primitive ideology, a feature that likely functions to retard the flow of personnel into "the life." Yet even within its primitive ideology, one finds the rudiments of moralization. Thus, like other low-prestige roles, the role of the prostitute can be viewed as making a valuable (*ergo*, moral) contribution to the larger society.

> We get 'em all. The kids who are studying to be doctors and lawyers and things, and men whose wives hate the thought of sex. And men whose wives are sick or have left them. What are such men going to do? *Pick on married women . . . or run around after underage girls?* They're better off with us. That's what we're for.
>
> ❋   ❋   ❋
>
> I could endure a surprising amount of humiliation for the *handicapped person*. . . . Most of the girls felt morally obliged to see the handicapped Johns and be unusually kind to them.
>
> ❋   ❋   ❋
>
> I think that the release of talking about an unhappy home situation may well have *saved many a marriage,* and *possibly even lives,* when nerves have been strained to a breaking point. It is well known that it is easier to unburden serious trouble onto a total stranger . . . Easier still to tell a girl whose time you have bought, whom nothing will surprise, and who is in no position to despise you . . . . (Quoted in Hirschi, 1962:44; italics added.)

(The claim made in the third quote is of particular interest, avowing, as it does, to provide a kind of lay psychiatry for the male public at large.) In a more explicitly moral vein, alternative moral values can be attended to in terms of which the deviant can then point to his own superiority. Among prostitutes, reference is made to the moral values in emotional honesty and in reasonably priced dealings that involve no duplicity.

And how about the society girls who marry older men they don't love—
who just happen to have money?   I'll say they're different from us.

✱   ✱   ✱

Let the poor bum figure up how many times a year she lets him have her,
divide it by what he gives her, and she'd see if she's not the higher-priced
whore.

✱   ✱   ✱

I was no "gold digger," who begged favors from a man *without giving
something in return* . . . . I had pride. (Quoted in Hirschi, 1962:44–45;
italics added.)

That is, in the same way that normal Others can develop a confirming evidential
sensitivity to Actor's deviance, Actor can develop a confirming evidential sensitivity to the immorality of normals.   As noted earlier, the behavior of all persons and the information which they emit to those around them are ambiguous
and subject to a variety of interpretations.   When the interpretative work is being done by deviants about normals, it appears to consist largely of imputations
of moral hypocrisy, naïveté, drabness and secret but frequent sinning.   To the
degree that normals engage in conduct that is amenable to such interpretations,
they support the moralization of deviance.[12]

TECHNICAL KNOWLEDGE AND SKILL

Closely related to, but not identical with, the facilitative provision of hardware and ideology is the matter of Others' making available to Actor the technical knowledge and skill required in the performance of a deviant role.   The
possession of physical means and ideologized motives without any accompanying technique makes for poor initial success in trying out a deviant identity and
can only retard its full assumption.   When the deviant category in question
entails skills not common in civil society, some sort of tutoring arrangement
must be devised in order most auspiciously to facilitate identity assumption.
Perhaps this escalation requirement can be best appreciated by pointing to
the poignant situation of those deviants upon whom progressive hardship has
been wrought by the technically innovating character of 20th-century America.

[12] Especially instructive on this point is Nettler's (1961) review of the empirical basis of
what normals take to be false and therefore sick cognitions (largely involving the immorality
of normals) of persons imputed to be deviant.   For further discussion of deviant ideologies
see Simmons, 1964; J. Lofland, 1966:Part III; Feldman, 1968.   Among more recent instances of highly complex ideologies of deviance, see the work of Genet, especially in *The
Thief's Journal* (1965).   Compare also the possibilities for ideological articulation inherent in
the means by which deviant acts among normals become subjectively available for performance, Chap. 4 of this text.

At one point in the development of engraving and printing, it was apparently quite possible to obtain tutoring in the skills (as well as to obtain the hardware) sufficient for the reasonably accurate counterfeiting of such items as stocks and bonds. In response to the relative ease with which counterfeiting could be accomplished, innovations in the production of real stocks, etc., were introduced which involved progressively esoteric and guarded skills and technology. At some point during the second or third decade of this century, there occurred the sad moment when the counterfeiters and their prospective apprentices had to confront fully the hard facts of a changing technology which entailed ever more difficult and out-of-reach skills (Lemert, 1958). With no one capable of providing adequate tutoring, a once-viable deviant identity began to disappear. But not only counterfeiters have suffered. Professional safecrackers, burglars, confidence men and the like (as well as normal artisans) have also experienced hardship in the face of an increasingly complex technology.[13]

The view sometimes promoted among normals that many forms of deviance are relatively easy, or represent an easy way out (especially in contrast with the supposed difficulties and heroic hardships of the normal's life), must be balanced with a closer appreciation of the fact that, although little skill may be required to try out or play at a role, considerable skill may be necessary to successfully perform it. In contrast to the notion that, for example, "prostitution comes perilously near the situation of getting something for nothing," more attention might be paid to the fact that the skills involved in prostitution—finding customers, maintaining a place of business, pleasing the clientele, collecting fees, guarding against disease, pregnancy and injury and avoiding the police— are not automatically acquired.[14]

So also the successful performances of even so seemingly simple a role as that of the contemporary hustler may involve a good deal of finesse.

> I used to carry my knife in my coat sleeve. I'd strap it around my arm in a little bag. And I had a rubber band that run up to my middle finger. When I'd stretch my hand as far as I could, wide open, and run my thumb between there, that would knock the latch off the little leather bag, and the knife would slide down into my hand. Everybody was carryin' them switch-blades then.

✿   ✿   ✿

Well, just as I passed by him I came up with my knife at his throat from

---

[13] See, for example, the now outmoded and therefore quaint techniques reported of professional thieves generally (Sutherland, 1937) and confidence men in particular (Maurer, 1962).   There is, however, a continuing dialectic between the technical and social innovations of normals, the subsequent decline of one sort of deviant role and the corresponding rise of deviant roles that prey on the new technology and social patterns.   Two such dialectics involving changes in the 19th century British systems of transport and money are chronicled in Tobias, 1967:Chap. 10.   See also Black's (1966) analysis of technological changes and "forms and reforms of whoredom."

[14] See Hirschi (1962), who explores the skills required for each of these occupational contingencies. See also the views presented in Bryan, 1965 and 1966.

the back, and I pulled him back. Now that's not the way you're supposed
to get a guy. You're supposed to put your arm around his neck, then put
your knee in his back, then pull him back to you and last put your knife
to his neck. (Williamson, 1965:153–54, 189.)

And, according to the same informant, even the uncomplicated robbery of a
store involves a number of technical matters.

See, you're not suppose to rob no place if there is more than one person in
there, and they're not standin' together. This is because you can't see
what they all doin' if they're apart. Now if you can get 'em together then
go ahead on and do it. Sometimes, if you're by yourself, you can go
in a place full of peoples and get a guy. This can only be done when you
can get the guy without attractin' the attention of the other peoples, and
when you're pretty sure that the guy ain't goin' a act no fool and holler.
You've got to have yourself in a position that if the guy do act the fool,
and wake the other peoples up to what's happenin', you can still do what
you want to do, and get on out of there.

                         ❊   ❊   ❊

I always liked to buy somethin' when I go into a place. I don't think I've
ever gone in a place to rob it where I didn't buy somethin'. I'd do it more
or less to put the person at ease, and then they're not expectin' nothin'.
Then I liked to get 'em just when they had opened the register to put my
money in. (Williamson, 1965:197, 191.)

Likewise, candidates for a skid row identity find that its successful assumption entails rather esoteric knowledge and skills, including a working acquaintance with the ways in which local institutions may be utilized. It is reported
that some skid row restaurants and taverns not only serve as sites in which to
eat and drink but perform a variety of rather technical functions for their
elderly clientele as well.

Many men have their retirement and disability checks sent directly to the
restaurant where they can have them cashed, purchase meal tickets and
leave some cash on deposit for safekeeping. This cuts down the possibility of being "jackrolled" and losing the funds one must live on for the
rest of the month. This practice also enables the man to establish some
credit against which he can borrow since the restaurant manager can take
the money owed him out of the next month's check when it arrives. For
many the restaurant becomes more of a home than their hotel. While a
man may switch hotels frequently, once he has found a restaurant that he
really likes, he usually sticks to it and it becomes a stable reference point
for him. Here he can continue to receive his checks and other mail without the serious interruptions which might otherwise result if he changed
residence on the street. Here the men receive mail from their families
and from each other. When a man is in trouble and away from the street,

he knows it is the one place through which he can get in touch with his friends and solicit their help. (Slosar, 1965:47–48.)

Of course, whatever the role, the knowledge and skills entailed in it must somehow be taught and learned. As is the case with conventional occupations, there are doubtless far more people who are disposed to do a job than can gain the training and many more who have access to the training than can master it. In the same way that there are occupations disproportionately populated by persons who did not master the technique of some more desired type of work, there are likely also conventional occupations overly populated by those who did not manually and intellectually measure up to one or another deviant career.[15]

CONCLUDING REMARKS ON THE ASSUMPTION OF DEVIANT IDENTITY

PROBLEMATICS

In presenting what seem to be facilitative conditions of escalation to a deviant identity, I have said little about the most facilitative *sequence* in which to introduce a given *strength* of one or another element for what *duration*. I have suggested only a very tentative ordering and implied only that all conditions should occur in order for identification of self as deviant to be most facilitated. Sequence, strength and duration are, nonetheless, problematic matters, particularly so because of the virtual absence of comprehensive descriptive materials upon which to draw. We do not have detailed accounts of a variety of escalation situations which will permit even a beginning attempt to isolate the relative contributions of given elements under varying degrees of strength and duration of the other elements. Any attempt here to provide such an assessment would involve almost sheer speculation.

Given such a limitation, the present goal is the more mundane one of making more articulate and specific the logical implications of the sociological conception of persons and, thereby, of suggesting the conditions under which persons may come to conceive themselves, specifically, in deviant terms. The emphasis is upon the articulation of what is, after all, a thesis of long standing. The following classic statement of Frank Tannenbaum was enunciated more than thirty years ago:

There is a great deal more delinquency practiced and committed by . . . young groups than comes to the attention of the police. The boy ar-

---

[15] Cf. the general summary statement by Cloward, 1959.

rested, therefore, is singled out in specialized treatment. This boy, no more guilty than the other members of his group, discovers a world of which he knew little. His arrest suddenly precipitates a series of institutions, attitudes and experiences which the other children do not share. For this boy there suddenly appear the police, the patrol wagon, the police station, the other delinquents and criminals found in the police lock-ups, the court with all its agencies such as bailiffs, clerks, bondsmen, lawyers, probation officers. There are bars, cells, handcuffs, criminals. He is questioned, examined, tested, investigated. His history is gone into; his family is brought to court. Witnesses make their appearance. The boy, no different from the rest of his gang, suddenly becomes the center of a major drama in which all sorts of unexpected characters play important roles. And what is it all about? About the accustomed things his gang has done and has been doing for a long time. In this entirely new world he is made conscious of himself as a different human being than he was before his arrest. He becomes classified as a thief, perhaps, and the entire world about him has suddenly become a different place for him and will remain different for the rest of his life.

      ❉   ❉   ❉

The first dramatization of the "evil" which separates the child out of his group for specialized treatment plays a greater role in making the criminal than perhaps any other experience. It cannot be too often emphasized that for the child the whole situation has become different. He now lives in a different world. He has been tagged. A new and hitherto non-existent environment has been precipitated out for him.

      ❉   ❉   ❉

There [may be then] a gradual shift from the definition of specific acts as evil to a definition of the individual as evil, so that all his acts come to be looked upon with suspicion. In the process of identification, his companions, hang-outs, play, speech, income, and his conduct, the personality itself, become subject to scrutiny and question.

      ❉   ❉   ❉

The process of making the criminal, therefore, is a process of tagging, defining, identifying, segregating, describing, emphasizing, making conscious and self-conscious; it becomes a way of stimulating, suggesting, emphasizing and evoking the very traits that are complained of. If the theory of relation of response to stimulus has any meaning, the entire process of dealing with the young delinquent is mischievous insofar as it identifies him to himself or to the environment as a delinquent person.

The person becomes the thing he is described as being. (Tannenbaum, 1938:19, 17, 19–20.)

Although Tannenbaum noted the components of Others, places, hardware and Actor and alluded to the more specific operation of more specific elements, he did not, as others have not, bring them to specific and separate consideration.

If it is now even remotely more possible directly to address the analytic task posed by him and by others before and after him, then my aim has been accomplished.[16]

SUMMARY

Consonant with that aim, the suggestions of Part II may be briefly summarized.

A. The initial identification of an Actor as a pivotal (or social) deviant is facilitated when a deviant category is:

1. widely known in a society;
2. widely believed to be reasonable;
3. implemented in an apparatus which increases the institutional and territorial number and prevalence of sensitive coders, namely, imputational specialists;
4. determined by simple indicators in the forms of a small number of necessary and a large number of alternatively sufficient ones; and
5. relatively congruent with the perceived acts and social categories of Actor.

The degree to which statements such as these appear obvious should not detract attention from the fact that these conditions appear to be among the major sources of variation in determining who gets called deviant about what. As others have noted, of equal or greater importance than what people do are such matters as where they do it, who knows about it and who is prepared to make what of it.

B. The escalation of an Actor to identification of himself as an instance of a pivotally deviant category is facilitated when:

1. Others are united in their imputations of Actor as an instance of a category of deviant person;
2. normals and deviants are both present in Actor's daily round;
3. Actor participates in an integrated place round;
4. all the places of Actor's round are publicly and formally defined as places frequented by and/or especially designed for his variety of deviant;
5. a wide range of hardware conventionally identified as "belonging with" some category of normal person is withdrawn;
6. a wide range of hardware conventionally identified as "belonging with" some category of deviant person is supplied;
7. Actor is disoriented;
8. Actor projects strong and positive affective bonds toward those imputing him to be pivotally deviant;

[16] Cf., again, Lemert, 1951 and 1967a; H. S. Becker, 1963:8–14, 25–39; Scheff, 1966; Sutherland and Cressey, 1966:373–75. Useful sets of empirical and conceptual materials are assembled in Scheff, ed., 1967; Rubington and Weinberg, eds., 1968. In addition, the logic and substance of Parts II and III are intended to reformulate and subsume, within a more generalized framework, the model of conversion presented in Lofland and Stark, 1965; and J. Lofland, 1966.

9. Actor's cognitive categories are congruent with those imputed to him;
10. the deviant identity imputed to Actor has attached to it a relatively comprehensive, articulate and moralized ideology; and
11. Others provide Actor with the technical knowledge and skill of the deviant identity.

Assuming that the foregoing specifies at least the rudiments of one way in which a deviant identity can be assumed, we can then inquire into the process by which Actor might be induced to return to a normal identity.

PART III

THE ASSUMPTION
OF NORMAL IDENTITY

By definition, of course, we believe the person with a stigma is not quite human.

ERVING GOFFMAN

There is no such thing as Jew and Greek, slave and freeman, male and female; for you are all one person in Christ Jesus.

"The Letter of Paul to the Galatians" (3:28)

Erving Goffman, *Stigma: Notes on the Management of Spoiled Identity*, p. 3.

We began previously with an Actor defined as normal and attempted to trace conditions facilitating his initial and then widespread identification as a pivotally deviant person and his escalation to identification of himself as deviant. In the same way we now begin with an Actor defined by himself and Others as deviant and inquire into conditions facilitating his initial and then widespread identification as pivotally normal and his escalation to belief in himself as a normal kind of person.

CHAPTER 9
SOCIAL IDENTIFICATION AS PIVOTALLY NORMAL

AN INVERSE MANUAL OF ROLE MANAGEMENT

A statement of conditions facilitative of identity assumption is a statement, in reverse, of conditions facilitative of *maintaining the preexisting identity*. Thus, as we proceed, I will be suggesting, by implication and by direct reference, conditions facilitative of maintaining social deviants in their roles. Indeed, the conditions facilitative of normal identity assumption might be conceived as potential "hazards" which social deviants might strive to avoid. In fact, what follows may be read by social deviants as a manual of situations devotedly to be skirted. The most general principles of this avoidance involve, as before, both (1) minimizing or ruling out the possibility of Others' making an initial and then widespread identification of one as an instance of a normal sort of person, and (2) arranging one's activities and outlook so as to minimize or rule out the possibility of undergoing escalation to identification of self as an instance of some normal label.

KNOWLEDGE

Categories of deviance come and go in the coding scheme of a society. Often they are known to only a portion of a population and/or are infrequently or irregularly activated. In contrast, categories of normality are widely known. A very high proportion of the population live out their lives under the cover of such categories, and they are activated continuously in the day-to-day dealings of a society. While categories of deviance are spectacular and irregularly present for much of the population, categories of normality are mundane and constantly present. It would appear, therefore, that from the point of view of sheer knowledge, the identification of a deviant Actor as an instance of some normal category is relatively unproblematic. The rich range of extant normal identities based upon occupation, religion (and voluntary associations generally), territoriality, family status, etc., is highly facilitative of initial identifica-

tion. In fact, considering only the available categories in the direction of
normality, it might be said that deviant Actors are highly vulnerable to initial
identification as normals. The apparent fact that entrance into deviance from
pivotal normality is much more frequent than entrance into normality from
pivotal deviance thus seems all the more ironic.

REASONABLENESS

Likewise, there would appear to be little issue surrounding the "reasonableness" of the categories of normality qua categories of objects in the world. By
"reasonableness," I mean the belief that it makes sense ever to construe *anybody* as an instance of a given category. Normal and deviant Others around
deviant Actor are likely to agree on almost any category of pivotal normality,
i.e., to agree that someplace there exist people for whom the category is a
reasonable designation. Any issue of reasonableness is likely, rather, to surround the justifiability of construing the particular deviant Actor as an instance
of some normal category. Among *normal* Others in Actor's round, this is likely
to involve a perception of complete incompatibility between Actor's particular
deviant identity and a particular normal category, as, for example, in the exclusion of convicted felons from admission to the bar. Among *deviant* Others in
Actor's round, arguments of unreasonableness seem likely to center upon *negative correlative* features attributed to the normal category. Thus social workers
and businessmen may be acknowledged to exist and to be reasonable labels for
some people, but such categories may also be felt to be "finks," hypocrites,
crooks, cowards or some such, thereby rendering it unreasonable for deviant
Actor ever to be an instance of these labels. Nevertheless, in terms of the sheer
reasonableness of normal categories qua categories, identification of a deviant
Actor as an instance of a normal type is highly facilitated.

SIMPLE INDICATORS

STRINGENT INDICATORS
AND NORMALS

Once an Actor has been publicly identified as deviant, it appears empirically
that a very large number of indicators of a wide variety of types is often needed
before an identification of him as an instance of a pivotal normal will be initiated. Long years of truly exemplary conformity or even hyperconformity and
stellar service to society may be required. Even outstanding conformity is
likely always to be greeted by the suspicion and fear in the minds and practices
of Others that at any time Actor might revert to type. The least indication of a
reversion or regression is likely to be read as indicative of his still being, "after
all," that kind of deviant. Thus heroin users who attempt to identify them-

selves as changed sorts of persons may find that Others—normal and deviant —continue to read their efforts at change as phony, feigning, unbelievable or implausible. A heroin user can thus report this kind of treatment from his family:

> My relatives were always saying things to me like "have you really quit using that drug now?" and things like that. And I knew that they were doing a lot of talking behind my back because when I came around they would stop talking but I overheard them. It used to burn my ass.[1]

Even when a publicly identified deviant Actor is seen as having been rehabilitated for many years, he may still be the recipient of patronizing acts said to be in his honor but which recall to everyone the fact of his inescapably deviant past and, therefore, his tainted present. So it is that the world conference of the Church of the Brethren doubtless felt proper in honoring Nathan Leopold and creating publicity of this kind:

> Nathan Leopold, convicted of first-degree murder in [a] Chicago slaying . . . 43 years ago, has been honored . . . for his "dedicated service of heart, hand and mind on behalf of humankind."
>   Leopold served 33 years in an Illinois state prison. (*Detroit Free Press,* June 26, 1967.)

The newspaper editor writing the headline for this story felt it appropriate, and perhaps cute, to caption the episode "Boy Killer Honored by Church."

The very stringent indicators of pivotal normality point to a central assumption about normality and deviance made by perhaps most persons. This central assumption is that once an Actor has become a deviant, he is likely to remain so. Logically grounded in some variety of personalistic perspective about the "real nature" of human objects, it is believed that deviant Actors are highly resistant to change, i.e., to becoming pivotal normals. The irony of this is, of course, that no such assumption is made about normals becoming deviants; instead there seems to be a strong propensity to believe that Actors are highly *vulnerable* to becoming fully deviant. However, one could as well believe that deviants are highly vulnerable to becoming normal and that normals are highly resistant to becoming deviant or that deviants and normals are equally resistant or equally vulnerable to change.

THE PROTECTIVE RELUCTANCE OF NORMALS

It is not difficult to decipher why Others do not practice equality in their beliefs about the changeability of normals and deviants. Let us ask what beliefs are safest for Others to have about Actors relative to deviance. It is

[1] Ray, 1961:138–39. See also the discussion and illustrations in Sutherland and Cressey, 1966:665–69 and Lindesmith, 1968:146–50.

clearly to their advantage to presume that people easily become deviant and are difficult to make normal. To presume the opposite is to make little effort to control and to manage those persons about whom suspicions have been aroused. Yet, once suspicions have been aroused, fear and anxiety over how they (the Actors) might harm or embarrass proximate Others are likely to be felt; given such feelings, it is altogether *irrational* for Others not to act in ways that increase their personal protection and defense. Actors identified as deviant are thought to be inexplicable, unpredictable, dangerous or unreliable. If such features are attributed to Actor, it is quite reasonable to be highly resistant to attributing a variety of normality to him. To attribute normality is to open oneself to the perceived possibility of being hurt, taken in, suckered, abused, put down or in some other way being made to seem a less-than-competent player of the social game. Nor is the danger entirely a matter of perception. On an *empirical* probability basis, people previously involved with deviance and, most especially, social deviants *are* more likely to be deviant in the future.[2] From the point of view of the persons who might hire, associate with or otherwise trust such persons, it is probablistically reasonable to avoid the class of Actors about whom such information is known. The managers who discriminated in the hiring of dishwashers in the Schwartz and Skolnick study mentioned previously (pp. 156–57) acted in an empirically rational manner.

Thus, if physical, psychic and social safety in social life is a paramount aim of social actors, then there is a *short-run* perceptual and empirical rationality in the typical beliefs in the vulnerability of normals to becoming deviants and in the resistance of deviants to becoming normals. The fundamental irony and *long-run* irrationality is, of course, that the very process of Others' acting quite rationally to protect themselves functions to promote Actors into pivotal deviance and to inhibit their return to pivotal normality—thus promoting that from which Others require protection.

Difficulties in transforming deviants into normals may have as much to do, then, with the fears of Others as with the propensities of Actors.

NORMAL-SMITHS

Having noted the large number of indicators typically necessary initially to identify a deviant Actor as an instance of a normal, we can then go on to see that there exists a minority of Others in American civilization who are not nearly so reticent about making imputations of normality. In the same way that there are specialists in taking minimal indicators to mean pivotal deviance, there exist, in the other direction, specialists in taking minimal indicators to

---

[2] There is, of course, a self-fulfilling prophecy operating here. The empirical danger is, at least in part, a function of the perception of danger. It is an empirical question, for which we have no data, as to how "real" the danger would be in a society where normals were seen as highly resistant to deviance and deviants as highly vulnerable to normality.

mean pivotal normality. And, in the same way that the social position of the specialist in identifying pivotal deviants can be crucial for spreading the deviant identification and escalating Actors to it, there are also crucially located specialists who can be important in initiating and spreading identification and in escalating Actors to normal identities. For convenience I will refer to these promiscuous imputors of pivotal normality as *normal-smiths*, a term which properly denotes the craftsman-like character of their work. Promiscuous imputors of pivotal deviance are, in complementary fashion, best designated *deviant-smiths*.

HUMANITY AND THE CAPACITY TO CHANGE

On encountering a deviant Actor, normal-smiths communicate to him the message that, despite what Actor thinks of himself, despite what normal and deviant Others think of him, there lurks within him—underneath, after all, essentially—a core of being that is normal. Despite Actor's deviant acts, however many there may have been, he is essentially a normal Actor. Normal-smiths may communicate this message not directly but indirectly through their aggressive imputation to Actor of a *capacity to change*. Considered generically, normal-smiths conceive human beings as those kinds of objects which are capable of profound or radical change within rather short periods of time. They believe that deviant Actors can be *quickly transformed* into a variety of normal.

ORGANIZED NORMAL-SMITHS

Under what conventional categories of normal Others are we most likely to find these normal-smiths? The most spectacular variety is found traveling in those versions of Christianity which are proselytizing and evangelical and which foster and practice the dictum of "hating the act but loving the sinner." Translated into a vocabulary of interpersonal imputation, this slogan and interaction practice demand that the believer *refuse* to define the indicators of the Actor's pivotal deviance as definitive of a *special, differentiated* deviant character. Such refusal is possible by means of the operating meaning of the concept "sinner." An Actor who is a "sinner" is *not* a special, differentiated deviant character. It is said, instead, that *all* humans are sinners. To be a sinner is to be a *normal human being*. To be a sinner is to be like everyone else. So say fundamentalists:

You Are by Nature a Sinner;
"There is none righteous, no, not one" (Romans 3:10)
"For all have sinned, and come short of the glory of God" (Romans 3:23).
(Moody Press, n.d.)

Thus the deviant Actor is brought into the pool of universally sinning mankind. That is, within a conception of persons such as this, the fact that a given Actor may have been more sinful—engaged in more deviant acts—than others pales in importance alongside what is defined as the *more fundamental fact* that all humans are sinners. Actors who think of themselves and who are thought of by Others as deviant are not, thereby, set apart from the rest of mankind. No matter how evil one's past and/or present actions, one remains essentially and irrevocably a "child of God" (or some similar designation), an instance of the category *humanity*. As long as everyone is guilty, of what importance are particular degrees of guilt? Given universal guilt, the only important thing is to be retrieved from it, that is, to be saved. And herein lies the relevance of this kind of belief for the imputation of normalcy. Normal-smiths who adhere to such a belief hold out to the deviant and sinful Actor (and to everyone else) the possibility and desirability of *radical and swift personal change*. There is proffered what is called "redemption" or "salvation" from the universal condition of human sin.[3]

Evangelical Christians are not, of course, the only believers in the radical and quick changeability of human objects. Of more recent vintage in American civilization are the variety of self-help groups which have a somewhat more restricted conception of *who* needs salvation but which are essentially similar in the "unreasonable" or "unsafe" character of the imputations they make of deviant Actors. I refer in particular to the largest and best-known of these groups, Alcoholics Anonymous (AA). AA and similar groups define considerably less than humanity itself as in need of salvation and restrict their definition of the sin from which Actors need to be saved. Instead of saving *all* humanity from *all* sin, self-help groups seek to save defined categories of humanity from defined varieties of sin. In the AA case the effort is to save alcoholics from the "sin" of excessive drinking and the acts and feelings felt to accompany it. Although self-help groups differ from evangelical Christianity in this way, the two types of collectivities are alike in their belief that the relevant human Actors *can change radically and quickly*.

To communicate to deviant Actors that they can change radically and quickly is, *at minimum,* to communicate to them that they are, after all, underneath, fundamentally, the kind of people who are not "trapped" in deviance by reason of fixed personal character. It is to say that, despite all evidence to the contrary, there is an essential core of normalcy that makes possible the living of

[3] Two of the emotions that deviant Actors impute to those who are "saving" them are "understanding" and "acceptance." Of Billy Graham, an alcoholic convert can say, "he knew what I was but he accepted me" (Gillenson, 1967). Of Jesus, it is sometimes asserted that he loves us in spite of anything we have done. Within the identity imputation framework offered here, terms such as understanding and acceptance mean most importantly that the Christian Other is aware of the identity imputed to Actor by himself and by a range of conventional third party Others but that he still imputes to Actor a different and nondeviant identity; namely that of fallen man who can be saved. Particularly rich case material on Christian normal-smithy is presented in Wilkerson, 1964:14, 68–69, 91–95, 121–30.

a reasonably normal life. Unlike some of the newer self-help groups, Alcoholics Anonymous promotes the conception that alcoholics are forever and irretrievably alcoholics; i.e., they can never again imbibe alcoholic beverages. In this limited sense AA does promote a conception of irrevocable character deviancy. Such a doctrine should not, however, be allowed to obscure the more fundamental imputation that AA people make of one another and of non-AA alcoholics. Despite this irrevocable deviant propensity, there is *still* a core of normalcy that makes possible the rapid assumption of a variety of normal life.[4]

Of more recent vintage, Synanon, an association of ex-drug addicts, imputes to its possible and actual membership the

> status or role of *"people"* rather than "ward," "inmate" or "prisoner" in the organization, and [addicts] can identify with its constructive goals. He [the addict] is in fact automatically an employee of the rehabilitation organization, and in this role he takes part in Synanon's management and development. (Yablonsky and Dederich, 1963:51.)

In defining "addicts" as instances of the very general category "people," there is the imputation—the expectation—that these "people" objects will act and feel properly, in terms of shared notions of what "people" do and feel. That is, it can be expected that they will behave as though they were instances of normal categories.[5]

Sometimes the conception of quick change takes on a very unusual cast but involves a fundamentally similar theme. Thus, among people like Dr. Timothy Leary, both when he was regarded as a "legitimate" psychologist and later, there may evolve the conception that

> We over-value the mind—that flimsy collection of learned words and verbal connections; the mind, that system of paranoid delusions with the learned self as center. (Leary, 1962:60.)

Combined with a conception of life as "game playing" and certain views of the eternal mystical, Dr. Leary derived the conception that, to change people, one need only shake them loose from their *learned games*, show them the ridiculousness of the games they play and substitute new "more satisfying" games. While acknowledging that many kinds of experiences could "shake people

---

[4] In this and the subsequent references to Alcoholics Anonymous without citation, I have drawn from observational materials collected in New York City, 1959–60. A part of these materials are reported in Lofland and Lejeune, 1960. See also, Gellman, 1964 and the comprehensive bibliography therein.

[5] A novice in Synanon who does construe himself as an instance of a special deviant character can thus be told in public: " 'You lying son of a bitch, you're so full of shit it's ridiculous!' With that, everyone in the group broke up in a loud roar of laughter." The leader, Charles Dederich, could comment further: "Here he was trying to rationalize away his bad behavior with this bull story he had dug out of Psychology I." (Yablonsky, 1965:150.)

loose," Dr. Leary, as is well known, came to advocate certain drugs as the "most efficient way to cut through the game structures of Western life." (Leary, 1962:59.) Whatever else may be said of Dr. Leary's views, they are one variant on the theme of defining persons as capable of quick and radical change. Before he was dismissed from Harvard and prior to his becoming involved in what is called the "psychedelic movement," he actually engaged in efforts to bring about such quick and radical change in prison convicts. (Leary, 1962:64–66.)

I do not wish to convey the impression that normal-smiths are found exclusively under rather unorthodox labels or in very esoteric settings, although this appears mostly to be the case. Here and there, now and again, Others who are members of the social control establishment undertake to depart from "deviant-smithy as usual" and begin making what are publicly defined as rather unusual imputations to the deviants with which they deal. Such little counter-ripples in the sea of deviant-smithy are even likely to receive notice in the conventional mass media. Thus *Time* noted in a psychiatry blurb the claim of Dr. Samuel Hadden of Philadelphia that "homosexuals can be cured." In addition to some other arrangements, Dr. Hadden's innovation appears to have involved "an understanding attitude toward his patients and confidence that their illness can indeed be treated." Dr. Hadden contrasts his view with the

> 45-year-old pessimism of Freud, who was convinced that the condition was discouragingly difficult to treat. Even when psychiatrists do try to aid homosexuals, their efforts are likely to be ineffectual because they themselves have too little confidence of success. (*Time*, February 12, 1965.)

Dr. Hadden's program appears to consist largely of aggressively imputing to homosexuals that they *can*, without enormous difficulty, be instances of normals. Using small groups of ex-homosexual normals who assist in fostering this imputation upon prospective normals, a definition of changeability is built up. (Hadden, 1967.)

LAY NORMAL-SMITHS

These examples of normal-smithy that come in the form of named groups or well-known labeled doctrines should not imply that organized types are the exclusive bearers of the orientation. Some recognition must also be accorded those few individuals found in most communities who, without benefit of Bibles, publications or specialized organization, are known to take unusual chances with local people whom everyone else has "given up on."[6] These in-

---

[6] Among other organized and labeled efforts, however, mention should be made of the "humanistic psychology" movement, a sprawling collection of dissenters from the psychological establishment who tend to make normal-smith assumptions. Statements by its prin-

clude the archtypical employers who give the local "ne'er-do-wells" and more
serious deviants a second or third or further chance to make good.   While the
local population grudgingly admires the chances that such employers and others take with deviants, they are not at all certain that they want personally to
run such risks.   Indeed, it seems that local laymen who would make imputations of normalcy to deviants—by giving them jobs and the like—tend themselves to be outstanding citizens in other regards.   If this were not the case,
association with deviant Actors would likely transform such normals themselves
into objects of suspicion.   After all, it is felt, "birds of a feather flock together"
(except when one of the birds is a stellar normal).   One might even say that the
famous imputors and the organizations of national repute are hardly at all the
true heroes of imputing normalcy.   The true heroes are, rather, local community people who put themselves on the line daily in the eyes of their fellow
citizens by treating a publicly defamed person in such a way as to enable the
more timid to make imputations of normalcy as well.   The offering of a job, an
invitation to a gathering, the selling or letting of a dwelling, the extension of
credit, the friendly conversation in a chance meeting—all become more possible
actions to take toward the "deviant" once such a hero has initiated the discernment of normality.

DEVIANT-SMITHS

The beliefs and imputations of normal-smiths are usefully contrasted with
those that typically prevail in the social control establishment.   The more "professional" stance of the social controllers involves making no "quasi-charlatan"
(some people would say) promises of radical and swift change.   According to
many professionals, one must have a proper appreciation of the difficulties and
uncertainties inherent in attempting to "cure" people of "illness," especially illness felt to be of a psychic variety.   About the most that can be promised is
that, given a long enough period of time, perhaps a little something can be
done.   Such a view is founded upon a theory of deep-lying, difficult to change,
deviant personal dynamics.   That is, the conception of humans as slow to
change fits together with theories of deviant personal character.   Indeed, given
the bureaucratic conditions under which such professionals labor, this is a
highly reasonable stance.   The irony is that the belief in slow and difficult

---

cipal exponents are brought together in Bugenthal, ed., 1967; and it is explicated from
within a more encompassing context by Halmos, 1966:especially 49–66. See also the special
set of articles on "the group phenomenon" in the magazine *Psychology Today*, December,
1967. See, in addition, Cooper, 1968; and Glasser, 1962, on what he refers to as "reality
therapy." (Glasser's work is further described in Langguth, 1967.) The argument for suicide
as a deviant identity also requiring normal-smith imputations for recruitment from it is presented in Kobler and Stotland's humanistically inclined study of that act. See, in particular,
their treatment of Carl Rogers and the imputations he recommends. (Kobler and Stotland,
1964:264–66.)

change, based on some corresponding theory of deviant personality, functions to retard identification of Actor as a variety of normal. As a result, the professionals of the social control establishment function largely as deviant-smiths.

SIMPLE INDICATORS RECALLED

Phrasing the efforts of normal-smiths in the language of categories and indicators, we can observe that normal-smiths have very "loose" indicators or requirements for coding a human as an instance of a normal. In the most extreme instance, that of conversionist Christianity, the *only* requirement necessary to begin predicating imputations of this object as an instance of a *normal* human being is that the object now viewed be recognizable as a *human being*, a not very difficult judgment to make. However, although most normal-smiths probably require a few more indicators before activating their variety of imputations as a normal, these are neither very numerous nor very elaborate. In Alcoholics Anonymous, for example, anyone who displays even the slightest interest in the organization for almost any announced reason (minimal indicators combined with a large number of alternative indicators) is likely to be immediately coded as one who is seeking help, and AA members begin at once to impute to Actor the normality of his feelings and his power to change. Protestations by Actor that he has been misinterpreted are met with knowing, sympathetic smiles which acknowledge that the AA member is well aware of the difficulties of self-revelation.

It might be said, then, that social identification as normal is facilitated by the presence of Others who have in their coding scheme normal categories for which the minimal indicator is merely *common humanity* or identification as a human being who suffers and can change or be redeemed. Phrased more generally, it can be said that identification as an instance of a normal is facilitated when normal categories have a small number of necessary and a large number of alternatively sufficient indicators.

PREVALENT SENSITIVITY

It must be recognized that the initiation of imputations of pivotal normality is a hazardous activity. Given the widespread beliefs about the resistance of deviants to change, persons who think of themselves as pivotal deviants and who are playing out that label are likely to continue to do so for a time in spite of any redefinition by Others. Before they change, to treat them as normal is to be open to exploitation, subterfuge or even physical danger. It is to lower one's guard against such dangers, to act "as if" such dangers did not exist. Since these dangers will likely in a measure exist, normal-smiths are, in the short-run sense, "irrational." A strong and articulate ideology of the merits of normal-smithy despite the danger is thus required. The perils of normality imputation are typically appraised as part of the price one pays for the privilege of making normals out of deviants—or, as one variety of normal-smith might put it, for the privilege of "winning souls for God."

NUMBERS OF
NORMAL-SMITHS

Because the vast bulk of a population is unlikely to espouse and practice a strong and articulate ideology which would allow them to discount or accept the dangers of this short-run irrationality, the *proportion* of intensive coders for normality in deviants is likely to be quite small. In contemporary American civilization, normal-smiths (taking together all the evangelical Christians, AA's and other self-help group members, as well as lay normal-smiths and those few in the social control establishment) probably constitute no more than a few per cent of the population. While in absolute numbers there may be several million, they constitute only a small stream relative to the sea of "safe" deviant-smiths.

STRATEGIC DISPERSION OF
NORMAL-SMITHS

Because of their ideology, however, normal-smiths tend to be institutionally dispersed such that their impact is magnified far out of proportion to their numbers. Embodying a sense of "cause," normal-smiths tend to act like traditional sorts of missionaries and proselytizers, fanning out into territories where deviants are presumably to be found. They set up headquarters in "deviant" neighborhoods, insinuate themselves into mental hospitals and prisons and make themselves available to go anywhere and speak before any sort of group that will issue an invitation. And within their more conventional round of life, normal-smiths tend to talk continually about their view of normality and to be always on the lookout for persons to whom it might be appropriately imputed. Evangelical Christians, of course, make imputations to everyone not already saved. The more restrictive normal-smiths, such as those in AA, confine themselves to being sensitive to possible problematic people of their "own kind."

Although typically viewed as a political phenomenon, the efforts of Saul Alinsky's Industrial Areas Foundation (IAF) is a model of aggressive normal-smithy, magnified in impact far beyond what would be expected from the tiny cadre involved. Founded on the premise that the only, or at least primary, problem of those called "the poor" is a lack of power and money, the IAF (upon sufficient invitation) sends into a slum area a cadre of organizers. One of this cadre's main tasks is to impute to the populous their essential normality and to communicate the possibility of rather quick and radical social and therefore personal change through mass organization. Fanning out through the area, the organizers are reported vigorously to impute to the residents their collective capacity to change their situation and, therefore, themselves.[7] (The resultant power politics and new sense of normal personal identity that these populations sometimes acquire must, of course, be contrasted with the results of the operations typically carried on by the American War on Poverty of the sixties, with its more timid and much less intensive imputations.)

To the degree, then, that normal-smiths display missionary intensity and accomplish institutional dispersion, the identification of a given deviant Actor as an instance of a normal is facilitated. There still remain, however, all the vicissitudes of escalation which for normal-smiths, as will be discussed shortly, are quite formidable.

DIFFERENTIAL VULNERABILITY TO IMPUTATION AS NORMAL

In the nature of the case, almost all social deviants are highly vulnerable to imputations of normality by normal-smiths. In line with the logic of tracing circumstances most highly facilitative of assuming normality, normal-smiths have become, and will continue to be, the central focus. However, it is not unreasonable also to mention marginal situations under which Others who code persons more conventionally might, too, begin construing Actor as normal. Or, put differently, mention can be made of *circumstances in which social deviants are vulnerable to—or, more neutrally, likely to be the objects of—imputations of normalcy from deviant-smiths and other conventionals.* These are, first, the chance circumstance of an Other's ignorance of Actor as a social deviant, and, second, the situation of Actor's possessing features highly incongruent with his identity as a social deviant.

[7] Silberman, 1964:Chap. 10; Sanders, 1965. See also the alignment between social science and aggressive normal-smithy initiated by Etzkowitz and Schaflander (1968). Further, relative to parties in conflicts of a more balanced or "political" kind (pp. 13–19 of this text), it is reasonable to conceive Mahatma Ghandi and Martin Luther King as outstanding utilizers of normal-smithy in power struggles of considerable social consequence. The context of conflict is different, but the normal-smith principles of interpersonal imputation—toward both followers and opponents—seem basically similar. Normal-smith imputations among and toward followers (but not toward opponents) seem to be found in a variety of social and revolutionary movements, including, in particular, many kinds of Black nationalism and self-help arising in the late sixties in America.

Ignorance of Actor's Pivotal Deviance

In recent years it has been fashionable to apprise all those interacting with a deviant Actor of his deviance. It is felt that everyone around the Actor should "get to know" his point of view, should understand how he conceives the world, should appreciate his "problems." The ironic effect of all this information sharing is that imputations of pivotal deviance may simply be reinforced. Normal Others who attempt to participate in the symbolic world of the deviant may find themselves also participating in *his* definition of the indicators taken to reveal his deviance. Knowing Others, however desirous they may be of imputing pivotal normality, can, because they are so knowledgeable about Actor's point of view, quite easily come to doubt their own imputations of normality. The general principle involved is, again, the fundamental ambiguity of human action. Because human emissions are so frequently ambiguous, full knowledge of conflicting definitions of the same item can very easily lead to making the "safe" definition of the item, i.e., that it is indicative of deviance. Any Other who approaches an Actor and "really gets close" to him easily finds that Actor has all manner of peculiar feelings and has engaged in all manner of peculiar acts. Note that I do not say here "normal Others approaching a deviant Actor." Almost *any* two people who get close are likely to find in the cognitive and action worlds of each other a variety of items that are at the very least "suspicious" in terms of their indicativeness for pivotal deviance. How much more corrosive is such closeness between two actors, one of whom is *already defined* as pivotally deviant?

It would seem, rather, that imputations of normality are most facilitated by the ignorance of normal Others. Not having rendered Actor an unambiguously deviant object, the ignorant Other is more likely to take Actor's situationally generated feelings of frustration, of anger, of despair or whatever, as instances of normal behavior.

One immediate implication of the facilitative character of ignorance is that those Actors whose deviance is not immediately visible are more likely to have imputations of normalcy made of them. Deviants who desire to *avoid* identification as normals are well advised to mutilate their bodies in some public and permanent way, to adopt distinctive dress or to practice special facial and body gestures. Those who fail to make their deviance immediately visible are, on that account, more vulnerable to becoming normals. Among particularly vulnerable categories are professional criminals such as confidence men, many alcoholics, neurotics and many schizophrenics (many of the latter are, however, protected by distinctive body language). And so it is that one finds differences in "recidivism" as a function of whether convicts' records of imprisonment are released with them upon parole to the Army (Mattick, 1956.) Among the least vulnerable to imputations of normalcy are those people called "the physically handicapped," Hell's Angels-type motorcyclists and hippies.[8]

INCONSISTENT DISPLAY

The initiation of an imputation of pivotal deviance is facilitated when Actor displays features that are inconsistent with normality but consistent with deviance. In the same way, imputation of pivotal normality is facilitated when Actor displays features that are inconsistent with deviance but consistent with normality. Non-normal-smith Others can be struck by some feature of Actor that is highly valued by normals and that is seen, therefore, as inconsistent with his pivotal deviance. Such inconsistencies not untypically involve intelligence, physical beauty or unusual leadership ability. Or, they may simply involve "niceness" or "being a good guy" or some other sort of personalistic feature. Deviants perceived by normals to have such high-value features are more likely to be singled out, to be noticed, to be the objects of special recognition and treatment—to be, in short, more likely to have imputations of normality made of them. They are, as a consequence (if other conditions come into play), more likely to be found among those ex-deviant normals who are paraded before the world as examples of successful "rehabilitation."

Persons who "work with" deviants are, of course, likely to attribute their "reform," at least in part, to such unusual qualities as those just mentioned. One thus hears it said that X was able to change because of his or her unusual intelligence, personality qualities or interpersonal skills. But it may be that it is not such qualities themselves that directly facilitate reform. Rather, they may simply function to bring the deviants who possess them to the attention of normals, who then use these qualities as a basis for predicating imputations of

---

[8] See further Goffman, 1963a:73–104. Relative to escalating Actor to a normal personal identity (Chap. 10 and 11 of this text), the imputations of ignorant Others, unaccompanied by the work of normal-smiths (who do "know all" and still impute normality), would not seem to be terribly facilitative. Actor is fully aware that these Others would treat him quite differently "if they only knew." Nevertheless, the very fact that he is able to pass may begin a crucial undercutting of his belief in his "essential deviance." Also relative to escalation, there exists an issue of the plausibility of pivotally normal imputations made by non-normal-smith Others. Between Actor and Others who know of his pivotal deviance, there is frequently played the game of what his feelings, properties and acts "really" mean. Normal Others will often go to great pains to redefine features of Actor as "really normal," even when, in fact, they have their own doubts about the case. This game is sometimes called patronizing or spurious interaction, and one of its important features is that Actor often *knows* that Others may be lying to him. Thus, because Others are known occasionally or frequently to misrepresent their actual impressions, he may have difficulty himself distinguishing between the normal and deviant meaning of his emissions. The intent of the normals' lying—to convince Actor and themselves of his normality—is a laudable one, to be sure. But unless they are very good liars, which very few people are, Actor is likely to view everything they say to him regarding his normality with skepticism. Ignorant Others, whom deviant Actor knows to be ignorant, are, on the other hand, *trustworthy* imputors of pivotal normality.

pivotal normalcy. If the ex-deviant normals of the world are more intelligent, better looking or more verbally and interpersonally skilled than are deviants generally, this may better reflect the propensities and selectivities of normals than the varying capacities of human beings defined as deviant.

In cases of inconsistent display, normals are more likely to become concerned over the waste of talent. They are more likely to feel that it "certainly is a shame" that some person, X, is a deviant. "She is such a wonderful girl." "He is so intelligent." It is a well-known folk theme, although insufficiently documented, that within the social control establishment of deviant-smithy as usual, now and again a "professional" takes a special interest in one or another of his charges (even to the point, in the case of children, of adoption or, in the case of adults, of eventual marriage). While, from within the perspective of the social control establishment, such interests are no doubt "nonprofessional," they do appear effective in bringing about normalcy. The interest of San Quentin Warden Clinton Duffy in Bill Sands, author of *My Shadow Ran Fast,* may well have hinged importantly on the fact that Sands was the son of a prominent southern California judge and attorney and, moreover, that he had the second highest I.Q. at San Quentin (exceeded only by C. Chessman). In addition, Sands was a proficient athlete, well built and perceived to be physically attractive. Of him it was surely said, "Isn't it a shame, given his background and all?"

Deviants who happen to be merely average in the mentioned regards would appear to be distinctively advantaged or disadvantaged (depending upon your point of view) vis-à-vis the initiation of imputation as a pivotal normal, for they are more likely to be perceived as fitting the stereotypic model of the pivotal deviant. And those who are *below* average seem especially unlikely candidates for imputations of normalcy. After all, by definition, deviants are a little bit stupid, ugly and incompetent, else why would they lead such foolish lives? Those who are, in fact, ugly, stupid or otherwise incompetent merely fulfill what is already imputed. It may well turn out, empirically, that sheer physical appearance—or more precisely, the imputations that others make of it—is one of the more crucial elements in the possibility of a deviant's being imputed as pivotally normal. Recent experiments in providing free plastic surgery to correct broken noses and the like for male and female convicts indicate that such surgery tends to be correlated with differences in postprison criminality (Abeles, Lewin and Mandell, 1965). While the effect of such corrections on the self-identification of Actor can be granted, one cannot overlook the effect of such changes—such new appearances of normalcy—on *Others,* normal and deviant as well.

Deviants who contrive to make themselves spectacularly visible in confirming ways protect themselves most against imputations of normality. To don special clothing or tattoo one's body in arcane ways is to draw the attention of normal Others to these items, deflecting attention from any high-value features that might also be displayed. In focusing attention on, and having concern over, Johnny's black jacket and his "born to raise hell" tattoo, normal Others are less likely to notice that Johnny is also handsome or brilliant or whatever. Homosexual "drag" garb and hippie costume serve a similar function.

These two points, again, apply primarily to prompting deviant-smiths and other conventionals to make imputations of pivotal normalcy. Normal-smiths seem not to require ignorance or contradictions of categorical display. The ideal-type normal-smith needs only the mere display of being a human. For him, to be human, regardless of all else, is to be fundamentally and after all a variety of normal.

Assuming that a socially deviant Actor has in the ways discussed been initially identified as a candidate normal, one can then ask how he might be brought to a conception of himself as some kind of normal who engages only in socially acceptable activities. An answer to this question involves, again, an analysis of escalation and its facilitants.

Assuming that identification of Actor as a pivotal normal has been initiated, we can inquire into conditions most facilitative of his escalation to identification of self as "truly" normal. I will assume that the escalation process from deviant to normal has much the same *formal structure* as escalation from normal to deviant. Only the substantive content of the imputations is changed. This must, however, be a tentative assumption that awaits closer investigation, especially in light of the differences in the "safeness" of imputing pivotal deviance or normalcy. If such an assumption can be made, it may then be asked: What arrangements of Others, places, hardware and Actors are most facilitative of escalating Actor to identification of himself as an instance of a normal? Within each of these categories I will employ the analytic concepts explicated in discussing the assumption of deviant identity. To minimize redundancy, I have assumed for the most part that the reader has a working knowledge of these concepts and their associated propositions.

FACILITANTS OF ESCALATION: OTHERS

UNANIMOUS IMPUTATION

NORMAL-SMITHS AND UNANIMOUS IMPUTATION

Continuing a focus on organized normal-smith enterprises, and bringing forth the previous postulate concerning the presence of unanimous Others, one may inquire into ways in which unanimity can be contrived or compromised. A first and defining fact about normal-smiths is that, because they make imputations of normalcy on the basis of minimal indicators—because they make "unsafe imputations"—more conventional Others are less than likely immediately to "buy" what they promote about a given Actor. Being a minority, normal-smiths can easily be but one category of imputors in Actor's total milieu, which might also include a variety of Others who are ignorant, doubtful, disbelieving or scoffing of the new imputation.

Residential Encompassment. Residential encompassment is one practical solution to the likelihood of imputational division. And it is precisely unanimity that is achieved by an organization like Synanon, which *requires,* as a condition of membership, that new charges live in a Synanon establishment. Initiates are prohibited from traveling outside or from contacting old friends, even by letter. Through such means (i.e., restriction of candidate normals to association with small, tight circles within which there is agreement), groups that are a tiny minority in the society at large can contrive unanimity. By being widely introduced, talked up and talked about within such a circle, the initial imputation is sold, although sold only among persons who are already in concord concerning identity types.

Divided Imputations. If a territorially encapsulating operation such as Synanon is not unique, it is at least rare. Other normal-smiths must traverse a more hazardous road, much more subject to imputational division. Foremost among these are the members of Alcoholics Anonymous who attempt to impute normality to Actor while he is still "at large" in civil society. Apparently appreciative of the importance of imputational unanimity, AA's do try to create it for candidates, at least initially. The central figure in this attempt is the "sponsor"—an AA who takes responsibility for the fledgling. In some AA groups an aggressive sponsor can come effectively to dominate, if not totally control, imputations received by Actor. The AA sponsor may take the "baby," as novitiates are called, to an AA meeting every night in the week; meet him for meals; travel many miles to pick him up to attend AA meetings; and cajole him into attendance if he is resistant. If the baby "slips"—takes a drink and goes on a "drunk"—the aggressive sponsor may run him down in a bar, drag him out, stay up all night with him and leave his job during the day to find and help him. In general the sponsor, and other helping AA's, working in relays, may undertake to control the baby's life, that is, to subject the Actor to the imputations of AA day and night.

However, because even AA members must make a living at some sort of conventional employment, division or conflict of imputation (as shown in Chart 10.1) is not untypical, and perhaps even usual. Unable to accomplish the withdrawal of Actor from the larger society and the resulting imputational unanimity achieved by Synanon-type organizations, AA and other similar efforts must contend with the continuing presence of Others who either do not know of the new imputations (the ignorant) or know of them but do not believe them to be reasonable (the challengers). Thus AA must contend with old drinking friends and spouses, both of whom may have an interest in Actor's being, and continuing to be, a deviant drinker. The supportive solicitude and/or *impugning* punishment (by spouses especially) that such Others continue to provide for deviant drinkers are a major kind of competition with AA imputations.

Strategies for Unanimity. It is apparently in response to such a problem that AA and similar organizations tend to form satellite or auxiliary groups of relevant normals and attempt to recruit Actors' kin and friends into them. Thus AA has Al–anon, a group for relatives, and even Alateen, an association for the teen-age children of both new and long-term AA's. The perspective of these groups is, of course, the AA view of normalcy and how it is achieved. Such

CHART 10.1. *SOME VARIATIONS IN WHO IS IMPUTING WHAT TO ACTOR: NORMAL IDENTITY*

Some Combinations of What Is Imputed	Some Combinations of Who Is Imputing		
	A. Normal and deviants are both typically encountered.	B. Only normals are typically encountered.	C. Only deviants are typically encountered.
1. Unanimous imputation of pivotal normalcy.	1A	1B	1C
2. Some impute normalcy; some are ignorant and impute deviance.	2A	2B	2C
3. Some impute normalcy; some are ignorant and impute deviance; some challenge an imputation of normalcy.	3A	3B	3C
4. Some impute normalcy; some challenge an imputation of normalcy.	4A	4B	4C

normal associations are instructed in a proper conception of human objects and proper imputations to make of them.

Within the worlds of normal-smithy, as contrived or compromised as they might be, there is also a distinct tendency to engage in what might be called *elevation ceremonies*. These serve publicly and formally to announce, sell and spread the fact of Actor's new kind of being. In the same way that the previously mentioned denunciation ceremonies can serve to sell deviance to the public at large, elevation ceremonies serve to sell new normalcy, at least within a particular world of normal-smiths. Ceremonies that announce new being, whether of degradation or elevation, differ in the degree to which they are organized and publicized, ranging from mere fleeting gestures made mostly in private and barely known about to enduring, complexly organized, enormously public and highly publicized undertakings. Because of the resources available to deviant-smiths, denunciation ceremonies tend toward the latter pole, while normal-smith ceremonies of elevation are more likely to be closer to the former pole. And, as is well known, deviants not in contact with normal-smiths are usually subjected only to denunciation ceremonies. The deviant Actor tends to be

> ushered into the deviant position by a decisive and often dramatic cere-mony, yet is retired from it with hardly a word of public notice. And as a result, the deviant often returns home with no proper license to resume a normal life in the community. Nothing has happened to cancel out the stigmas imposed upon him by earlier commitment ceremonies; from a formal point of view, the original verdict or diagnosis is still in effect. It should not be surprising, then, that the members of the community seem reluctant to accept the returning deviant on an entirely equal footing. (Erikson, 1962:310.)

Among normal-smiths, devices, such as public appearance before a formally assembled group, the public profession of one's personal transformation, or-ganized congratulation on membership and write-ups in a group's newspaper, newsletter or magazine, function, however tentatively, to solidify unanimity and therefore a new conception of self. That such occurrences tend not to be as thoroughly organized and publicized as ceremonies of denunciation presum-ably limits the degree to which they are facilitative.

DIVIDED IMPUTATIONS AND
PROFESSIONAL ENTERPRISE

In recent years within the social control establishment itself, there have been some sporadic attempts at normal-smithy. The operation and fate of these efforts offer some instructive insights into the difficulties of achieving unanim-ity of imputation as normal. Under the rubrics of "guided group interaction" and similar titles, the federal and state governments have undertaken, in a small way, the enterprise of normal-smithy *in the context* of a deviant-smith estab-lishment. While a few such efforts have managed, at least for awhile, to insu-late themselves from the larger context of deviant-smithy from which they derive their legitimacy,[1] many have not. In situations where insulation has not been achieved, division or conflict over what kind of imputations to make of deviant Actors has ensued. For the deviants involved, such divisions and con-flicts have created a very confusing and alienating world and have served to alienate them from conventional categories even more than routine subjection to the kind of processes outlined in Part II.

As a form of normal-smithy, central features of "guided group interaction" include the conception that deviant Actors can change in response to changed life situations. An important part of implementing such change is the subjec-

---

[1] E.g., McCorkle, Elias and Bixby, 1958. See also the parade of difficulties encountered by the Provo experiment, reported by Empey, 1967.

tion of deviant Actors to imputations of this possibility and the provision of viable objective possibilities for acting normally. As it has been implemented in some places, however, that segment of the resident staff who offer such imputations find themselves confounded and contradicted by (1) other segments of the staff and (2) higher-level administrative units who dictate on-the-scene policy. In one such federal program for juvenile offenders in Chicago, a proportion of the staff was recruited from "various juvenile and adult correctional institutions, some maximum security" (Dickson, 1966:6). Such a strategy of personnel recruitment well ensured that the staff would—and did—impute pivotal deviance to their charges. Because the larger federal system was committed to a mixture of "treatment technologies," the Chicago effort at normal-smithy had imposed upon it from above the requirement of administering "technologies" in addition to guided group interaction. The week had to be filled, it was felt; so it was filled by the "darlings" of deviant-smithy, especially "client-oriented" private meetings with staff.

A similar kind of pattern prevailed in a "halfway house" for adult narcotic users in Los Angeles. Although the program was intended as an experiment in normal-smithy, a proportion of the staff was composed of deviant-smiths, in this case, "parole agents." These normals were perceived by the resident deviant Actors to impute only pivotal deviance. Who but pivotal deviants are subjected to the kind of treatment that would bring the following response from a resident?

> When we ask you a question, why can't you give us an answer instead of acting like a psychologist or sociologist . . . instead of sitting back and acting like you are so smart. After all, you're just a cop. . . . Why don't you act like you're supposed to act? (Fisher, 1965:192.)

The author of the report on this halfway house relates more generally:

> Residents interpret this behavior by staff as treating them like children, and contend that an individual who asks a straight-forward question deserves a straightforward answer. It suggests that they are not being treated like "men." (Fisher, 1965:192.)

In the eyes of the deviant-smiths, deviant Actors are, of course, and by definition, not "men." They should therefore not be treated as such, or as any other category of pivotal normality. This effort seems, indeed, to have been less of a case of divided imputations than of almost unanimous imputations of pivotal deviance, despite the fact that the overt, formal and public goals (and the persuasions of a part of the staff) were in the direction of normal-smithy. The deviant-smith portion of the staff even managed to instigate the following kinds of arrangements, nicely serving to confound and contradict any attempted imputations of normalcy.

> The resident perception that the place is "just like the joint" [in spite of claims to the contrary] is based on certain policies and standard operating procedures. First, the appearance of the place is a constant matter of staff concern, and residents are obligated to meet staff demands for maintaining a neat-appearing establishment. Staff demands on this issue are much as they are in prison and military establishments. Second, certain security measures must be taken in the House, such as maintaining twenty-four hour coverage by official personnel. Third, a timetable for arising in the morning and for lights out at night is maintained. Fourth, attendance is mandatory for the group counseling sessions. Fifth, week-night passes are not allowed. These are among the features of the Halfway House program which are frequently cited by its resident population as justification for viewing it as [just] another "joint." (Fisher, 1965:192.)

In addition, a portion of the staff engaged in personalistic imputations of pivotal deviance of this kind:

> One staff member commented on the failure of some residents to seek work who were permitted to do so as follows: "I think it is symptomatic of a much deeper personality disturbance that the majority of these men have. Obtaining and retaining employment has been difficult for, I am sure, that vast majority of every parolee addict that we will come in contact with. He will not have a stable employment record. This will be part of the pathology, part of the symptom of the whole thing . . . ." (Fisher, 1965: 192.)

In line with the *official* normal-smithy of this place, the deviant Actors:

> object to and deny the implication that they are "sick" or that they have "problems" of which their actions in the Halfway House, or elsewhere, are symptomatic. They frequently claim that their actions have to do with their current social situation, particularly the demands of the Halfway House program. They also claim that staff is unwilling, or unable, to see this. (Fisher, 1965:192.)

Dr. Timothy Leary's early efforts to identify convicts as instances of normals and to escalate them to a variety of normal pivotal identity also labored under contradictory and divided imputations. The group with which he worked, as reported by Dr. Leary,

> has become [a] workshop for planning future games. Some prisoners are being trained to take over the functions of research assistants. They are performing the tasks of a vocational guidance clinic—preparing occupational brochures for inmates about to be released, making plans to act as rehabilitation workers after their release, for organizing a halfway house for ex-convicts. Other convicts are using their time to prepare for the games to which they will return—the family game, their old job.
> The psilocybin experience made these men aware of the stereotyped

games in which they had been involved, the game of "cops and robbers," the game of being a tough guy, the game of outwitting the law, the game of resentful cynicism. "My whole life came tumbling down, and I was sitting happily in the rubble." But insight is the beginning, and the more demanding task is to help these men choose new games, help them learn the rules, the roles, the concepts, the rituals of the new game.

Our work progresses slowly and against strong opposition. Our new game of allowing criminals to take over responsibility and authority and prestige as experts on "crime and rehabilitation" brings us into competition with the professional middle class. Anger and anxiety are aroused. (Leary, 1962:66.)

NORMALS AND DEVIANTS PRESENT

NEW AND PHANTOM DEVIANTS IN NORMAL-SMITH GROUPS

Significantly, normal-smith groups are almost all organized so as to provide for the presence of both pivotal normals and pivotal deviants. These groups are in the business of seeking ever-new deviants to whom to impute their variety of normal identity. This means that the groups will almost always have around them prospective or candidate deviant Actors contemplating or beginning the particular identity. These ever-new Actors view anyone who has arrived previous to them as part of the enterprise they are now beginning to view. The deviant Actor of focus becomes included, in the view of the more newly arrived prospects, as one of the group. Even if the difference in arrival is only a matter of a few hours or a few days, the most immediately arrived deviant must impute to any, even slightly, "older" arrivee some minimal standing as part of the local body of imputors. That is, he imputes pivotal normality to candidate Actor.

In organizations such as Synanon and AA, such a process is a continual one. Because of the imputations of pivotal normality that such ever-new deviant Actors provide for persons already arrived, it might even be said that the worst thing that can happen to normal-smith groups is to exhaust the category of their potential membership. As an aside, it might be noted that, if such groups should deplete the category they are committed to save, the organization would either wither from lack of a major goal or be forced to redefine the category of persons in need of salvation. Since Christians take all of humanity, they would indeed have a problem, although space travel may open up new categories of objects to be saved. (And Synanon has already begun to redefine and broaden its relevant categories of persons, expanding to include more kinds of crime and immorality generally.)

Normal-smith groups conceived and conducted by ex-deviants have a second source of present deviants. Although the members are no longer so, each *was* a deviant; each embodies in himself, in a special way, both pivotal normality and pivotal deviance. Each member is, in effect, two people: a deviant person that he *was* and a normal person that he *is*. The deviant person that he was is kept very much alive through the practice of relating, even *ad nauseam,* the character of the deviant person he used to be. In this sense the live *social* membership of a normal-smith group is actually twice the number of human bodies.

The stream of new deviants and the phantom or social membership of past pivotal deviants accomplish, then, the rather massive presence of both normals and deviants in normal-smith groups. Taking the present and previous facilitants in combination, it can be said that the strongest situation is conjoint production of unanimous imputations of pivotal normality in the presence of both normals and deviants. This situation is graphically represented as cell 1A of Chart 10.1. As one moves either down or across the chart of who is imputing and what is imputed, the possibility of escalation is progressively less likely.

ATTENUATED SITUATIONS

The situation of only normals present should perhaps be ranked second strongest in facilitating escalation. There are in this condition viable models of activity to be *learned.* There are persons who can be identified with, thus increasing the probability of identification of self as an instance of the same category. Some of the more recent efforts to send young Black males with extensive records of delinquency to college illustrate this situation. The stress, appropriately, is on the possibility of *learning* the technical and social routines of a given variety of normality. It is in this respect that the presence of deviants only, even if unanimously imputing pivotal normality to deviant Actor, is the least facilitative. The deviants-only condition may conduce to a pivotally normal conception of self, but it less viably presents the possibility of learning and performing the routines that follow from the category.

It must, of course, be recognized that, outside a normal-smith setting, unanimity on normality among normals and deviants who are both present seems a highly unlikely occurrence. However unlikely, something of the sort is possible and seems to have been at least partially the case in the situation of the previously mentioned Bill Sands, a young man serving a sentence in San Quentin. Sands had developed a warm relationship with Warden and Mrs. Duffy, from whom he was receiving imputations of normality. Concurrently, his relation to "the toughest con in the joint" led to the following encounter, an engagement that could well serve as a type case of imputational facilitation, irrespective of its standing as a touching moment of human contact.

> One day [in the yard] I looked up to see a massive figure making its way, unmistakably toward me. A path opened voluntarily for him, for bearing down on me was, indisputably, the toughest con in the joint.

He was Bob Welles. A four-time loser, doing life for murder, without possibility of parole. Legends of him were legion . . . . I knew Bob and liked him, as I did several other bad boys of San Quentin. Bad, but solid. I had, at first, been drawn naturally to this group. Recently, however, my studies had taken all my free time. As the huge man approached, I wondered if he thought I had turned my back on the clique of tough, solid cons. But my animal wariness, which I had learned to trust more than any other faculty, told me there was no danger here.

"Bill-boy." My own sizeable hand was lost in his great black paw. "Hear you been studyin'."

"That's right. Studying hard." There was a long pause as the huge, solid muscled Colossus worked to put his thoughts into sentences. Talking came hard to him.

"Someday you oughta be getting out—and if you do, then you oughta *stay* out."

I waited in silence.

"You listen to my words, Bill-buddy, 'cause I don't often come out with 'em." Since this was true, I paid strict attention with as much respect for the effort that he was making as curiosity about his motives.

With one great blunt finger, he tapped the book I had been reading.

"Schoolin' ain't the whole story, 'cause if it was, you wouldn't be here in the fust place. But you got somethin' besides schoolin' and it's good—if it don't kill you." He pointed to his own face. "Now look at me a minute, boy. Take a good, long look . . . ."

I obeyed. Only by rigid self-control could I keep my face expressionless. The big Negro was a shambling remnant of tremendous physique, a battered engine of endless vitality and strength. His naturally prominent frontal bones were humped and swollen from blows, protruding so that his eyes were almost obscured. His wide nose literally had been pounded into his face, broken more than a hundred times, torn and mutilated until it was a declivity instead of a protuberance, looking like the end of a double-barreled shotgun. As he spoke, snaggly broken teeth were visible in a mouth surrounded by scar tissue that obliterated the original lip line. But worst of all was the frightful, liver-colored scar that clove his face diagonally. Half an inch wide in places, it ran from his forehead, down across the place where his nose had been, over cheek and jawline.

"You wanna look like this, huh?"

I couldn't help uttering a low-voiced, embarrassed, "No."

"Well, you better make up your mind then. 'Cause you gonna look like this sure as you standing there if you don't stay out after you once make it out." In his earnestness, Welles gripped my upper arm in one bear-trap hand.

"That's 'cause you tough, Bill. Real tough. Most guys who think they tough—they not tough, they just mean. But you tough, boy. I'm tough and bad both, but I ain't never been just plain mean. And, boy, you gonna go the same way I done if they ever get you in a joint again. 'Cause they know only way anyone ever gonna break you is kill you. You know it, and they know it, too. Now that's good on the outside—it's good when you're bein' good. But in here it's murder—and murder is what I mean.

"Before Warden Duffy, my stretches before this here one, them bulls left me for dead many a time. So fur, I always got up again. But someday when they leave ol' Bob for dead, that's just what he'll be. You, too, boy. Lessin you stay outa joints and quit lookin' up to men like me.

"I'll tell you this—bein' the toughest con in the joint don't make the time no easier. I gets awful . . . lonesome . . . ."

Then he was gone. But that soft, deep voice has come back to me many times since—times when it may have made the difference. I looked down at the book in my hand. I had been reading that Christ said every man had His Divine spark. So for counsel that has lasted me all my life since—and for the Spark that prompted that tough old con to quit "doing his own time" long enough to give it—I offer my belated thanks to Bob Welles. (Sands, 1964:55–56.)

FACILITANTS OF ESCALATION: PLACES

INTEGRATED PLACE ROUND

The complement of places frequented by an Actor can be distinguished in terms of the degree to which information about him flows between and among the Others of these places. The two extremes of this continuum can be labeled integrated and segregated place rounds. Total institutions of deviant-smithy, such as prisons and mental hospitals, were previously said to be especially potent instances of integrated place rounds. They are characterized by the circulation of written information, an emphasis on order and simultaneousness of action and a resultant increase in the range of items that take on a moral significance, i.e., that can be defined as having "symptomatic significance" for the imputed pivotal deviance. Such places, it was earlier suggested, are strongly facilitative of escalation to pivotal deviance. Changing only the *content* of the imputation, it can be suggested that integrated place rounds, particularly of the total institution variety, are also most strongly facilitative of escalation to pivotal normality. The social processes that make deviant-smith total institutions so potent are essentially the same formal processes that make normal-smith total institutions so potent.

INTEGRATED PLACE ROUNDS: THE
CASE OF SYNANON

The Synanon organization is among the more spectacular of normal-smith contrivers of integrated place rounds. Similar to many deviant-smith enterprises, Synanon requires its new and candidate members to live in one of its residential establishments. Volkman and Cressey report:

> the daily program has been deliberately designed to throw members into continuous mutual activity. In addition to the free, unrestricted interaction in small groups called "synanons," the members meet as a group at least twice each day. After breakfast, someone is called upon to read the "Synanon Philosophy," which is a kind of declaration of principles, the day's work schedule is discussed, bits of gossip are publicly shared, the group or individual members are spontaneously praised or scolded by older members. Following a morning of work activities, members meet in the dining room after lunch to discuss some concept or quotation that has been written on a blackboard. Stress is on participation and expression; quotations are selected by Board members to provoke controversy and examination of the meaning, or lack of meaning, of words. Discussion sometimes continues informally during the afternoon work period and in "synanons," which are held after dinner. . . . In addition, lectures and classes, conducted by any member or outside speaker who will take on the responsibility, are held several times a week for all members who feel a need for them. Topics have included "semantics," "group dynamics," "meaning of truth," and "Oedipus complex." There are weekend recreational activities, and holidays, wedding anniversaries and birthdays are celebrated. (Volkman and Cressey, 1963:135.)

"Continuous mutual activity" in mental hospitals creates a high vulnerability to a high rate of imputations of deviance and increases the number of items that can be taken as indicative of such. In the same way the intensive interaction of Synanon and similar groups creates a high vulnerability to a high rate of imputation of pivotal normality and an increase in the number of items so indicative. There are intense mutual monitoring and intense exposure to Others, permitting the possibility for, and the actuality of, all manner of information about Actor becoming known.

Moreover, the special practice in normal-smith groups such as Synanon of demanding honesty and truth in interpersonal dealings requires that imputations be intensively conducted and intensively circulated. In Synanon:

> Each member is urged: "Be yourself," "Speak the truth," "Be honest."

❋   ❋   ❋

> The Synanon sessions differ from everyday honesty by virtue of the fact that in these discussions one is expected to *insist* on the truth as well as to tell the truth. . . . The sessions seem to provide an atmosphere of truth-seeking that is reflected in the rest of the social life within the household so that a simple question like "How are you?" is likely to be answered by a five-minute discourse in which the respondent searches for truth. (Volkman and Cressey, 1963:135, 139.)

Such practices—highly destructive as they are of everyday dramaturgical customs—when conducted in the context of an integrated place round, provoke an added imputational potency.

More generally it might be noted that, in terms of the concerns of policy-oriented citizens, the issue would not seem to be one of being "for" or "against" integrated place rounds—total institutions—per se but, rather, a question of *what* is imputed within such rounds or institutions.

QUASI-INTEGRATED PLACE ROUNDS

While Synanon and some varieties of evangelical religion, such as the Salvation Army, have been able to create territorially homogeneous foundations for integrated place rounds, most normal-smith groups labor under the disadvantage of territorial dispersion. Despite this, some normal-smith groups have managed to create the possibility of at least quasi-integrated place rounds.

Integration in Alcoholics Anonymous. Among such groups, Alcoholics Anonymous is, again, the most prominent. The necessity for AA members to continue in conventional employment crucially undercuts the creation of a fully integrated place round. Nonetheless, it is possible, in some cities, for AA people to absorb themselves almost completely in a highly complex social world—in an "underground" *community* centered on sobriety. In New York and other large cities it is possible to participate in AA places at almost any time of the day or night. A booklet simply listing days and times of New York City meetings runs to many pages. Yet meetings are only the substratum around which all manner of other activities flourish. Cliques of meeting attenders develop; AA *club* membership is possible; holding an office is likely; sponsorship of "babies" is supported; "twelfth-step work" of speaking and responding to calls from alcoholics is fostered. Special meetings and dinners, speakers, anniversaries of sobriety, service at an intergroup office and participation in Al–anon and Alateen groups punctuate time in the AA world and provide meaning and involvement.

Information flow among these places is not, however, nearly so intensive as in an organization like Synanon. High integration seems, rather, to be *voluntarily* achieved by those few who choose to confine themselves to a limited number of regularly frequented places. And for those few who happen also to *work* with AA people, AA approaches the integration of Synanon and perhaps the escalation effects. But for the majority, whether new participants or older members, territorial dispersion and the compromise of conventional employment make the segregated place round the more common situation. For some, the fact of their AA membership may even be a secret at their place of work.[2]

---

[2] However, AA's high public repute has led, in more recent years, to emphasizing that anonymity applies primarily to occasions of being before the public at large, namely, in the mass media.

By contrast, in Synanon the degree to which Actor's place round is integrated is not a matter of personal choice. The Actor allows his places to be fully integrated, or he is out of the organization altogether. The fact that AA candidates can choose for themselves the degree of their place-round integration, and that most choose relative segregation, would seem to attenuate escalation possibilities.

Techniques of Integration in Other Settings. There are, nonetheless, techniques that can be employed to keep up a high level of information flow despite territorial dispersion. One of the more unique and effective of such contrivances was employed by a nonresidential organization for "delinquent" boys in Provo, Utah. Under a regime of "guided group interaction," the subjected youth spent only a minor portion of their day in a house called "Pinehills." Most of their time was spent either in school (while in session), employment (during the summer) or otherwise at large in the community. Although out of audio-visual range of the Pinehills adult authorities and most of their peers for much of their typical days, they were not, in fact, beyond the possibility of information flow about them. Guided group interaction involves "recruiting" the boys themselves to be monitors of each other's activities. Even if a youth did not directly witness the activities of one or another boy in the program, he was likely to hear from nonprogram Others about him. Since the youths met almost daily at the Pinehills house (in guided group interaction sessions), what was witnessed or heard of was likely to become a matter of accusation, recrimination and discussion *among the youthful peers.* The process is called guided group interaction precisely because "authorities" (adult supervisors in this case) mostly remain silent in the sessions and enter only new and then to "guide" the interaction. Discussion is carried on primarily by the delinquent youths themselves who are in the process of *mutually* "reforming" one another. This enterprise had, in plain words, something of a spy system in action. It was, however, a spy system with a difference: persons of one's "own kind" spied on one in the name of one's own good. Moreover, this was a matter of *reciprocal* spying; each boy was fully licensed to "spy" on each other boy, thereby avoiding the consequences that flow from having only one category licensed to spy on another category (e.g., guards can spy on prisoners, but prisoners are not supposed to spy on guards). In contrast to such a situation Pinehills encouraged promiscuous spying (Empey and Rabow, 1961).

It is in the context of integration-segregation of place rounds, too, that one can at least partially understand efforts to field a cadre of "street club workers" who "hang around" with juveniles in their so-called "gangs." The young men who play out the category of street club worker sometimes come centrally to integrate information about a small number of adolescent males and, *partially* because of this position, come to be instrumental in imputing pivotal normality to their charges (Riccio and Slocum, 1962). A similar phenomenon of being an integrating node of information is sometimes also found in priests and political agitators who undertake, with considerable effort, to involve themselves in the lives of deviants (J. D. Harris, 1965; Wilkerson, 1964).

ATTENUATED SITUATIONS

AA and many other normal-smith groups have no prohibition against wide and diffuse contacts among their members. The leaders, through formal declarations and conscious efforts at new organization, indeed, seek to foster a high level of involvement, that is, a high informational integration of place rounds through high levels of physical engrossment. AA members mutually encourage one another to stay in the presence of other AA's for as many hours of the day as possible. At least one normal-smith group has, however, attempted to stride a different, and probably less facilitative, route. This is Recovery, Inc., a mental illness will-training organization, which has, in contrast to an earlier position, sought to limit contact among members. The architect of Recovery, Dr. Abraham Low, theorized that persons can be too involved with members of their "own kind," such that effective coping with normal Others is inhibited. Thus Recovery's current position is that attending a few meetings a week is proper; making phone calls to other members in emergency situations, with a five-minute limit, is proper; reading Recovery documents alone is proper; but high *social* involvement with other members is improper. All this is a marked reversal of Dr. Low's earlier stand and apparently of the character of Recovery. Writing during and about the original arrangement, Low described the following kind of high place-round integration in Recovery groups:

> The members know one another; they meet frequently and regularly in classes and at parties; they get together in family gatherings and consort socially; they form sewing clubs, bowling parties and dancing teams; many of them spend evenings or Sundays together, dining or visiting theaters and |amusement| places. (Low, 1950:15.)

To the degree that such diffuse involvements—integration of place rounds— have actually ceased in Recovery, one must predict that the probability of escalation has decreased.

Indeed, the place segregation undertaken by Recovery begins to approximate the *formal* character of the typical social arrangement of professional social controllers and deviant Actors. While many establishment professionals are deviant-smiths, some do, within the medical model of the "helping professions," attempt normal-smithy. That is, they expose themselves to the Actors they are presumably making normal for one, two, three or so hours a week. They are likely to be doing this in the privacy of their own "offices," sites which are usually quite thoroughly segregated from the rest of Actors' places. On the basis of the conception offered here, such normal-smiths probably have little impact at all upon an Actor who defines himself as pivotally deviant.[3]

NORMAL PLACES

The imputed character of an Actor derives in part from the imputed character of the places he frequents. Similar to the way in which "clothes make the man" or *are* the man, an Actor's places serve to communicate a part of what he "is." Escalation to pivotal normality is facilitated through participation in a complement of places which do *not* give rise to presumptive suspicions about the Actor's normal character.

TYPICAL DEVIANT-SMITHY

It is, of course, well documented that Actors defined as deviants are quite likely to experience difficulty in gaining access to the kinds of places presumptively frequented by normals. Actors defined as mental patients frequently have difficulty obtaining conventional employment (Miller, 1967). Actors defined as ex-convicts (read "criminals") not only experience similar difficulties but are even formally barred in some locations from specified occupational and civic roles. It is reported that the medical and legal professions bar ex-convicts. In some states Actors with records of some types of criminal convictions are denied entrance to such skilled trades as physical therapist, nurse, barber and guide-dog trainer. Within the political realm, for Actors convicted of what are defined as "serious crimes," there occur prohibitions on jury duty, on holding political office and on voting.[4] These and other formal deviant-smith practices, combined with a wide range of informal exclusions, serve to promote participation in places (and with Others) that will accept the suspect Actor, namely, suspect places (and Others).

NORMAL-SMITHY

Normal-smiths, on the other hand, seek to encompass candidate Actor in a round of formally and informally defined normal places. Missionary normal-smiths of the Christian and AA variety seek not only to foster participation in

---

[3] There may, however, be considerable impact upon Actors who define themselves as pivotally normal and as simply having one or another sort of "problem." Evidence for this possibility is summarized in Halmos, 1966; Berelson and Steiner, 1964:287–94. See also Koegler and Brill, 1967.

[4] President's Commission . . . *Corrections*, 1967:32–34, "Employment"; 81–89, "Civil Rights." Of the category of "Hell's Angels" created by the press, Thompson (1967:73) reports: "The publicity also had a bad effect on their employment. At the end of 1964 perhaps two-thirds of the outlaws were working, but a year later the figure was down to about one-third. . . . Motorcycle outlaws . . . [were not] . . . now much in demand on the labor market."

presumptively normal places defined for "their kind"—such as churches and clubhouses—but also to persuade employers to give the candidate Actor "a chance" by providing employment. Members of such groups who happen also to be employers, or employers to whom members have persuasive access, may even find their places of business disproportionately populated with Actors who are being given, or have been given, a chance to "prove themselves." Such contriving of access to formal normal places seems, indeed, a crucial step in the possibility of escalating to normal identity. One study of "parole success" after release from federal prisons thus found that the factor most strongly predictive of *not* returning to prison was the securing of reasonable employment (Glaser, 1964). Studies of those released from mental hospitals similarly find that the gaining of employment is the strongest predictor of not being rehospitalized. (Maisel, 1967. See also Dinitz, *et al.*, 1961.)

Employment is one of the major bases upon which lives are organized in American civilization. Work is a primary pivotal category in terms of which people identify one another and themselves. Type of work (or lack thereof) is very frequently the pivotal category of Other-imputed and self-imputed normality (or lack thereof). Being in a presumptively normal work place, of course, exposes Actor to Others who *may* be making unanimous imputations of him as a pivotally normal worker; but more to the point here, this kind of *place* frequence is itself a salable commodity to yet Others at other times and in other places. The mere mention of the place where Actor works gives rise to presumptions as to his pivotal character, apart, even, from the particular job he performs. So it is perhaps understandable that keypunch operators traffic in saying only that they "work for IBM" and file clerks traffic in reporting only that they "work for General Motors downtown in the Fisher Building." The imputations arising from reporting presumably normal, or even prestigious, places of work serve not only to conduce Others to impute pivotal normality to Actor but also to conduce Actor to impute to himself pivotal normality, perhaps in part out of pride over the prestige (if any) so conferred upon him by his work place. In a like manner, imputations by Others and self of pivotal normality can arise from place of residence; from having a standard family constellation with whom one lives (a spouse and children intact); and from frequenting some voluntary association in a given place, such as a church, recreational or social action group.

Within such presumptively normal places as stores, plants, schools and homes, it is unlikely that expressions of role distance arising from the restrictions and vexations of the moment will be construed as symptomatic of Actor's pivotally deviant character.[5] Because the Actor who is candidate for pivotal normality is engaging in such expressions of distance in the midst of, or along with, normal Others who are doing the same thing, his expressions are more likely to be taken as a feature of "interaction as usual." An Actor who is responded to in terms of acceptable "interaction as usual" is thereby imputed to be a pivotal normal in the situation.

[5] See pp. 163–65 of Chap. 7.

In recent years in America the professionals of the social control establishment have attempted to move toward what is sometimes called the "commu-
nity-oriented rehabilitation" of pivotal deviants. Elements of the federal "war
on poverty" have organized programs of job training, retraining and skill up-
grading which are intended to get deviant Actors into normal places. Interestingly enough, these and other efforts are reported to have a tendency to accept
for "treatment" exactly those Actors who are defined as *least* pivotally deviant.
Having a quite understandable interest in high rates of success (enduring job
placement or other "social adjustment" after the program), such establishment
professionals are partial to recruiting and accepting Actors who are on the margin between pivotal deviance and normality. The character of such timid
normal-smithy is best comprehended when contrasted with the aggressive nor-
may-smithy of an organization such as Employment Enterprises Development
Corporation (EEDCO) of Ann Arbor, Michigan. EEDCO provides private
employment for Actors cast as mental patients, convicts, drop-outs and as general "unemployables." Ironically, it prefers deviant Actors who either have
failed or could not pass the admittance examinations for the Federal Manpower Development and Training Act programs. No admittance tests are
given, since it is reasoned that:

> Tests [scare] away prospective applicants. The people we are trying to
> reach have been failing tests all their lives. Many are afraid to be tested
> because they think they would be weeded out once again. Since we want
> them to know we believe they can be a success from the start, we don't
> give tests. (Rapoport, 1967.)

On the basis of such an initial imputation of a capacity to act as a pivotal
normal in an employment place, EEDCO puts people to work in one of its sub-
sidiaries or with a cooperating employer. Such enterprises include a gas station and janitorial service. The candidate Actors for pivotal normality are
reported to

> usually work with EEDCO for a week to three months before using it as
> an effective job reference for employers who wouldn't normally be inter-
> ested in hiring a former inmate or convict. (Rapoport, 1967.)

This effort to get pivotally deviant types into normal places (and hence normal roles) is founded upon a set of normal-smith beliefs such as the following,
expressed by its "normal" architects:

> Companies are setting employment standards too high and creating seri-
> ous underemployment and civil rights problems. There are a lot of people
> in mental institutions, jails and pool halls who would do a good job if
> employers lowered their standards a bit.
> In many cases we've been able to get people going again by merely re-

vitalizing a lost skill and re-establishing confidence and a desire to work.

The hard-core "unemployables" are often needlessly victimized by a system that finds it easier to put them away than to put them to work. (Rapoport, 1967.)

Unless caught intentionally destroying property or stealing, no EEDCO worker is fired. Failure to show up for work and failures on the job are not construed as indicative of pivotal deviance for which an Actor must be banished. There are, instead, continued imputations of the Actor's capacity to act "properly" in work places. The EEDCO people report that they have been able to place 50 per cent to 60 per cent of their people successfully, while the Manpower Development Training Act (working with more "success-prone" persons) has some 45 per cent to 50 per cent success.

NORMAL PLACES WITHIN DEVIANT PLACES

It should not be surmised that deviant Actors situated in deviant sites are always and necessarily cut off from normal sorts of places. Even within the most discrediting of deviant places, a few Actors are sometimes situated such that normal imputations can be made of them. Within prisons and mental hospitals there have come to be specialized territories (and corresponding roles) wherein those few inmates who can be located in them can have pivotally normal imputations made of them. I refer in particular to the elite office jobs, to the jobs with newspapers and radio stations and other such activities found in some total institutions for deviants. Such territories are a little bit of the normal world imported into a pivotally deviant place. One wonders, for example, if the so-called spectacular "rehabilitation" of Bill Sands at San Quentin was not importantly facilitated by the presence of a radio station with which he became involved. Like other "elite inmates," Sands also lived in special separate quarters apparently reserved for the higher-level office help. Upon assignment to such an office job, he was transferred from the cell blocks to

the Old Spanish Cell Block, a section of the original adobe constructed in the 1870's. I was directed to one of the dormitories, each set up for occupancy by sixteen men. The dormitory at [the] Preston [institution for juvenile delinquents where he was previously incarcerated] had seemed forbidding, but after San Quentin's two-man barred cell, this one looked good. Here three large rooms were connected by low archways. Plumbing had been installed. We could shower every day instead of only twice a week. (Sands, 1964:58–59.)

The imputations arising from this "more normal" place were combined with the trust and advantage communicated by his job. While time dragged when Sands was merely an inmate among the thousands in San Quentin, "Now my days passed swiftly. I worked in an office with a pleasant view from an *un-barred* window" (Sands, 1964:59; italics added).

However facilitative they may be, such territorial slots can absorb only a minuscule proportion of a total institution's population. One would not expect massive recruitment from pivotal deviance on their account.

MULTIPLE FACILITANTS RECALLED

It must be stressed that the availability of normal territories per se, out of the context and existence of *all the other elements*, does not ensure identity change. Thus in the Bill Sands case participation in radio and a special job and quarters were combined with an intense relation with Warden Duffy and his wife and a variety of other special peculiarities that began, even within the context of San Quentin, to approximate the model explicated here.[6] In quite another context, some persons have for thirty years urged that the delinquency problem would be solved if only playgrounds and recreation were provided for slum youths. Such territorial provisions were undertaken only to find that they often became sites for the plotting and commission of delinquent acts. The technical point missed by such reformers, leading some of them to disillusionment, is that identity change must be hinged upon change in Others, hardware and Actor, as well as in places. Focusing upon any one of these classes of variables to the exclusion of any other simply fails to meet the technical requirements of identity change.

Viewed analytically, efforts such as EEDCO (and others) function to place what were defined as pivotally deviant Actors into publicly and formally defined normal places. They promote the possibility of pivotally normal imputations by Others, and hence by Actors themselves, based upon sheer association with a reputable type of place. Such placement may, of course, serve other functions as well, as we have seen already and will see in the next chapter.

[6] See the discussion of Sands on pp. 253–54.

CHAPTER 11

ESCALATION TO NORMAL IDENTITY: HARDWARE AND ACTOR

NORMAL HARDWARE

The more or less movable physical objects affixed to or associated with Actor—his hardware—are a basis upon which he and Others can make imputations of his character. The character or self of a human being is an elusive, ghostly object. While the core is believed hidden within a flesh casing, it is at the same time "radioactive," for it emits "waves" that are thought to affect the objects with which the flesh casing is in contact. Therefore, humans scrutinize these objects as aids in discerning the essential features of one another's flesh-contained characters or selves. Typically, essentiality is read from physical attire, apparel maintenance devices, grooming equipment, feeding and sleeping equipment, place furnishings, occupational and recreational equipment and ideological artifacts. That is, the quality and quantity of these items associated with an Actor are part of the physical foundations of his imputed identity, whether imputed by Others to Actor or by Actor to himself.

WITHDRAWAL AND SUPPLY

To facilitate escalation to a category of pivotal normality, then, these physical foundations should be congruent with, or supportive of, the category of normality. Escalation is facilitated through the reciprocal processes of *withdrawing* hardware associated with the deviant identity and *supplying* hardware associated with the candidate category of normality. For a social deviant, withdrawal of hardware typically occurs under circumstances of apprehension, incarceration and perhaps conviction by agents of the social control establishment. Guns, knives, needles, automobiles, special attire and the like are quickly and forcibly foregone. Less frequently there occurs a metaphorical "apprehension" by agents of a normal-smith organization, and, likewise, efforts are made to separate the deviant and his supportive hardware. AA's attempt to separate an alcoholic from his alcohol; members of Synanon attempt to separate addicts from their drugs and their equipment for using them. Lacking the state-backed power of the social control establishment, however, normal-smiths find such separations much more difficult to accomplish and maintain. Members of Alcoholics Anonymous sometimes place their identity candidates in a jail or hospital precisely to accomplish such separations because of their own (AA's) inability (legally) to do so.

While normal-smiths and deviant-smiths are similar in their attempts to withdraw deviant hardware, they are, by definition, quite different regarding what new hardware will be supplied. Deviant-smiths escalate the deviant identity by supplying the hardware of a more serious, more extreme deviant identity. Actor may be supplied the hardware of an inmate, convict, juvenile delinquent, patient, etc. Normal-smiths, in contrast, seek to supply Actor with hardware that will physically communicate his candidate pivotal normality. They seek to provide a physical basis upon which he and Others can more easily impute to him an identity defined as acceptable.

Indeed, for some normal-smith enterprises such supply may require considerable resources and become a rather central task. Alcoholics and addicts especially are quite often lacking in much of any items of normal hardware. They may have sold or lost or had stolen almost everything denoting normality, and normal-smiths may have to start from scratch. It is reported[1] about one normal-smith center for alcoholics that the staff spent a significant portion of their time begging and buying such basic items as shoes (some alcoholics lose even these), false teeth, glasses, driver's licenses, Social Security cards, hearing aids and the standard array of apparel. Alcoholics with previous training that would facilitate imputations of them as normal office workers or white-collar workers had to be supplied with suits, white dress shirts and ties—items, it turns out, which are considerably more expensive and difficult to obtain on a limited budget than is the hardware of the normal category "worker."

IDEOLOGICAL ARTIFACTS AND NORMAL-SMITHY

The range of ideological artifacts supplied with a normal category are particularly prominent and important. In Alcoholics Anonymous these items include wallet and purse cards printed with identity slogans, which are read and recalled by members during moments of stress, desire, anxiety and fear. Such artifacts are claimed to, and probably do, serve as sources of self-imputation of the new category. In AA there are separate cards for slogans such as the following:

Easy does it.
Live and let live.
First things first.
There but for the Grace of God go I.
God grant me the serenity to accept the things I cannot change, the courage to change the things I can, and the wisdom to know the difference.

Private normal-smith groups other than AA have wallet card slogans such as these:

If the "outside" world only matched our "inside" dreams, then not one of us would ever return to prison.

[1] L. H. Lofland.

Happiness is a direction—not a place.
Think realistically.
Know the truth, and the truth shall make you free. (Sands, 1964:184.)

Identity slogans, of course, derive their coherence from a larger body of ideology about the character of the relevant category of persons. Some aspects of this ideology were discussed previously, and others will be discussed subsequently.[2] Here we need merely observe that such ideology is available and is used as an item of hardware in many normal-smith groups. Boiled down to a set of interrelated slogans or "principles," the perspective becomes part of the operating equipment of Actor. Alcoholics Anonymous has been the much-imitated progenitor of the practice of printing in small type an elaborate set of principles which can be made to fit neatly on one side of a wallet-size card.

THE TWELVE STEPS

STEP ONE: We admitted that we were powerless over alcohol—that our lives had become unmanageable.

STEP TWO: Came to believe that a Power greater than ourselves could restore us to sanity.

STEP THREE: Made a decision to turn our will and our lives over to the care of God as we understand Him.

STEP FOUR: Made a searching and fearless moral inventory of ourselves.

STEP FIVE: Admitted to God, to ourselves and to another human being the exact nature of our wrongs.

STEP SIX: Were entirely ready to have God remove all these defects of character.

STEP SEVEN: Humbly asked Him to remove our shortcomings.

STEP EIGHT: Made a list of persons we had harmed and became willing to make amends to them all.

STEP NINE: Made direct amends to such people whenever possible, except when to do so would injure them or others.

STEP TEN: Continued to take personal inventory and when we were wrong promptly admitted it.

STEP ELEVEN: Sought through prayer and meditation to improve our conscious contact with God as we understood Him, praying only for knowledge of His will for us and the power to carry that out.

STEP TWELVE: Having had a spiritual awakening as a result of these steps, we tried to practice these principles in all our affairs.

Drawn up in 1938 by a cofounder of AA, a variety of other groups designed for other categories of pivotal deviants have since adopted the above, sometimes bodily and without change, sometimes with only a slight modification. Some groups have tinkered more massively with, but still adhered to, the notion of ideological principles available in the form of handy hardware. The following is one of the more revisionist formulations conceived under the guidance of Bill Sands, who became a professional normal-smith for convicts after leaving San Quentin.

[2] Pp. 197–99; pp. 290–92.

1. *Facing* the truth about ourselves and the world around us, we decided we needed to change.
2. *Realizing* that there is a Power from which we can gain strength, we have decided to use that Power.
3. *Evaluating* ourselves by taking an honest self-appraisal, we examined both our strengths and our weaknesses.
4. *Endeavoring* to help ourselves overcome our weaknesses, we enlisted the aid of that Power.
5. *Deciding* that our *freedom* is worth more than our resentments, we are using that Power to help free us from those resentments.
6. *Observing* that daily progress is necessary, we set an attainable goal toward which we could work each day.
7. *Maintaining* our *freedom*, we pledge ourselves to help others as we have been helped. (Sands, 1964:183–84.)

The similarity between these and the AA steps is evident, the change arising importantly from a desire that the first letter of each of these latter steps spell out the word "Freedom." (That is, there is believed to be freedom in pivotal normality.)

While somewhat less convenient than wallet cards, normal-smith groups also promote other bulkier ideological artifacts, including placards, signs ("suitable for framing"), books, magazines and a variety of tracts and leaflets on specialized topics. But even bulkier items are designed so as to facilitate omnipresence. The AA magazine *Grapevine*, for example, is produced in a pocket-size format that can easily be carried about and read during free moments. Sometimes called a "monthly meeting in print," the *Grapevine* is a particularly complex form of handy identity hardware. Its most prominent feature is the personal confession profession. Each issue typically contains a succession of statements by members who serve as the pegs upon which are hung AA ideology in personalized form. Consider the following titles and quotations.

THE HAPPIEST YEAR

. . . I can be ever thankful to AA and its teachings, which have shown me not only how to get sober and how to stay sober but also how to make life worth the living. (*Grapevine*, May, 1960.)

THE SEARCH

We are the lucky ones. In AA we learned that our search [for perfection in all things] was hopeless because we lived within ourselves, in our own little dream world. . . . We came to AA and we found that, though we refused to admit our weakness, our only hope lay in just that—an admission that we alone were helpless and a belief that a power greater than ourselves could make us whole again. (*Grapevine*, May, 1960.)

MY DAUGHTER IS MY SPONSOR

When she drove me through those gates [of the hospital], we faced together the new and wonderful friends [in AA], who accepted me as I now learned to accept them . . . . (*Grapevine*, July, 1959.)

Professing confessions, available as handy hardware, are also and more generally "lessons" or explications of "principles to live by." They promote, in easily available form, instructions in the "correct" definitions of personal experience.

IS PRIDE TABOO?

What is the substitute and the antidote for pride? It is boundless gratitude. If we are grateful for being sober, we shall not be proud of our sobriety. (*Grapevine*, July, 1959.)

THE UNENDING PURSUIT OF HUMILITY

So I am finally and with some difficulty coming to accept the fact that I am not automatically entitled to succeed in everything, or, indeed, in anything. I am, thank God and AA, no longer a superior individual, but simply a sober individual. (*Grapevine*, July, 1959.)

Hardware of pivotal normality, then, provides a physical foundation for the possibility of an escalating personal belief by Actor in the normality of his self. Within a normal-smith group such as Alcoholics Anonymous, ideological artifacts can serve to impute the normal identity even more forcefully.

ACTOR

DISORIENTATION

The degree to which Actor is oriented or disoriented has to do with his subjective sense of the degree to which events of his world are manageable. As discussed, Actors who are least vulnerable to the possibility of disorientation are likely to be so because they possess complex, articulated and self-consciously justified or moralized cognitive systems. A highly complex cognitive system is one in which a wide range of possible occurrences are anticipated. Articulated and self-consciously justified systems are those in which the occurrence of unanticipated events is likely to lead to extrapolation of previously developed principles of coping and management. Actors who have developed a cognitive system with these properties are also likely to be highly cathected to the system so that its short-run failures to code and manage occurrences successfully will not quickly lead to doubt about its viability. It will not easily become meaningless. By contrast, Actors with more simple, unarticulated, unselfconsciously justified or unmoralized cognitive systems to which they are weakly cathected are more vulnerable to the possibility of disorientation.

Low education and youth and old age have been mentioned as major social locations for the relatively high frequency occurrence of weak orientation and vulnerability to disorientation. A range of situational or more or less contemporaneous events observed to induce at least temporary, and sometimes rather spectacular, disorientation have also been discussed (pp. 181–83). It needs now to be said that exactly the same kinds of events that may precipitate disorientation in an Actor such that he is vulnerable to escalation to a deviant identity can also precipitate disorientation which will facilitate his escalation to a normal identity.

DEVIANT IDENTITIES AND DISORIENTATION

Recognizing these already explicated sources of disorientation, some circumstances connected in particular to the dissolution of deviant identity can additionally be explored. Such specially connected circumstances include: (1) the structural character of some deviant roles themselves; (2) incarceration by the social control establishment; and (3) formally organized efforts to disorient social deviants or to intensify their existing disorientation. Relative to these circumstances, it is best to keep in mind that large numbers of social deviants who become involved in them may already be rather weakly oriented. Many deviant identities appear to have attached to them only very simple, unarticulated, and unself-consciously justified or unmoralized cognitive systems. On that account we would expect Actors possessing such identities to be quite vulnerable to disorientation.

Disorienting Deviant Identities. That delicate object called the self requires, for the maintenance of its identity, feedback from Others that supports and validates whatever that identity is thought by an Actor to be. A continuing system of identity imputations is not only empirically common; it is necessary. It is necessary, moreover, that there be relative agreement between Actor and at least *some* Others on the character of the identity of his self. It happens that roles generally, and deviant roles in particular, vary in the degree to which they allow or permit continuing supportive imputational feedback once they have been assumed. What Lemert has called "the systematic check forger" is one such deviant role. The nature of the deviant acts involved in the performance of the role conduces to Actor's increasing isolation from almost all supportive Others. To write bad checks for a living is, by necessity, to be geographically mobile, to be forever "getting out of town." Names must constantly be changed to avoid detection, and Others who might come to know who one "really is" must be avoided. Even when "laying off" (not writing bad checks), systematic check forgers tend not to assume their "true identities" but, rather, pose as the occupant of some other occupation under some other name. The world thus becomes a kaleidoscope of briefly known Others who impute to Actor a variety of normal identities, none of which is enduring and none of which is "really" him; that is, none of which is composed of the terms in which he sees himself. As a consequence, these Actors live in a world where there are few or no persons who validate who they "really are." They come to live almost entirely in a world of "pretend identities." Lacking in supporting Others to validate their identities, their fears and anxieties rise. And, given the same lack of supportive Others, there is no one to help them cope with those fears and anxieties. Finally, as Lemert puts it:

> The self becomes amorphous and without boundaries; the identity sub-structure is lost. Apathy replaces motivation, and in phenomenological terms, "life" or "this way of life" is no longer worth living. This is the common prelude to the forger's arrest. (Lemert, 1967a:31.)

One check forger phrased the situation in this way:

> I could not rid myself of the crying need for the sense of security which social recognition and contact with one's fellows, and their approval fur-nishes. I was lonely and frightened and wanted to be where there was someone who knew me as I had been before. (Quoted in Lemert, 1967a:126.)

The social or unsocial character of a role such as that of the systematic check forger is to be contrasted with criminal or deviant roles built around more intimate and enduring relations. Of the check forger in contrast to, say, the confidence man, Lemert comments:

> . . . The latter retains a locus of the self by means of intimate interaction with other con men. Identity is further maintained by interaction with lesser criminals, and paradoxically, through accommodative relationships with police. Gambling, drinking and sexual display for the con man tend to take place in the context of primary groups. As such they appear to be more efficient means for relaxing tensions and are less likely than with the forger to generate . . . [further] anxieties. In some cases con men have been able to integrate their criminal forays with a relatively stable family life. (Lemert, 1967a:129.)

The role-entailed seclusiveness, geographical mobility and pseudonymity leading to the intolerable anxiety and disorientation described by Lemert ap-parently conduce to the short career of systematic check forgers. While some are caught through no overt mistake of their own, many, at the point of dis-orientation, turn themselves in or stop taking the precautionary measures necessary to avoid apprehension. These last forgers remain

> where they are, knowing full well that police or detectives will soon catch up with them [and are found] in a resigned mood awaiting their arrival. Still other forgers, like fabled animals wending back to their mythical graveyard to die, return to their home community, there either to court arrest or to arrange for the inevitable in familiar surroundings. In more complex cases an otherwise accomplished check man makes a mistake,

knowing at the time that it is a mistake which will probably land him in jail or prison. (Lemert, 1967a:125.)

The disorientation that appears to be a frequent product of this deviant role itself means, from the point of view of escalating to pivotal normality, that, immediately at the time of apprehension, many such Actors are highly vulnerable to a new identity. The identity they typically have imputed to them, and typically assume, however, appears to be a deviant one.

> His apathy or carelessness and subsequent arrest function to end his anxiety. . . . [Arrest] . . . solve[s] his identity problem; arrest immediately assigns the forger an identity, undesirable though it may be, as a jail or prison inmate. In effect, he receives or chooses a *negative identity*, . . . which despite its invidious qualities, is nearest and most real to him. At this juncture he is much like the actor who prefers bad publicity to none at all, or the youth who is willing to be a scapegoat for the group rather than not be part of the group at all. (Lemert, 1967a:132.)

A second role may be mentioned as inherently productive of disorientation: that of the problem drinker. Unlike the systematic check forger, however, the problem drinker is not isolated for long periods in the sense of having few or no people making identity imputations to him. Indeed, he often appears to experience imputations as a problem drinker over rather long periods of time and from many sources. The character of his deviance (intoxication with inappropriate frequency at inappropriate times and places) ensures, in contrast to the systematic check forger, that it will be known to Others who will begin making imputations in those terms. Spouses can impute in terms of rebukes and threats of divorce; police can impute in terms of arrests and jailings; priests and ministers can impute in terms of admonishments; employers can impute through lay-offs and firings; doctors and hospitals can impute in terms of "rehabilitative" incarcerations; relatives and friends can impute both by shaming and abetting.

The problem drinker is also likely to be subject to vacillating cycles of attempts by Others to help, followed by their disenchantment and rejection. Both help and rejection impute to him the identity of "problem drinker" or alcoholic. He may "run through" a long series of relationships with Others, each of whom, because the object of their assistance continues to become inappropriately intoxicated, plays out the full cycle. Such a pattern of aid and rejection is conduced by the effect of alcohol itself on the human body. A human can remain continuously intoxicated for only a limited period of time. Imbibing alcohol to the exclusion of other liquids and solid foods (the typical pattern during a "bender") eventually undermines physical capability. While in some cases a bender may last several months, hallucinations and delirium tremens eventually will set in. Unconsciousness or other physical immobilization will occur. Such incapacitation is typically followed by some kind of "drying out" and at least a temporary period of sobriety. With sobriety, some of Actor's Others may want to aid him not to drink in such a manner again. Yet other Others may already have rejected him for having betrayed them by the last bender.

At the point of just coming off a bender and *beginning* to get sober, some problem drinkers, under certain circumstances, are highly *disoriented*. They feel remorseful and full of shame and guilt. They feel that they have reached "the end of the line." Such feelings sometimes occur in the context of there being, *this* time, no one who will any longer provide possibilities for future action and meaning by giving aid or by bothering to rebuke. Instead of threatening or pleading, the spouse may leave and file for divorce. Instead of threatening, the employer may terminate employment. Or, such feelings may occur in the context of "coming to" for the first time in the drunk tank of a jail, with no one to bail him out, or on the "flight deck" (ward) of a mental hospital. At these times Actors are amenable to escalation to pivotal normality (or, for "unidentified" problem drinkers, to pivotal deviance). The fact that AA members in some localities make regular rounds promoting AA to the just-sobered-up inmates of drunk tanks and mental hospitals suggests their intuitive appreciation of the key point at which to introduce a new identity.

The period of disorientation appears, however, to be rather brief. Most typically, Actors quickly reorient themselves to drinking again, and normal-smiths who would escalate them must wait for the next point of sober disorientation. As a result, for AA members, for example, 12th-Step work is often a game of catching the alcoholic at a point of disorientation sufficient for AA to begin to "make sense" to him. Since disorientation is a variable state—sometimes mild, sometimes profound—AA's find that the alcoholic they could not "convert" at one point may, at a later time, be highly amenable and may subsequently become a turned-on "sober alcoholic" and AA member. In AA this period of disorientation is labeled "bottom," and the Actor experiencing it is said to "have reached bottom." It is believed, probably correctly, that an Actor's first experience of "bottom" is unlikely to make him amenable to the AA identity. Two or more such experiences, each more strongly disorienting than the former, are felt to be required to bring the alcoholic to the point of requisite "vulnerability."

In this context we need to recall again that what will be experienced as disorienting is largely a function of the scheme of categories Actor uses in coding experience. Just when "bottom" will be reached is, in part, a function of what has been experienced in what kind of cognitive scheme. For the white-collar, upper-middle-class male who views himself as a problem drinker but who has had no contact with agencies of law enforcement, the trauma, discontinuity and strangeness of waking up for the first time with the "bums" in the local drunk tank may be sufficient to induce profound disorientation. A lower-class male with long and extensive experience with agencies of law enforcement may find his first time in the same drunk tank merely a slight and insignificant variation on a familiar theme and code the experience as "more of the same," suffering, thereby, little disorientation.

Disorienting Social Control Practices. Possessing a near monopoly on the use of coercive sanctions, i.e., physical force, the social control establishment is in a highly advantageous position to induce disorientation in social deviants. It has the right to apprehend and force deviant Actors to leave their complement of imputors and place rounds. It has the right to force Actors into new ways of life.

The act of yanking people from their accustomed rounds is often (depending upon the degree of categorical discontinuity involved) sufficient to induce disorientation. However, it appears empirically the case that very often such disorientation is utilized by the social control establishment (inadvertently to be sure) to escalate Actors to pivotally deviant identities or to reinforce and support a previously assumed deviant identity. It is important to keep in mind, nonetheless, that disorientation induced in an institution of deviant-smithy does not inevitably lead to a pivotally deviant identification of self (or to reinforcement of a prior identification) and that, most important here, disorientation is not per se an experience that is "bad." Even, or perhaps most especially, experiences of disorientation arising from solitary confinement in prisons are rather famous for their role in identity change—to either pivotal normality or deviance. For Bill Sands the disorientation induced by solitary confinement turned out to be instrumental in his escalation to normality. Sands described it in this way:

So this was The Shelf, as it was known to the cons. A cell, about four-and-a-half feet wide by ten feet long and seven high, contained a steel bunk, without a mattress or other bedding, and a toilet, lidless and seatless. That was all.

Except me.

I lay on my back on the slab, thinking little, feeling nothing. . . . After awhile I slept. After awhile I awoke. All was the same. Silence—thick, heavy, dull. There should be some mechanical sound from somewhere, I thought, some distant hum from the elevator. Something should drift up from the prison that was pulsing far below. But there was nothing. I clicked my fingernails against the concrete wall to be sure I had not lost my hearing. They clicked. I coughed. So much for that.

There was no way of keeping track of time with no clock in view. The light bulbs burned perpetually, and there was little daylight. But finally I heard the steel door at the end of the row being unlocked. It swung open silently. I could see nothing and could hear only the vaguest pad-pad of slippered feet on the paved floor. They stopped. There was a slight grating noise. A trusty wearing felt slippers stopped in front of my cell. He shoved a tin bowl and two pieces of thick bread along the floor through a four-or-five-inch space between the bottom of the cell door and the floor. Then he padded off.

Bread and water. I could live on that, but I wasn't interested in nourishment or living. I expected momentarily to be informed that I had killed that [guard he had attacked] and to be hauled off to some local jurisdiction for trial. Maybe I'd be lucky enough to get the gas chamber, although, curiously, many prison killings seemed to net the perpetrators only more time. In the latter case, however, I could not beat the long monotonous years that stretched ahead. If I were given the gas chamber, at least I would have a definite date when my time ended.

Eventually, I slept. After an interminable time, I received more bread and water, although the first was untouched. I figured it must have been twenty-four hours between meals—figured it by the tiny, muted sounds of the screws changing shifts, three eight-hour watches a day. I had no way of being positive, of course, of changes that occurred when I was asleep, but the subtle changes in the remote daylight gave me slight clues of passing time.

For awhile I wished I could shave; the crawling stubble on my jaws annoyed me. I would have liked to bathe my face in cold water. There was the toilet, but I wasn't tempted. I knew it wasn't shaving or facewashing I wanted—I would gladly have foregone both for the rest of my life just to hear the sound of a human voice. I lay there thinking, listening by the hour. Thinking of what? Listening for what?

I was filled with revulsion and self-loathing to discover that the worst punishment that could be meted out to me was to be confined exclusively with myself. God, what lousy company I made.

Why don't we die when there is no reason to live?

I remembered thinking the same thing the night I learned of my parents' pending divorce. Eight years ago. Was it only eight? Too bad I hadn't died then. I would have saved everyone, including myself, a lot of grief.

Was there any use in anything? Trying again? For what? I knew I still had spirit left . . . they hadn't been able to break me. But what good was it? Even if I wanted to try, I wouldn't know where to begin. No one would believe it, no one believed in me. I wished my dad were still . . . [alive] . . . . If only I could talk to him for just a few minutes, maybe we could figure out what was wrong. Maybe I could start again. How I'd love to hear his voice . . . any voice . . . . (Sands, 1964:46–47.)

While solitary confinement per se as a concrete social arrangement cannot be said to facilitate disorientation and hence the possibility of escalation to pivotal normality, the *analytic meaning* of measures such as solitary confinement (combined with other measures) would appear to do so.

Disorienting Normal-Smith Practices. In recent years some normal-smith innovators within the social control establishment have come explicitly to recognize the technical necessity of disorientation as an element of identity change and have set out intentionally to provoke it. The previously mentioned Provo, Utah, experiment in guided group interaction has been among the more articulate and forthright of these efforts. The "clientele" of the experimenters were male youths defined as pivotally delinquent, aged 15–17, who, by the time they reached the Pinehills establishment, had been:

cajoled, threatened, lectured and exhorted—all by a variety of people in a variety of settings: by parents, teachers, police, religious leaders and court officials. As a consequence, most have developed a set of manipulative techniques which enabled them to "neutralize" verbal admonitions by appearing to comply with them, yet refraining all the while from any real adherence. (Empey and Rabow, 1961:689–90.)

Exposure to such treatment had provided these Actors with what was in some sense a "successful" repertoire of coping strategies, partly on the basis of which they predicated their delinquency. Empey and Rabow therefore reasoned that "before they can be made amenable to change, they must be made anxious about the ultimate utility of . . ." participating in delinquency (Empey and Rabow, 1961:688).

The Pinehills organization was designed to provoke anxiety and disorientation in the delinquent Actor from the first moment he set foot therein. Upon his arrival,

Instead of meeting with and receiving an orientation lecture from authorities, he receives no formal instructions. He is always full of such questions as, "What do I have to do to get out of this place?" or "How long do I have to stay?", but such questions are never answered [by the adult authorities]. They are turned aside with, "I don't know," or "Why don't you find out?" Adults do not orient him in the ways that he has grown to expect, nor will they answer any of his questions. He is forced to turn to his peers.

      ❖   ❖   ❖

As he begins to associate with other boys he discovers that important informal norms do exist, the most important of which makes inconsistency rather than consistency the rule. That which is appropriate for one situation, boy or group may not be appropriate for another. Each merits a decision as it arises. (Empey and Rabow, 1961:686.)

Although the authorities would not provide detailed formal rules or engage in one-to-one "counseling," they did define Pinehills as "not a place to do time." They made it clear that each boy must become "involved" in the guided group interaction sessions, the groups themselves having considerable power to sanction.

From within the present perspective, the Pinehills effort may be seen as involving a set of forced events that fell outside or between the categories of reality coding and coping strategies developed by the youths. Pinehills was, in plain words, "like nothing they have ever seen before." But it was more than that. It was not simply a new, clearly defined system, such as would be encountered upon entering another culture, but an intentionally ambiguous and capricious system. As such, it was an assault upon personal identity, making that identity "unworkable" or unmanageable.

However, the Provo enterprise was mild relative to the measures sometimes used by other innovators in the game of identity change. More recent work under the rubric of "behavior therapy," especially with autistic children, has involved intense slapping, yelling and even the utilization of rooms laid with metal strips for administering electric shock on bare feet (Lovaas, 1968). Physical assaults of this kind upon barely or newly symbolic human animals seem, moreover, to bring about a good deal of change (when combined with other elements).[3]

Before Dr. Timothy Leary was required to leave Harvard University, he, too, was engaged in an intentional effort to precipitate disorientation among pivotally deviant Actors in order to make them more amenable to escalation to pivotal normality. Working with inmates of a maximum-security prison, he and his associates introduced to their "subjects" some notions about society being a "game" and about each individual's being a player of "games." Leary imputed to his inmates their capacity to stop playing "cops and robbers" or whatever and to take up a different scheme. According to Leary, one could change by "getting beyond the game structure" (Leary, 1962:58). One could change by first transcending all games and then self-consciously choosing what social game to play. That is, disorientation facilitates identity change. And, as Leary saw, there are many ways in which disorientation could be precipitated, or, as he put it, "many methods for expanding consciousness beyond the game limits."

> Have a psychotic episode. (This is to say, stop playing the social game for awhile and they'll call you insane, but you may learn the great lesson.) Or expose yourself to some great trauma that shatters the gamesmanship out of you. Birth by ordeal is a well-documented phenomenon. The concentration camp experience has done this for some of our wisest men. Physical trauma can do it. Electric shock. Extreme fatigue. Live in another and very different culture for a year where your roles and rituals and language just don't mean a thing. Or separate yourself from the game-pressure by institutional withdrawal. Live for awhile in a monastic

[3] Despite the proclivity of "behavior therapy" for a learning-theory terminology, it might be enlightening, indeed, to conceive the social organizations constructed in the name of that cause as a form of normal-smithy and thereby as a game of identity transformation. Important steps in the direction of a sociologically founded version of behaviorism and behavior therapy have been taken by Halmos, 1966:67–73; and by Burgess and Akers, 1966; Akers, Burgess and Johnson, 1968. Among works by behavioral therapists, see: Grossberg, 1964; Ullmann and Krasner, 1965; Wolpe, Salter and Reyna, 1964.

cell. Or marry a Russian. Sensory deprivation does it. Sensory deprivation cuts through the game. (Leary, 1962:58.)

As previously mentioned, Leary advocated the use of certain drugs as "the
most efficient way to cut through the game structure of Western life" (Leary,
1962:59).

> The nongame visionary experiences are, I submit, the key to behavior
> change. Drug-induced *satori*. In three hours under the right circum-
> stances the cortex can be cleared: the games that frustrate and torment
> can be seen in the cosmic dimension. (Leary, 1962:61.)

He and his associates administered psilocybin to volunteer inmates.

> The psilocybin session was followed by three discussions. Then another
> drug session. Then more discussions. At this point the inmates have
> taken the drug an average of four times. There has not been one moment
> of friction or tension in some forty hours of egoless interaction. Pre-post
> testing has demonstrated marked changes on both objective and projec-
> tive instruments. Dramatic decreases in hostility, cynicism, depression,
> schizoid ideation. Definite increases in optimism, planfullness, flexibility,
> tolerance, sociability. (Leary, 1962:65.)

Unfortunately, perhaps, Dr. Leary did not long continue this line of endeavor
because of certain pivotally deviant imputations made to him. Before he became a different "kind of person," however, he may have been on the track of
at least one way in which disorientation can be induced and utilized without
the enormous trauma and physical and/or psychic pain that so typically accompanies it. Determination of whether or not this is empirically the case will now
presumably have to wait for a change in the legal stance toward extensive
experimental work of this kind.[4]
  Operating outside the social control establishment, organizations like AA
and Synanon must "take what they can get" in terms of disorientation. As we
have seen, AA relies upon the difficulties generated by prolonged and intense
drinking itself to produce the requisite personal disorientation, and, upon re-
ceipt of an alcoholic, they immediately attempt orientation to a new scheme of
life. Perhaps because of their residential operation, with its potentially exploitable offering of bed and board, Synanon members are somewhat more
cautious and undertake "tests" to assure themselves that an addict who appears

---

[4] See, however, Ditman, 1968; Kurland, Shaffer and Unger, 1966; Abramson, ed., 1966.
It can be noted also that one should not be surprised when experiences with such drugs as
LSD (as disorienting and reorienting experiences) do not in and of themselves produce
"rehabilitation" of social deviants. Drug experiences should be expected to effect fundamental transformations of identity only in circumstances where all the facilitants explicated
are present in reasonable strengths. An experiment in which the LSD experience was employed in the seeming absence of other facilitants is described in Ludwig, *et al.*, 1968.

at their door is indeed as disoriented as he may claim.   They undertake, in fact, to disorient him even more as a means of ensuring his vulnerability and good faith.   A Synanon member reports the following kind of interaction in "admissions interviews":

> When a new guy comes in we want to find out whether a person has one inkling of seriousness.   Everybody who comes here is what we call a psychopathic liar.   We don't take them all, either.   We work off the top spontaneously, in terms of feeling.
>
>   We ask him things like "What do you want from us?" "Don't you think you're an idiot or insane?" "Doesn't it sound insane for you to be running around the alleys stealing money from others so's you can go and stick something up your arm?"
>
>   Mostly, if people don't have a family outside, with no business to take care of, they're ready to stay.   They ain't going to have much time to think about themselves otherwise. . . .   Not when he's got problems, when he's got things outside, if he's got mickey mouse objections, like when you ask him "How do you feel about staying here for a year?" and he's got to bargain with you, like he needs to stay with his wife or his sick mother—then we tell him to get lost.   If he can't listen to a few harsh words thrown at him, he's not ready.   Sometimes we yell at him "You're a goddamned liar!"   If he's serious he'll take it.   He'll do anything if he's serious.   (Quoted in Volkman and Cressey, 1963:132.)

Generalizing about the admissions encounter, Volkman and Cressey report:

> It forces the newcomer to admit, at least on a verbal level, that he is willing to try to conform to the norms of the group, whose members will not tolerate any liking for drugs or drug addicts.   From the minute he enters the door, his expressed desire to join the group is tested by giving him difficult orders—to have his hair cut off, to give up all his money, to sever all family ties, to come back in ten days or even thirty days.   (Volkman and Cressey, 1963:132.)

This procedure serves to

> weed out men and women who simply want to lie down for a few days to rest, to obtain free room and board or to stay out of the hands of the police.

                    ✿   ✿   ✿

> [In order to be admitted] he must be willing to give up all ambitions, desires and social interactions that might prevent the group from assimilating him completely.   (Volkman and Cressey, 1963:132.)

Having, by such means, assured themselves of the addict's disorientation and lack of outside orienting commitments, there follow (aside from positive orientation to Synanon) further efforts to intensify disorientation. Among these is a

> strong taboo against what is called "street talk." Discussion of how it feels to take a fix, who one's connection was and where one took his shot, the crimes that one has committed or who one associated with is severely censured. (Volkman and Cressey, 1963:133.)

Personal identity is founded fundamentally upon a body of linguistic terms, upon categories that discriminate, distinguish and categorize experience. In Synanon, apparently, the linguistic foundations of the addict identity are withdrawn, serving forcefully and further to disorient an Actor who has employed that identity. Any and all indications or possibility that the Actor might "revert" to his addict self are met with swift and strong sanctions intended to disorient any action taken in terms of an addict identity. What is called the "haircut" session (sometimes meant literally, sometimes figuratively) is a prime medium of such sanctioning. A Synanon member who made a date with and met a former girl friend who was still on drugs could be subjected to the following:

> I called the house the next morning and came back. I got called in for a haircut. I sat down with three Board members in the office. They stopped everything to give the haircut. That impressed me. Both Y and Z, they pointed out my absurd and ridiculous behavior by saying things like this—though I did not get loaded, I associated with a broad I was emotionally involved with and who was using junk. I jeopardized my *own* existence by doing this. So they told me, "Well, you fool, you might as well have shot dope by associating with a using addict." I was given an ultimatum. If I called her again or got in touch with her I would be thrown out.
>
>   ❖   ❖   ❖
>
> To top that off, I had to call a general meeting and I told everybody in the building what a jerk I was and I was sorry for acting like a little punk. I just sort of tore myself down. Told everybody what a phony I had been. And then the ridiculing questions began. Everybody started in. Like, "Where do you get off doing that to us?" That kind of stuff. (Volkman and Cressey, 1963:134–35.)

In addition to formal "haircuts," there are, as well, "spontaneous denunciations and . . . denunciations in general meetings" (Volkman and Cressey, 1963:134). "Any weapon, such as ridicule, cross-examination or hostile attack, is both permissible and expected" (Volkman and Cressey, 1963:139).

> After the synanon sessions, the house is always noisy and lively. [Sometimes] members sulk, cry, shout and threaten to leave the group as a result of conversation in the synanon. (Volkman and Cressey, 1963:141.)

Summing up the foregoing, it has been suggested that a state of disorientation is facilitative of escalation. Expanding upon the social locations and situational sources of weak orientation and disorientation identified in Part II,
some features of deviant roles, practices in the social control establishment and
efforts of normal-smith organizations have been reported as further sources of
disorientation. Disorientation itself serves to bring into doubt the morality
and utility of being a pivotal deviant. More than simply confusing Actor—
although it can do that—disorientation precipitates a questioning of the deviant
role itself as a valid or reasonable way in which to conceive oneself and organize one's life. It promotes disaffection with deviance.

All this is perhaps most meaningful when seen in contrast to a primary pattern of effort within the social control establishment. I refer to the practice of
sending troublesome Actors to some kind of counselor or parole officer for one
or a few hours a week. Despite the fact that many of these Actors conceive of
themselves as pivotally deviant, they are required to spend only minutes in the
presence of a benign "people changer." It is not surprising that they return to
"real life" massively untouched. While this arrangement may bring about solutions to particular problems in troubled people, it does not appear to fulfill the
technical requirements for identity transformation of pivotally deviant Actors.
This arrangement seems, in particular, to have little power to provoke disorientation. (See Meyer and Borgotta, 1965.)

A CAUTION

It needs to be stressed again that disorientation per se is not necessarily
facilitative of escalation to pivotal normality (or deviance). Disorientation (and
all the other elements) assumes a facilitative significance only in the context of,
and in combination with, the elements explicated previously and those that
remain to be explicated. Disorientation, occurring completely apart from other
elements, may lead merely to Actor's complete "autistic" withdrawal.[5] The
more spectacular of such instances have involved sailors shipwrecked and cast
alone on an island. It is reported that many of them appear, quite literally, to
lie down and die. Even where natural vegetation could have provided the
materials of easy survival, the absolute absence of Others to impute and support an identity of any kind conduced to a diffusion and disintegration of self.
Such isolates have no categorical and linguistic construct upon which to predicate action and organize activity. Natural experiments of this sort and a variety of laboratory experiments on "sensory deprivation"[6] point strongly to the
truth of the proposition that, in order to be social persons at all, human beings
need stable social points of orientation. In the absence thereof, they tend to

[5] Because this or some similar outcome is sometimes the product of solitary confinement
or other punishment, some reformers have been led to argue that social deviants should not
be subjected to serious pressures. (Sutherland and Cressey, 1966:670–71.)

[6] E.g., Solomon, et al., eds., 1961. See also the references of note 5, Chap. 8.

fall apart. The crucial question, then, is: once disorientation is provoked, how is it managed most effectively to facilitate escalation to pivotal normality? A part of the answer is contained in the foregoing analysis of who is present making what kind of imputations within what kind of place round in the midst of what kind of hardware. We now turn to other parts of an answer.

AFFECTIVE BONDS

Assuming the existence of the most facilitative conditions already enumerated, what kind of regard for Others on the part of deviant Actor further facilitates escalation? Recalling the suggested connection between truth and emotional attachment, it can be said that Actor is most "vulnerable" to accepting as true the imputations which emanate from those Others for whom he has a strong and positive affective regard. What is true would appear be a highly social affair.

> The formation of a new perspective and the concomitant transformation of behavior patterns—in conversions, in social mobility, in deviant behavior and in the quest for independence among adolescents—are facilitated when there are conjunctive sentiments toward those who represent the new standpoint.[7]

If such is the case, there is then the question: upon what factors, in turn, do the development and maintenance of positive affective bonds depend? Phrased differently, what kind of actions on the part of Others are most conducive to Actor's developing positive emotive attachments to these Others? Operationally, this is the task of, in a sense, "conning" Actor into believing that he has high regard for a set of Others who are making imputations of pivotal normality to him.

Especially under circumstances of disorientation, Actor may come to worry or to be suspicious that no one cares about him and that no one is concerned for his welfare. Such a worry or suspicion may be factually correct; but whether it is or not is less important than his belief that he has been cast out, that he is without Others who, to put it plainly, give a tinker's damn about him. It is at this point that Actor is most vulnerable to any reality promoted by Others whom he believes sincerely care for him. That famous savior of mankind William Booth, founder of the Salvation Army, had an acute, if quaint, appreciation of this point. As reported by William James, Booth believed, "The first vital step in saving outcasts consists in making them feel that some decent human being cares enough for them to take an interest in whether they are to rise or sink."[8] Thus the question becomes: what actions on the part of Others are

[7] Shibutani, 1961:590 and his discussion on pp. 588–92; see further, J. Davis, 1963.
[8] James, 1958:167, note 8, copyright, 1902.

most conducive to Actor's believing that they care and that they are therefore objects to be positively cathected?

FACILITANTS OF AFFECTIVE BONDS

Working within the assumptions about interpersonal relations and deserved affect that prevail in American civilization, it is possible to point to at least five practices that seem highly facilitative of "conning" Actor in this manner. These involve the generic dimensions of (1) exposure, (2) practical aid, (3) actual or potential peership, (4) understanding and (5) warmth. The maximization of values of each of these dimensions toward Actor by Others would seem to maximize the likelihood that he will be convinced that they care and are therefore deserving of positive affective regard. Given the development of affective bonds, Actor is more likely to accept as true the view of the world that is sponsored by whatever Others are the objects of this regard. The most facilitative values of each of these five dimensions derive their potency from *cumulative and concomitant* presence. The existence of any one alone is only minimally facilitative. Each strongest value of each dimension that is additionally brought to bear increases the likelihood that Actor will respond with strong emotional cathexis toward the Others.

Before explicating and illustrating each of these five dimensions, it is necessary to insert a disclaimer of sorts. I here stride ground that has been marched across countless times by moralists, religionists and social workers, among many others. Occupants of these social categories have not untypically paraded under the banner of moral right and Christian ethics and in the name of "love thy neighbor" and "the golden rule." Stripped of all refinement, what follows amounts to a similar kind of slogan. But there is a crucial difference between those who enunciate such slogans as morally proper and ethically superior and what is said here. The assertions below rest upon a claim of empirical truth and technical adequacy relative to the process of transforming identity in human beings. Therefore, even though it is necessary to line up, in one respect, with the dewy-eyed and the sentimental, this collusion takes place on technical and not moral grounds.

Exposure. Exposure refers to (1) the amount of time per day, week, month or other unit that Actor and Others are in one another's presence; and (2) the number of settings in which Actor and Other conjointly participate. In a polar condition of low exposure, Actor and Other (1) meet one or fewer hours per week or month, and (2) always come together in the same setting, whether it be an office, a hallway, park, home, bus, etc. In a polar condition of high exposure, Actor and Other (1) are in one another's presence many hours—possibly twenty-four—per day, and (2) completely share all the settings in which each of them participates. In total conjointness, they might work, eat, sleep and participate in recreation together.

A reasonably high degree of exposure appears to be a strongly facilitative, if not a necessary, condition of Actor's projecting affective bonds toward Others. One of the meanings of high exposure is exactly the *sharing* it entails. Even if the participants are divided into superordinates and subordinates, high exposure generates a sense of *common fate* or *common lot*. And even where there is concern merely that all the participants in this sharing physically survive their days and weeks, care must be taken and regard manifested for the welfare of each. More often there is a much broader mutual concern involved in Actor's and Others' sharing. To sloganize the point, "to share is of necessity to care" in many kinds of ways.

It was noted, in connection with unanimity of imputations, that residential arrangements around Actor in total institutions or integrated place rounds serve to promote high exposure. Synanon is perhaps a prime example of the high-exposure situation because of the literal sharing of work, eating, sleeping and recreation that is therein contrived. The Synanon situation should again be contrasted with a prominent practice within the social control establishment. The latter's pattern of dyadal "people change" is based upon a condition of low exposure precisely to inhibit entanglements and any sense of shared fate. Of social workers, Wilensky and Lebeaux relate:

> The worker typically does not "make friends" with the client. He does not reveal his personal life, entertain the client socially in his home or visit with the client on a social basis. As far as possible, the social worker insists that service be given in the office rather than in the home, because the latter threatens a more extensive personal involvement than is good for professional relationship. The client is kept to a strict appointment schedule, symbolizing formality of relationship and measuring restriction of contract. (Wilensky and Lebeaux, 1958:299–300.)

Or, as Yablonsky has written:

> . . . In professional group therapy, the group members usually come from various walks of life, convene for a session and then return to their private worlds. This kind of treatment can become a therapeutic game, not closely related to basic life situations, since the group's members do not live in similar environments. (Yablonsky, 1965:152.)

Aside from considerations of professional propriety, there are of course organizational reasons for this kind and degree of exposure. Not untypically, members of the social control establishment have such large "case loads" that they "must" choose to see many people briefly rather than a few people extensively. For this reason alone, exposure is limited, and, therefore, so is the range of possible ways that Actor and Other can come to feel about one another—the range of possible emotions that can possibly be evoked.

The escalation to pivotal normality of someone like Bill Sands is of particular interest here, suggesting again the peculiar and wide range of circumstances under which relatively high exposure (and other elements promoting affect) to pivotal normals can be effected. Upon inventing and having accepted the notion of a prison-wide weekly radio "Interview Time with Warden Duffy," Sands became the interviewer who had to plan the show with Duffy himself. After a time the show originated from Duffy's home on the San Quentin grounds, and Sands began frequenting this place to plan and conduct the interview.

> It took a while to break down my reserve, not because of distrust, but because I was in the habit of being a con's con, solid, forceful, grim, doing my own time. Warden Duffy understood. The Duffys met me about halfway, not wanting to hurry either me or themselves. But gradually our conversations branched out beyond the radio program. We had many stimulating discussions on philosophy, religion, analyzing the forces that drive people to violence, wrongdoing and drink. . . . We searched for qualities men must have in order to be good. I was anxious to hear everything the Duffys thought about these matters. Not only was it an opportunity for me to discuss the anatomy of faith with people who already had demonstrated so conclusively that they truly possessed it—but it was a matter of the survival of my own mind.
>
> [For their sessions] Mrs. Duffy . . . brought in the coffee service . . . and we settled in our . . . places—the Warden in his big leather chair, Mrs. Duffy on the couch by the low table and myself in a comfortable chair across from the Warden.
>
> *   *   *
>
> To these warm, honest people, who really cared, not only about me, but about everyone inside and outside the prison, I could at last relieve my mind and unload my heart.
>
> *   *   *
>
> During perhaps five hours of the 168 hours in the week, I felt more like part of a family, this good family, than I did like a convict. The pendulum within me swung wider, as I had to return from the warmth and gentility of the Duffy home to the world of violence, with its gray pasts and its grayer futures.[9]

Practical Aid. While relatively high exposure provides the ecological possibility of Actor's projecting affective bonds toward Others, additional elements are needed in order most strongly to facilitate this possibility. Like exposure, practical aid can be distinguished in terms of degrees or amount. A large amount of practical aid involves such practices as the cueing in to the "ropes" of a new place; the loan of objects or money when needed; the offering of advice on how to manage some impending event; the provision of support in Ac-

---

[9] Sands, 1964:70. The five hours refers only to being directly in the Duffy home. Sands had other contact with Duffy in the prison itself.

tor's management of even mildly disturbing circumstances; and the opening up of employment, recreational and other role possibilities through introductions, recommendations and other exercises of influence on Actor's behalf. A small amount of practical aid implies the converse of such practices.

Humans are those sorts of creatures who tend to cathect other humans who help them. This is not to imply that they feel positively about Others who try to do a wide variety of things *for* them. Overly helpful Others tend merely to communicate, by their actions, a belief in Actor's incompetence, or, in the present context, Actor's pivotal deviance. Partly in the name of not being overly helpful and in order to foster Actor's "independence," some professionals of the social control establishment have indeed advocated that little or no practical aid be offered. However, while there may be an ambiguous division between aiding Actor and replacing him, not very many Others in contact with pivotal deviants seem in danger of overextending themselves. The standard sort of relation to Actors among members of the social control establishment seems, in fact, to fail to promote affective bonds, partly because of the small amount of practical aid that is extended.

The character and amount of possible practical aid is of course highly correlated with the degree of exposure. Deviant Actors, seen infrequently in a single setting, can have little done to help them in a practical way. They might, of course, submit lists of their needs, but such a practice would appear rather presumptuous under any circumstances, perhaps most especially with a professional social controller who is, socially speaking, little more than a stranger. Practical aid is likely to be most effectively extended under conditions of high exposure where events can be dealt with quickly—and even casually—at the time they come up. Other than in groups like Synanon and AA, where this occurs continually, priests and others who take to the slums to "work with" juveniles or drug addicts are well known for their strength in the offering of practical aid.[10]

The willingness or unwillingness to offer practical aid is perhaps most vividly symbolized by normal Others' definitions of an unexpected phone call from Actor. Others who prefer to offer little practical aid view Actor's unexpected call for advice or help as an illegitimate intrusion or demand. Actor should, after all, be "independent," and social controllers should always be "professional." A call from a tearful or otherwise distressed or lonely Actor announcing his temptation to "revert" or that he has "reverted" or his fears over one thing or another is therefore seen as out of order. Actor should not ask Other to meet him across town in ten minutes or come down to the county jail and bail him out or make any other plea that would necessitate Other's leaving his office or home. Indeed, it is reported[11] that social workers within the social control establishment who so inconvenience themselves are the objects of dis-

[10] See, for example, Wilkerson, 1964; J. D. Harris, 1965; Riccio and Slocum, 1962; and the review of aggressive religious programs in Fitzpatrick, 1967:323–28.

[11] L. H. Lofland.

paragement by their peers because of the belief that such conduct is highly "unprofessional." In contrast, the unexpected phone call in the middle of the night, most especially, is the *sine qua non* of those who are high on practical aid. These types come to expect to run here and there at a moment's notice, to help in whatever way they can. In an organization like Alcoholics Anonymous, such calls and running about are a routine and *expected* part of the "good AA's" role.

Practical aid is a form of *commitment* by Others, a form of putting oneself on the line for Actor. If Other does not put himself on the line in many small ways, as well as in a few large ones, Actor can begin to question why such an Other should be deserving of strong and positive regard. And, if he is not so deserving, why believe what he claims about Actor or any other object? Indeed, the contradiction between the supporting words of some professionals and their lack of committing deeds makes such Others especially vulnerable to Actor's defining them as "hypocrites." As one parolee put it: "I never listened to the advice of my parole agent. I figured he was being paid for doing his job and that he would always give me the sort of advice he was paid to hand out."[12]

Potential and Actual Peership. Intimate interaction and affective bonds seem to occur more easily between humans who are actual or potential peers than between humans who are, in a variety of ways, massively different in the social categories they wear. There are least likely to be affective bonds between a deviant Actor and an Other when the Other actually or potentially shares no, or very few, identity categories with Actor. For a pivotally deviant Actor the first and primary category that an Other may or may not share with him is his deviant identity. An Other who has never been a prostitute, a criminal, a delinquent, a drug addict, mentally ill or an alcoholic, but yet desires to foster affective bonds between himself and humans in any of these categories, stands at the outset in the position of a superordinate, not a peer. To the Actor or Actors involved, he represents the superordinate category of the chaste, the law-abiding, the prudent, the nonaddict, the mentally healthy or the normal drinker. Yet his distance from Actor is even greater than the superordinate-subordinate relationship, involving merely differences in power and influence, would suggest. For his location within the relevant acceptable and even lauded category of normality involves *moral* superiority as well. Actors defined as "mentally healthy" do not simply "outrank" or stand in a superordinate position to the mentally ill in the more neutral sense that foremen outrank workers or teachers outrank students. Normals outrank deviants in a more drastic sense, involving the moral scheme of types of persons permissibly existing in a social world. Added to this initial *moral* outranking are yet additional categorical superordinations of Other over Actor. It is not untypical for Others who

---

[12] Scott, 1965:17. See also the theoretical perspectives provided by Strauss, 1959:100–108, on "coaching"; Gouldner, 1960; B. Schwartz, 1967; H. S. Becker, 1960.

"work with" deviants also to outrank them in terms of education, income, occupational prestige and, perhaps, age, religion and laudability of their family and community participation.

The important point is not simply, however, *initial* outranking or lack of peership. The crucial point is whether such differences, if existing, are assumed to be, or defined to be, *temporary* or *permanent*. While a superordinate Other *may* (but it is not likely) define Actor's pivotal deviance as temporary, and thus anticipate that he and Actor will soon share some category of normality, their potential relationship may depend crucially on how he defines the *other* categories they may not at the moment share. Is it expected that they will come to be relatively similar in education, income, occupational prestige and in other categories such that they will be *peers?* Even if it is not expected that they will know one another in the future, is it expected that they will participate in a similar kind of world? Or, in contrast (and more typically), do Other and Actor expect that each will return to his respective world, having met briefly on an artificial and contrived margin of overlap between those different worlds? Since social worlds are founded on differences in education, income and occupation, especially, expectations concerning the permanence of such differences are crucial in determining the kind and degree of emotional involvement not only that Actor can have with Other but that Other can have with Actor.

It would appear that members of the social control establishment frequently do not have expectations of categorical sharing in this broader sense, much less in the specific matter of whatever pivotal deviance is at issue. It may indeed be unreasonable to fault psychiatrists and other psychotherapeutic types for confining themselves to "people change" with humans who are already quite similar to themselves in education, income, occupational prestige and the like. Out of those similarities there do in fact sometimes come to be peer relations. In general, "people changers" who are "advantaged" in a variety of categories and who attempt to spawn affective bonds with social devants who are "disadvantaged" in a variety of ways are likely to find themselves resented more than loved and avoided more than sought—*unless* the categorical dissimilarities are defined as temporary.[13]

Relations between the generally superordinate and the social deviant who is *older* but generally subordinate have a special poignancy. The categories of education, income and occupation that a human can feasibly attain in American civilization are determined by decisions made relatively early in life. Human Actors who are beyond their twenties and early thirties are likely to be presumed to be "set" in whatever categories they occupy. The fatalism that fol-

[13] Reciprocally, the professional may have attenuated regard for the client. See, e.g., Hollingshead and Redlich, 1958:253–303, 344–51. Although professional people changers usually outrank their "clients" in the social class system, relations may be equally difficult when the client socially outranks the professional—as when upper-class persons undertake therapy with merely upper-middle-class psychotherapists. (Hollingshead and Redlich, 1958: 353–55.)

lows from such a presumption serves to make relations between superordinate normal Others and subordinate deviant Actor particularly pathetic. It is only in relation to young social deviants that superordinate Others feel that they can legitimately hold out the prospect of categorical sharing or eventual peership. It is perhaps not accidental that the peership which came eventually to exist between Mr. and Mrs. Clinton Duffy and the reformed Bill Sands was founded, in the beginning, on Sands' youth. Although he spent two years and three months in San Quentin, upon release he had only just passed his twenty-third birthday. (Sands, 1964:75.)

A *high* degree of actual or potential peership involves, in the polar and clearest instance, Actor's and Other's (1) *sharing* a category of pivotal deviance and (2) being relatively similar in education, income, occupation and so forth.

It seems most facilitative for escalation to pivotal normality for Others not to be pivotally deviant at the time when they intersect with Actor but to have been so previously. With such backgrounds, they are living examples of the transformation (of identity) that is possible. Unlike mobility to peership with normals who have never been Actor's kind of deviant (or any kind of deviant), mobility to peership with the formerly pivotally deviant is a *replication* of such Others' careers. It may be the case that humans find it less difficult to replicate the identity career of Others they esteem than to attempt to achieve the identity of esteemed Others whose careers they are not replicating. Identity career replication appears to be the rule rather than the exception in human societies generally. Would-be doctors, lawyers, plumbers and electricians replicate the identity careers of esteemed persons in those categories. When the apprenticeship gets tough, it is possible to say, "He did it, so can I." A would-be identity model derives *legitimacy* from his having traversed the same route. To expect deviants to have affective bonds for—to take as identity models— Others who have not had that career is to expect an atypical, unusual and treacherous identification. Perhaps only deviants are expected to be so unusually responsive to persons different from themselves. The rest of us, the normals, are expected only to copy, to imitate, to replicate. The situation of the pivotal deviant relative to a *never* deviant Other might be compared to that of a medical student who is expected to come to conceive of himself as a doctor when none of his teachers ever attended or graduated from medical school.[14] It is in part because of the recognized importance of role models that many universities permit only people who have attained the Ph.D. to offer any kind of graduate instruction.

Synanon and other more recent experiments in identity transformation build in the possibility of actual or potential peership. The bulk of imputing Others have themselves already traversed escalation to pivotal normality. Deviant Actor is made clearly aware of this and has impressed upon him that he also is capable of the same transformation, that he *can* be a peer. This ability is im-

---

[14] Note, indeed, the difficulties that arise in the first two years of medical school because few of the teachers are M.D.'s. (E.C. Hughes, 1959.)

puted from the moment of acceptance into Synanon, at which point it becomes
mandatory that Actor withdraw from drugs, that is, "kick the habit." "Kicking" is done "on the davenport in the center of the large living room [in the
Santa Monica residence], not in a special isolation room or quarantine room.
Life goes on around him." (Volkman and Cressey, 1963:136.)

> Although a member will be assigned to watch him, he soon learns that his
> sickness is not important to men and women who have themselves kicked
> the habit. In the living room, one or two couples might be dancing, five
> or six people may be arguing, a man may be practicing the guitar and a
> girl may be ironing. The kicking addict learns his lesson: These others
> have made it. (Volkman and Cressey, 1963:136.)

From time to time during the process of kicking, his potential peers stop by to
chat with him. Their comments and advice serve to impress upon him that,
while he may be feeling desperately ill at the moment, he can soon be as well
and happy as the persons in his presence:

"We have all been in the shape you are in."

"Mike was on heroin for twenty years and he's off."

                    ❋   ❋   ❋

"It's OK, boy. We've all been through it before."

"For once you're with people like us. You've got everything to gain and
nothing to lose."

"You think you're tough. Listen, we've got guys here who could run
circles around you, so quit your bull———."

"You're one of us now, so keep your eyes open, your mouth shut and try
to listen for a while. Maybe you'll learn a few things." (Quoted in Volkman and Cressey, 1963:135–36.)

Commenting on such imputations and expectations of peership, Volkman and
Cressey twittingly note: ". . . none of [these] . . . comments could reasonably
have been made by a rehabilitation official or professional therapist." (Volkman and Cressey, 1963:136.)
    Actual and potential peership relative to the important dimensions of edu-
cation, income and occupation is a somewhat trickier matter and is diversely
managed. Some groups are characterized by dedication to a spartan, missionary style of life such that normal Others are neither very "rich," "cultured" or
manifestly educated, relative to even the most impoverished of deviant Actors
who are being escalated. The Salvation Army and other fundamentalist Christian organizations tend to prefer this solution to the peership problem. Synanon appears to have achieved a different solution in organizing an internal

occupational and income hierarchy. It is expected that all members will eventually work their way through all five of the income-responsibility-prestige grades. (See Volkman and Cressey, 1963:137.) It remains to be seen whether some people will become permanently immobile at lower levels while those at the highest level will become highly educated, attain very good jobs and earn large amounts of money. To the degree that rate of mobility through the stages becomes low such that there are large categorical differences between top and bottom, Synanon (and other organizations of its kind) can expect to have more difficulty promoting affective bonds.

Where pivotal deviants in question are relatively young and are drawn from modest occupational and income levels and are exposed to likewise modestly "well-off" formerly deviant normals, affective bonds are not so difficult to spawn. In contrast, a type of deviance such as alcoholism tends to occur at many levels of income, education and occupational prestige. Such a spread is then reflected in the Actors who come into contact with Alcoholics Anonymous, which is itself internally diverse on income, occupation and education. It becomes quite possible, for example, for a "lower-class" deviant Actor to encounter a "higher-class" AA and vice versa. Such dissimilarities are not productive of a sense of actual or potential peership. The AA "solution" to this categorical diversity has been social class specialization of its groups. The "birds of a feather" tend to "flock together," increasing the possibility of a sense of peership. In Manhattan, the groups on the Upper East Side tend to meet in upper-class churches, to have piped music, showmanship and the conspicuous presence of expensive furs on females. These are sometimes called "snob groups" and are avoided by persons who are members of the more modest units meeting in more modest surroundings and who consider themselves to be "real AA." The Upper East Side types tend, reciprocally, to practice their own avoidance. (Lofland and Lejuene, 1960.) In the larger metropolitan settlements there has tended also to be racial segregation within AA. It is highly functional for affiliation that potential AA's are advised to visit and are taken around to visit what are euphemistically called "many different kinds of groups" in order to see which "kind" the candidate AA might like best. Indeed, in New York City, AA goes even further, with formerly organized groups fostering membership from among particular occupations and sexes. There have been groups for seamen only, for actors only, for men only and for women only. One group observed by the author in lower Manhattan even appeared to be developing informally into a group for AA's who were also homosexuals.

In a similar manner, identity transformations within evangelical Christianity tend to take place within economically and racially homogeneous groups. In contrast to the modesty and relative poverty of such groups as the Salvation Army and their "clienteles," groups allied with Billy Graham appear to pitch themselves to the more advantaged sectors of the population. In one recently published collection of tales exemplifying Billy Graham's saving power, all seven transformations involved persons of considerable economic standing, education and/or public acclaim. The seven converts had, of course, a much higher average standing than Graham's converts as a whole. The point is, rather, that Graham gave his blessing to a popular work that would so represent the character of his "ministry" and clientele (Gillenson, 1967).

While segregation into groups of categorical similarities of these kinds may run counter to at least some moral principles, it must also be said that peership is nonetheless promoted by such segregation. Segregation, considered more generically than simply racial segregation, is, after all, more comfortable than integration. It assures a common universe of discourse and a common body of similar problems that have been and have to be faced.

A further, oft-noted aspect of peership in "self-help" groups needs also to be mentioned. More than simply being escalated to a pivotally normal identity, the deviant Actor in such groups quite soon has the opportunity and the obligation to enact or play out the role of the pivotally normal category. He is not simply being "treated"—whatever that might mean—but he comes rather quickly to be among the *administrators* of "treatment." At the same time that he is escalating to pivotal normality, he must act in terms of that pivotal normality toward even newer candidates as well as toward those who outrank him in the group. "The roles of patient and therapist are interchangeable," as Yablonsky has said of Synanon.[15] The initial and known possibility of such "interchangeability" is potential peership; the relatively early possibility of such interchangeability is actual peership.

Situations of actual or potential peership are situations where Actors can, without too much fear or threat, reveal their personal failings to one another. And, when situations of peership are combined with situations of high exposure, it becomes likely that personal failings will become known and not have to be merely "revealed." In American civilization it would appear that peers have a stronger license than do superordinates vis-à-vis their subordinates to preach, to advise and to admonish one another without producing alienation. (Cf. Jourard, 1964.)

Understanding. Human beings tend to have positive affective regard for Others who are believed to "understand" them. "Understanding" (or lack thereof), as a quality that persons impute to one another, appears to mean that an Other can (or cannot) "put himself in your place." He can conceive and perceive what the world is like through Actor's eyes, from within Actor's perspective. To be understood is to be not alone. To be understood is to have one or more Others who also see things that way. Given the typically disintegrating consequences of being alone, either physically or socially, it can be expected that humans will have high regard for Others who rescue them from social isolation; that is, for Others who appear to understand. However, the attitudes and practices of most normal Others toward social deviants make it

[15] Yablonsky, 1965:151. See further Cressey, 1955:118–19, on retroflexive rehabilitation, and 1965:55–56. See also National Institute of Mental Health, 1963.

particularly difficult for the latter to achieve an arrangement of their lives wherein they feel they are understood by normals. Deviant Actors who have encountered a period of disorientation and who are experiencing doubt regarding the efficacy of their pivotal deviance are likely to have an acute sense that no one "understands" them.

If affective bonds are to be fostered, the question is raised as to what social categories of Others are most likely (although not exclusively) to be imputed by Actor to be "understanding." A major part of the answer is already contained in the discussion of actual or potential peership. Understanding, as an interpersonal imputation, is, like peership, founded most frequently and easily upon the sharing of social categories. Persons who have lived out their lives within relatively similar sets of social categories are likely to define problems, events, possibilities, etc., in a relatively similar manner. Their categorical similarity is the structural basis of their "psychic empathy." Similarity of a deviant life trajectory makes the revelation of past experience and troubles and current difficulties and problems "explicable." The revelation "makes sense" to such a similar Other. He can "understand" what Actor "has gone through" for he has "been through" perhaps identical experiences himself. In Alcoholics Anonymous the following type of exchange occurs between members and potential members. Paraphrased and condensed, it goes:

> I am an alcoholic. We are all alcoholics; we know what you have gone through, what you are going through; and we know the problems you will meet. If you think you have had it bad, let me tell you about myself. I was . . . . I, too, felt humiliation and disgrace. We understand you. This is the only place you can be understood.

Although understanding as an interpersonal construct is highly correlated with categorical similarity, and hence peership, it is nonetheless important to make a distinction between the two. The imputation of Others' understanding is sometimes made by deviant Actors toward those who are not and have not been any kind of pivotal deviant. It must be recognized that there are a few unconventional heroes of empathy who, despite their always having been quite "straight" in almost every way, still manage to project themselves into deviant Actor's perspective. More accurately, some Others manage themselves in such a way that deviants impute to them extraordinary understanding. Whether this imputed understanding is, in fact, of the same order as that offered by yet another Other who was or is deviant is not known. Nor does it matter, as long as Actor believes in the understanding of such normal heroes of empathy.

Preachers, priests and psychotherapists are among the most prominent of categories that produce exemplars of understanding on the part of normals. And, it must be said that the instances of these social categories that are most likely to have deviants impute understanding to them are also likely to be persons (1) who have high exposure to deviants and (2) who engage in a large amount of practical aid. By such extraordinary exposure and assistance, they are perhaps able to overcome the limitations of being variously dissimilar, categorically, from the people with whom they "work."

Warmth. A final cumulating quality which appears productive of affective bonds is, of those mentioned, the most elusive. It is, in large part, an imputed quality that derives from activity undertaken along all the previous elements. Even though largely derivative, it does not appear to be perfectly correlated with or totally dependent upon them and must therefore be separately considered. I refer here to the mystical quality of "warmth" which Actor may impute to an Other. Imputed warmth and coldness are not simply constructs toyed with by arcane social psychologists (e.g., Asch, 1952), but assessments that persons make of one another in everyday life. The issue of how warm or cold Others are seems, even, a particularly sensitive matter between pivotal deviants and their complements of Others. Whatever may constitute warmth and whatever its sources may be, all Actors, including deviant ones, seem to like it very much and to be responsive to being its recipient.

To approach this elusive quality, it is useful to indicate some associated imputations that are often confused or associated but not identical with it. Warmth does not mean only niceness or gentleness. Although some people imputed to be warm may be "nice" or "gentle," many persons so imputed are not seen as such. While there may be little old ladies who are "just as nice as they can be" and who are seen as warm, there are also warm persons who are viewed as being gruff or as "anything but sweet." Nor is warmth synonymous with a cheerful countenance, nor with being permissive or accepting. Some people who are imputed to be warm smile very little, and many are not seen as particularly permissive or laissez faire.

While acknowledging that there are people imputed to be warm who are also imputed to have any or all of these mentioned qualities, the generic meaning of warmth has to do with something broader than any of them. The nice and the gruff, the permissive and the strict, the smiling and the somber who are imputed to be warm appear to be alike in the degree to which they communicate to Actor qua human being and in the degree to which they project themselves qua human beings. They appear to care *about Actor* as a *full person* or whole being. They appear to project *themselves* as full or whole human beings: they are genuine and sincere.

A hurried disclaimer is immediately necessary. The concept of the whole or full person has been used so much and by so many naïve idealists and moralists that it has become almost "corny" and has lost practically all meaning. Be that as it may, it is nonetheless necessary here to perform a technical salvage job. As long as human beings are concerned about being treated as, and treating others as, "whole" or "full" persons, such notions must be of technical interest to social science.

Viewed technically, warm persons are those who rarely, in the current vernacular, play games. To play games is to toy with identities, to flit from one to another interaction gambit and to be perceived as intentionally creating ambiguity about what one "really thinks."[16] To play games is to be fully socialized in and adept at the necessary political strategies of everyday life. In everyday life it is in the interest of a person never to be fully honest about himself and his thoughts, feelings and positions. And it is functional for the maintenance of certain kinds of social systems that human beings be socially supple and ambidextrous. The prototype of the successful and socially necessary gamesman is, of course, the international diplomat. But that role merely epitomizes the necessary skill for, and requirements of, all "normal" social relations. Warm persons are, in a sense, inept gamesmen, although in small numbers, they are also necessary for the maintenance of a social system. Other inept gamesmen gravitate to them, some to become warm persons, others to learn how to be good gamesmen and more comfortable politicians in everyday life.

Warm Others who project a sense of being real or genuine, of coming on as whole persons, tend also to treat Actor as a whole person and as real. The gamesmanship of Actor is turned aside; there is a tendency, as it is said, to "come down to cases," to "get down to it." Jointly, there is a tendency for Actor and such Others to make the social game and social gamesmanship themselves the objects of discussion—to "step outside of" or verbally suspend their social categories and their social commitments, at least to the small degree that this is possible among human beings. Warm Others appear, to use the banal phrase, to care about Actor as a human being. But such caring may well involve being judgmental, and it may involve sanctioning, as well as the more celebrated—and necessary—practices of emotional support and practical aid. Suspension of imputed gamesmanship and the imputation of warmth imply, then, a degree of imputed intimacy. To suspend games, to "get down to it," is to make Actor and Other both more vulnerable because of the mutual revelations implied by a suspension of representations in terms other than the most immediate categories of identity.

Within this sort of perspective we can understand how it is that warmth can be imputed to persons who sometimes treat others in what appears, superficially, to be a quite ruthless and cold manner. This superficial paradox is quite spectacular in an organization such as Synanon. As we have seen, members are evidently (from an outsider's perspective) quite "mean" to one another. At the same time they think of one another as warm, and one hears "frequent repetition of some comment to the effect that 'This is the first home I ever had'" (Volkman and Cressey, 1963:135). The paradox is resolved when it is recognized that Synanon members are engaged in the task of caring about one another as human beings. They do this with whatever devices may be necessary to conduce one another to "be oneself" and to be "truthful." This is, of course,

---

[16] See the technical explications by Goffman, 1959; Berne, 1961 and 1964.

also a social game, at least in the sense that it is organized within a set of rules. It is different, however, in that there is a suspension of the "run and hide," "flit and play" character associated with the concept of "gamesmanship" popularized by Stephen Potter and Eric Berne.[17]

Summarizing, it has been suggested that the development of affective bonds between Actor and Other or, more particularly, the development of positive affect by Actor toward Other is facilitated by the cumulative and joint existence of a high degree of mutual exposure of Actor and Other; a relatively large amount of practical aid rendered to Actor by Other; a reasonable degree of actual or potential peership between them; and a degree of understanding and a reasonable amount of warmth imputed to Other by Actor. There remains, of course, the question of how much of any combination of these elements is necessary for Actor actually to respond with positive affect toward Other. It could be, for example, that high exposure combined with a large amount of practical aid and actual peership can suffice to overcome an Other's weak degree of understanding and warmth or vice versa (although this latter seems, on the face of it, unlikely).

AFFECTIVE BONDS AND SOCIAL
CONTROL PROFESSIONALS

Even though there are a large number of unasked and unanswered empirical questions concerning various minimal conditions of affective bonds, it is already possible provisionally to suggest at least one kind of relation within the social control establishment that is not, typically, productive of them. I refer to the dyadal relation so widespread in social work and psychotherapy—a type of relation commented on previously that can now be addressed more directly. The following characterization of the relation between social workers and mental patients is not untypical of relations generally between professional social controllers and other types of pivotal deviants.

Patients are seen by appointment, usually at the worker's convenience and in the worker's office where a desk and a formal procedure somehow structures or dominates the interactions. The patient may be seen only infrequently and formally. Patients do not enter the home or the private life of the worker, nor do they violate the worker's forty-hour week. To reach the worker, the patient must act through intermediaries, i.e., receptionists, secretaries, etc. Further, the services given to the patient have undergone segmentation via a division of labor; i.e., if the patient requires financial assistance, he is "referred" to another agency, perhaps located even in another town; if he needs a job, still another referral is

17 On warmth, see further Halmos, 1966:Chap. 3; Rausch and Bordin, 1957; Gardner, 1964; Rogers, 1957; Goldstein, Heller and Sechrest, 1966:73–145. Some means by which Goffmanesque reserve and flitting are more typically developed in dyadic change relations are explicated in Blum and Rosenberg, 1968.

needed—and so on for a myriad of social services. The use of the community resources of an artistic or educational nature are largely overlooked or untouched by the ex-mental patient. (Miller and Blanc, 1964:4.)

Yet despite such low exposure, compromise of practical aid, low degree of peership and high degree of formality, there is the expectation that Actor will allow this professional Other to be privy to the intimate parts of his life. There is the expectation—indeed, the demand—that Actor will reveal precisely those things about himself that he would prefer not be known by strangers such as this. "Inquiry into the client's life is defined as legitimate, not as snooping" (Wilensky and Lebeaux, 1958:299–300).

The combination of these social arrangements and this expectation sets up a very special and peculiar type of human relationship. It sets up a special kind of dilemma between intimacy and distance, between commitment and detachment.

> All human relations blend social nearness and distance; and the dilemma of involvement and detachment is not new to our time. But never before has it been built into a society and labeled "job." For social work (as well as psychotherapy) the term "objectivity" (or emotional neutrality) takes its place beside "rapport" as a characterization of the client-professional relationship. Together they comprise in Mannheim's words a "strange combination of intimacy and objectivity, nearness and distance, attraction and repulsion, friendship and estrangement," a combination which the professional in training (especially one who works in an intimate field like social work) finds difficult to comprehend and incorporate into his habit patterns. When it is grasped and "learned in the muscles," then the novitiate has developed the essence of the "professional self." (Wilensky and Lebeaux, 1958:300–1.)

Professionalism and Spurious Intimacy. In American civilization, relationships of this peculiar character are reserved especially for, and recommended especially to, humans defined as deviant. To coax or force persons into such relations is to define them as meriting only *spurious intimacy*. It is to define them as less than or other than normal. A "proper" relation to a professional Other is one which defines Actor as less than deserving of the professional's personal friendship. It is one which defines him as less than deserving of the more diffuse concern that is the hallmark of affective bonds between human beings and the foundation of social truth. Professional social controllers are specialists in the compromise of involvement in the lives of others. By excluding Actor from friendship, in the conventional meaning of that term, they foster and sustain a conception of him as a pivotal deviant. And, by demanding, in the face of all this distance, a kind of intimacy, they are likely to promote alienation and ambivalence, if not intense dislike, more than positive affective regard.

Independence and Professionalism. Built into this type of relation, moreover, is what might be called the "doctrine of independence." It is believed
that therapeutic treatment is not completed or successful unless and until the
Actor becomes independent of it, unless and until he no longer needs the professional or team of professionals. Within a broadened conception of "therapy"
and "therapeutic" endeavor, this doctrine amounts to saying that Actor is not
cured until he no longer needs some organizing system of meaning and set of
significant Others in relation to whom he plays out his life.

The doctrine of independence is, of course, useful in the construction of
mass men who can successfully live out their lives in the presence of interchangeable others with whom they have no important affective ties. It contributes to the possibility of a society of atomized and socially and geographically mobile Actors who are nonetheless responsive to the controls exerted by
changing sets of relatively anonymous others. And, in a technological society
such as the American one, if the kind of social organization conduced by its
technological system is to be sustained, this may well be a "functionally necessary" belief. The doctrine of independence may be, in addition, functionally
necessary to the maintenance of the social control establishment itself. Very
few Actors possess the resources requisite to sustained "treatment" by it. Because many "patients" cannot afford it, and few can afford it for very long, if a
living is to be made from the enterprise, there must be a relatively high turnover of treated clientele. The doctrine of independence is a polite device
through which to promote "patient" turnover. It is at least more polite and
dignified than simply telling such Actors that they are a drag on the economy
of the social control establishment.

Within the view taken here, permanent attachment to a therapy, such as a
religious commitment or a commitment to Synanon or AA, is not indicative of
failure. Being "hooked" on the therapy itself indicates, rather and merely, the
fundamental need of social man to participate in a system of meaning—a system
of action possibilities. It is generically no different from becoming committed
to or being hooked on the business game if one is a businessman, the family
game if one is a family man, the scholar's game if one is a scholar or the psychotherapy game if one is a therapist.[18]

Serving the Servers. The societal and organizational functions of the doctrine of independence raise the more general question of additional ways in
which Other is served by dyadal relations of spurious intimacy. And intertwined with that question are issues of how, historically, professional social
controllers came to be served in the manner they are.

[18] On the psychotherapy game, see Hollingshead and Redlich, 1958:165; Rieff, 1966:98–
107. On the relation between urban-technological social orders and the idea of therapeutic
independence see further Rieff, 1966: especially Chaps. 1–4 and 8; and, more generally, Bennis and Slater, 1968. The ambivalence of professional controllers themselves toward the
doctrine of independence (and other central features of their enterprise) is brilliantly analyzed in Halmos, 1966: especially 146–75 and Chap. 4.

Historians of dyadal relations, in particular, have observed that the conception is borrowed from the practice of medicine, from the model of a "doctor" and a "patient." First taken over by persons who called themselves "psychiatrists" and "psychoanalysts," it was subsequently imitated by people who called themselves "psychologists" and "social workers" and various kinds of "counselors" (Szasz, 1961). This adoption of an occupational model occurred in an historical context of the bureaucratization and professionalization of all manner of work activities. In the first half of the 20th century in American civilization, occupations competed for the power and prestige of being "professional," for the right to set their own terms of "service." Amidst this jostling, social work was particularly vigorous in its claims to "professionalism," that is, in its claim to control over the conditions under which its member would render a service. Social workers wanted to be respectable, to be white collar, and to work a forty-hour week.

Social work and kindred social control occupations have largely succeeded in their efforts to forge an occupation similar to other middle-class occupations. They are becoming accustomed to having a house in the suburbs, even if they have to commute to the inner city or the rural mental hospital or prison camp to encounter a parade of deviants between the hours of nine and five. They are becoming accustomed to returning home at an appointed late afternoon hour and eating with their spouses and children; to attending community events; and to spending considerable hours a week on the maintenance and improvement of their bodies, their houses and their grounds. They are becoming accustomed to watching certain television programs nearly every week; to rising at much the same time each weekday and weekend morning and to routing themselves through a relatively predictable day. They are becoming accustomed to the family celebration of holidays and to the yearly family vacation. They are becoming accustomed, in short, to living the standard, segregated life of the American. One part, the "working" portion, is devoted to making imputations to deviant Actors (and, not untypically, imputations of deviance) and another part is devoted to "family," "community" and "leisure." Writing about occupations in general, and social work in particular, Martin Rein has summed it up in this manner:

> When a group of persons who perform a service band together to control the body of persons who may legitimately perform that service, certain inevitable consequences follow: a striving to raise their own prestige and rewards; a tendency to overdefine the skills needed to do the work; a limit on those who may do it, and to whom it may be done; and an increasing concern with "professional standards," personal satisfaction and income. The danger is that the interests of the recipients can easily become subverted to serve the interests of the dispensers. (Rein, 1964:4.)

The self-serving tendencies of occupations which collectively promote their own interests do not, of course, escape the notice of other categories of persons at whose expense this self-serving is accomplished. Unions are aware of it with regard to management, and management is aware of it with regard to unions. University students are aware of it with regard to professors and administrators, and professors and administrators are aware of it with regard to students (and so also for the relations of professors and administrators). To the point here, deviant Actors amenable to change are likely aware of it with regard to their professional "helpers," "therapists" and other keepers. Even if not verbalized, they can hardly escape the message communicated by the typically segregated life of their controllers. It seems unlikely that pivotal deviants are not in some sense aware of the essential absurdity of a situation in which persons tinker with the fundamentals of their lives—with the intimate contents of their selves—while avoiding meaningful involvement in their lives. It seems unlikely that pivotal deviants are not at some level aware of this compromise of commitment, that they are not aware that "professional" relations communicate tenuous, partial or even peripheral "interest" in what they are and what they can be. If so, affective bonds—and the social truth that rests upon them—are not facilitated.

SOCIAL ROLES FACILITATING AFFECTIVE BONDS

Let me emphasize that the foregoing characterization of the relations between professional social controllers and social deviants is constructed vis-à-vis the earlier suggestions regarding conditions most conducive to affective bonds. Lest I appear to be unreasonably skeptical of professional social controllers, let me state more clearly the kind of life that is implied for a normal Other who would meet the conditions most facilitative of affective bonds. In order to illustrate maximal states of the five elements most conducive of affective bonds, I have had to make frequent reference to Synanon and other "turned-on" styles of life. The major feature of such lives, from the point of view of persons who would live them, is that they are *highly demanding*. They demand enormous absorption in sheer time, in physical energy and in emotional investment, leaving little or no time, energy or emotional capacity for anything else. Such lives are not unsimilar to that of a mother to several children under age five and are perhaps even more demanding. Mothers, after all, begin with little animals upon whom initial identities as humans and as some more particular categories are to be impressed; normal-smiths must supplant identities already impressed.

It is because of this enormous and necessary investment that normal-smiths who effect affective bonds are found to be drawn disproportionately from certain social locations, while other social locations are disproportionately underrepresented. The cutting line between overrepresented and underrepresented social locations would appear to be the possession of spouse and children. When particular normal-smiths have such encumbrances, either special arrangements are made to absorb them into the normal-smith enterprise or they are rendered altogether irrelevant and family tension ensues.

The occupants of what social locations are least likely to have spouses and children? First and most obvious are priests and nuns, and we indeed find instances of these categories disproportionately involved with deviants, often as normal-smiths. Father Flanagan who founded Boys' Town in Omaha, Nebraska, is among the best known of such committed types. (See further, e.g., J. D. Harris, 1965.) Second are the young of either sex before they have had time to acquire family commitments. Best known are perhaps the young males who take up positions as "street club workers" (e.g., Riccio and Slocum, 1962). It should be noted that the career of the street club worker is typically quite short. Lacking the organizational security and ideologization of the religious orders, the occupation of the street worker, it is said, has no future. After a few years on the street, the young men marry, have children and become social workers, professors or some such. An equivalent kind of commitment and irregular life are demanded also of those who would undertake guided group interaction. Indeed, its founders and initial promoters have not remained in the practice of guided group interaction but have spawned families and become high level bureaucrats or college professors. They, quite reasonably, one supposes, satisfy their missionary urges through writing textbooks and articles about it. Third, there are reformed deviants who have never collected family commitments (or have absconded from them because of their deviance). This is the case with some members of Synanon and Alcoholics Anonymous.

Among those who have family commitments and are still "turned-on" normal-smiths, arrangements are often made to absorb the family into the enterprise. The Salvation Army does this through encouraging marriage within the Army and arranging for the rearing of children. Other evangelical Christians accomplish accommodation also through involving the entire family in the enterprise. (See, e.g., Wilkerson, 1964.) When absorption of the family does not take place, family units frequently come into jeopardy. This problem is most acute in Alcoholics Anonymous, where the spouse is sometimes seen less by his family than when he was drinking. If the family is not absorbed into Al-anon or Alateen, chronic family conflict is sometimes the plight of an AA, unless he decides to ignore his family altogether.

Considering the difficulties and requirements of this kind of life and the definition of a normal life and normal pleasures in American civilization (viz., a job, family and leisure), it should be no surprise that there are so few occupants of the turned-on normal-smith's role who can spawn affective bonds and affect identity transformations. It must be understood, too, that the compromise of involvement engaged in by professional social controllers is only the normal compromise of work and family that is typical and expected. The compromise of the professional social controllers is different only in that the objects of their compromise are not materials, products and assembly lines but people. Materials, products and assembly lines can be attended to on shifts and are not aware of nor resentful over vacations, families and unrelated voluntary activities. People are a different kind of object altogether; they are aware of part-time, peripheral and casual involvement, and they respond to it. Let us not, however, fault the professional social controllers for their desire to lead normal lives of compromise. It is more fitting to empathize with such a dilemma.

Cognitive Congruence

Content congruence

Bringing forward the previous distinctions between personalistic, interpersonalistic and superpersonalistic cognitive systems, it can also be said here that congruence or similarity of Actor's and Others' perspectives facilitates escalation. Escalation is facilitated not only by general similarity or congruence of realms but also by the congruence vis-à-vis more specific formulations of postulates within realms. The fact of facilitation does not, again, rule out the possibility of changes in general perspective. Such changes are only less likely and more difficult to accomplish.

The integration of biography and self

Of more interest in relation to the question of escalating pivotal deviants to pivotal normality is a matter of a rather different kind of congruence. A system of cognitive categories designates objects or aspects of reality toward which humans can act. For the believer in, or espouser of, a system of categories, the objects so designated have "meaning" or are "meaningful." An object which is meaningful or has meaning is one that denotes or reveals possibilities for action. To say that things are "meaningless" or "lack meaning" is to say that they lack action possibilities and that they do not provide a vehicle on the basis of which the organism can project a course of conduct. Meaningless objects can be so, either because they reveal to the Actor no possibilities at all for action or because the action they reveal is distasteful to him for any of a variety of reasons. Following from the above, one can ask if there are any further facilitating differences between potentially proffered systems. Given congruence, are all proffered systems of categories equally facilitative of escalation to a personal identification of self as a pivotal normal? Considering the systems of cognitive categories—the character of the meaningful worlds—that ex-deviant normals come to espouse, I am inclined to propose that escalation to pivotal normality is facilitated by some, rather than other, already generally congruent perspectives.

The Problem of Discontinuity and Guilt. Pivotal deviants who have lived with stigma and have undergone disorientation display at least two features that conduce them to be differentially sensitive to proffered congruent cognitive systems. Although neither of these features is experienced only by them, they seem untypically combined in such social deviants. First, there are the profoundly shaking concomitants of the disorientation itself. Disoriented persons have suffered or are suffering what is for a human being a fate worse than death: the stripping of identity and therefore of meaning system. Human beings seem, indeed, to be the only creatures who can feel they are dead, or should be dead, while still being physically alive. Such social nakedness seems to provoke a deep sense of worthlessness, a sense of a deeply blemished being. At the time, and in retrospect, the period of social nakedness is viewed in grim terms, as an experience hopefully never to be encountered again, despite the fact that it may have led or be leading to a glorious "new being."

Second, social deviants typically combine the first experience with a sense of shame and degradation over their past deviance. In the midst of imputations of moral normality, the deviant period of the biography is defined as a long stretch of acts that are incompatible with the proffered and candidate self. Actor can come to feel *guilt* over his history of deviance. He has, in one sense or another, "sinned," and the fact of this sinning in the past must be dealt with —defined and managed—in the present. There is, in particular, the problem of how to relate the *past* period as a social deviant to his *present* candidacy for pivotal normality and to his *future* as a pivotal normal. How can an apparently discontinuous life trajectory be made a related, meaningful train of events?

These two features (and others) pose, from the perspective of Actor, a problem of meaning, of definition and of management. Thus conceived, the question of congruence is a question of what kinds of perspectives most facilitatively or most easily integrate and make meaningful a life that is experienced as discontinuous, radically changing and full of shame and guilt and that is felt or feared to be worthless. What kinds of perspectives provide possibilities for Actor's acting toward, and in terms of, such a life?

Moral Heroism. Viewing the range of normal-smith enterprises, one finds in them a common, if not universal, theme. Without attempting entirely to capture the character of this theme, or interrelated set of themes, it seems to consist importantly of a sense of *heroic endeavor* or *extraordinary worth.* The normality assumed by such former deviants is not simply worthwhile, it is *inordinately worthwhile.* If normal-smith groups are not overtly out to save the world (which some are), what they are doing does not seem to fall very short of it. Transformed deviants tend to become not merely moral but hypermoral. They are not simply "reformed" or "rehabilitated" into regular people with regular jobs and regular lives. They become extraregular people, have extraregular jobs (even if the job is not the way they make a living), and live extraregular lives. They take on a relatively fervent moral purpose. This theme (or themes) is most spectacular and most easily seen in former deviants who are converts to one or another variety of evangelical Christianity. Chronicles of gunmen, punks, addicts and alcoholics who "got religion" and who now preach salvation rank, indeed, among the folk tales of American civilization.

Evangelical Christianity is, however, only one such perspective that facilitates the integration of biography and self through a sense of heroic mission and inordinately worthwhile personal identity. In the second third of the 20th century there has been a proliferation of more specialized possibilities for hypermoral and heroic selves. The ideological and organizational model for this has been provided by Alcoholics Anonymous,[19] but heroic selves have been or are now being provided for practically every form of popularly identified deviance. In AA, members can come to feel so integrated, so moral and so worthwhile that it is possible for some to say that they are glad they were problem drinkers; otherwise they would not be able to participate in the warm wonders of AA. "Alcoholism is turned into an asset instead of remaining a source of shame and guilt" (Ripley and Jackson, 1959:48). Of Synanon, a leader and promoter wrote:

> The residents of Synanon, unlike prisoners or inmates, are involved with the growth and development of their own organization. Because the residents generally believe that "Synanon saved our lives," the *esprit de corps* and involvement in the organization are quite powerful. (Yablonsky and Dederich, 1963:52.)

THE PROLIFERATION OF SELF-HELP MORAL HEROISM

In the late fifties, O. Hobart Mowrer, a psychologist, became interested in the proliferation of "self-help groups" (so-called because they are undertaken apart from, and are even scornful of, professional therapists). Publishing and speaking widely on them, he began and continues publicly to articulate the heroic theme that unites their endeavor. Mowrer's position, however, is less that of an analyst *of* them and more that of a leading spokesman *for* them. One of his inexpensive paperback promulgations, *The New Group Therapy*, contains passages such as these:

> Primitive (Apostolic) Christianity was essentially a small-group movement and had, it seems, many of the characteristics we today see in the spontaneously emerging self-help therapeutic groups. But, over the centuries, the vision and vitality of the Early Church has been so far lost that there is a real question whether the Modern Church is going to have the discernment to claim these groups as its own.

❀   ❀   ❀

[19] Of somewhat more than historical interest is the fact that AA itself grew out of the tenets and organization of the Moral Rearmament Association, an enterprise dedicated to moral heroism for the less than pivotally deviant. See Gellman, 1964:Chap. 1; Eister, 1950.

. . . The "new" group therapy is . . . a "historical necessity" in this day of personal estrangement and "mass culture" . . . without it our very survival may be in jeopardy.

❖   ❖   ❖

. . . It is, I submit, only through a "spiritual" (or "ideological") revival of massive proportions that we have any assured prospect of retaining our traditional form of society and civilization.

❖   ❖   ❖

. . . We have lost the strong sense of community and commitment which characterized early Christianity and have become disastrously individualistic, independent and isolated. Now, the great salvationist scheme is one which energetically condemns individualism and extols personal dedication.

❖   ❖   ❖

The current upsurge of interest and involvement in therapeutic self-help groups is, clearly, a rebuke both to religion and to psychology and psychiatry for our self-interest and lack of imagination and courage. In short, a *revolution* is quietly in progress. We psychologists can oppose or aid and encourage it. For myself, I hope we will choose the latter course. (Mowrer, 1964:v, vi, 23, 24, 99.)

We have in these passages the beginnings of the logical extension of what began as more modest and limited moral heroism. Moral salvation becomes more than simply personal salvation; it means, as well, the salvation of civilization itself. This latter theme is, of course, common and well known among enterprises identified as social, political or revolutionary movements. What is new is the appearance of the same theme among the ranks of the organized ex-deviants of the world. (Mowrer is himself a member of a self-help group, having undergone, it appears from his reports, disorientation and guilt similar to the general case described above. See Mowrer, 1964:65, 108.) It remains to be seen whether a significant number of the self-help groups will form any kind of politically significant coalition.

I have referred above to the possibility of a deviant Actor's becoming normal—nay, hypernormal—through personal identification in the terms of some ongoing group. All groups, of course, have a beginning. Someone at some time was, of necessity, an *identity entrepreneur*. This route remains a possible and potent one in American civilization. As did Clifford Beers, author of *A Mind That Found Itself* (1921), it is still feasible to construe one's mental hospitalization as an appropriate experience upon which to found and head a movement to reform mental hospitals—a moral cause indeed. And groups of ex-deviants are still not numerous enough to make unfeasible the founding of further groups of ex-deviants dedicated to reforming their former kind. The two founders of AA only showed the way. Bill Sands may be among the most recent of well-known identity entrepreneurs, but there are likely to be more after him (Sands, 1964, 1967).

One might also expect increased defection to heroic enterprises among the professional social controllers. O. Hobart Mowrer is but one variety of normal-smith defector. Dr. Timothy Leary's early efforts at moral heroism among convicts are likely to be replicated as drugs of the "consciousness-expanding" type come more widely into use. At least in the early phases of their introduction, such drugs provide cognitive systems and styles of life for transformed deviants which depict them as the vanguard of a moral revolution. Indeed, almost any somewhat resisted innovation about which one can feel morally righteous can potentially provide a morally heroic identity. Where the innovation is only slightly resisted and has a solid foothold in legitimacy, such transformed deviants are only a variety of normal. Such has been the case for AA and Synanon. Where the identity transformation involves a weakly legitimated heroic identity, the Actor becomes merely another kind of deviant, albeit one who is more solid in his deviance because he may now be part of the vanguard of history. Such was the fate of Malcolm X, who went from pivotally criminal to pivotally Black Muslim.

A general point to be made, then, is that the facilitative character of the cognitive system may depend less upon the specific terms of transformation than upon whether or not it involves moral heroism which serves to make a chaotic life of shame and guilt coherent and full of high moral purpose. Timothy Leary's early successes with administering psilocybin to convicts may have less to do with psilocybin per se than with the function of the experience in producing a heroic, integrated, revealed and purposeful life. Religion, AA, Synanon or a variety of other cognitive systems can serve the same function, within the limits of preexisting congruence.

EXCURSUS ON THE RISE OF SELF-HELP MORAL HEROISM

Shifting the focus, the intriguing rise of morally heroic groups of ex-deviants justifies, I think, a brief excursion into the related matter of why and how this has occurred only in modern times. Their recent proliferation can usefully be viewed as corresponding to and reflecting more general tendencies to identity proliferation and specialization in complex societies. Within the last two hundreds years of Western civilization there has been a proliferation not only of occupational identities but also of medical diseases and, important here, of psychiatric or psychological disabilities and types of possible crime. Corresponding to many of these new categories of deviance there have come to be specialized modes of identifying, punishing and treating each. Neurotics, psychotics, alcoholics, drug addicts, juvenile delinquents and others are relatively new categories in the world, in the sense that normals have only recently worked them up and sought, organizationally, to identify, process and thoroughly treat Actors in their terms. This is not to say that activity which might be construed as fitting one or another of these categories has not previously existed, only that such thoroughly organized social recognition and response are rather recent to any society. The fact of Others' more differentiated identification and response provides, then, the categories of identity in terms of which Actors so treated can organize themselves. We begin, in the 20th century, to witness the birth of Alcoholics Anonymous, Synanon, Neurotics Anonymous, Phobics Anonymous, Gamblers Anonymous, Recovery, Inc., Divorcees Anonymous, Mental Aid Fellowships, X-Patient Groups and a host of others, in response to, or on the basis of, the larger society's having more thoroughly and forcefully discriminated extant kinds of deviants.[20]

Prior to the current rationalization, formalization and bureaucratization of social life, problematic people were a more undifferentiated lot. Defined more vaguely and generally, such Actors thought of themselves in more general terms. As such, they were more "vulnerable" to identification and escalation processes undertaken by correspondingly more generalized perspectives. Given the prominence of religious perspectives in the premodern Western world, problematic Actors were perhaps more likely to be converts to religious movements that offered a sense of moral renewal and heroism. In early Christianity, for example, the Apostle Paul remarked of and to his followers:

> My brothers, think what sort of people you are, whom God has called. Few of you are men of wisdom, by any human standard; few are powerful or highly born. Yet to shame the wise, God has chosen what the world counts folly; and to shame what is strong, God has chosen what the world counts weakness. He has chosen things low and contemptible, mere nothings, to overthrow the existing order. (The First Letter of Paul to the Corinthians 1:25–28, *NEB*.)

While Paul doubtless also spoke of the simply poor, it seems clear that all manner of those who would today be defined in more differentiated deviant terms were among the early Christians and other cultists of the time and since.

In modern times the decline of superpersonal perspectives and more heroic interpersonalistic perspectives and the growth of a differentiated conception of what kind of deviants exist produced, temporarily, an identity vacuum. The decline produced an undersupply of morally heroic identities in terms of which disoriented social deviants might conceive themselves, attain moral purpose and bring coherence into discontinuous lives. That vacuum was not filled by the bland "steady-bloke" categories of identity offered by the social control establishment. The social control establishment had defined Actors as specific kinds of problematic persons, typically in personalistic terms, thus rendering them, by and large, unavailable for political or religious moral heroism (Halmos,

---

[20] Jackson, 1962, is a partial census of such groups.

1966:Chaps. 1–2). Rendered inert, such Actors continued to float or drift as pivotal deviants. It is in this social context that there began to form groups catering to specific categories of deviant persons. The important and ironic point is that the identity categories sponsored by self-help groups are the same as the ones sponsored by the social control establishment.

Beyond the way in which such groups have filled an identity vacuum for moral heroism, it is important to see also that what is called "deviance" has ultimately a political meaning. Persons who define themselves as pivotal deviants —the specific terms provided by the social control establishment—are thereby *unavailable for overt political activity.* Among the conditions that account for the relative stability of Western societies, one must perhaps count the neutralization provided by convincing so many otherwise politically available Actors that they have personal "problems" that have nothing to do with political process and social power. Hundreds of thousands, perhaps millions, of Actors who believe or at least fear that they are psychiatrically "sick" are not thereby strongly disposed to undertake political activity. There is a sense in which the social control establishment is "functional" to American civilization in reducing the pool of persons likely to be available for hypermoral politics. And, normal-smith self-help groups are similarly functional in draining off moral heroism from politics into proselytization for groups that look inward rather than outward to the world of politics and power. The vaguely political talk of people like O. Hobart Mowrer and the reported territorial aspirations of organizations like Synanon may yet mean, nonetheless, that the identity vacuum so filled will turn back on its progenitors and make political demands.

If this connection between deviance and the social control establishment on the one hand and politics on the other seems farfetched, consider in the same light the early and careful efforts of the U.S. Congress to ensure that the sixties' War on Poverty monies would be spent on programs embodying a personalistic perspective. Some of the early funds were, perhaps inadvertently, channeled into efforts to organize the poor politically through rent strikes and other interpersonalistic political measures. That and other programs of its kind were terminated forthwith, and the War on Poverty was never again that type of political problem.

Terminating this excursus, the central suggestion regarding cognitive congruence may be recalled and summarized. It has been said that perspectives offering some sort of moral heroism or even moral superiority and moral purpose are the most facilitative of escalation to pivotal normality. The life experience of pivotal deviance, of disorientation, of discontinuity and of shame and guilt appear to create in human beings the need for heroic identity. Heroic moral identity serves to make acceptable, explicable and even meritorious the guilt-laden, "wasted" portions of an Actor's life. Heroic identity and mission serve to redeem the Actor for what he feels to be his sinful past. It serves to render such past sins relevant and morally acceptable by convincing him that he could not be the current hero he is without having had such a sinful past. It would appear, therefore, that the social control establishment likely runs a poor second against such identity competition. The identity that its agents typically offer is bland and pallid in comparison. They specialize in proffering the category of "steady bloke." They proffer the "Nowhere Man," as John Lennon and Paul McCartney have called him, who works from eight to five in a nondescript job. For Actors who have known the excitement of pivotal deviance (let us not deceive ourselves), the horror of identity nakedness and the shame and guilt of repentance, that identity seems pale indeed. It fails to meet the special integrative and morally justifying needs of persons who have experienced drastic change. (I leave aside the question of what such an identity does to even faithful normals—the Eleanor Rigbys of the world—a question of intense concern in popular discourse and moral polemics.)

FURTHER FACILITANTS AND OTHERS

BIOGRAPHICAL INTEGRATION AND NORMAL OTHERS

The foregoing refers to Actor's personal problem of integrating his biography into a meaningful trajectory and to some means by which this integration can be accomplished. Actor's own problem of a believable and meaningful integration is, however, only half the story. The believable integration performed by normal-smith groups also has consequences for how normal and never-deviant Others will subsequently view him. A large proportion of lay and professional deviant-smiths, as well as the uninvolved public, happen *also* to believe that normal-smith groups can accomplish moral transformation of social deviants. To the degree that they do, any newly established normal identity will be supported by these Others when they are subsequently encountered (cf., unanimous imputation, pp. 225–28). Thus it can be said that normal-smiths serve not only Actor's need but the need of never-deviant normals as well, for an account which believably integrates Actor's discontinuous biography. The solid assumption of a normal identity by Actor is thereby facilitated. There is now available an acceptable account of transformation that normals can produce for themselves and for each other as justification for admitting Actor to normal places, for providing him normal hardware, for extending him cordial relations and the like.

An important aspect of all this is that endorsement by well-known normal-smith groups makes *credible* an Actor's claim to transformation. Merely individual claims of privately accomplished change carry little weight. (Cf., Ray, 1961; and pp. 210–11 of this text.) But consider the case of a nineteen-year-old male who claimed in court his conversion and renewal after listening to Billy Graham and then confessed to forty burglaries. His claim was ratified by the Graham organization and his account accepted by his father and the judges.

> The magistrates who heard Harvey confess to burglarizing forty business places were told that he had been leading the life of a criminal since he was fifteen and that his father had thrown him out of the family home because of his lawlessness.
>
> Also in the courtroom was Harvey's father, who said he had talked to the youth in his cell and now wanted the youth home.
>
> "I didn't appear to be talking to the same son," the bewildered father told the magistrates. "He has completely changed. I cannot grasp it."
> (*Detroit Free Press,* July 10, 1966.)

A part of providing conventional normal Others with a sense of Actor's being "completely changed" resides in the new vocabulary of motives, ideology and affiliation, provided by the normal-smith group, that Actor now produces. The transformation is signaled not merely by current conformity and resolutions to be normal but also by production, in the presence of conventional normals, of a *rhetoric*—a set of concepts—that is discontinuous with Actor's past. He speaks now of "salvation," "the love of Christ," "one day at a time," his "sponsor" or whatever.

And, ironically, it is in the context of normal-smith-ratified transformation that *normals* begin to distinguish between "being a deviant" and having merely "led the life of a deviant." Note that the reporter above refers to Mr. Harvey as formerly "leading the life of a criminal." Under circumstances of simple apprehension, Mr. Harvey would likely have been characterized as "being a criminal." His imputed renewal makes possible and even necessary a distinction between personal character and style of life. If previous style of life continued to define personal character, the claims of Mr. Harvey and the Graham organization could not be honored. Nonetheless, the practice of imputing personal character continues. The newly normal Actor is now imputed by normals to have the sort of personal character that made it possible for him to reform.

To repeat, it is normal-smith groups that perform the operations that make it easier for conventional normals to honor claims of reformed personal character and to view biography as credibly integrated. The reader can, again, contrast this with operations performed by the social control establishment. This contribution does not, however, exhaust the facilitating work of normal-smith Others. We turn now to consideration of two further services which they render in the task of escalating deviant Actors to normal personal identities.

ARTICULATE, COMPREHENSIVE IDEOLOGY

FORESTALLING DOUBT

A belief system or ideology that is successful, in the sense of having few defectors and of avoiding existential crises among its adherents, is one in which fundamental questions of meaning do not arise. They do not, because of the system's capacities to forestall them among both adherents and identity fledglings. By avoiding fundamental questionings, I mean that the following class of topics does not become anguishingly problematic:

> What shall I do?
> What may I hope?
> What can I know?
> What *is* man?[21]

This is not to say that such questions may not be asked, but that, when asked, the ideology provides relatively complex and comprehensive answers that have rather direct implications for practical everyday action. Comprehensiveness of ideology is most easily identified in systems of meaning that we conventionally identify as "religious," especially those seen as being Christian "fundamentalist." But we see something of the same features in the ideologies of self-help groups, where, in the oldest and more articulated, Alcoholics Anonymous, one encounters the claim that an answer to any question can be found in the AA "Bible"—"the big book."

It is the task of all functioning systems of social life to field social actors who do not become problematically aware of or "bogged down" in topics of existential concern. This is a difficult and treacherous task, for any set of answers to the "fundamental" questions has a fragile character. In an era of known and competing sets of ideologies, and because of the fundamental features of the human condition itself, any set of answers can rather easily be confounded. In mentioning the "fundamental features of the human condition itself," I introduce a postulate hitherto assumed but which must now be made explicit. Human identities and human meanings are arbitrary constructs imposed upon a reality that is essentially without meaning. As such, all systems of meaning, of human reality, are continuously subject to breakdown and rupture. Beyond or behind the social fictions, on the basis of which humans order their social world, lie the chaos and anguish of confronting infinity.[22] It is in moments of con-

---

[21] E. Becker, 1964:9–35.

[22] The sociological implications of taking seriously such a postulate are most explicitly developed in Berger, 1961, 1963, 1966 and 1967; Berger and Luckmann, 1966; E. Becker, 1962 and 1964. Such implications are, of course, implicit in other works and traditions.

fronting the anguish and chaos of infinity—of an essentially meaningless world
—that human beings can come to ask themselves: What shall I do? What may
I hope? What can I know? What is man?

POWERFUL PRINCIPLES

One of the most important features of facilitative comprehensiveness is the
existence of a set of principles, deduced from the overall grandiose ideology,
that are at once simple, complex and powerful in the practical matter of managing the moment-to-moment events of everyday life. In AA, considerable mileage is apparently gained from such widely applicable everyday dictums as:
"Easy Does It," "Live and Let Live," "First Things First," "There But for the
Grace of God Go I," and "God grant me the serenity to accept the things I cannot change, the courage to change the things I can, and the wisdom to know
the difference." These dictums are derived from a relatively elaborate and
formally stated (i.e., written down) set of principles. And these latter are given
frequent expression in the formally organized ritual expression of the belief
system called the AA meeting.

It can be tentatively suggested that we do not find so clearly these features of
articulate and complex comprehensiveness in many ideologies associated with
the more mundane varieties of normal identities. The variety of normal identity summed up in the concept of the "steady bloke" or the "working stiff" or
the "everyday guy" lacks much articulate coherence and ideologized guide to
practical action. Yet it is this sort of identity that agents of the social control
establishment would impute to deviants who are to be made normal.

IDEOLOGY AND AFFECTIVE BONDS

These points about comprehensive and articulate ideology do not gainsay
the even more fundamental role of affective bonds to other espousers as the
first line of offense in generating beliefs and as the first line of defense against
the precipitation of doubt and eventual disbelief or defection. The matter of
the comprehensiveness and articulate character of ideology is perhaps best
viewed as a secondary feature that operates within the constraints or possibilities already set up by the character of the affective bonds within which Actor is
enmeshed. There may even come to be a struggle between what are seen as
cognitive gaps or lapses in the ideology and Actor's high positive regard for the
Others who espouse it. Actor's subsequent direction is a function of the severity of the cognitive gap or lapse in the world view and the strength of his
emotional ties to these Others who believe in it. (Cf., J. Lofland, 1966:50–57.)
The most highly facilitative circumstance is, of course, the one in which cognitive gaps or lapses do not occur and affective bonds to Others are very strong.

It is in the context of the ways in which articulated and comprehensive ideologies and affective bonds can vary that one can appreciate the facilitative

importance of intensive and quick teaching of the ideology and its practical application to the identity fledgling. Identity categories—primarily normal-smith groups—which have *de facto* or formally intended arrangements for *tutoring* the identity fledgling in his new and tentative view of the world and of himself would appear to be most potent in escalation. In addition, the tutoring (or small group) circumstance heightens possibilities for diffuse interaction and affective bonds.

Technical Knowledge and Skills

I have spoken of the imputation of pivotal normality by Others in the context of an integrated round of normal places where deviant hardware is withdrawn and normal hardware is supplied to an Actor who has undergone disorientation, projected affective bonds and learned from Others a comprehensive and articulate ideology associated with a category of normality. At least one additional element must be "built in" in order most strongly to facilitate the fielding of a pivotal normal—of an Actor who will be enduringly normal and who will reliably play his part in acceptable social games. Tutoring in a comprehensive and articulate ideology and practice in the role management strategies associated with the ideology of the normal identity may provide a sufficient repertoire of *social* skills in managing the events of everyday life. But such efforts do not necessarily ensure that Actor will acquire sufficient *technical* skills, in the sense of the knowledge of, and practice in, matters necessary to earn some kind of stable and living wage.

Massive imputation, enormously strong affective bonds and all the rest mean little if it is not also possible to translate a new and pivotally normal self into system payoffs. One requirement for acquiring such payoffs is the possession of occupationally relevant technical skills. While some former pivotal deviants might already have acquired such skills (e.g., some alcoholics once held good jobs), many have not. For those who have not, Others must undertake to provide the requisite tutoring.

Making normality worth it

Actor's identification of himself as a pivotal normal and the durability of that identification are thus facilitated by the provision of technical skills by means of which a normal self can literally be "worth more" than a deviant self. Hollywood movies notwithstanding, whether or not "crime pays" is very much a matter of where one is situated in the social system. For those who are advantageously placed in the social order and encumbered by well-paying jobs, homes, cars and families, most sorts of deviance are unlikely to be profitable. Unsurprisingly, it is these "privileged" who like most frequently to remind us that "crime does not pay." While that slogan may be more or less true for people like them, it is not at all clearly true for those who have little. Those with little thereby have little to lose and much to gain through pivotal deviance. For pivotal normality to be worth the bother (and it can, after all, get to be something of a drag), it is most facilitative for it to be "worth it" not only in the sense of the moral heroism that some can derive but in dollars-and-cents terms as well. And since dollars-and-cents terms are so highly associated with imputed moral worth and respect *among normals*, pivotal normality is also made "worth it" in terms of the sense of dignity that *can* be derived from occupational enmeshment.

NORMALS LIKEWISE BOUGHT OFF

It needs to be said more generally that one of the fundamental tasks of a social order is to "buy off" all its participants, not just those who are defined as pivotally deviant and whom at least some Others desire to make pivotally normal. It is the job of a social order, if it is to be stable, to *compromise* any countercommitments or tendencies among its participants. It does this by burdening them with prestige, possessions and power to which they become attached and which give them something to lose if they engage in significant deviance. It is the compromising entanglements of prestige, possessions and power that serve to keep people more or less in line. The empirical association between these and economic and political conservatism is an association between compromising entanglements in the social order and being bought off by that order. Prestige, possessions and power are the foundations upon which rest both the famous sense of "responsibility" that more advantaged persons sponsor and their likewise famous sense of "respect for law and order."

To suggest, then, that former pivotal deviants must be bought off and that normality must be made worth it is not to suggest anything peculiar. It is only to say that those Actors defined as deviant must be treated (if they are to become pivotal normals) pretty much like normals are treated (relative, here, to matters of dollars and cents, but also more generally). The fact that many normals sell themselves—that is, their identity and their conformity—to the prevailing social order for rather low prices and in disadvantageous terms is only indicative of a less-than-acute sense of bargaining. The fact that some pivotal deviants, in contrast, demand rather high prices as the terms of their selling out indicates a rather acute sense of the cost of pivotal normality and compensations proper to its assumption.

These remarks on the facilitative significance of providing occupational skills should not be interpreted as in themselves an endorsement of existing conceptions of "vocational education," "technical training programs" or other efforts at occupational training, such as even promoting formerly deviant Actors into medical or law schools. The promoters of such existing efforts and enterprises have tended to take a rather narrow view of their mission, in the sense that the inculcation of technical skill per se has been central to the operating definition of their task. A broader view would argue that the inculcation of technical skill is most facilitative when performed in the context of all the heretofore enumerated elements. The rather important extent to which occupational training programs have not met the expectations that their advocates have had of them may be best accounted for through an examination of the character of these programs in their "extratechnical" aspects, aspects such as those I have tried to explicate.

DEVIANTS MAY BE CHEAPER

In order ultimately to be facilitative, whatever technical skills are provided must be ones for which there exists a demand in the social order. To be trained and unemployable is hardly better than to be untrained and unemployable. Despite the acute shortages of trained personnel in some sectors of the economy and in some occupations, the larger fact seems to be that there are more bodies in American civilization than are needed to man its economic system. Unless there is a large change in conceptions of what it is worth paying people to do, as automation increases, the gap between population size and employment capacity of the economy is likely to grow larger. The consequences and responses to such a development are impossible to foresee, but it may ultimately be decided that provision of technical skills and useful employment for would-be former deviants merely increases the job competition and adds to the already surplus normal population on the labor market. In such an event it will perhaps be seen as cheaper, in a variety of ways, simply to maintain Actors as pivotal deviants rather than to flood an already glutted society with yet more normals.

CONCLUDING REMARKS ON THE ASSUMPTION OF NORMAL IDENTITY

In concluding, it should be reiterated that this exposition has been directed primarily to the question of facilitating the assumption of normal identity among Actors who are *social deviants*. More attenuated and less intensive circumstances may well suffice in order to tinker with the identities of the variety of Actors who are only marginally deviant, e.g., Actors with ambivalent or low attachment to their deviant selves or Actors who are never defined as deviant by more than a few and tenuously significant Others. But to the degree that social deviants are involved, conjoint activation of the foregoing elements seems most facilitative.

That there are few such facilitative efforts within the social control establishment reflect, I think, some almost inevitable consequences of its bureaucratization and formalization of the identity change business. Rationalization of activity (in the Weberian sense) has narrowed the range of what its staff and its house scholars can contemplate as the fundamental elements of people change. They come to think in terms of what is feasible, real and possible only within a world of formal and bureaucratic organizations. As a result, they evolve highly elaborate theories and programs that are addressed to a quite limited range of "independent variables." Namely, they come to think only, or mostly, in terms of "independent variables" that can be "programmed" or manipulated by means of formal organizations. They think in terms of civil service jobs for which specifications and requirements can be written and to which bodies can be recruited. Out of this focus on what can be readily set up in an organization for which there exists a labor pool from which to draw a "staff," one gets, I think, a more accurate expression of the kinds of formal organizations and staffing that are possible than of what is required to make deviants normal. We must, in fact, leave open the possibility that formalized and bureaucratic apparatus as typically construed and constrained may be incompatible with identifying and escalating deviant Actors to a variety of normal identity.

As is obvious, I have here attempted to take a broader view than that imposed by the practicalities of state planning.[23]

Bracketing the substance of Part III within a broader historical context, it is possibly the case that Western civilization is moving toward the kind of social order in which the technical requirements of identity transformation will be created with progressively decreasing frequency. According to sociohistorical analyses such as those performed by Philip Rieff, the historical drift may be away from "transformative experiences" and "therapies of commitment" and toward "informative experiences" and "analytic therapy" (Rieff, 1966:especially Chaps. 3 and 8). To the degree that there is actually occurring a "triumph of the therapeutic," as Rieff terms it, one should expect to see decreasing rates of return from pivotal deviance.

A last observation: Once an Actor has identified himself as a variety of normal, what then? The answer seems to be for ex-deviants as it is for everyone else: more of the same. More of the same, except, of course, disorientation and facilitative exposure to yet a different category of identity. Ex-deviants, and human beings generally, get to be "normal" (or deviant) and remain what they are because their lives are arranged to maximize consistency, intensity and duration of united imputations in the midst of appropriate place rounds and hardware which are supported by ideology and affective bonds. This is at least one sense in which Actors of all *social* sorts are, in the final analysis, of the same *human* sort.

[23] See also Frank, 1961; Kiev, ed., 1964; Sarbin, 1964; Halmos, 1966; Lifton, 1963:Part IV; Studt, Messinger and Wilson, 1968.

CHAPTER 12

CONCLUDING REMARKS

I should like to conclude with a series of remarks which do not summarize what has been said but, rather, elaborate latent themes or explicate logical implications. These remarks relate, on the one hand, to theory and method in the study of deviance and, on the other, to paradoxes and ironies implicit in the study of deviance and social life.

THEORY, METHOD AND DEVIANCE

EMPHASIS IN THE EXPLANATION OF ACTION

The analysis offered here is an instance of a more general approach to sociology and social science. It may be considered an instance of a *situational* or interactionist emphasis or approach. As an aid to the reader in assessing the present work, three features which *conjointly* specify this approach will be stated and contrasted with features of other emphases.

First, a situational emphasis tends to employ a processual rather than a static model of causation. A processual model of causation focuses upon successions of dependencies through time; upon ways in which prior conditions may or may not develop into succeeding conditions of a given outcome or may or may not culminate or eventuate in a given outcome. Attention is focused upon ways in which alternatives may or may not be present; upon ways in which, and the degree to which, action may be constrained. Particular attention is given to the cumulation of factors—each factor being a condition of an outcome but not sufficient for it; each factor making an outcome merely possible or more probable but not yet determined. In contrast, a static model of causation tends to assume that "causes" operate more or less simultaneously, or at least that temporal occurrence or activation of causes is of relatively little importance. A static model leads easily to static statistical profiles of the "characteristics" associated with an outcome. Or, more particularly, it may lead to profiling the characteristics of "types of persons," such as Republicans, murderers or juvenile delinquents.[1]

Second, a situational emphasis tends to take the phenomenology of the actor rather seriously and to be concerned with discovering and depicting it in its own terms. There is openness to the possibility that at least a part of the "reasons" for action have to do with what actor says they have to do with. Within a situational emphasis, *not* to be so concerned is:

---

[1] See further H. S. Becker, 1963:Chap. 2, on simultaneous and sequential models, and Chap. 3; Cressey, 1953; Lemert, 1951:75 and 1953 and 1962; Turner, 1953. On the *logic* of "value added" models see also, Smelser, 1963:12–21, 1959:29–32, 60–62, 138–39.

to risk the worst kind of subjectivism—the . . . observer is likely to fill in the process of interpretation with his own surmises in place of catching the process as it occurs in the experience of the acting unit which uses it.[2]

In contrast, a variety of other emphases tend to minimize the import of the actor's own account of himself, of his perspective and of his verbalized reasons for acting the way he does or did. There is a tendency to view actor's phenomenology as epiphenomenal, as masking the "real" or "in fact" or "actual" reasons for conduct. This may take the form of ignoring actors' accounts altogether, as in research focusing on correlations among social categories. Or, it may take the form of "standing close" to actors and eliciting their phenomenologies but discounting their own terms in the search for "deeper meanings," as in psychoanalytic accounts.

Third, a situational emphasis tends to highlight processual and phenomenological explanatory variables whose operation is relatively proximate to that for which an account is being given. Proximate variables evoke the character and consequences of current and relatively immediate interaction situations. Attention is directed to deciphering the channeling effects of ongoing, face-to-face interaction systems in spatiotemporally bounded contexts. The compel - ling reality of the immediate and its imperatives for action are highlighted. In the words of one situationalist: ". . . The behavior of a person depends above all upon his momentary position. Often the world looks very different before and after an event which changes the region in which a person is located."[3] In contrast, other emphases tend to focus upon variables that are spatiotemporally and conceptually remote. Thus, for example, the slaying of a man by a friend during a barroom altercation may be explained by prime reference to a tradition (or "culture") of violence in American civilization. Such a variable has the character of being widely diffused in space and time and being removed many levels of conceptual abstraction from the barroom and its internal events. Explanatory variables, such as socioeconomic conditions in that city, occupational opportunities, relations among ethnic groups, etc., are likewise spatially and conceptually remote from the event. The conceptualization of long-past events in the biographies of the participants as prime operative determinants is a similar evocation of remote—in this case, temporally remote—explanatory units. Viewed more generally, the focus on remote variables tends to sponsor an imagery of fixed or long-past characteristics of actors or looming and massive features of their settings (i.e., features of a city or an entire culture) as immediately operative features that reasonably account for action.

Taken *together*, then, *processual, phenomenological* and *proximate* explanatory units might be said to constitute some important features of a situational or interactionist approach to the explanation of action. Of course, such an ap-

---

[2] Blumer, 1962:188. See also Blau and Scott, 1962:81–83; and, more generally, Blumer, 1956 and 1966.

[3] Lewin, 1951:137, quoted in Briar and Piliavin, 1965:37.

proach has its limitations, which are precisely the strengths of the other approaches and vice versa.

Despite this conciliatory complementarity, it should also be mentioned that, when viewed from within more general and philosophic perspectives, the situ-ational approach tends to move in a different moral direction from that of its alternatives. It embodies a rather different conception than they of the kind of objects that humans are and can be.[4]

SPECIAL THEORY AND DEVIANCE

While deviance has been the concrete phenomenological substance of this volume, it should be made clear that the concepts, social processes and propo-sitions explicated herein are not unique to deviance. Discussions and analyses of such matters as the social act, social and personal identities, identity assump-tion, processes of social identification, escalating interaction processes, arrange-ments of others around an actor, types of place rounds, etc., are applicable far beyond the narrow confines of the sociology of deviance. The foregoing is a perspective on deviance or a "theory" of deviance *only* in the sense that the empirical materials used to illustrate the analytic themes have had to do with various kinds of deviance. The present synthesizing effort is *not* a theory of deviance in the sense of being a special body of theory applicable only (or most pertinently) to it. While a few of the concepts, processes and propositions may be uniquely relevant to the study of deviance, the perspective here explicated seems useful as well in the analysis of social acts and of identity assumption (or maintenance) more generally.

DEVIANCE AND SOCIAL ORGANIZATIONAL THEORY

The foregoing has been rather massively psychosociological in the sense that I have conceived the world from the point of view of a few selected categories of actors. I hope, however, that I have done so in such a way that the analytic emphasis here pursued is easily linked to the more social systemic pursuits of such areas as organizational and societal analysis.

---

[4] For discussion, see Jean Paul Sartre's explication of the contrast between what might be called the "essentialist" and "existentialist" conception of humans. (Sartre, 1956.) Further, a situational emphasis must be kept separate from any retreat from premises of scientific positivism. A situational emphasis does *not*, by its logic, constitute such a retreat, although some of its practitioners have apparently felt that it does. For an analysis in which a situ-ational emphasis apparently is taken to imply attenuated positivism, "soft determinism" and an element of something similar to free will, see Matza, 1964: especially Chaps. 1, 2 and 6. See also Bruyn, 1966.

The study of organizations per se constitutes the next level or layer of variables within which are nested or contained many of the kinds of processes which have been of central focus in the present work.   It is possible, for example, to focus on a prison, a police department, a social work agency, etc., as an *organization*—as a consciously conceived, formally conducted instrumentality —in terms relevant to the type of themes here pursued at more microscopic levels.   What I have here taken to be independent variables become, within the perspective of organizational analysis, dependent variables.   Attention is turned to factors at the organizational level upon which the development of each of these depends.   In the foregoing I have provided only some rather limited illustrations of a few of these possible connections.

Beyond organizations and at the level of interorganizational analysis, one enters the areas of the sociology of politics, of collective behavior and social movements, of population movements and the like.   That is, one enters the level of analysis of the contending components of a society as a unit.

I have spoken here of relatively intimate, microscopic, face-to-face processes. But such processes do not exist in a vacuum.   They are, rather, very much a function of the successive layers of social organizational processes within which they are nested.   The properties and directions of microprocesses are only the endpoints of a long chain of connections that extend outward in space and time and upward in level of analytic unit, ultimately involving the entire history and organization of the cosmos.   Put more plainly and familiarly, everything is related to everything else.

It is equally true that the postulate that "everything is related to everything else" is not a very useful one.   If analysis is actually to be accomplished, effort must be delimited and specialized.   But such specialization is most usefully performed with the recognition that there do exist interconnections which must ultimately be explicated.   It is my hope that the present specialized and delimited effort is of a character such that others can more easily trace those connections—especially the connections between the processes focused upon in the present work and the intraorganizational and interorganizational processes within which they are nested.

METHOD, DATA AND
DEVIANCE

While available empirical materials appear consistent with the conceptual apparatus here constructed, I have moved somewhat beyond available material to chart out what is logically implied from what is already known.   Such projection of the logical implications of extant concepts and data seems necessary because of the inherent methodological difficulties involved in (1) the study of the analytic processes addressed, and in (2) the particular character of the materials of deviance.

Relative to the analytic processes at issue, we are here dealing with rather fundamental variables and with changes in them that involve almost the full range of their possible variance. That is, the reconstitution of an identity is a rather fundamental matter, and it involves the inducement of rather massive changes. Aside from moral prohibitions—and there are, of course, strong moral taboos against such undertakings—it is clear that the time and effort required to manipulate the relevant component variables have not encouraged social scientists to undertake the necessary experimental manipulations.

Be that as it may, there are, additionally, difficulties involved in the very character of the empirical materials classified under the topic of deviance. Deviance, by definition, is disapproved, and it therefore occurs in secret or at least is carried on in a very circumspect manner. Moreover, the study of episodic or isolated deviant acts is seriously hampered by their unpredictability. How, for example, would one arrange to study interaction scenes of homicide? There is little doubt that sound and film records of the interaction in the hours before the occurrence of acts of assault, rape, robbery, embezzlement or homicide would be of enormous value in understanding the constraining character of immediate space-time-bound locales. But it is less than clear how one is to know where and when to be in order to make such observations. Even if the "who, where and when" were foreknown, it is less than clear how one would arrange to be present without changing the entire situation and conducing some different outcome. And, of course, there are further issues of morality involved in such close research. (See, e.g., Shils, 1959; Erikson, 1967.)

Because of all these difficulties, then, if they are to talk about deviance at all, scholars must often "make do" with less than the fullest, most precise and most systematically assembled data. Indeed, some are inclined to the stance that, since they do not have the best materials, they should say nothing at all. Given the rather bizarre theories (and the unrepresentative facts used to support them) that are spawned in a situation of imprecise, partial and unsystematic data, I am highly sympathetic with this kind of agnostic pleading. I think, however, that such purity of methodological conscience is too costly. I think so for two reasons. First, one must face the fact that, regardless of any agnostic stance and of concern for methodological purity, laymen, specialists in the practical management of "deviants" and a variety of pseudoscientific types are going to talk about these materials anyway. To remain silent is to abandon these matters to precisely those persons who are least likely to talk about them in a reasonably dispassionate manner. It is to abandon them to persons who are likely to have the least regard for standards of evidence and who are most involved in defending and promoting some enterprise directly engaged with deviance. Second, although available materials very infrequently meet the highest standards, this does not mean that, when taken together, they add up to no knowledge at all. It does not mean that they cannot be legitimately collated into a generalized and testable framework of concepts and propositions.

It is in the light of such considerations (and others) that I have thought it reasonable (despite current data difficulties) to undertake the present work. The reader will have noted that, as mentioned at the outset, the character and quality of the material I have utilized vary widely. While much of it is drawn from reliably performed social scientific studies, a significant proportion comes from newspapers, autobiographies, general reflections and the like. But in view of the matters just discussed, this situation is currently unavoidable. As long as the aforementioned methodological difficulties and moral prohibitions exist, our knowledge will remain highly partial.

Indeed, the moral implications of the methodological requirements of full, precise, systematic knowledge of deviance convince me that the moral price we would have to pay for full knowledge is much higher than the value of that knowledge. I, for one, would not be willing to condone—in fact, would actively oppose—the initiation of a series of precise experimental manipulations aimed at sorting out the exact effects of the various factors involved in the reconstitution of personal identity. Nor could I countenance the invasion of privacy that would be required for the natural-setting study of homicide, embezzlement or other deviant acts. The "research" activities of Nazi Germany taught us (or should have) very well that there are definite moral limits on what can be done in the name of science. In matters as fundamental as identity change and deviance, we must, as moral men who happen also to be social scientists, make what we can of the variations that occur in the natural world and that we can discover without undue invasions of privacy. We must hold in check our impulse to implement our research technology in ways that violate our beliefs about the essential dignity and inviolate character of human beings. And too, a variety of episodes in the 20th century occurring under totalitarian (and not so totalitarian) regimes have made quite clear the untenable character of arguments which justify some present condition of human debasement, degradation, suffering and even death for the sake of "enormous" benefits that will accrue to future generations—whether these benefits are to derive from knowledge gained or from something else. Ironically, of course, some such claims of future good based on present evil are probably true. But their truth or falsity is quite beside the point. The point is, rather, that, with few exceptions (as perhaps when the future ends are quite concrete and immediate and as when the present suffering is voluntarily undertaken), the sacrifice of human beings for laudable ends is not morally acceptable.

PARADOX, DEVIANCE AND IDENTITY

The questions addressed in this study and the perspective employed in dealing with them contain a large number of implicit moral paradoxes or ironies. In closing, I should like to mention a few of these.

CREATION, CONTROL AND
FUNCTIONS

Efforts to define and control problematic behavior can *create* persons who define themselves as one or another sort of deviant. Certain strengths of some combinations of elements that can produce this effect were explicated in Part II. Having so defined themselves, it thus becomes possible for such persons to sustain a commitment to a conception of deviant character and thus to increase the frequency with which they perform deviant acts.

That this is a possible and highlighted consequence of the way in which processes of social control can sometimes operate should not detract attention from another and perhaps more typical outcome. Insofar as Actor experiences punishment, and insofar as he does so under highly attenuated strengths of the elements sketched, the exercise of control likely functions as a *deterrent* to deviance. It does so through the instillation of fear of punishment itself and/or through the instillation of fear of the self-defining implications of any subsequent involvement with formal or informal agents who might apply punishment. (See, e.g., Cameron, 1964:159–70; Chambliss, 1967b.) The fact that the exercise of control can produce a more or less stable set of permanent deviants should not obscure the likely larger and more important fact that the routine application of punishment can "keep in line" or "put back in line" a very large proportion of the population. Without rules and punishment, social order simply could not be maintained.

From a moral or policy standpoint, then, the question is hardly one of exercising or not exercising control and punishment. Rather, the question is one of the desirability or feasibility of exercising the larger punishment and deterrent function without at the same time creating a pool of permanent deviants. Ironically, it is not at all clear whether a society can effectively perform the former without also accomplishing the latter. Indeed, while a pool of more or less permanent deviants may be a consequence of the exercise of control, it may also be true that such a pool is socially "necessary." It may serve functions that are rather independent of the control processes that brought it into being.

Without a conception of deviant types of persons (and, therefore, without the existence of "deviants"), how effectively might the boundaries be drawn between the "good life" and the "bad life"? How effectively might the limits of acceptable behavior be dramatized and communicated without a continuing supply of "degenerate" sorts who personify all that which is to be avoided? Without a conception of deviant types of persons (and, therefore, without the existence of "deviants"), how effectively might a population discharge the inevitable residue of hostility and frustration arising out of socialization and out of everyday life? Deviant persons provide convenient objects for the venting of hostility in the classic scapegoat manner and, at the same time, make possible the affirmation of the normality of the prosecutors. As Coser observes, "It is against the ground of their deviance that the righteous achieve the comforting affirmation of their normality. Inasmuch as 'our' innocence is contingent upon 'their' guilt, dereliction by others provides occasion for self-congratulations."[5] Without a conception of deviant types of persons (and, therefore, without the existence of deviants), how effectively might a sense of solidarity—of common moral community—be sustained? How effectively might the otherwise-conflicting cleavages of class, religion, sex, age, race, occupation and the like be overridden? The very existence of deviant types provides a common enemy against which otherwise-conflicting groups can unite—a function served also by the existence of chronic international conflict, especially war.

If defining persons as deviant serves such functions more effectively than does simply railing against *acts*, then we need not be surprised by a massive lack of interest in transforming "deviant types" into normals. The meager support, despite lip service, given to normal-smith enterprises may be appropriately equilibrated to the social necessity of deviants. Unless equivalent means of meeting the functions they serve are developed, one should perhaps not expect to see any considerable change in the belief in the existence of, and therefore in the existence of, deviant persons.

THE SOCIAL AND HUMAN PERSPECTIVES

From the distance achieved by bracketing and making problematic the varying ways in which human beings categorize and construct themselves, one is struck by a sense of the arbitrary, contrived and fictive character of it all. Observation of the stripping and simplification which occur in the process of categorizing and constructing, and of the injustice that is a necessary concomitant of this process, can produce, from such a distance, a sense of how simultaneously comic and tragic, pathetic and heroic is the social construction of "society." When so viewed, the social order takes on an aura of phoniness. It begins to appear like a gigantic version of the classic confidence game. There we are, each of us, busily conning ourselves, and even more busily conning others, about our respective social characters.

Viewing the social order from such a distance, one is struck by the irony implicit in the realization that it can be no other way. One is struck by the irony implicit in the realization that the primordial and prime directives of any social order—getting enough to eat, constructing shelter and perpetuating the species—make necessary a division of labor; and a division of labor makes necessary a division into social categories. All that follows from such division,

[5] Coser, 1962:174. See also, on the functions of deviance, Durkheim, 1950:64–75 (first published 1895); Mead, 1928; Kluckhohn, 1967:Part II (first published 1944); Dentler and Erikson, 1959; Erikson, 1962 and 1966; Lofland and Lofland, 1968.

especially the necessity to exercise control and punishment, follows naturally. Perhaps the fullest thrust of the irony is achieved when one additionally appreciates that historical and continuing attempts to surmount such divisions in the name of humanity, brotherly love or the welfare of all seem mostly to succeed in creating yet-newer bases of division and conflict.[6]

Social categorization and its social psychological concomitants would appear, then, to be in the nature of necessary evils. But efforts to transcend any given set of them are, perhaps, equally necessary. It may be that the perspective of the social—of social categorization and control—is destined always to be in a continuing dialectic with the perspective of the human; the latter always maintaining that, despite all socially constructed and managed differences, we are all, ultimately, only human. From the human perspective, the fact of common humanity is enormously more important in determining the sort of treatment we ought to accord one another than is the fact of the convenience which social categories provide in coping with our various proximate problems. This is true whether the problem is operating an economic enterprise, waging a war or managing persons guilty of deviance.

The perspective of the human is idealistic and visionary and inconvenient. Against it, in taking the social perspective, we organize ourselves to cope with demanding "realities" and we attune ourselves to the practical and the pragmatic. Yet, without the existence of the human perspective—inconvenient and impractical as it may be—the social order might be even more the con game, more fictive, more unjust, than is now the case.

PERSONAL IDENTITY AND SOCIAL DISTRUST

It is in the context of this dialectic between the social and human perspectives that one can best appreciate another irony: the apparently supportive relation between one's feeling of distrust toward, and moral superiority over, others and one's stable personal identity.

Humans tend to imbue their respective social locations with an aura of moral correctness and to view other social locations as less than morally proper. The married tend to look down on the unmarried; the unmarried tend to look down on the married. Domestic women tend to look down on career women; career women tend to look down on domestic women. Social deviants tend to look down on conventionals; conventionals tend to look down on social deviants. Intellectuals tend to look down on nonintellectuals; nonintellectuals tend to look down on intellectuals. And so on and on throughout social life.

Such feelings appear to have a socially stabilizing consequence in those complex societies heavily based on an achievement ethic and on a belief in personal

[6] E.g., the divisions and conflict flowing from the humanitarianism of Christianity, Communism, hippydom and youthful radicalism.

responsibility for "what one is." For a human to be sympathetic toward and
accepting of others who wear different identities (especially different achieved
identities) is to open himself to the possibility of taking up those identities.
Because change of identity may not be feasible (and may be highly disruptive
to standing arrangements), such sympathy opens humans to frustration. Alternatively, a belief in the moral superiority of what one is, is highly protective of
a sense of the validity of one's own identity. People who are too sympathetic
toward doctors are too likely to want to be doctors. Too much kindly feeling
toward doctors could produce too many actual doctors or too many frustrated
would-be doctors.[7] If there were a high level of kindly feeling toward identities other than their own, humans would be very changing entities, indeed.
They would constantly desire to become the latest thing toward which they
feel most kindly; they would constantly be torn between a variety of things
toward which they feel affection; or, simply, they would be frustrated much of
the time because of the practical obstacles to easy identity change.[8] Distrust
and suspicion toward others and a conviction of one's own moral superiority
help to solidify the social order by helping to keep people where they are.
(Such consequences must not, of course, be construed as causes. Nor should
an "is" be confused with an "ought.")

Moreover, differences in identity often represent differences in their possessors' wealth, power and degree of discretion in the organization of their days
and lives. Ideologies of social location help to accommodate occupants to their
location's disadvantages and constrictions. The claim of moral superiority contained within these ideologies serves to minimize occupants' perceptions of the
limitations of their locations and to exaggerate their perceptions of the benefits.
To become sympathetic with another identity, especially one that is less disadvantaged and less personally limiting than one's own, is more easily to lose
one's hold upon the identity-ideology that keeps one where one is.[9]

Suspicion, distrust, a conviction of moral superiority, dislike, distaste and
tut-tutting are, conveniently (and not unreasonably), major themes of interaction *between* wearers of different identities and major points of consensus
among wearers of the same identity. Identity stability (and, hence, social stability) in complex, achievement-oriented societies appears, then, to be supported by a modicum of hate. The "downs" are kept more satisfied with being
down, and the "ups" are kept more self-righteously justified in being up by a
reciprocal display of hate, or, at least, by a reciprocated belief that each is in
some ways crucially defective.

---

[7] On popular distrust of and hostility toward medical doctors and other occupations, see
Gamson and Schuman, 1963; and more generally, pp. 13–23, above.

[8] Except, of course, where one identity is defined as inferior to another *and* humans in
the inferior identity are defined as live candidates for the superior identity such as obtains
between parents and children, between journeymen and apprentices of all kinds and between normal-smiths and social deviants (pp. 266–71, above).

[9] The more advantaged identity toward which a person feels kindly will, of course, likely
have its own set of disadvantages and limitations relative to yet still other identities.

Further, liking and sympathy despite identity difference seem most typically to occur only when one social category takes on the world view of another category. Professors of education are viewed sympathetically by public school teachers when they have taken on the identity-ideology of public school teachers. Fondness is generated on the basis of their efforts to articulate and reinforce the identity-ideology of public school teachers. Professors of other subjects who feel kindly toward businessmen, federal officials or social welfare professionals tend to do so on the basis of having taken on the identity-ideologies of these social categories. In contrast, contacts among all these identities which are less empathetic tend to be so because each does not surrender to the others' view of their respective social locations and to their respective identity-serving view of the world.

Kindly feeling across identities seems typically to occur in American civilization, then, when humans in one category come to take on the standards, desires and objective interests of some other category; when one party surrenders the objective interests and standards of his own social location. (Cf. that famous figure, "Uncle Tom.") While Marx assumed that such surrender or "false consciousness," always meant exploitation (and often it does), it is also clear that humans can sometimes gain more than they lose in such exchanges, whether these exchanges be "up" or "down" in the identity scheme of things.

It might be said, therefore and in general, that while love makes American civilization "go round," it is hate that seems importantly to keep it straight.[10] And, in the context of deviance, normality is importantly supported by hate toward social deviants; social deviance is importantly supported by hate toward normals.

IDENTITY AND THE
"TRUE SELF"

There are yet other ironies, requiring less distance for their appreciation. Some humans, whether designated "humanist" or "hippy" or whatever, seem to believe that to know oneself or others in terms of social categories is, in some sense, not "really" or "fully" to know oneself or others at all. While this may be true, it seems also to be true that the only way there can be anything "there" for oneself or others to know is through definition in terms of these self-same categories. For, at the same time that social categories limit a sense of "fully knowing," they seem also to be the only way in which one can achieve any sense of "knowing" in the first place. The frustration in knowing oneself or others which is generated by the constriction of social categories can itself arise only through employing social categories. They make possible an initial

[10] Some of the many ways in which love makes the world "go round"—or, more accurately, can be disruptive of a standing social order—are explored in Goode, 1959.

sense of "knowing" that makes possible a subsequent sense of being thwarted in "truly knowing."

Further, the report by humans that they have succeeded in "truly knowing" themselves or others would suggest that they have succeeded only in casting themselves or others into one of the variants of the social category "real person." The term used will vary, depending on whether it is embedded in some category of social organization (e.g., Synanonist or "free men") or adopted apart from organized and named true-self enterprises. In either event, the selves so "revealed" or "discovered" or "truly known" are merely instances of social categories within which people believe it possible to be truly known or truly to know. All selves are social performances. Moreover, the revealed "true," and therefore "unique," self is the furthest extreme from anything unique. Rather, the most common of things is revealed: the fact of common humanity.

———————

These kinds of paradoxical mischief created by social categories are, then, among the mischievous ironies implicit in the study of deviant identities and identities more generally. While it is sometimes difficult to live with such ironies, it is also difficult to see how humans could live without both social categories and the mischief they create.

Nonetheless, and again, these and many other cruel paradoxes do not vitiate a strong and continuing need for exercise of the human perspective. Whether it be called the precarious vision, the sociological imagination, the quest for human unity[11] or the human perspective, a view of social categories (and therefore of "society") as a human-made fiction that must continuously be transcended seems ultimately the best route to more just and authentic social orders.[12]

[11] Berger, 1961; Mills, 1959; Gouldner, 1968:116, respectively. See also E. Becker, 1968; Halmos, 1966:164–75.
[12] Such a view has been translated into programmatic possibility by Etzioni (1968a). See in particular, and within the context of the entire book, Chap. 20, especially 604–8, and Chap. 21, especially 647–55.

Italicized numbers following each entry
identify the pages of this text on which the
reference is cited.

BIBLIOGRAPHIC
INDEX

ABELES, H., M. LEWIN AND W. MANDELL,
*Interim Progress Report: Surgical and
Social Rehabilitation of Adult Offend-
ers.* September, 1965. *223*

ABRAHAMSON, M., *Interpersonal Accommodation.* Princeton, N.J.: D. Van Nostrand Company, Inc., 1966. *147*

ABRAMSON, H. A., editor, *The Use of LSD
in Psychotherapy and Alcoholism.* Indianapolis, Ind.: The Bobbs-Merrill
Co., Inc., 1966. *257*

AKERS, R. L., R. L. BURGESS AND W. T.
JOHNSON, "Opiate Use, Addiction and
Relapse." *Social Problems*, 15:459–69 (Spring, 1968). *256*

ALLPORT, G., *The Person in Psychology: Selected Essays.* Boston: Beacon Press,
Inc., 1968. *137*

AMBER, G., AND P. AMBER, *Anatomy of Automation.* Englewood Cliffs, N.J.: Prentice-Hall, Inc., 1962. *32*

AMERICAN CIVIL LIBERTIES UNION, Board of Directors, "Civil Disobedience." *Civil
Liberties*, 254:4 (March–April, 1968). *86, 93*

AMIR, M., "Patterns of Forcible Rape," in M. Clinard and R. Quinney, editors, *Criminal Behavior Systems: A Typology.* New York: Holt, Rinehart & Winston, Inc.,
1967, pp. 60–75. *75*

ANDERSON, N., *The Hobo: The Sociology of the Homeless Man.* Chicago: University
of Chicago Press, 1923. *29*

ANNAN, N., "A Very Queer Gentleman." *The New York Review of Books*, Vol. X,
No. 11, June 6, 1968, pp. 8–12. *166*

APPLEY, M. H., AND R. TRUMBULL, *Psychological Stress: Issues in Research.* New
York: Appleton-Century & Appleton-Century Crofts, 1967. *181*

ARONSON, E., AND J. MILLS, "The Effect of Severity of Initiation on Liking for a
Group." *Journal of Abnormal and Social Psychology*, 59:177–81 (September,
1959). *181*

ASBURY, H., *The Gangs of New York: An Informal History of the Underworld.* New
York: Alfred A. Knopf, Inc., 1927. *65*

ASCH, S. E., *Social Psychology.* Englewood Cliffs, N.J.: Prentice-Hall, Inc., 1952. *273*

BACKMAN, C. W., "Resistance to Change in the Self-Concept as a Function of Consensus Among Significant Others." *Sociometry*, 26:102–11 (1963). *155*

BECKER, E., *The Birth and Death of Meaning: A Perspective in Psychiatry and Anthropology.* New York: The Free Press of Glencoe, Inc., 1962. *44, 178, 290*

——, *The Revolution in Psychiatry: The New Understanding of Man.* New York:
The Free Press of Glencoe, Inc., 1964. *290*

———, *The Structure of Evil: An Essay on the Unification of the Science of Man.* New York: George Braziller, Inc., 1968. *7, 307*

BECKER, H. S., "Notes on the Concept of Commitment." *American Journal of Sociology,* 64:32–40 (July, 1960). *159, 266*

———, *Outsiders: Studies in the Sociology of Deviance.* New York: The Free Press of Glencoe, Inc., 1963. *9, 18, 19, 26, 42, 74, 133, 134, 204, 296*

———, editor, *The Other Side.* New York: The Free Press of Glencoe, Inc., 1964. *7, 8*

———, "Deviance and Deviates," in D. Boroff, editor, *The State of the Nation.* Englewood Cliffs, N.J.: Prentice-Hall, Inc., 1965, pp. 73–82. *21*

———, "Whose Side Are We On?" *Social Problems,* 14:239–47 (Winter, 1967). *7*

BEERS, C., *A Mind That Found Itself.* New York: Doubleday, Doran & Co., 1921. *284*

BELKNAP, I., *Human Problems of a State Mental Hospital.* New York: McGraw-Hill Book Company, 1956. *165*

BEM, D. J., "When Saying is Believing." *Psychology Today,* 1:21–25 (June, 1967). *181*

BENNIS, W. G., E. H. SCHEIN, D. E. BERLEW AND F. I. STEELE, "Personal Change Through Interpersonal Relationships," in W. G. Bennis, *et. al.,* editors, *Interpersonal Dynamics: Essays and Readings on Human Interaction.* Homewood, Ill.: The Dorsey Press, 1964, pp. 357–94. *181*

BENNIS, W. G., AND P. E. SLATER, *The Temporary Society.* New York: Harper & Row, Publishers, 1968. *277*

BERELSON, B., AND G. A. STEINER, *Human Behavior: An Inventory of Scientific Findings.* New York: Harcourt, Brace & World, Inc., 1964. *239*

BERGER, P. L., *The Precarious Vision.* New York: Doubleday & Company, Inc., 1961. *12, 290, 307*

———, *Invitation to Sociology: A Humanistic Perspective.* New York: Doubleday Anchor, Inc., 1963. *290*

———, "Identity as a Problem in the Sociology of Knowledge." *European Journal of Sociology,* 7:105–15 (1966). *129, 290*

———, *The Sacred Canopy: Elements of a Sociological Theory of Religion.* New York: Doubleday & Company, Inc., 1967. *290*

BERGER, P. L., AND T. LUCKMANN, *The Social Construction of Reality: A Treatise in the Sociology of Knowledge.* New York: Doubleday & Company, Inc., 1966. *290*

BERNE, E., *Transactional Analysis in Psychotherapy.* New York: Grove Press, Inc., 1961. *274*

———, *Games People Play.* New York: Grove Press, Inc., 1964. *274*

BESS, D., "The High Church Heresy." *The Nation,* September 28, 1963. *186*

BETTELHEIM, B., "Individual and Mass Behavior in Extreme Situations." *Journal of Abnormal and Social Psychology,* 38:417–52 (October, 1943). *181*

BINSWANGER, L., "The Case of Ellen West," in R. May, E. Angel and H. F. Ellen-berger, editors, *Existence*. New York: Basic Books, Inc., Publishers, 1958, pp. 237–364. *57*

BITTNER, E., "Radicalism and the Organization of Radical Movements." *American Sociological Review*, 28:928–40 (December, 1963). *149*

BLACK, D. J., "Forms and Reforms of Whoredom: Notes on the Sociology of Prostitution and Moral Enterprise." Working Paper Number 15, Center for Research on Social Organization, The University of Michigan, March, 1966. *200*

———, "Police Encounters and Social Organization." Unpublished Ph.D. dissertation, Department of Sociology, University of Michigan, 1968. *144*

BLAKE, R. R., AND J. S. MOUTON, "Conformity, Resistance and Conversion," in I. A. Berg and B. M. Bass, editors, *Conformity and Deviation*. New York: Harper & Row, Publishers, 1961. *183*

BLAU, P. M., AND W. R. SCOTT, *Formal Organizations*. San Francisco: Chandler Publishing Company, 1962. *297*

BLUM, A. F., AND L. ROSENBERG, "Some Problems Involved in Professionalizing Social Interaction." *Journal of Health and Social Behavior*, 9:72–85 (March, 1968). *275*

BLUM, R., and associates, *Utopiates: The Use and Users of LSD 25*. New York: Atherton Press, 1964. *112*

BLUMER, H., "Sociological Analysis and the 'Variable.'" *American Sociological Review*, 21:683–90 (December, 1956). *26, 297*

———, "Society as Symbolic Interaction," in A. Rose, editor, *Human Behavior and Social Processes: An Interactionist Approach*. Boston: Houghton Mifflin Company, 1962, pp. 179–92. *297*

———, "Sociological Implications of the Thought of George Herbert Mead." *American Journal of Sociology*, 71:535–44 (March, 1966). *37, 297*

BORDUA, D. J., "Delinquent Subcultures: Sociological Interpretations of Gang Delinquency." *The Annals of the American Academy of Political and Social Science*, 338:119–36 (November, 1961). *47*

———, "Recent Trends: Deviant Behavior and Social Control." *The Annals of the American Academy of Political and Social Science*, 369:149–63 (January, 1967). *8*

BOULDING, K. E., "Toward a General Theory of Growth." *The Canadian Journal of Economics and Political Science*, 19:326–40 (August, 1953). *33*

BREED, W., "Suicide and Loss in Social Interaction," in E. S. Shneidman, editor, *Essays in Self-Destruction*. New York: Science House, 1967, pp. 188–202. *48*

BRIAR, S., AND I. PILIAVIN, "Delinquency, Situational Inducements and Commitment to Conformity." *Social Problems*, 13:35–45 (Summer, 1965). *102, 297*

BRIM, O. G., JR., AND S. WHEELER, *Socialization After Childhood*. New York: John Wiley & Sons, Inc., 1966. *121*

BROWN, C., *Manchild in the Promised Land*. New York: The Macmillan Company, Publishers, 1965. *46–47, 94, 160, 165*

BROWN, R., *Social Psychology*. New York: The Free Press of Glencoe, Inc., 1965. *125*

BROWNFIELD, C. A., *Isolation: Clinical and Experimental Approaches.* New York: Random House, Inc., 1965. *181*

BRUYN, S. T., *The Human Perspective in Sociology.* Englewood Cliffs, N.J.: Prentice-Hall, Inc., 1966. *298*

BRYAN, J. H., "Apprenticeships in Prostitution." *Social Problems,* 12:287–97 (Winter, 1965). *200*

————, "Occupational Ideologies and Individual Attitudes of Call Girls." *Social Problems,* 13:441–50 (Spring, 1966). *200*

BUGENTHAL, J. T., editor, *Challenges of Humanistic Psychology.* New York: McGraw-Hill Book Company, 1967. *217*

BURGESS, R. L., AND R. L. AKERS, "A Differential Association-Reinforcement Theory of Criminal Behavior." *Social Problems,* 14:128–47 (Fall, 1966). *256*

CAMERON, M. O., *The Booster and the Snitch: Department Store Shoplifting.* New York: The Free Press of Glencoe, Inc., 1964. *302*

CHAMBLISS, W. J., "A Sociological Analysis of the Law of Vagrancy." *Social Problems,* 12:67–77 (Summer, 1964). *133*

————, "Two Gangs: A Study of Societal Responses to Deviance and Deviant Careers," ms., 1967a. *138–39*

————, "Types of Deviance and the Effectiveness of Legal Sanctions." *Wisconsin Law Review,* 1967:703–19 (Summer, 1967b). *302*

CHEIN, I., D. L. GERARD, R. S. LEE, E. ROSENFELD, with the collaboration of D. M. Wilner, *The Road to H.* New York: Basic Books, Inc., Publishers, 1964. *49, 74*

CICOUREL, A. V., *The Social Organization of Juvenile Justice.* New York: John Wiley & Sons, Inc., 1968. *144*

City of Ann Arbor, Michigan, *Ordinance Code.* Ann Arbor: Municipal Codification Service, Inc., 1957. *64*

CLAUSEN, J., et al., *Socialization and Society.* Boston: Little, Brown and Company, 1968. *121*

CLINARD, M. B., *The Black Market.* New York: Holt, Rinehart & Winston, Inc., 1952. *73, 83, 85*

————, editor, *Anomie and Deviant Behavior: A Discussion and Critique.* New York: The Free Press of Glencoe, Inc., 1964. *26*

————, *Sociology of Deviant Behavior.* New York: Holt, Rinehart & Winston, Inc. (3rd ed.), 1968. *95, 135*

CLINARD, M. B., AND R. QUINNEY, editors, *Criminal Behavior Systems: A Typology.* New York: Holt, Rinehart & Winston, Inc., 1967. *26, 100*

CLOWARD, R. A., "Illegitimate Means, Anomie, and Deviant Behavior." *American Sociological Review,* 24:164–76 (April, 1959). *202*

CLOWARD, R. A., AND L. E. OHLIN, *Delinquency and Opportunity.* Glencoe, Ill.: The Free Press, 1960. *6, 10*

COHEN, A. K., *Delinquent Boys.* Glencoe, Ill.: The Free Press, 1955. *6, 10, 147*

————, "The Study of Social Disorganization and Deviant Behavior," in R. K. Merton, L. Broom and L. S. Cottrell, editors, *Sociology Today*. New York: Basic Books, Inc., 1959, pp. 461–84. *6, 15, 147*

————, *Deviance and Control*. Englewood Cliffs, N.J.: Prentice-Hall, Inc., 1966. *16, 27, 133*

COHEN, A. K., AND J. F. SHORT, JR., "Research in Delinquent Subcultures." *Journal of Social Issues*, 14:20–37 (1958). *115*

COLEMAN, J. V., "Some Factors Influencing the Development and Containment of Psychiatric Symptoms," in T. J. Scheff, editor, *Mental Illness and Social Processes*. New York: Harper & Row, Publishers, 1967, pp. 158–68. *184*

COOLEY, C. H., *Human Nature and the Social Order*. New York: Schocken Books, 1964 (copyright 1902; revised 1922). *vii*

COOPER, D., "The Anti-Hospital: An Experiment in Psychiatry," in F. Lindenfeld, editor, *Radical Perspectives on Social Problems*. New York: The Macmillan Company, Publishers, 1968, pp. 369–80. *217*

COOPERSMITH, S., *The Antecedents of Self-Esteem*. San Francisco: W. H. Freeman & Co., Publishers, 1967. *48, 181*

COSER, L. A., "Some Functions of Deviant Behavior and Normative Flexibility." *American Journal of Sociology*, 68:172–81 (September, 1962). *303*

COXE, S., "Public Letter to Roger Gordon." Youth Conservation Services, Philadelphia, Pa., February 4, 1964. *140–41*

CRAIG, M., AND S. GLICK, *A Manual of Procedures for Application of the Glueck Prediction Table*. New York: New York City Youth Board, 1964. *144*

CRESSEY, D. R., *Other People's Money*. Glencoe, Ill.: The Free Press, 1953. *46, 51–52, 58, 70, 73, 75, 83, 84, 86, 87, 95, 112, 296*

————, "Changing Criminals: The Application of the Theory of Differential Association." *American Journal of Sociology*, 61:116–20 (September, 1955). *271*

————, editor, *The Prison: Studies in Institutional Organization and Change*. New York: Holt, Rinehart & Winston, Inc., 1961. *165*

————, "Role Theory, Differential Association and Compulsive Crimes," in A. Rose, editor, *Human Behavior and Social Processes*. Boston: Houghton Mifflin Company, 1962, pp. 443–67. *91, 98*

————, "Social Psychological Foundations for Using Criminals in the Rehabilitation of Criminals." *Journal of Research in Crime and Delinquency*, 2:49–59 (July, 1965). *88*

DAHRENDORF, R., "Out of Utopia: Towards a Re-Orientation of Sociological Analysis." *American Journal of Sociology*, 64:115–27 (September, 1958). *7*

DAVIS, F., "Deviance Disavowal: The Management of Strained Interaction." *Social Problems*, 9:120–32 (Fall, 1961). *29*

DAVIS, J. A., "Structural Balance, Mechanical Solidarity and Interpersonal Relations." *American Journal of Sociology*, 68:444–62 (January, 1963). *155, 181, 261*

DAVIS, K., "Mental Hygiene and the Class Structure." *Psychiatry*, 1:55–65 (February, 1938). *133*

DEMERATH, N. J., III, AND R. A. PETERSON, editors, *System, Change and Conflict: A*

Reader on Contemporary Sociological Theory and the Debate Over Function-alism. New York: The Free Press of Glencoe, Inc., 1967. *7*

DENNIS, N., *Cards of Identity.* New York: Meridian Books, Inc., 1960 (copyright 1955). *129*

DENTLER, R. A., AND K. T. ERIKSON, "The Functions of Deviance in Groups." *Social Problems,* 7:98–107 (Fall, 1959). *303*

DICKSON, D. T., "Guided Group Interaction: The Organizational Implementation of an Experimental Treatment Technology," ms., 1966. *229*

———, "Bureaucracy and Morality: An Organizational Perspective on a Moral Crusade." *Social Problems,* 16:143–56 (1968). *18, 133*

DINITZ, S., M. LEFTON, S. ANGRIST AND B. PASAMANICK, "Psychiatric and Social Attributes as Predictors of Case Outcome in Mental Hospitalizations." *Social Problems,* 8:322–28 (Spring, 1961). *240*

DINITZ, S., F. R. SCARPITTI AND W. C. RECKLESS, "Delinquency Vulnerability: A Cross Group and Longitudinal Analysis." *American Sociological Review,* 27:515–17 (August, 1962). *149*

DITMAN, K., "The Use of LSD in the Treatment of the Alcoholic," in R. Fox, editor, *Alcoholism: Behavioral Research, Therapeutic Approaches.* New York: Springer Publishing Company, Inc., 1968, Chap. 23. *257*

DOHRENWEND, B. P., AND E. CHIN-SHONG, "Social Status and Attitudes Toward Psychological Disorder: The Problem of Tolerance of Deviance." *American Sociological Review,* 32:417–33 (June, 1967). *132*

DOUGLAS, J. D., *The Social Meanings of Suicide,* Princeton, N.J.: Princeton University Press, 1967. *47*

———, "The General Theoretical Implications of the Sociology of Deviance," in J. C. McKinney and E. A. Tirakian, editors, *Theoretical Sociology: Perspectives and Developments.* New York: Appleton-Century & Appleton-Century-Crofts, 1969. *8, 19, 26*

DOWNES, D. M., *The Delinquent Solution: A Study in Subcultural Theory.* New York: The Free Press of Glencoe, Inc., 1966. *114*

DURKHEIM, E., *The Rules of Sociological Method.* Glencoe, Ill.: The Free Press, 1950 (copyright 1895). *303*

DWORKIN, R., "On Not Prosecuting Civil Disobedience." *The New York Review of Books,* 10, No. 11, June 6, 1968, pp. 14–21. *86, 87, 88*

EATON, J. W., in collaboration with R. J. Weil, *Culture and Mental Disorders: A Comparative Study of Hutterites and Other Populations.* Glencoe, Ill.: The Free Press, 1955. *173*

EDGERTON, R. B., *The Cloak of Competence: Stigma in the Lives of the Mentally Retarded.* Berkeley and Los Angeles: University of California Press, 1967. *189*

EISTER, A. W., *Drawing-Room Conversion: A Sociological Account of the Oxford Group Movement.* Durham, N.C.: Duke University Press, 1950. *283*

ELLIOTT, M., AND F. E. MERRILL, *Social Disorganization.* New York: Harper & Brothers, 1934. *3–4*

EMPEY, L. T., "The Provo Experiment: Introduction, Research and Findings," in H.

Gold and F. R. Scarpitti, editors, *Combatting Social Problems: Techniques of Intervention.* New York: Holt, Rinehart & Winston, Inc., 1967, pp. 371–74, 395–404. *228*

EMPEY, L. T., AND J. RABOW, "The Provo Experiment in Delinquency Rehabilitation." *American Sociological Review*, 25:679–95 (October, 1961). *237, 255*

ERIKSON, K. T., "Notes on the Sociology of Deviance." *Social Problems*, 9:307–14 (Spring, 1962). *228, 303*

————, *Wayward Puritans: A Study in the Sociology of Deviance.* New York: John Wiley & Sons, Inc., 1966. *133, 135, 136, 139, 144, 149, 156, 158, 179, 303*

————, "A Comment on Disguised Observation in Sociology." *Social Problems*, 14:366–73 (Spring, 1967). *300*

ETZIONI, A., *The Active Society: A Theory of Societal and Political Processes.* New York: The Free Press of Glencoe, Inc., 1968a. *12, 307*

————, "Shortcuts to Social Change." *The Public Interest*, No. 12:40–45 (Summer, 1968b). *71*

ETZKOWITZ, H., AND G. M. SCHAFLANDER, "A Manifesto for Sociologists: Institution Formation—A New Sociology." *Social Problems*, 15:399–408 (Spring, 1968). *220*

FARBEROW, N. L., "Crisis, Disaster and Suicide: Theory and Therapy," in E. S. Shneidman, editor, *Essays in Self-Destruction.* New York: Science House, 1967, pp. 373–98. *181*

FELDMAN, H. W., "Ideological Supports to Becoming and Remaining a Heroin Addict." *Journal of Health and Social Behavior*, 9:131–39 (June, 1968). *114, 115, 199*

FESTINGER, L., AND J. M. CARLSMITH, "Cognitive Consequences of Forced Compliance." *Journal of Abnormal and Social Psychology*, 58:203–10 (March, 1959). *181*

FISHER, S., "The Rehabilitative Effectiveness of a Community Correctional Residence for Narcotics Users." *Journal of Criminal Law, Criminology and Police Science*, 56:190–96 (June, 1965). *229–30*

FISKE, D. W., AND S. R. MADDI, *Functions of Varied Experience.* Homewood, Ill.: The Dorsey Press, 1961. *115*

FITCH, J. M., *American Building, 1: The Historical Forces That Shaped It.* Boston: Houghton Mifflin Company (2nd ed.), 1966. *66*

FITZPATRICK, J. P., "The Role of Religion in Programs for the Prevention and Correction of Crime and Delinquency," in The President's Commission on Law Enforcement and Administration of Justice, *Task Force Report: Juvenile Delinquency and Youth Crime.* Washington, D.C.: U.S. Government Printing Office, 1967, Appendix P, pp. 317–30. *265*

FOOTE, N. N., "Identification as the Basis for a Theory of Motivation." *American Sociological Review*, 16:14–21 (February, 1951). *129*

FOUCAULT, M., *Madness and Civilization: A History of Insanity in the Age of Reason.* New York: New American Library, 1967. *133*

FOWLER, H., *Curiosity and Exploratory Behavior.* New York: The Macmillan Company, Publishers, 1965. *115*

FRANK, J. D., *Persuasion and Healing: A Comparative Study of Psychotherapy.* Baltimore, Md.: The Johns Hopkins Press, 1961. *295*

FRIEDSON, E., "Disability as Social Deviance," in M. B. Sussman, editor, *Sociology and Rehabilitation.* Washington, D.C.: American Sociological Association, 1966, pp. 71–99. *26*

GAMSON, W. A., AND H. SCHUMAN, "Some Undercurrents in the Prestige of Physicians." *American Journal of Sociology,* 68:463–70 (January, 1963). *305*

GANS, H. J., *The Urban Villagers.* New York: The Free Press of Glencoe, Inc., 1962. *90–91*

GARDNER, G. G., "The Psychotherapeutic Relationship." *Psychological Bulletin,* 61:426–37 (1964). *275*

GARFINKEL, H., "Conditions of Successful Degradation Ceremonies." *American Journal of Sociology,* 61:420–24 (March, 1956). *158, 188*

GEBHARD, P. H., J. H. GAGNON, W. B. POMEROY AND C. V. CHRISTENSON, *Sex Offenders: An Analysis of Types.* New York: Harper & Row, Publishers, 1965. *63, 75, 79–80, 80–81*

GEIS, G., "White Collar Crime: The Heavy Electrical Equipment Antitrust Cases of 1961," in M. B. Clinard and R. Quinney, editors, *Criminal Behavior Systems: A Typology.* New York: Holt, Rinehart & Winston, Inc., 1967, pp. 139–51. *93*

———, editor, *White-Collar Criminal: The Offender in Business and the Professions.* New York: Atherton Press, 1968. *73*

GELLMAN, I. P., *The Sober Alcoholic.* New Haven, Conn.: College & University Press, 1964. *215, 283*

GENET, J., *The Thief's Journal.* New York: Bantam Books, Inc., 1965 (copyright 1949). *199*

GIBBONS, D. C., *Changing the Lawbreaker: The Treatment of Delinquents and Criminals.* Englewood Cliffs, N.J.: Prentice-Hall, Inc., 1965. *26, 165*

———, *Society, Crime and Criminal Careers.* Englewood Cliffs, N.J.: Prentice-Hall, Inc., 1968. *26*

GIBBS, J. P., "Conceptions of Deviant Behavior: New and Old." *Pacific Sociological Review,* 9:9–14 (Spring, 1966). *8*

GILLENSON, L. W., *Billy Graham and Seven Who Were Saved.* New York: Trident Press, 1967. *214, 270–71*

GLASER, B. G., AND A. L. STRAUSS, *The Discovery of Grounded Theory: Strategies for Qualitative Research.* Chicago: Aldine Publishing Company, 1967. *25*

GLASER, D., *The Effectiveness of a Prison and Parole System.* Indianapolis, Ind.: The Bobbs-Merrill, Co., Inc., 1964. *240*

GLASSER, W., *Reality Therapy: A New Approach to Psychiatry.* New York: Harper & Row, Publishers, 1962. *217*

GLUECK, S., AND E. GLUECK, *Unraveling Juvenile Delinquency.* Cambridge, Mass.: Harvard University Press, 1950. *115*

GOFFMAN, E., "The Nature of Deference and Demeanor." *American Anthropologist,* 58:473–502 (June, 1956). *146, 162*

———, *The Presentation of Self in Everyday Life.* New York: Doubleday Anchor, Inc., 1959. *15, 142, 162, 274*

———, *Asylums.* New York: Doubleday & Company, Inc., 1961a. *130, 158, 162, 163–64, 170, 175, 190*

———, *Encounters: Two Studies in the Sociology of Interaction.* Indianapolis, Ind.: The Bobbs-Merrill Co., Inc., 1961b. *15*

———, *Stigma: Notes on the Management of Spoiled Identity.* Englewood Cliffs, N.J.: Prentice-Hall, Inc., 1963a. *2, 16, 25, 29, 207, 222*

———, *Behavior in Public Places.* New York: The Free Press of Glencoe, Inc., 1963b. *64*

———, *Interaction Ritual.* New York: Doubleday & Company, Inc., 1967. *15, 115*

GOLDMAN, N., *The Differential Selection of Offenders for Court Appearance.* Washington, D.C.: National Research and Information Center and National Council on Crime and Delinquency, 1963. *144*

GOLDSTEIN, A. P., K. HELLER AND L. B. SECHREST, *Psychotherapy and the Psychology of Behavior Change.* New York: John Wiley & Sons, Inc., 1966. *275*

GOODE, W. J., "The Theoretical Importance of Love." *American Sociological Review,* 24:38–47 (February, 1959). *306*

GOSLIN, D. E., editor, *Handbook of Socialization Theory and Research.* Chicago: Rand McNally and Company, 1968. *121*

GOULDNER, A. W., "The Norm of Reciprocity: A Preliminary Statement." *American Sociological Review,* 25:161–78 (April, 1960). *266*

———, "Anti-Minotaur: The Myth of Value-Free Sociology." *Social Problems,* 9:199–213 (Winter, 1962). *5, 7*

———, "The Sociologist as Partisan: Sociology and the Welfare State." *The American Sociologist,* 3:103–16 (May, 1968). *7, 12, 307*

GROB, G. N., *The State and the Mentally Ill: A History of the Worcester State Hospital in Massachusetts, 1830–1920.* Chapel Hill, N.C.: University of North Carolina Press, 1966. *173*

GROSSBERG, J. M., "Behavior Therapy: A Review." *Psychological Bulletin,* 62:73–88 (August, 1964). *256*

GURSSLIN, O. R., R. G. HUNT AND J. L. ROACH, "Social Class and the Mental Health Movement." *Social Problems,* 7:210–18 (Winter, 1959–60). *133*

GUSFIELD, J. R., *Symbolic Crusade: Status Politics and the American Temperance Movement.* Urbana, Ill.: University of Illinois Press, 1963. *134*

———, "Moral Passage: The Symbolic Process in Public Designations of Deviance." *Social Problems,* 15:175–88 (Fall, 1967). *23, 134*

HADDEN, S. B., "A Way Out for Homosexuals." *Harper's Magazine* (March, 1967), pp. 107–20. *216*

HALL, J., *Theft, Law and Society.* Indianapolis, Ind.: The Bobbs-Merrill Co., Inc., 1939. *133*

———, "Social Change and Status Protest." *Phylon*, X:58–65 (1949). *125*

———, "Stress and Strain in Professional Education." *The Harvard Educational Review*, 29:319–29 (Fall, 1959). *268*

HUGHES, H. M., editor, *The Fantastic Lodge*. Boston: Houghton Mifflin Company, 1961. *75*

JACKSON, M. P., *Their Brother's Keepers—A Directory of Therapeutic Self-Help Groups, Intentional Communities, and Lay Training Centers*. Mimeographed: Department of Psychology, University of Illinois, Urbana, Ill., and Berkeley Baptist Divinity School, Berkeley, Calif., 1962. *286*

JACOBS, J., *The Death and Life of Great American Cities*. New York: Vintage Books, 1963. *66–68*

JAMES, W., *The Varieties of Religious Experience*. New York: Mentor, 1958 (copyright 1902). *261*

JANIS, I. L., "Anxiety Indices Related to Susceptibility to Persuasion." *Journal of Abnormal and Social Psychology*, 51:663–67 (November, 1955). *181*

JASPAN, N., with H. Black, *The Thief in the White Collar*. Philadelphia: J. B. Lippincott Co., 1960. *72, 73*

JEWELL, D. P., "A Case of a 'Psychotic' Navaho Indian Male," in D. Apple, editor, *Sociological Studies of Health and Illness*. New York: McGraw-Hill Book Company, 1960, pp. 107–17. *143*

JOHNSON, E. H., *Crime, Correction and Society*. Homewood, Ill.: The Dorsey Press, 1964. *65, 126, 144*

JOURARD, S. M., *The Transparent Self*. Princeton, N.J.: D. Van Nostrand Company, Inc., 1964. *271*

KANTER, R. M., "Utopia: A Study in Comparative Organization." Unpublished Ph.D. dissertation, Department of Sociology, The University of Michigan, 1967. *177*

KATZ, F. E., "Occupational Contact Networks." *Social Forces*, 37:52–55 (October, 1958). *166*

KATZ, J., J. GOLDSTEIN AND A. M. DERSHOWITZ, editors, *Psychoanalysis, Psychiatry and Law*. New York: The Free Press of Glencoe, Inc., 1967. *143*

KENISTON, K., *The Uncommitted*. New York: Harcourt, Brace & World, Inc., 1965. *112*

———, *Young Radicals: Notes on Committed Youth*. New York: Harvest Books, 1968. *187, 190, 194*

KESEY, K., *One Flew Over the Cuckoo's Nest*. New York: Signet, 1962. *195*

KIEV, A., editor, *Magic, Faith and Healing*. New York: The Free Press of Glencoe, Inc., 1964. *295*

KINCH, J. W., "A Formalized Theory of the Self-Concept." *American Journal of Sociology*, 68:481–86 (January, 1963). *121*

KINSEY, A. C., W. B. POMEROY AND C. C. MARTIN, *Sexual Behavior in the Human Male*. Philadelphia: W. B. Saunders Company, 1953. *27*

KITSUSE, J. I., "Societal Reaction to Deviant Behavior: Problems of Theory and Method." *Social Problems*, 9:247–56 (Winter, 1962). *125, 149*

KITSUSE, J. I., AND A. V. CICOUREL, "A Note on the Uses of Official Statistics." *Social Problems*, 11:131–39 (Fall, 1963). *136*

KLAUSNER, S. Z., editor, *Why Man Takes Chances: Studies in Stress-Seeking.* New York: Doubleday Anchor, Inc., 1968. *115*

KLUCKHOHN, C., *Navaho Witchcraft.* Boston: Beacon Press, Inc., 1967 (copyright 1944). *303*

KOBLER, A. L., AND E. STOTLAND, *The End of Hope.* New York: The Free Press of Glencoe, Inc., 1964. *34, 46, 48, 49, 52, 56, 57, 76–79, 217*

KOEGLER, R. R., AND N. Q. BRILL, *Treatment of Psychiatric Outpatients.* New York: Appleton-Century-Crofts, 1967. *239*

KUHN, M. H., AND T. S. MCPARTLAND, "An Empirical Investigation of Self-Attitudes." *American Sociological Review*, 19:68–76 (February, 1954). *129*

KUHN, T., *The Structure of Scientific Revolutions.* Chicago: University of Chicago Press, 1962. *7*

KURLAND, A. A., J. W. SHAFFER AND S. UNGER, "Psychedelic Psychotherapy (LSD) in the Treatment of Alcoholism." Proceedings of the Vth International Congress of the Collegium Internationale Neuropsychopharmacologicum, *Excerpta Medica International Congress Series*, No. 129:435–40 (1966). *257*

LANGGUTH, J., "California's Gift to Psychotherapy." *Harper's Magazine* (June, 1967), pp. 52–56. *217*

LAUD HUMPHREYS, R. A., "They Meet in Tearooms: A Preliminary Study of Participants in Homosexual Encounters." Paper presented to the Society for the Study of Social Problems, August, 1967. *112*

LEARY, T., "How to Change Behavior," in G. S. Nielson, editor, *Clinical Psychology, Proceedings of the XIV International Congress of Applied Psychology, Vol. 4.* Copenhagen: Munksgaard, 1962, pp. 50–68. *215–16, 230–31, 256–57*

LEEPER, R. W., AND P. MADISON, *Toward Understanding Human Personalities.* New York: Appleton-Century & Appleton-Century-Crofts, 1959. *112*

LEIGH, M., *The Velvet Underground.* New York: Macfadden Books, 1963. *83, 112*

LEIGHTON, D. C., *et al.*, *The Character of Danger.* New York: Basic Books, Inc., Publishers, 1963. *27*

LEMERT, E. M., *Social Pathology.* New York: McGraw-Hill Book Company, 1951. *26, 27, 82, 121, 140, 142, 147, 159–60, 184, 196, 204, 296*

———, "An Isolation and Closure Theory of Naïve Check Forgery." *Journal of Criminal Law, Criminology and Police Science*, 44:296–307 (1953). *41, 48, 52, 58–59, 72, 83, 95, 296*

———, "The Behavior of the Systematic Check Forger." *Social Problems*, 6:141–49 (Fall, 1958). *200*

———, "Paranoia and the Dynamics of Exclusion." *Sociometry*, 25:2–20 (March, 1962). *144, 148, 149, 152–53, 196, 296*

———, *Human Deviance, Social Problems and Social Control.* Englewood Cliffs, N.J.: Prentice-Hall, Inc., 1967a. *vii, 27, 147, 204, 249–51*

———, "The Juvenile Court—Quest and Realities," in The President's Commission on Law Enforcement and Administration of Justice, *Task Force Report: Juvenile*

Delinquency and Youth Crime. Washington, D.C.: U.S. Government Printing Office, 1967b, Appendix D, pp. 91–106. *143, 144*

LERMAN, P., "Individual Values, Peer Values, and Subcultural Delinquency." *American Sociological Review,* 33:219–35 (April, 1968). *114*

LEWIN, K., *Field Theory in Social Science.* New York: Harper & Brothers, 1951. *297*

LIFTON, R. J., *Thought Reform and the Psychology of Totalism: A Study of "Brainwashing" in China.* New York: W. W. Norton & Company, Inc., Publishers, 1963. *55, 188, 295*

LINDER, R., *Must You Conform?* New York: Grove Press, Inc., 1961. *100*

LINDESMITH, A. R., *Addiction and Opiates.* Chicago: Aldine Publishing Company, 1968. *42, 71, 133, 149, 211*

LINDESMITH, A. R., AND A. L. STRAUSS, *Social Psychology.* New York: Holt, Rinehart & Winston, Inc. (3rd ed.), 1968. *133*

LIPSET, S. M., AND N. SMELSER, "Change and Controversy in Recent American Sociology." *British Journal of Sociology,* XII:41–51 (March, 1961). *7*

LOFLAND, J., *Doomsday Cult: A Study of Conversion, Proselytization and Maintenance of Faith.* Englewood Cliffs, N.J.: Prentice-Hall, Inc., 1966. *29, 167, 186–87, 189, 193, 194, 199, 204, 291*

————, "The Youth Ghetto." *Journal of Higher Education,* XXXIX:121–43 (March, 1968). *52*

LOFLAND, J., AND R. LE JEUNE, "Initial Interaction of Newcomers in Alcoholics Anonymous." *Social Problems,* 8:102–11 (Fall, 1960). *215, 270*

LOFLAND, J., AND L. H. LOFLAND, "Some Benefits of Crime and Other Nonconformity." *Forum, The University of Houston,* 6:41–45 (Spring, 1968). *303*

LOFLAND, J., AND R. STARK, "Becoming a World-Saver: A Theory of Conversion to a Deviant Perspective." *American Sociological Review,* 30:862–75 (December, 1965). *204*

LOFLAND, L. H., "In the Presence of Strangers: A Study of Behavior in Public Settings." Working Paper Number 19, Center for Research on Social Organization, The University of Michigan, December, 1966. *142*

LORBER, J., "Deviance as Performance: The Case of Illness." *Social Problems,* 14:302–10 (Winter, 1967). *154*

LOVAAS, O. I., "A Behavior Therapy Approach to the Treatment of Childhood Schizophrenia," in *Minnesota Symposium on Child Psychology.* Minneapolis, Minn.: University of Minnesota Press, 1968. *256*

LOW, A. A., *Mental Health Through Will-Training.* Boston: The Christopher Publishing House, 1950. *238*

LUDWIG, A., J. LEVINE, L. STARK AND R. LAZAR, "A Clinical Study of LSD Treatment in Alcoholism." Paper presented at the 124th Annual Meeting of the American Psychiatric Association, Boston, Mass., May 13–17, 1968. *257*

LYND, R. S., *Knowledge for What?* Princeton, N.J.: Princeton University Press, 1939. *7, 99*

MAISEL, R., "The Ex-Mental Patient and Rehospitalization: Some Research Findings." *Social Problems*, 15:18–24 (Summer, 1967). *240*

MANIS, J. G., "The Sociology of Knowledge and Community Mental Health Research." *Social Problems*, 15:488–501 (Spring, 1968). *7*

MATTICK, H. W., "Parole to the Army: Military Experience as a Factor in Parole Success." Unpublished M. A. thesis, Department of Sociology, University of Chicago, 1956. *221*

MATZA, D., "Subterranean Traditions of Youth." *The Annals of the American Academy of Political and Social Science*, 338:102–18 (November, 1961). *88*

———, *Delinquency and Drift*. New York: John Wiley & Sons, Inc., 1964. *47, 88, 92, 95, 102, 115, 188, 298*

MATZA, D., AND G. M. SYKES, "Delinquency and Subterranean Values." *American Sociological Review*, 26:712–19 (October, 1961). *88, 99*

MAURER, D. W., *The Big Con*. New York: Signet, 1962. *166, 200*

MCCALL, G. J., AND J. L. SIMMONS, *Identities and Interactions*. New York: The Free Press of Glencoe, Inc., 1966. *125*

MCCORKLE, L. W., A. ELIAS AND F. L. BIXBY, *The Highfields Story*. New York: Holt, Rinehart & Winston, Inc., 1958. *228*

MCDONALD, H. J., Series on Mental Hospitals in Michigan, *Ann Arbor News*, May 3–6, 1965. *170*

MCKAY, H. D., "Report on the Criminal Careers of Male Delinquents in Chicago," in President's Commission on Law Enforcement and Administration of Justice, *Task Force Report: Juvenile Delinquency and Youth Crime*. Washington, D.C.: U.S. Government Printing Office, 1967, Appendix F, pp. 107–13. *171*

MEAD, G. H., "The Psychology of Punitive Justice." *American Journal of Sociology*, 23:557–602 (1928). *303*

MERTON, R. K., "Social Structure and Anomie." *American Sociological Review*, 3:672–82 (October, 1938). *6*

———, *Social Theory and Social Structure*. Glencoe, Ill.: The Free Press, 1949 (revised and enlarged 1957). *6, 26*

MEYER, H., AND E. BORGOTTA, *Girls at Vocational High*. New York: Russell Sage Foundation, 1965. *168, 200*

MILLER, D., "Retrospective Analysis of Posthospital Mental Patients' Worlds." *Journal of Health and Social Behavior*, 8:136–40 (June, 1967). *239*

MILLER, D., AND E. BLANC, "Concepts of 'Moral Treatment' for the Mentally Ill: Implications for Psychiatric Social Work With Post-Hospital Patients," ms., 1964. *275–76*

MILLER, D., AND M. SCHWARTZ, "County Lunacy Commission Hearings: Some Observations of Commitments to a State Mental Hospital." *Social Problems*, 14:26–35 (Summer, 1966). *180*

MILLS, C. W., "Situated Actions and Vocabularies of Motive." *American Sociological Review*, 5:904–13 (December, 1940). *179*

———, "The Professional Ideology of Social Pathologists." *American Journal of Sociology*, 49:165–80 (September, 1942). *3, 5*

————, *The Sociological Imagination.* New York: Oxford University Press, Inc., 1959. *6, 12, 196, 307*

————, "The Big City: Private Troubles and Public Issues," in I. L. Horowitz, editor, *Power, Politics and People: The Collected Essays of C. Wright Mills.* New York: Ballantine Books, 1963, pp. 395–402. *196*

Moody Press, "How To Become a Christian," tract, n.d. *213*

Moss, L. M., and D. M. Hamilton, "Psychotherapy of the Suicidal Patient," in E. Shneidman and N. Farberow, *Clues to Suicide.* New York: McGraw-Hill Book Company, 1957. *56, 76*

Mowrer, O. H., *The New Group Therapy.* Princeton, N.J.: D. Van Nostrand Company, Inc., 1964. *283–84*

Murphy, F. J., M. M. Shirley and H. Witmer, "The Incidence of Hidden Delinquency." *American Journal of Orthopsychiatry,* 16:686–96 (October, 1946). *27*

Myrdal, G., with the assistance of R. Sterner and A. Rose, *An American Dilemma: The Negro Problem and Modern Democracy.* New York: Harper & Brothers, 1944. *7*

National Institute of Mental Health, *Experiment in Culture Expansion,* Report of a conference on "The use of products of a social problem in coping with the problem," California Rehabilitation Center, Norco, Calif., July 10–12, 1963. *271*

Nelson, S. E., "History Repeats Itself." *Contemporary Psychology,* 12:516 (October, 1967). *173*

Nettler, G., "Good Men, Bad Men, and the Perception of Reality." *Sociometry,* 24:279–94 (September, 1961). *199*

Newcomb, T. M., R. H. Turner and P. E. Converse, *Social Psychology.* New York: Holt, Rinehart & Winston, Inc., 1965. *125*

Parsons, T., *The Social System.* Glencoe, Ill.: The Free Press, 1951. *6, 26, 147*

Phillips, D. L., "Rejection: A Possible Consequence of Seeking Help for Mental Disorders." *American Sociological Review,* 28:963–72 (December, 1963). *157*

Pike, L. O., *A History of Crime in England.* London: Smith, Elder, 1873–1876. *158*

Piliavin, I., and S. Briar, "Police Encounters with Juveniles." *American Journal of Sociology,* 70:206–14 (September, 1964). *144*

Porterfield, A. L., *Youth in Trouble.* Fort Worth, Texas: Leo Potishman Foundation, 1949. *27*

President's Commission on Law Enforcement and Administration of Justice, *Task Force Report: Corrections.* Washington, D.C.: U.S. Government Printing Office, 1967. *170, 239*

————, *Task Force Report: Crime and Its Impact—An Assessment.* Washington, D.C.: U.S. Government Printing Office, 1967. *144*

Rapoport, R., "Wanted in Ann Arbor: 'Unemployables.'" *The Wall Street Journal,* May 14, 1967. *241–42*

Rausch, H. L., and E. S. Bordin, "Warmth in Personality Development and in Psychotherapy." *Psychiatry,* 20:351–63 (November, 1957). *275*

RAY, M., "The Cycle of Abstinence and Relapse Among Heroin Addicts." *Social Problems*, 9:132–40 (Fall, 1961). *211, 289*

RECKLESS, W. C., *The Crime Problem*. New York: Appleton-Century & Appleton-Century-Crofts (3rd ed.), 1961. *144*

RECKLESS, W. C., S. DINITZ AND B. KAY, "The Self Concept in Potential Delinquency and Potential Nondelinquency." *American Sociological Review*, 22:566–70 (October, 1957). *149*

REIN, M., "The Social Service Crisis." *Trans-Action*, 1:3–8 (May, 1964). *278*

REISS, A. J., JR., "Delinquency as the Failure of Personal and Social Controls." *American Sociological Review*, 16:196–207 (April, 1951). *114*

————, "The Study of Deviant Behavior: Where the Action Is." *The Ohio Valley Sociologist*, 32:1–12 (Autumn, 1966). *8*

————, *Studies in Crime and Law Enforcement in Major Metropolitan Areas, Volume I*. Washington, D.C.: U.S. Government Printing Office, 1967. *63–64*

RIEFF, P., *The Triumph of the Therapeutic: Uses of Faith After Freud*. New York: Harper & Row, Publishers, 1966. *277, 295*

RIESMAN, D., N. GLAZER AND R. DENNEY, *The Lonely Crowd: A Study of the Changing American Character*. New Haven, Conn.: Yale University Press, 1950. *142*

RICCIO, V., AND B. SLOCUM, *All the Way Down: The Violent Underworld of Street Gangs*. New York: Ballantine Books, 1962. *237, 265, 280*

RIPLEY, H. S., AND J. K. JACKSON, "Therapeutic Factors in Alcoholics Anonymous." *American Journal of Psychiatry*, 116:44–50 (July, 1959). *283*

ROACH, J. L., "A Theory of Lower-Class Behavior," in L. Gross, editor, *Sociological Theory: Inquiries and Paradigms*. New York: Harper & Row, Publishers, 1967, pp. 294–314. *180*

RODMAN, H., AND R. GRAMS, "Juvenile Delinquency and the Family: A Review and Discussion," in President's Commission on Law Enforcement and Administration of Justice, *Task Force Report: Juvenile Delinquency and Youth Crime*. Washington, D.C.: U.S. Government Printing Office, 1967, Appendix L, pp. 188–221. *102*

ROEBUCK, J. B., AND M. L. CADWALLADER, "The Negro Armed Robber as a Criminal Type: The Construction and Application of a Typology." *Pacific Sociological Review*, 4:21–26 (Spring, 1961). *115*

ROGERS, C., "The Necessary and Sufficient Conditions of Therapeutic Personality Change." *Journal of Consulting Psychology*, 21:95–103 (1957). *275*

ROKEACH, M., *The Three Christs of Ypsilanti*. New York: Alfred A. Knopf, Inc., 1964. *154, 196*

ROSENBERG, M., *Society and the Adolescent Self-Image*. Princeton, N.J.: Princeton University Press, 1965. *48, 181*

ROSENTHAL, R., AND L. JACOBSON, "Teachers' Expectancies: Determinants of Pupils' IQ Gains." *Psychological Reports*, 19:115–18 (1966). *149*

RUBENSTEIN, R., R. MOSES AND T. LIDZ, "On Attempted Suicide." *AMA Archives of Neurology and Psychiatry*, 79:103–12 (1958). *56*

RUBINGTON, E., AND M. S. WEINBERG, editors, *Deviance: The Interactionist Perspective.* New York: The Macmillan Company, Publishers, 1968. *29, 204*

SAMUELS, G., "A Summons Instead of an Arrest." *The New York Times Magazine,* July 26, 1964. *158*

SANDERS, M. K., "Conversations with Saul Alinsky, Parts I & II." *Harper's Magazine* (June, 1965), pp. 37–47; (July, 1965) pp. 50–59. *220*

SANDS, B., *My Shadow Ran Fast.* New York: Signet, 1964. *175–76, 223, 232–34, 242–43, 247, 253–54, 264, 268, 284–85*

———, *The Seventh Step.* New York: New American Library, 1967. *285*

SARBIN, T., "Role Theoretical Interpretation of Psychological Change," in P. Worchel and D. Byrne, editors, *Personality Change.* John Wiley & Sons, Inc., 1964, pp. 176–219. *295*

SARTRE, J. P., "Existentialism as a Humanism," in W. Kaufmann, editor, *Existentialism from Dostoevsky to Sartre.* New York: Meridian Books, Inc., 1956, pp. 287–311. *298*

SCHAFER, W. E., AND K. POLK, "Delinquency and the Schools," in President's Commission on Law Enforcement and Administration of Justice, *Task Force Report: Juvenile Delinquency and Youth Crime.* Washington, D.C.: U.S. Government Printing Office, 1967, Appendix M, pp. 222–77. *147, 158*

SCHEFF, T. J., "The Role of the Mentally Ill and the Dynamics of Mental Disorder: A Research Framework." *Sociometry* 26:436–53 (December, 1963). *151, 183*

———, "Social Conditions for Rationality: How Urban and Rural Courts Deal with the Mentally Ill." *American Behavioral Scientist,* 7:21–27 (March, 1964a). *143*

———, with the assistance of D. M. Culver, "The Societal Reaction to Deviance: Ascriptive Elements in the Psychiatric Screening of Mental Patients in a Midwestern State." *Social Problems,* 11:401–13 (Spring, 1964b). *141, 143*

———, *Being Mentally Ill,* Chicago: Aldine Publishing Company, 1966. *82, 125, 144, 181, 184, 185, 204*

———, editor, *Mental Illness and Social Processes.* New York: Harper & Row, Publishers, 1967. *204*

SCHEIN, E. H., "The Chinese Indoctrination Program for Prisoners of War." *Psychiatry,* 19:149–72 (May, 1956). *55, 181*

———, "Reaction Patterns to Severe, Chronic Stress in American Army Prisoners of War of the Chinese." *Journal of Social Issues,* 13:21–30 (1957). *55, 181*

———, *Coercive Persuasion.* New York: W. W. Norton & Company, Inc., Publishers, 1961. *55, 181*

SCHUR, E., *Crimes Without Victims.* Englewood Cliffs, N.J.: Prentice-Hall, Inc., 1965. *20, 96*

SCHWARTZ, B., "The Social Psychology of the Gift." *American Journal of Sociology,* 73:1–11 (July, 1967). *266*

SCHWARTZ, R. D., AND J. H. SKOLNICK, "Two Studies of Legal Stigma." *Social Problems,* 10:133–42 (Fall, 1962). *157, 212*

Scott, C. S., "Can You Get a 'Peep' Out of People?" *Federal Probation*, XXIX:13–18 (March, 1965). *266*

Scott, M. B., and S. M. Lyman, "Accounts." *American Sociological Review*, 33:46–62 (February, 1968). *47, 88, 90, 179*

Secord, P. F., and C. W. Backman, *Social Psychology*. New York: McGraw-Hill Book Company, 1964. *125*

Seeley, J. R., "Social Science? Some Probative Problems," in M. Stein and A. Vidich, editors, *Sociology on Trial*. Englewood Cliffs, N.J.: Prentice-Hall, Inc., 1963, pp. 53–65. *11*

Sellin, T., *Culture Conflict and Crime*. New York: Social Science Research Council, Bulletin 41, 1938. *85, 95*

Shaw, C. H., *The Natural History of a Delinquent Career*. Chicago: University of Chicago Press, 1931. *106–7*

Shibutani, T., *Society and Personality*. Englewood Cliffs, N.J.: Prentice-Hall., Inc., 1961. *187, 261*

Shils, E. A., "Social Inquiry and the Autonomy of the Individual," in D. Lerner, editor, *The Human Meaning of the Social Sciences*. New York: Meridian Books, Inc., 1959, pp. 114–57. *300*

Short, J. F., and F. I. Nye, "Extent of Unrecorded Delinquency." *Journal of Criminal Law, Criminology and Police Science*, 49:296–302 (December, 1958). *27*

Short, J. F., and F. L. Strodtbeck, "The Response of Gang Leaders to Status Threats." *American Journal of Sociology*, 67:571–79 (March, 1963). *47*

——, *Group Process and Gang Delinquency*. Chicago: University of Chicago Press, 1965. *26, 52*

Silberman, C. E., *Crisis in Black and White*. New York: Vintage Books, 1964. *220*

Silver, A., "The Demand for Order in Civil Society: A Review of Some Themes in the History of Urban Crime, Police, and Riot," in D. Bordua, editor, *The Police: Six Sociological Essays*. New York: John Wiley & Sons, Inc., 1967, pp. 1–24. *22*

Simmons, J. L., "On Maintaining Deviant Belief Systems." *Social Problems*, 11:250–56 (Winter, 1964). *29, 199*

——, with the assistance of H. Chambers, "Public Stereotypes of Deviants." *Social Problems*, 13:223–32 (Fall, 1965). *9–10, 125*

Simon, W., and J. H. Gagnon, "The Lesbians: A Preliminary Overview," in J. H. Gagnon and W. Simon, with the assistance of D. E. Carns, editors, *Sexual Deviance*. New York: Harper & Row, Publishers, 1967, pp. 247–82. *29*

Skolnick, J. H., and J. R. Woodworth, "Bureaucracy, Information and Social Control: A Study of a Morals Detail," in D. Bordua, editor, *The Police: Six Sociological Essays*. New York: John Wiley & Sons, Inc., 1967, pp. 99–136. *137–38*

Slosar, J., "The Skid Row Community," ms., 1965. *201–2*

Smelser, N. J., *Social Change in the Industrial Revolution*. Chicago: University of Chicago Press, 1959. *296*

——, *Theory of Collective Behavior*. New York: The Free Press of Glencoe, Inc., 1963. *42, 296*

SMITH, R. A., *Corporations in Crisis*. New York: Doubleday & Company, Inc., 1963. 87

SOLOMON, P., *et al.*, editors, *Sensory Deprivation*. Cambridge, Mass.: Harvard University Press, 1961. *181, 260*

SOMMER, R., "Patients Who Grow Old in a Mental Hospital." *Geriatrics*, 14:581–90 (September, 1959). *169*

SROLE, L. T., *et al.*, *Mental Health in the Metropolis*. New York: McGraw-Hill Book Company, 1962. *27*

STARK, R., "On the Incompatibility of Religion and Science." *Journal for the Scientific Study of Religion*, 3:3–20 (October, 1963). *194*

———, "Class, Radicalism and Religious Involvement in Great Britain." *American Sociological Review*, 29:698–706 (October, 1964). *196*

STENGEL, E., AND N. G. COOK, *Attempted Suicide*. London: Chapman & Hall, Ltd., 1958. *56*

STRAUSS, A. L., *Mirrors and Masks: The Search For Identity*. Glencoe, Ill.: The Free Press, 1959. *129, 149, 266*

———, *Images of the American City*. New York: The Free Press of Glencoe, Inc., 1961. *3*

———, editor, *The American City: A Sourcebook of Urban Imagery*. Chicago: Aldine Publishing Company, 1968. *3, 166*

STREET, D., R. D. VINTER AND C. PERROW, *Organization For Treatment*. New York: The Free Press of Glencoe, Inc., 1966. *165*

STUDT, G., S. L. MESSINGER AND T. P. WILSON, *C-Unit: Search for Community in Prison*. New York: Russell Sage Foundation, 1968. *295*

SUCHMAN, E. A., "The 'Hang-Loose' Ethic and the Spirit of Drug Use." *Journal of Health and Social Behavior*, 9:146–55 (June, 1968). *112*

SUDNOW, D., "Normal Crimes: Sociological Features of the Penal Code in a Public Defender Office." *Social Problems*, 12:255–76 (Winter, 1965). *125*

SUDOMIER, B., "Teens Face World as Publishers." *Detroit Free Press*, March 15, 1965. *124*

SUTHERLAND, E. H., *The Professional Thief*. Chicago: University of Chicago Press, 1937. *166, 190, 200*

———, "White-Collar Criminality." *American Sociological Review*, 5:1–12 (February, 1940). *73*

———, *White Collar Crime*. New York: Holt, Rinehart & Winston, Inc., 1949. *73, 83*

———, "The Diffusion of Sexual Psychopath Laws." *American Journal of Sociology*, 56:142–48 (1950). *133*

SUTHERLAND, E. H., AND D. R. CRESSEY, *Principles of Criminology*. Philadelphia: J. B. Lippincott Co. (7th ed.), 1966. *88, 95, 121, 158, 165, 204, 211, 260*

SUTTLES, G. D., *The Social Order of the Slum*. Chicago: University of Chicago Press, 1968. *47, 50, 67, 80, 113–14, 127, 165*

SYKES, G., AND D. MATZA, "Techniques of Neutralization: A Theory of Delinquency."

American Sociological Review, 22:664–70 (December, 1957). *86, 88, 89, 91, 93, 98*

Szasz, T. S., *The Myth of Mental Illness*. New York: Hoeber-Harper Books, 1961. *133, 278*

———, *Law, Liberty and Psychiatry: An Inquiry into the Social Uses of Mental Health Practices*. New York: The Macmillan Company, Publishers, 1963. *143*

———, *Psychiatric Justice*. New York: The Macmillan Company, Publishers, 1965. *143, 156, 179*

Taft, D. R., and R. W. England, Jr., *Criminology*. New York: The Macmillan Company, Publishers (4th ed.), 1964. *95, 116*

Tagiuri, R., and L. Petrullo, editors, *Person Perception and Interpersonal Behavior*. Stanford, Calif.: Stanford University Press, 1958. *125*

Tannenbaum, F., *Crime and the Community*. Boston: Ginn and Company, 1938. *156, 202–3*

Tarsis, V., *Ward 7: An Autobiographical Note*. New York: E. P. Dutton & Co., Inc., 1965. *195*

Thompson, H. S., *Hell's Angels*. New York: Ballantine Books, 1967. *115, 132, 133, 239*

Thrasher, F., *The Gang*. Chicago: University of Chicago Press, 1927. *113, 116*

Tobias, J. J., *Crime and Industrial Society in the 19th Century*. London: B. T. Batsford, Ltd., 1967. *65, 66, 70, 165, 190, 200*

Toby, J., "Affluence and Adolescent Crime," in President's Commission on Law Enforcement and Administration of Justice, *Task Force Report: Juvenile Delinquency and Youth Crime*. Washington, D.C.: U.S. Government Printing Office, 1967, Appendix H, pp. 132–44. *114*

———, "A Reply to Harris." *Social Problems*, 15:508–9 (Spring, 1968). *149*

Tumin, M. M., "In Dispraise of Loyalty." *Social Problems*, 15:267–79 (Winter, 1968). *7*

Turner, R. H., "The Quest for Universals in Sociological Research." *American Sociological Review*, 18:604–11 (December, 1953). *42, 296*

Tyhurst, J. S., "The Role of Transition States—Including Disasters—in Mental Illness," in *Symposium on Preventive and Social Psychiatry*. Washington, D.C.: U.S. Government Printing Office, 1957, pp. 149–69. *181*

Ullmann, L., *Institution and Outcome: A Comparative Study of Psychiatric Hospitals*. New York: Pergaman Press, 1967. *165*

Ullmann, L., and L. Krasner, *Case Studies in Behavior Modification*. New York: Holt, Rinehart & Winston, Inc., 1965. *256*

Vaz, E. W., editor, *Middle-Class Juvenile Delinquency*. New York: Harper & Row, Publishers, 1967. *114*

Vestal, B., "How Wallace Carries Out His 'Spoiler' Campaign." *Ann Arbor News*, June 22, 1967. *16, 142*

Vold, G. B., *Theoretical Criminology*. New York: Oxford University Press, Inc., 1958. *23, 95*

Volkman, R., and D. R. Cressey, "Differential Association and the Rehabilitation of

Drug Addicts." *American Journal of Sociology*, 69:129–42 (September, 1963). *235, 258–59, 269, 270, 274*

WADE, A. L., "Social Processes in the Act of Juvenile Vandalism," in M. B. Clinard and R. Quinney, editors, *Criminal Behavior Systems: A Typology.* New York: Holt, Rinehart & Winston, Inc., 1967, pp. 94–109. *102, 107*

WALLACE, S. E., *Skid Row as a Way of Life.* Totowa, N.J.: Bedminster Press, Inc., 1965. *158*

WALLERSTEIN, J. S., AND C. J. WYLE, "Our Law-Abiding Law-breakers." *Probation*, 25:107–12 (April, 1947). *27*

WARD, D. A., AND G. KASSEBAUM, "Homosexuality: A Mode of Adaptation in a Prison for Women." *Social Problems*, 12:159–77 (Fall, 1964). *52*

———, *Woman's Prison.* Chicago: Aldine Publishing Company, 1965. *149, 165*

WEBER, M., *From Max Weber: Essays in Sociology*, translated by H. H. Gerth and C. W. Mills. New York: Oxford University Press, Inc., 1946. *5*

WEINBERG, S. K., editor, *The Sociology of Mental Disorders: Analyses and Readings in Psychiatric Sociology.* Chicago: Aldine Publishing Company, 1967. *165, 181*

WERTHMAN, C., "The Function of Social Definitions in the Development of Delinquent Careers," in The President's Commission on Law Enforcement and Administration of Justice, *Task Force Report: Juvenile Delinquency and Youth Crime.* Washington, D.C.: U.S. Government Printing Office, 1967, Appendix J, pp. 155–70. *114, 115, 144, 147*

WERTHMAN, C., AND I. PILIAVIN, "Gang Members and the Police," in D. Bordua, editor, *The Police: Six Sociological Essays.* New York: John Wiley & Sons, Inc., 1967, pp. 56–98. *144*

WESTLEY, W. A., "Violence and the Police." *American Journal of Sociology*, 59:34–41 (July, 1953). *52*

WESTWOOD, G., *A Minority.* London: Longmans, Green & Company, Ltd., 1960. *91*

WHEELER, S., "Sex Offenses: A Sociological Critique." *Law and Contemporary Problems*, 25:258–78 (Spring, 1960). *27*

———, "Deviant Behavior," in N. J. Smelser, editor, *Sociology.* New York: John Wiley & Sons, Inc., 1967, pp. 601–66. *70, 137*

WILDE, W. A., "Decision-Making in a Psychiatric Screening Agency." *Journal of Health and Social Behavior*, 9:215–21 (September, 1968). *143*

WILENSKY, H. L., AND C. N. LEBEAUX, *Industrial Society and Social Welfare.* New York: Russell Sage Foundation, 1958. *263, 276*

WILKERSON, D., with J. and E. Sherrill, *The Cross and the Switchblade.* New York: Pyramid Publications, Inc., 1964 (copyright 1963). *214, 238, 265, 280*

WILKINS, L. T., *Social Deviance.* Englewood Cliffs, N.J.: Prentice-Hall, Inc., 1965. *70*

WILLIAMSON, H., edited by R. L. Keiser, *Hustler.* New York: Doubleday & Company, Inc., 1965. *115, 200–1*

WILSON, J. Q., "The Police and the Delinquent in Two Cities," in S. Wheeler, editor,

Controlling Delinquents. New York: John Wiley & Sons, Inc., 1968, pp. 9–30. *137*

WINICK, C., "Physician Narcotic Addicts." *Social Problems,* 9:174–86 (Fall, 1961). *71*

WOLFGANG, M. E., "Victim Precipitated Criminal Homicide." *The Journal of Criminal Law, Criminology and Police Science,* 48:1–11 (May–June, 1957). *42–43*

———, *Patterns in Criminal Homicide.* Philadelphia: University of Pennsylvania Press, 1958. *43, 59, 69–70, 92, 94*

———, "The Culture of Youth," in President's Commission on Law Enforcement and Administration of Justice, *Task Force Report: Juvenile Delinquency and Youth Crime.* Washington, D.C.: U.S. Government Printing Office, 1967, Appendix I, pp. 145–54. *47, 115*

WOLFGANG, M. E., AND F. FERRACUTI, *The Subculture of Violence.* London: Tavistock, 1967. *94*

WOLPE, J., A. SALTER AND L. J. REYNA, *The Conditioning Therapies.* New York: Holt, Rinehart & Winston, Inc., 1964. *256*

X, MALCOLM, with the assistance of A. Haley, *The Autobiography of Malcolm X.* New York: Grove Press, Inc., 1966 (copyright 1964). *190–91*

YABLONSKY, L., *The Tunnel Back: Synanon.* New York: The Macmillan Company, Publishers, 1965. *215, 263, 271*

YABLONSKY, L., AND C. E. DEDERICH, "Synanon: As a Program for Training Ex-Offenders," in National Institute of Mental Health, *Experiment in Culture Expansion.* Report of Proceedings of a Conference on "The use of products of a social problem in coping with the problem," held at the California Rehabilitation Center, Norco, Calif., July 10–12, 1963. *215, 283*

YARROW, M., C. SCHWARTZ, H. MURPHY AND L. DEASY, "The Psychological Meaning of Mental Illness in the Family." *The Journal of Social Issues,* 11:12–24 (1955). *136*

YOUNG, F. W., *Initiation Ceremonies: A Cross-Cultural Study of Status Dramatization.* Indianapolis, Ind.: The Bobbs-Merrill Co., Inc., 1965. *158*

ZIMBARDO, P. G., "The Psychology of Police Confessions." *Psychology Today,* 1:16–27 (June, 1967). *181*